CONTEMPORARY'S

GED

SCIENCE

Robert Mitchell

Reviewers

Judith Diamond,
Educational Consultant
Adult Learning Resource Center
Des Plaines, Illinois

Theresa Hutchinson, Instructor
Correctional Education Program
Arizona Department of Corrections
Phoenix, Arizona

Miriam Petrowsky, Adult Educator
Office of Adult and Continuing Education
New York City Board of Education
Brooklyn, New York

Margaret A. Rogers
Vice Principal
San Juan Unified Adult Education
Sacramento, California

Peggy Stubbs, CASAS/Curriculum Specialist
Basic Skills Program
Fayetteville Technical Community College
Fayetteville, North Carolina

Editor: Jennifer Krasula
Executive Editor: Linda Kwil
Creative Director: Michael E. Kelly
Marketing Manager: Sean Klunder
Production Manager: Genevieve Kelley
Manager of Editorial Services: Sylvia Bace

Interior Design by Think Design Group LLC

 **Wright Group**

Send all inquiries to:
Wright Group/McGraw-Hill
8787 Orion Place
Columbus, OH 43240

ISBN 0-8092-2230-2

11 12 13 14 15 WDQ 12 11 10 09

Table of Contents

PART TWO: READINGS IN LIFE SCIENCE

Acknowledgments

Photo of compound microscope and cork cells on page 101: © Lester V. Bergman/CORBIS

Photo of red blood cells magnified 50x on page 102: © Lester V. Bergman/CORBIS

Photo of red blood cells magnified 1,500x on page 102: © Science Pictures Limited/CORBIS

Photo of large red blood cells on page 102: © Mark L. Stephenson/CORBIS

Photo of Martian surface on page 103: © NASA

Photo of UNIVAC 1 on page 104: © Bettmann/CORBIS

Photo of ENIAC on page 104: © Bettmann/CORBIS

Photo of iMAC on page 104: Photo courtesy of Apple Computer, Inc./Mark Laita, Photographer

Photo of Einstein on page 141: © Bettmann/CORBIS

Photo of Pasteur on page 141: © Hulton-Deutsch Collection/CORBIS

Photo of Mendeleyev on page 141: © Bettmann/CORBIS

Photo of nebula on page 342: Image acquisition by Arne Henden (USNO); image processing
    by Al Kelly (NASA).

Photo of Grand Canyon on page 362: © Tom Bean/CORBIS

Photo of Asteroid 243 IDA on page 371: © NASA/Roger Ressmeyer/CORBIS

Photo of Halley's Comet on page 371: © Bettmann/CORBIS

Photo of spiral galaxy on page 377: Jason Ware, galaxyphoto.com.

Photo of elliptical galaxy on page 377: © AFP/CORBIS

Photo of Apollo astronaut on page 421: © NASA

To the Student

If you're studying to pass the GED Tests, you're in good company. In 1999, the most recent year for which figures are available, the American Council on Education GED Testing Service reported that over 750,700 adults took the GED Test battery worldwide. Of this number, more than 526,400 (70 percent) actually received their certificates. About 14 percent of those with high school credentials, or about one in seven, have a GED diploma. One in twenty (5 percent) of those students in their first year of college study is a GED graduate.

The average age of GED test-takers in the United States was over 24 in 1999, but nearly three quarters (70 percent) of GED test-takers were 19 years of age or older. Two out of three GED test-takers report having completed the tenth grade or higher, and more than a third report having completed the eleventh grade before leaving high school.

Why do so many people choose to take the GED Tests? Some do so to get a job, to advance to a better job, to attend college, or to qualify for military service. More than two out of every three GED graduates work toward college degrees or attend trade, technical, or business schools. Still others pursue their GED diplomas to feel better about themselves or to set good examples for their children.

More than 14 million adults earned the GED diploma between 1942 and 1999. Some well-known graduates include country music singers Waylon Jennings and John Michael Montgomery, comedian Bill Cosby, Olympic gold medalist Mary Lou Retton, Delaware Lieutenant Governor Ruth Ann Minner, Colorado's U.S. Senator Ben Nighthorse Campbell, Wendy's founder Dave Thomas, Famous Amos Cookies creator Wally Amos, and Triple Crown winner jockey Ron Turcotte.

This book has been designed to help you, too, succeed on the test. It will provide you with instruction in the skills you need to pass and plenty of practice with the kinds of test items you will find on the real test.

What Does GED Stand For?

GED stands for the Tests of **General Educational Development.** The GED Test Battery is a national examination developed by the GED Testing Service of the American Council on Education. The certificate earned for passing the test is widely recognized by colleges, training schools, and employers as equivalent to a high school diploma. The American Council reports that almost all (more than 95 percent) of employers in the nation employ GED graduates and offer them the same salaries and opportunities for advancement as high school graduates.

The GED Test reflects the major and lasting outcomes normally acquired in a high school program. Since the passing rate for the GED is based on the performance of graduating high school seniors, you can be sure your skills are comparable. In fact, those who pass the GED Test actually do better than one-third of those graduating seniors. Your skills in communication, information processing, critical thinking, and problem solving are keys to success. The test also places special emphasis on questions that prepare you for entering the workplace or higher education. Much that you have learned informally or through other types of training can help you pass the test.

Special editions of the GED Test will include the Spanish language, French language, Braille, large print, and audiocassette formats. If you need special accommodations because of a learning or physical disability, your adult education program and testing center can assist you.

What Should You Know to Pass the Test?

The GED Test consists of five examinations called Language Arts, Writing; Social Studies; Science; Language Arts, Reading; and Mathematics. On all five tests, you are expected to demonstrate the ability to think about many issues. You are tested on knowledge and skills you have acquired from life experiences, television, radio, books and newspapers, consumer products, and advertising. Your work or business experiences may be helpful during the test. You can expect the subjects to be interrelated. This is called interdisciplinary material. For example, a mathematics problem may include a scientific diagram. Or a social studies question may require some mathematical skills.

Keep these facts in mind about specific tests:

1. The **Language Arts, Writing Test** requires you in Part I to recognize or correct errors, revise sentences or passages, and shift constructions in the four areas of organization, sentence structure, usage, and mechanics (capitalization and punctuation). Letters, memos, and business-related documents are likely to be included.

   In Part II you will write an essay presenting an opinion or an explanation on a topic familiar to most adults. You should plan and organize your ideas before you write, and revise and edit your essay before you are finished.

2. Three of the five tests—**Social Studies, Science,** and **Mathematics**—require you to answer questions based on reading passages or interpreting graphs, charts, maps, cartoons, diagrams, or photographs. Developing strong reading and critical thinking skills is the key to succeeding on these tests. Being able to interpret information from graphic sources, such as a map or cartoon, is essential.

3. The **Language Arts, Reading Test** asks you to read literary text and show that you can comprehend, apply, analyze, synthesize, and evaluate concepts. You will also read nonfiction and show that you can understand the main points of what you are reading.

4. The **Mathematics Test** consists mainly of word problems to be solved. Therefore, you must be able to combine your ability to perform computations with problem-solving skills.

   Part I of the Mathematics Test will permit the use of the Casio fx-260 calculator, which will be provided at the test site. The calculator will eliminate the tediousness of making complex calculations. Part II will not permit the use of the calculator. Both parts of the test will include problems without multiple-choice answers. These problems will require you to mark your answers on bubble-in number grids or on coordinate plane graphs.

Who May Take the Tests?

About 3,500 GED Testing Centers are available in the fifty United States, the District of Columbia, eleven Canadian provinces and territories, U.S. and overseas military bases, correctional institutions, Veterans Administration hospitals, and certain learning centers. People who have not graduated from high school and who meet specific eligibility requirements (age, residency, etc.) may take the tests. Since eligibility requirements vary, you should contact your local GED testing center or the director of adult education in your state, province, or territory for specific information.

What Is a Passing Score on the GED Test?

A passing score varies from area to area. To find out what you need to pass the test, contact your local GED testing center. However, you should keep two scores in mind. One score represents the minimum score you must get on each test. The other is the minimum average score on all five tests. Both of these scores will be set by your state and must be met in order to pass the GED Test.

Can You Retake the Test?

You are allowed to retake some or all of the tests. The regulations governing the number of times that you may retake the tests and the time you must wait before retaking them are set by your state, province, or territory. Some states require you to take a review class or to study on your own for a certain amount of time before retaking the test.

THE GED TESTS

Tests	Minutes	Questions	Content/Percentages
Language Arts, Writing Part I: Editing (multiple choice) Part II: the Essay	 75 45	 50 1 topic: approx. 250 words:	Organization 15% Sentence Structure 30% Usage 30% Mechanics 25%
Social Studies	70	50	World History 15% U.S. History 25% Civics and Government 25% Economics 20% Geography 15%
Science	80	50	Earth and Space Science 20% Life Science 45% Physical Science 35% (Physics and Chemistry)

Language Arts, Reading	65	40	Literary Text 75%
			Poetry 15%
			Drama 15%
			Fiction 45%
			Nonfiction 25%
			    Informational Text
			    Literary Nonfiction
			    Reviews of Fine and Performing Arts
			    Business Documents

Mathematics
 	
Part I
  Calculator
 	
Part II
  No Calculator
	
	45
	
	45
		
		25
		
		25
			Number Operations and Numbers Sense 20–30%
			Measurement and Geometry 20–30%
			Data Analysis, Statistics, and Probability 20–30%
			Algebra, Functions, and Patterns 20–30%

	Total: $7\frac{1}{4}$ hours	Total: 240 questions and essay	

How Can You Best Prepare for the Test?

Many community colleges, public schools, adult education centers, libraries, churches, community-based organizations, and other institutions offer GED preparation classes. While your state may not require you to take part in a preparation program, it's a good idea if you've been out of school for some time, if you had academic difficulty when you were in school, or if you left before completing the eleventh grade. Some television stations broadcast classes to prepare people for the test. If you cannot find a GED preparation class locally, contact the director of adult education in your state, province, or territory.

What Are Some Test-Taking Tips?

1. **Prepare physically.** Get plenty of rest and eat a well-balanced meal before the test so that you will have energy and will be able to think clearly. Intense studying at the last minute probably will not help as much as having a relaxed and rested mind.

2. **Arrive early.** Be at the testing center at least 15 to 20 minutes before the starting time. Make sure you have time to find the room and to get situated. Keep in mind that many testing centers refuse to admit latecomers. Some testing centers operate on a first come, first served basis; so you want to be sure that there is an available seat for you on the day that you're ready to test.

3. **Think positively.** Tell yourself you will do well. If you have studied and prepared for the test, you should succeed.

4. **Relax during the test.** Take half a minute several times during the test to stretch and breathe deeply, especially if you are feeling anxious or confused.

5. **Read the test directions carefully.** Be sure you understand how to answer the questions. If you have any questions about the test or about filling in the answer form, ask before the test begins.

6. **Know the time limit for each test.** The Science Test has a time limit of 80 minutes (1 hour 20 minutes). Work at a steady pace; if you have extra time, go back and check your answers.

7. **Have a strategy for answering questions.** You should read through the reading passages or look over the materials once and then answer the questions that follow. Read each question two or three times to make sure you understand it. It is best to refer back to the passage or graphic in order to confirm your answer choice. Don't try to depend on your memory of what you have just read or seen. Some people like to guide their reading by skimming the questions before reading a passage. Use the method that works best for you.

8. **Don't spend a lot of time on difficult questions.** If you're not sure of an answer, go on to the next question. Answer easier questions first and then go back to the harder questions. However, when you skip a question, be sure that you have skipped the same number on your answer sheet. Although skipping difficult questions is a good strategy for making the most of your time, it is very easy to get confused and throw off your whole answer key.

   Lightly mark the margin of your answer sheet next to the numbers of the questions you did not answer so that you know what to go back to. To prevent confusion when your test is graded, be sure to erase these marks completely after you answer the questions.

9. **Answer every question on the test.** If you're not sure of an answer, take an educated guess. When you leave a question unanswered, you will always lose points, but you can possibly gain points if you make a correct guess.

10. **Clearly fill in the circle for each answer choice.** If you erase something, erase it completely. Be sure that you give only one answer per question; otherwise, no answer will count.

11. **Practice test-taking.** Use the exercises, reviews, and especially the Posttest and Practice Test in this book to better understand your test-taking habits and weaknesses. Use them to practice different strategies such as skimming questions first or skipping hard questions until the end. Knowing your own personal test-taking style is important to your success on the GED Test.

How to Use This Book

Step 1: Take the Pretest. This will give you a preview of the actual GED Science Test. And, it will help you pinpoint types of questions you need the most work on. Even if you do well on the pretest, we strongly suggest you work through the whole book to best prepare yourself for the GED Test.

Step 2: Read and study the twelve chapters in this book. Not only will this thoroughly prepare you for the GED Test, it will also prepare you for further study as you continue your education.

Step 3: Take the Posttest. The Posttest is a simulated GED Test and presents questions in the format, at the level of difficulty, and in the percentages found on the actual GED Test.

Step 4: Take the Practice Test. The Practice Test is a second simulated GED Test and can be used as a final indicator of your readiness for the actual GED Test. You are now ready to take the test.

Features of the New GED Science Test

The new GED Science Test is based on the National Science Education Standards of the National Academy of Sciences. In accordance with these standards, a major emphasis of the new GED Science Test will be on the interdisciplinary themes—themes that thread through all subjects of scientific inquiry:

- Unifying Concepts and Processes
- Science as Inquiry
- Science and Technology
- Science in Personal and Social Perspectives
- History and Nature of Science

Part One of *Contemporary's GED Science* thoroughly prepares you for questions arising from these themes.

Parts Two, Three, and Four emphasize the traditional subject areas of science. Woven into every chapter are the interdisciplinary themes of Part One.

- Part Two: Life Science (Plant and Animal Science; Human Biology)
- Part Three: Physical Science (Chemistry; Physics)
- Part Four: Earth and Space Science (Earth Science; Space Science)

Special Features of This Book

Contemporary's GED Science has a number of features designed to make your test preparation easier, more effective, and more enjoyable.

- **Thinking About Science** exercises enable you to review the material you have just read.

- **GED Practice** exercises provide actual GED Test preparation.

- **Chapter Reviews** provide comprehensive reviews of the concepts presented in each chapter with questions written in GED format.

- **Writing Activities** provide opportunities to use critical thinking skills, applying scientific knowledge to a variety of real-life topics. Topics are written in the format of the GED essay.

- A **Science Almanac** provides lists and tables of useful scientific information, along with Web sites pertaining to the major divisions of science.

- The **Answer Key** explains the correct answers for the exercises. If you make a mistake, the answer key can help you understand your error.

- The **Glossary** provides an accessible list of important terms.

- Throughout the chapters you'll see references to **www.GEDScience.com** This Web site has been designed to accompany this book. Check it out for additional instruction and practice!

A Short Course in Science Preparation

Many students are on a limited time schedule and need to prepare for the GED Science Test in a relatively short time. For these students, studying the entire GED Science book may not be possible. If you are one of these students, we have designed a short course for you. The short course is approximately one-third the length of the entire book and emphasizes the interdisciplinary standards—the themes of science, supported by three full-length practice tests: the Pretest, Posttest, and Practice Test.

Short Course in Preparing for the GED Science Test

- Full-length Pretest, pages 1–24

- Themes in Science, pages 25–156
    Concepts and Processes in Science
    Science as Inquiry
    Science and Technology
    Science in Personal and Social Perspectives
    History and Nature of Science

- Full-length Posttest, pages 387–407

- Full-length Practice Test, pages 409–431

By completing this short course, you will experience every type of question you will see on the GED Science Test. For additional GED practice, we suggest you do the end-of-chapter reviews. Additional concentrated practice can also be found in McGraw-Hill/Contemporary's *GED Science Exercise Book.*

Preparing for General Knowledge Questions in Science

Many questions on the GED Science Test will be general knowledge questions—questions that test your specific knowledge of core scientific facts, concepts, and processes. The short course outlined above will prepare you for many of these questions.

To be more fully prepared, however, you are strongly encouraged to read as much of the reading selections in Parts Two, Three, and Four as your time permits. These reading selections are designed specifically to round out and strengthen your general knowledge of science. The **Thinking About Science** and **GED Practice** questions have been carefully chosen to focus on the types of questions that appear on the GED Test.

Good luck on your quest for the GED. We hope you enjoy your study of science.

Science

Before you begin to work with this book, take this Pretest. The purpose of the Pretest is to help you determine which skills you need to develop to pass the GED Science Test.

Directions: Choose the <u>one best answer</u> to each question. The questions are based on reading passages, charts, graphs, maps, and cartoons. Answer each question as carefully as possible. If a question seems to be too difficult, do not spend too much time on it. Work ahead and come back to it later when you can think it through carefully.

Pretest Answer Grid

1 ① ② ③ ④ ⑤	18 ① ② ③ ④ ⑤	35 ① ② ③ ④ ⑤
2 ① ② ③ ④ ⑤	19 ① ② ③ ④ ⑤	36 ① ② ③ ④ ⑤
3 ① ② ③ ④ ⑤	20 ① ② ③ ④ ⑤	37 ① ② ③ ④ ⑤
4 ① ② ③ ④ ⑤	21 ① ② ③ ④ ⑤	38 ① ② ③ ④ ⑤
5 ① ② ③ ④ ⑤	22 ① ② ③ ④ ⑤	39 ① ② ③ ④ ⑤
6 ① ② ③ ④ ⑤	23 ① ② ③ ④ ⑤	40 ① ② ③ ④ ⑤
7 ① ② ③ ④ ⑤	24 ① ② ③ ④ ⑤	41 ① ② ③ ④ ⑤
8 ① ② ③ ④ ⑤	25 ① ② ③ ④ ⑤	42 ① ② ③ ④ ⑤
9 ① ② ③ ④ ⑤	26 ① ② ③ ④ ⑤	43 ① ② ③ ④ ⑤
10 ① ② ③ ④ ⑤	27 ① ② ③ ④ ⑤	44 ① ② ③ ④ ⑤
11 ① ② ③ ④ ⑤	28 ① ② ③ ④ ⑤	45 ① ② ③ ④ ⑤
12 ① ② ③ ④ ⑤	29 ① ② ③ ④ ⑤	46 ① ② ③ ④ ⑤
13 ① ② ③ ④ ⑤	30 ① ② ③ ④ ⑤	47 ① ② ③ ④ ⑤
14 ① ② ③ ④ ⑤	31 ① ② ③ ④ ⑤	48 ① ② ③ ④ ⑤
15 ① ② ③ ④ ⑤	32 ① ② ③ ④ ⑤	49 ① ② ③ ④ ⑤
16 ① ② ③ ④ ⑤	33 ① ② ③ ④ ⑤	50 ① ② ③ ④ ⑤
17 ① ② ③ ④ ⑤	34 ① ② ③ ④ ⑤	

When you have completed the test, check your work with the answers and explanations on page 22. Use the evaluation chart on page 24 to determine which areas you need to review most.

Questions 1 and 2 refer to the following passage.

Commercially prepared food that is sold in the United States often contains one or more types of food additives. Preservatives are chemicals that are placed in food to retard spoilage by bacteria. Artificial coloring is placed in food to change its color, while artificial flavoring and sweeteners are added to improve taste.

In recent years medical researchers have discovered that certain kinds of food additives, when they are eaten in very large amounts, can cause cancer in laboratory animals. However, scientists have not been able to prove that small amounts of these additives are harmful to people. Yet, even without medical evidence of danger to consumers, many companies now sell foods that contain no preservatives, artificial coloring, or artificial flavoring.

1. Which of the following is not mentioned in the passage as a reason that additives are placed in food?

   (1) to retard spoilage
   (2) to improve its taste
   (3) to lower its cost
   (4) to change its color
   (5) to slow down the growth of bacteria

2. What assumption is made by food companies that sell food that is advertised as being 100 percent natural (containing no artificial additives)?

   (1) Food additives do not cause cancer.
   (2) Out of concern for their health, many consumers will buy only food that is 100 percent natural.
   (3) Many consumers feed their pets scraps of food, and 100 percent natural food will be safer for these pets.
   (4) Food that is 100 percent natural contains fewer calories than food in which additives have been placed.
   (5) Food that is 100 percent natural has a better appearance than food in which additives have been placed.

PRETEST

3. Two identical negatively charged spheres are suspended by string from support stands. Which of the drawings below correctly illustrates how the charged spheres will react when the stands holding them are moved close together?

(1)

(2)

(3)

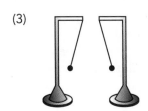

(4)

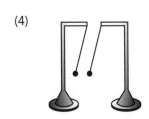

(5)

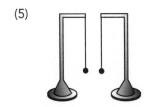

Questions 4 and 5 refer to the graph below.

AVERAGE LIFE EXPECTANCY
(years)

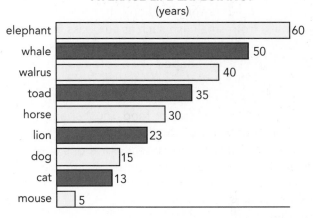

4. A general rule for animals is that the larger an animal is, the longer its life expectancy will be.

According to the bar graph, what animal is an exception to this rule?

(1) walrus
(2) dog
(3) horse
(4) toad
(5) mouse

5. How many years longer is the average life expectancy of a whale than the average life expectancy of a dog?

(1) 13 years
(2) 24 years
(3) 28 years
(4) 35 years
(5) 50 years

Questions 6 and 7 are based on the following passage.

Sharks, the most feared of the large fish, are mainly predators that feed on other marine animals, from small fish such as sea bass and salmon to marine mammals such as elephant seals and whales. Shaped like a torpedo, sharks move swiftly through water and capture and rip their prey with rows of razor-sharp teeth. To aid in their endless search for food, most sharks have a keen sense of smell, particularly for blood. Sharks can even detect vibrations in the water caused by an injured animal swimming.

6. What survival advantage does a torpedo-like shape give a shark?

   (1) strength
   (2) tough skin
   (3) flexibility
   (4) keen vision
   (5) speed

7. One type of shark, the great white shark, is known for its tendency to attack swimmers and even small fishing boats. Suppose a scientist wants to know whether the great white shark is in danger of becoming extinct. Which of the following would the scientist most likely be interested in knowing?

   (1) the number of great white sharks alive today compared to 20 years ago
   (2) the number of swimmers killed each year by great white sharks
   (3) the types of sharks that are already extinct and the dates they became extinct
   (4) the number of teeth in a great white shark
   (5) the diseases that affect great white sharks

Question 8 refers to the following chart.

CALORIE NEEDS PER DAY	
Very active man	4,500
Inactive man	3,000
Very active woman	3,000
Inactive woman	2,500
Teenage boy	3,200
Teenage girl	2,800
Children 1–6	1,200–1,600

8. Which of the following statements is best supported by information presented in the chart above?

   (1) Teenagers need more calories each day than young children because teenagers get more daily exercise.
   (2) On the average, men are physically larger than women.
   (3) Both male and female adults need more calories each day than children or teenagers regardless of their activity level.
   (4) It is more difficult for a man to lose weight than it is for a woman.
   (5) The daily calorie need of an adult increases as activity level increases.

PRETEST

9. At room temperature, hydrogen gas mixes freely with oxygen gas. A flame or an electric spark can cause this quiet mixture of gases to explode violently.

What is the best rule for storing a container of oxygen gas and a container of hydrogen gas?

(1) A danger sign should be placed next to each container.
(2) The containers should be stored at least six feet away from each other.
(3) Smoking should be permitted only near one of the containers.
(4) One container should be stored in a room that is separate from the room in which the other container is stored.
(5) The containers should be stored together in a room with concrete walls.

Questions 10 and 11 refer to the diagram below.

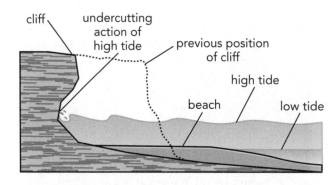

10. Which phrase below is the best title for the above diagram?

(1) Cliffs Overlooking an Ocean
(2) Cliff Erosion Caused by Tides
(3) The Movement of Sand Along a Beach
(4) Growth and Decay of Sand Dunes
(5) Changing Tide Levels on a Beach

11. What is one result of the action of the high-tide waves on the cliff?

(1) an increase in the amount of beach
(2) a decrease in the amount of beach
(3) an increase in the height of the cliff
(4) a decrease in the height of the cliff
(5) an increase in the height of the high tide

Questions 12 and 13 refer to the following passage.

You may have heard a meteorologist, or weather forecaster, talk about a temperature inversion and the dangers of air pollution that accompany it. To understand what a temperature inversion is, you must first know that when weather conditions are normal, air temperature decreases with increasing altitude. In other words, the higher up you go, the colder it is. During an inversion, the opposite is true: the air gets warmer as altitude increases.

A temperature inversion occurs when a layer of warm air passes over a layer of cooler air next to the ground. The layer of cooler air, which may be several hundred feet thick, traps air pollutants and holds them close to the ground. The layer of warm air above prevents the pollutants from dispersing at a higher altitude, as they normally would. This situation is especially dangerous in and around large cities where pollution from automobile exhausts and industrial smoke can be at a health-threatening level even when atmospheric conditions are normal.

12. During a temperature inversion, what is a city most likely to be bothered by?

   (1) snow
   (2) hot weather
   (3) air pollution
   (4) water pollution
   (5) congested traffic

13. During a temperature inversion in and around a heavily polluted large city, what is the best advice that the mayor can give to the city's residents?

   (1) Don't drive your car unless necessary.
   (2) Wear warm clothes outdoors.
   (3) Stay inside until the inversion is over.
   (4) Leave the city for a few days.
   (5) Write letters to the weather bureau.

PRETEST

Questions 14–16 refer to the following information.

An important principle in biology is that each living thing is adapted (physically suited) to survive best in the conditions present in its home environment. As illustrated below, one adaptation shown by birds is foot structure.

FOOT STRUCTURE VARIATIONS OF COMMON BIRDS

A   B   C   D   E

| wading (Heron) | grasping (Hawk) | perching (Warbler) | swimming (Duck) | running (Rhea) |

14. Which of the five birds represented is most suited to use its feet to pick up and carry small land animals?

(1) heron
(2) hawk
(3) warbler
(4) duck
(5) rhea

15. Which two drawings would be of most interest to someone studying birds that get their food from rivers and lakes?

(1) A and C
(2) C and E
(3) B and E
(4) A and D
(5) D and E

16. The drawings would have the least relevance to a person interested in what type of study?

(1) the walking abilities of birds
(2) the dietary habits of birds
(3) illustrations of wildlife
(4) the climbing ability of birds
(5) the soaring ability of birds

Questions 17–20 refer to the following passage.

Chemists working in medical research have developed quite a number of pain-relieving drugs. They have also discovered that the human body produces its own pain relievers. Evidence shows that these natural painkillers, chemicals called endorphins, are produced by the body in response to the stress of tiring exercise. Chemists believe that endorphins are probably responsible for "runner's high," a feeling of calm and absence of pain experienced by athletes during long periods of strenuous running. What's more, although medical evidence is not conclusive, some chemists point out that the short-term depression many people feel when they must give up exercising on a regular basis may be a form of natural drug withdrawal!

After reading the paragraph above, three students made the following statements:

A. Even though endorphins are natural body chemicals, endorphin withdrawal is a serious drug problem.

B. Endorphins are types of chemicals produced by the body in response to strenuous exercise.

C. The reason I'm moody today is that I'm experiencing endorphin withdrawal from all the exercise I got yesterday.

17. Which of the statements is a correct restatement of information given in the passage?

   (1) A only
   (2) B only
   (3) C only
   (4) A and B only
   (5) B and C only

18. Which of the statements is a hypothesis (a possible explanation of an observed fact or condition)?

   (1) A only
   (2) B only
   (3) C only
   (4) A and B only
   (5) B and C only

19. Which of the following is the most reasonable prediction that can be made from the information given in the passage?

   (1) Further research will show that there is no such thing as endorphin withdrawal.
   (2) The adverse side effects of all pain-relieving drugs will someday be eliminated.
   (3) Chemists will someday discover that endorphins are present only in the bodies of people who are drug abusers.
   (4) Learning to control a person's endorphin level may someday give doctors a new method of relieving pain.
   (5) Further research will show that taking aspirin also causes the body to produce endorphins.

20. Considering what is now known about endorphins, for what symptom would synthetic endorphins most likely be recommended if they someday become a safe medicinal drug?

   (1) chest pain due to a cold
   (2) a headache due to a hangover
   (3) an upset stomach
   (4) a broken bone
   (5) body soreness due to physical labor

Questions 21–23 refer to the diagram below.

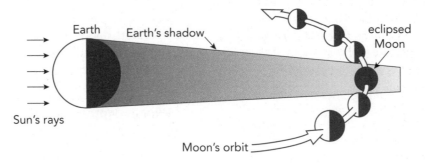

**LUNAR ECLIPSE
(ECLIPSE OF THE MOON)**

Earth · Earth's shadow · eclipsed Moon · Sun's rays · Moon's orbit

21. Looking at the diagram, what can you infer is the meaning of the phrase *Moon's orbit*?

(1) size of the Moon
(2) path of the Moon
(3) temperature of the Moon
(4) reflected light off the Moon
(5) rotation speed of the Moon

22. How often does an eclipse of the Moon occur?

(1) once every month
(2) once every year
(3) only when Earth is directly between the Sun and the Moon
(4) only when the Moon is directly between Earth and the Sun
(5) only when the weather is clear on Earth and no clouds block the sunlight

23. Knowing that moonlight is reflected sunlight, what can you conclude happens during an eclipse of the Moon?

(1) For a few minutes, the Moon turns dark and seems to disappear from the sky.
(2) For a few minutes, the bright daytime Sun turns dark and seems to disappear from the sky.
(3) The Moon, which otherwise is only partly visible as a crescent, slowly becomes a full Moon for a few minutes.
(4) The Moon, which otherwise is not visible at all during that evening, slowly appears overhead as a full Moon.
(5) The otherwise bright daytime Sun becomes much dimmer, similar to when it is hidden behind a cloud layer.

24. Heat and light are forms of energy that almost always occur together. Usually, a consumer product is designed primarily to provide either heat or light energy, not both. For example, after you strike a match, both heat and light are given off, but the main purpose of a match is to make something start burning. You would use a match to light a darkened room only if there were no other source of light available.

For which two products below would heat be the least useful form of energy produced?

A. a cigarette lighter
B. a desk lamp
C. an electric oven
D. a candle

(1) A and C
(2) A and D
(3) B and C
(4) B and D
(5) C and D

25. Friedrich Wöhler (1800–1882) was a pioneer in the field of organic chemistry. Wöhler showed that urea, a waste product created by living organisms, could be created in a laboratory from ammonium cyanate, a chemical substance that did not come from living organisms. Before Wöhler's discovery, scientists had believed that organic substances—substances made by living organisms—could be made only from other organic substances.

What is another way of stating Wöhler's contribution to modern chemistry?

(1) All nonliving substances come from living substances.
(2) All living substances were once nonliving substances.
(3) All living substances eventually break down into nonliving substances.
(4) There is no difference between living and nonliving substances.
(5) Nonliving substances are the basic building blocks of living substances.

Questions 26 and 27 are based on the graph below.

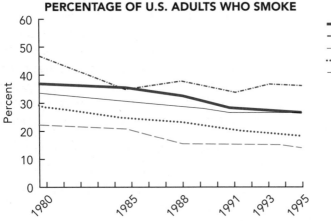

PERCENTAGE OF U.S. ADULTS WHO SMOKE

— African Americans
–·–·– Native Americans
– – – Asian Americans
········· Hispanics
——— Caucasians

26. Which group had the greatest number of smokers between 1980 and 1995?

(1) African Americans
(2) Native Americans
(3) Asian Americans
(4) Hispanics
(5) Caucasians

27. For what purpose might a scientist use the information in this graph to design programs to help people quit smoking?

(1) to determine which groups most need health information about smoking
(2) to design experiments that find ways to discourage people from smoking
(3) to decide which groups most deserve to receive health care
(4) to select a sample of females to target with antismoking information
(5) to choose a geographic region in which to offer classes to stop smoking

Questions 28 and 29 refer to the following passage.

During the 1910s, Alfred Wegener, a German meteorologist, advocated the idea that at one time, perhaps 200 million years ago, all the continents were joined as a single landmass. Wegener based his theory on the observation that the east coast of South America seems to fit the west coast of Africa, much like pieces of a jigsaw puzzle.

Wegener's theory was not backed by scientific evidence until the discovery in the 1960s of seafloor spreading. Additional geological evidence linked features found on the west coast of Africa with the east coast of South America. The theory of continental drift is now an accepted part of the modern theory about the evolving Earth.

28. What is continental drift?

   (1) a slow moving apart of continents
   (2) the shrinkage of continents
   (3) the growth of continents
   (4) the formation of new continents
   (5) a slow coming together of continents

29. Based on the passage, which of the following conclusions can you draw?

   (1) A scientific theory is not announced until confirming evidence is discovered.
   (2) A scientific theory is usually not correct unless confirming evidence is available.
   (3) A scientific theory can be considered correct even if evidence does not support it.
   (4) Most correct scientific theories do not have evidence to support them.
   (5) A scientific theory may be announced before it is confirmed by evidence.

Questions 30–32 refer to the following passage.

A storm cloud is much like a giant electric generator. When the cloud forms, electric charges within the cloud separate. A positive charge accumulates near the top of the cloud, and a negative charge accumulates near the bottom. As the cloud passes overhead, the negatively charged lower part of the cloud causes a large positive charge to appear on the ground below. Because positive and negative charges are strongly attracted to each other, the ground charge follows the cloud like a shadow. Both the negative charge in the cloud and the positive charge on the ground increase as the storm cloud grows.

Before lightning strikes the earth, the air between the cloud and the ground acts as an insulator and does not allow electricity to pass through it. However, when the electrical force pulling the cloud's negative charge toward the earth's positive charge becomes strong enough, it overcomes the resistance of the air. When this happens, lightning occurs: the negative charge rushes down from the cloud to meet the positive ground charge.

When lightning strikes the earth, it takes the path of least resistance. This path is most often just the shortest distance from the cloud to anything touching the ground. That's why lightning frequently strikes the highest point of an area—usually a tall tree, a high tower, or a skyscraper. People have also been struck, often when walking in an open area such as a field or when boating on a lake. In fact, the National Center for Health Statistics reports that about 125 Americans are killed by lightning each year, and more than 500 are injured.

Although lightning can't be prevented, there are ways to protect tall buildings from its destructive power. The most common way is with a lightning rod, a sharply pointed rod that runs from the highest point of the building down into the ground. The lightning rod is made of material such as copper that conducts electricity rather than resisting it. If lightning strikes the rod, the electricity safely flows to the ground without damaging the building or harming the people inside.

30. For what reason is a lightning rod placed on a tall building?

(1) to help prevent lightning storms from occurring in the sky over the building
(2) to prevent lightning from striking near the building
(3) to protect the building from lightning by providing a high-resistance, safe electrical path to the ground
(4) to protect the building from lightning by providing a low-resistance, safe electrical path to the ground
(5) to cause cloud-to-cloud lightning bolts instead of cloud-to-earth bolts

31. When lightning strikes an object such as a tree, the object is heated as electricity passes through it.

Which of the following could be caused by lightning?

(1) a warm-weather front
(2) positive electric charges accumulating on the ground
(3) negative electric charges accumulating in a cloud
(4) a forest fire in a hot, dry area
(5) the separation of electric charges within a cloud

32. Imagine that you're unexpectedly caught in a violent lightning storm while hiking in the countryside, thirteen miles away from your car. Of the options listed below, what is the safest course of action?

(1) Hike back to your car as quickly as possible.
(2) Go to the lowest point of an open area and lie down, preferably in a ditch or depression.
(3) Climb up a tree in order to get out of contact with the ground.
(4) Go to the highest point of an open area and wait for the storm to pass.
(5) Seek shelter under the highest tree you can find.

Question 33 is based on the drawing below.

Question 34 is based on the drawing below.

33. What is the instrument above designed to measure?

   (1) air pressure
   (2) wind direction
   (3) air pollution
   (4) air temperature
   (5) wind speed

34. What symptom is the instrument shown above designed to measure?

   (1) sore throat
   (2) blister
   (3) fever
   (4) infection
   (5) sore joint

Question 35 is based on the drawing below.

wings

35. The wings on a penguin are used to perform the same function in water as which of the following body parts?

   (1) the snout of a dolphin
   (2) the wings of a seagull
   (3) the tail of a monkey
   (4) the arms of a human
   (5) the gills of a salmon

36. Scurvy is a disease characterized by body weakness, loose teeth, tender joints, and ruptured blood vessels. Before 1800, scurvy was prevalent among British sailors who spent weeks, or even months, at sea without fresh fruit or vegetables. Dutch sailors who had citrus fruits on board, did not suffer the same affliction. It was only after 1795, when lime juice began to be given to British sailors, that outbreaks of scurvy lessened. Today it is known that scurvy is a disease caused by a lack of vitamin C.

What type of diseases did the reports of sick British sailors help identify?

   (1) exercise-deficiency diseases
   (2) vitamin-deficiency diseases
   (3) water-deficiency diseases
   (4) sleep-deficiency diseases
   (5) blood-pressure diseases

Questions 37 and 38 refer to the passage below.

One of the great natural disasters that coastal cities face is the tsunami. A tsunami is an ocean wave generated by an undersea earthquake or a volcanic eruption. A tsunami starts as a set of circular waves similar to the waves caused by an object dropped into water.

The wavelength of a tsunami is usually between 60 and 120 miles long. The tsunami may travel hundreds of miles while reaching speeds up to 500 miles per hour. The height of the wave may be only one or two feet while far out in the ocean, but grows to 50 feet or higher when it reaches the shallow waters near a coast. A ship at sea will most likely not feel a tsunami pass beneath it.

Most tsunamis occur along the Ring of Fire, a string of volcanoes that encircles the Pacific Ocean. Since 1800, more than 40 tsunamis have struck the Hawaiian Islands and Japan. When a tsunami strikes, a coastal city can be destroyed as the huge wave passes over it.

37. What is the danger that residents in coastal cities face when a tsunami strikes?

(1) death by starvation
(2) death by hazardous waste
(3) death by strong winds
(4) death by epidemic disease
(5) death by drowning

38. Suppose a strong underwater earthquake is detected about 1,000 miles from Japan. About how much early warning time is it possible to give coastal cities about a possible tsunami?

(1) 2 minutes
(2) 2 hours
(3) 2 days
(4) 2 weeks
(5) 2 months

39. In discovering the laws of falling bodies, Galileo (1564–1642) proposed several hypotheses, some of which he abandoned after conducting experiments to test them.

First hypothesis: If an object falls twice as far, it will reach twice the speed. Galileo proved that the first hypothesis is false.

Second hypothesis: In an equal length of time, all objects fall the same distance. Galileo proved that the second hypothesis is false.

Third hypothesis: If an object falls for twice the length of time, it will fall four times the distance. For example, an object that falls for 2 seconds will fall 4 times (2×2) as far as an object that falls for 1 second. Galileo's experiments proved that the third hypothesis is true.

Which statement best points out a feature of science demonstrated by Galileo?

(1) Scientific discovery builds on hypotheses that are tested and then abandoned if found to be false.
(2) Science is the art of good guessing with the hope of eventual success.
(3) Some scientific hypotheses are based on asking the wrong question.
(4) Scientists often try to make discoveries by first proposing hypotheses that are known to be false.
(5) Correct scientific results show that previous scientists were not educated.

Questions 40 and 41 refer to the following passage.

Methane (CH_4), also called natural gas, is commonly used as fuel for heating and cooking. When methane burns, it combines with oxygen gas (O_2) and produces carbon dioxide gas (CO_2) and water (H_2O). The equation for this chemical reaction is written as:

$$CH_4 + 2O_2 \longrightarrow CO_2 + 2H_2O + energy$$

40. For each molecule of methane gas that burns, how many molecules of CO_2 gas form?

   (1) one
   (2) two
   (3) three
   (4) four
   (5) six

41. Which of the following statements about the reaction equation above is true?

   (1) There are more atoms of oxygen on the left side of the arrow than on the right side.
   (2) There are fewer atoms of oxygen on the left side of the arrow than on the right side.
   (3) There is an equal number of molecules of oxygen gas on each side of the arrow.
   (4) There is an equal number of atoms of oxygen on each side of the arrow.
   (5) No oxygen gas is represented in the reaction equation.

42. An important principle of science is that matter is neither created nor destroyed during physical or chemical changes. Rather, matter is changed from one form to another. Which of the following is not an example of matter changing from one form to another?

   (1) gasoline in a car engine changing into a mixture of hot exhaust gases
   (2) burning wood changing into ashes
   (3) food being digested
   (4) a plucked guitar making sound
   (5) heated bread changing into toast

43. Addiction is the body's dependence on a drug, caused by continual use of the drug over a period of time. Which of the following is <u>not</u> an example of addiction?

   (1) Lian still takes a painkiller, even though her broken arm no longer hurts.
   (2) Sean has smoked for 23 years and now plans to quit.
   (3) Richard eats 4,000 calories each day when he works in temperatures below freezing.
   (4) Elise, hooked on heroin, is seeking treatment in a drug rehabilitation center.
   (5) Feroz drinks three bottles of beer each night, but says he can stop.

Questions 44 and 45 refer to the passage and chart below.

From person to person, differences exist in the surface proteins found in red blood cells. Because of these differences, each person can have any one of four types of blood. These four blood types are named A, B, AB, and O. The chart below shows which kinds of blood transfusions are possible. A transfusion is the use of one person's donated blood in the body of a second person.

BLOOD TYPES AND TRANSFUSION POSSIBILITIES

Blood Type	Can Receive Blood from	Can Donate Blood to
A	O, A	A, AB
B	O, B	B, AB
AB	A, B, AB, O	AB
O	O	A, B, AB, O

44. What blood type(s) can receive a transfusion of blood type B?

(1) blood type B
(2) blood type O and blood type B
(3) blood type AB and blood type B
(4) blood type O and blood type A
(5) blood type A and blood type AB

45. A person who can give blood to any blood type is called a universal donor. A person who receives blood from all types is called a universal recipient. Which of the following conclusions can be drawn from the chart?

(1) Blood type A is a universal donor, and blood type AB is a universal recipient.
(2) Blood type B is a universal donor, and blood type O is a universal recipient.
(3) Blood type AB is both a universal donor and a universal recipient.
(4) Blood type AB is a universal donor, and blood type O is a universal recipient.
(5) Blood type O is a universal donor, and blood type AB is a universal recipient.

Questions 46 and 47 refer to the following passage.

Rhythms are patterns of behavior that take place periodically. Communities of living organisms exhibit daily, seasonal, and annual rhythms. An example of a daily rhythm is shown by hawks and owls. Hawks are diurnal animals and hunt only during the day while owls are nocturnal animals and hunt only at night.

Migration is a seasonal rhythm. Animals migrate to find a warmer climate and new sources of food or to find a more suitable place to nest and produce their young. For example, ducks migrate at the start of winter from Canada to regions of warmer climate nearer the equator. When the winter is over, the ducks return to Canada.

Hibernation, an annual rhythm, is a deep type of sleep that many animals undergo during winter months. A true hibernating animal does not wake up during hibernation. Woodchucks and ground squirrels are true hibernators. Bears are not. Although bears sleep most of the winter, they do wake up often. Frogs, snakes, and lizards are also not true hibernators. However, they do spend their winters buried in mud, in a similar deep sleep.

46. What type of rhythm is the act of sleeping every afternoon?

    (1) a daily rhythm
    (2) a seasonal rhythm
    (3) an annual rhythm
    (4) true hibernation
    (5) a nocturnal behavior pattern

47. Which of the following is a conclusion that can be drawn from the passage?

    (1) Woodchucks go hunting more often in winter.
    (2) Bears sleep throughout the entire winter.
    (3) Salmon migrate each year in order to breed.
    (4) Owls migrate only at night.
    (5) Ducks migrate to seek a warmer climate.

Question 48 is based on the following passage and diagram.

The word *asteroid* refers to any of the small celestial bodies found primarily between the orbits of the planets Mars and Jupiter.

The diagram shows distance in astronomical units. (One astronomical unit is the distance between Earth and the Sun, about 93 million miles.)

THE MAIN ASTEROID BELT
(orbits drawn approximately to scale)

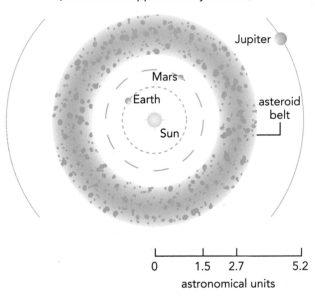

48. What is the approximate distance between the center of the main asteroid belt and the Sun?

    (1) about 251 million miles
    (2) about 1,395 million miles
    (3) about 4,836 million miles
    (4) about 93 million miles
    (5) about 5.2 million miles

Questions 49 and 50 refer to the following passage and drawings.

The volume of an odd-shaped object such as a small ceramic statue can be measured by the immersion method, the steps of which are given below.

STEP 1. Partially fill a measuring cup with a volume scale along its side with water. Measure the volume of the water at its surface and label it *Level A.*

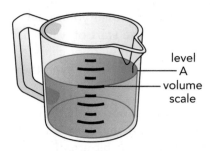

STEP 2. Place the statue in the measuring cup. Notice that the water level rises.

STEP 3. Measure the new level of the water at its surface and label it *Level B. Level B* is the combined volume of the water and the statue.

STEP 4. Subtract *Level A* from *Level B.* The difference equals the volume of the statue.

49. Which of the following must be true if the volume of the statue is to be measured accurately?

(1) The volume of the statue is less than the volume of water.
(2) The volume of the statue is greater than the volume of water.
(3) The weight of the statue is equal to the weight of the water.
(4) The water level does not rise above the top of the statue.
(5) The statue is totally covered by water.

50. Which of the following would be the greatest source of error when using the immersion method to measure the volume of the clay in the statue?

(1) the use of a liquid other than water
(2) the unknown fact that the statue is hollow inside
(3) a change in water temperature during the measurements
(4) the spilling of water when the statue is removed from the container
(5) a mistake in an earlier measurement of the statue's weight

Answers are on page 22.

Answer Key

1. (3) Cost is the only factor listed that is not mentioned in the passage.

2. (2) Food companies correctly assume that there is a growing number of health-conscious people who do not want additives in food.

3. (3) The spheres carry <u>like charges</u> and will push away from each other. This follows the principle that like charges repel and unlike charges attract.

4. (4) The toad is the exception because it has a longer life expectancy than the cat, dog, lion, and horse.

5. (4) The difference in life expectancy is 50 years minus 15 years which equals 35 years.

6. (5) According to the passage, the torpedo-like shape of a shark is related to the shark's ability to move swiftly.

7. (1) Long-term population change determines whether an animal is in danger of becoming extinct. Choices (2), (3), and (4) are not relevant. Choice (5) is not correct: all the sharks may be killed by one disease, or they may be killed by hunters.

8. (5) Although choices (1) and (2) may also be true, only choice (5) is supported directly by information from the table.

9. (4) Because of the explosive nature of these two gases, the best rule is to store them as far away from one another as possible.

10. (2) The diagram shows how wave action erodes a cliff, slowly moving the edge of the cliff farther inland and creating more beach.

11. (1) As the cliff is undercut and worn away, the depth of the beach increases. Neither the height of the cliff nor the height of the high tide is affected by wave action.

12. (3) During a temperature inversion, the air temperature is cooler but not necessarily cold, eliminating choice (1). As the passage states, air pollution is the main concern.

13. (1) Because some air pollution comes from automobile exhausts, city residents should be advised to leave their cars at home.

14. (2) Of the foot structures shown, the grasping ability of the hawk is the most suitable for picking up and carrying small land animals.

15. (4) The birds most apt to get food from rivers and lakes are birds most adapted for wading or swimming.

16. (5) Of the choices listed, (5) refers to the person whose interest is least likely to involve foot shape, structure, or function.

17. (2) Statement A is an opinion. Statement C is a hypothesis that cannot be proved.

18. (3) Only statement C is a hypothesis, offering an explanation for the feeling of moodiness.

19. (4) Choice (4) is a reasonable prediction based on the currently known effects of endorphins. Choices (2), (3), and (5) are not supported by information given in the passage. Choice (1) is not as reasonable a prediction as choice (4).

20. (5) The discomfort of overall body soreness is similar to the discomfort felt in strenuous exercise.

21. (2) The diagram indicates that the Moon's orbit refers to the changing position of the Moon (or path of the Moon).

22. (3) An eclipse of the Moon occurs only when the Moon passes in the shadow of Earth. An eclipse can happen only when Earth is directly between the Sun and the Moon.

23. (1) When it moves into Earth's shadow, the Moon is no longer struck by sunlight, and it turns dark and disappears from view.

24. (4) The main use of both a desk lamp and a candle is to produce light. Heat is also produced by each.

25. (5) Wöhler's discovery showed that a nonliving substance (ammonium cyanate) could combine to create a living substance (urea).

26. (2) The top data line indicates that Native Americans had the greatest number of smokers.

27. (1) The graph could be used by scientists to support the need for health information for specific groups. None of the other uses are supported by information in the graph—designing experiments, female smokers, geographic regions.

28. (1) Continental drift is still taking place, although at a very slow rate.

29. (5) As in Wegener's case, a scientific theory may be announced before confirming evidence is found.

30. (4) Lightning cannot be controlled, but buildings can be made safe through the use of a lightning rod—a low-resistance electrical path to the ground.

31. (4) When lightning strikes a tree, the tree may catch fire and a forest fire may result. Choices (2), (3), and (5) are all causes of lightning, not effects.

32. (2) During a lightning storm, you do not want to be in a tree, next to a tree, or near a high point in an open area. Choice (2) is the safest of the listed places.

33. (1) A mercury barometer is used to measure air pressure.

34. (3) A medical thermometer is used to measure human body temperature. A fever is elevated body temperature.

35. (4) The wings of a penguin are like flippers and are used for swimming, in a way similar to how arms are used by humans for swimming.

36. (2) The discovery that scurvy could be easily prevented by diet helped lead to the discovery of the importance of vitamins in preventing disease.

37. (5) Residents in coastal cities may find themselves underwater when a tsunami strikes. Death by drowning is likely.

38. (2) A tsunami may travel as quickly as 500 miles per hour, crossing a distance of 1,000 miles in about 2 hours.

39. (1) Galileo had to abandon two hypotheses before discovering evidence that this third hypothesis was correct.

40. (1) The term CO_2 is not preceded by a number, indicating only one (1) molecule.

41. (4) The number of atoms (not molecules) of each element must be the same on each side of the arrow. This is because no atoms of any element are destroyed in a reaction.

42. (4) When a guitar string vibrates, the string itself does not undergo any physical or chemical change. In each of the other choices, matter changes from one form to another.

43. (3) Eating a large amount of calories while working in cold weather is done in response to the body's needs, not an addiction.

44. (3) See the second and third data rows in the chart.

45. (5) See the third and fourth data rows in the chart.

46. (1) Daily rhythms occur each day, such as the act of sleeping every afternoon.

47. (5) Only choice 5 is based on the passage. Choices (1), (2), and (4) are not true. Choice (3) is not mentioned in the passage.

48. (1) This distance is about 2.7 astronomical units ($93,000,000 \times 2.7 \approx 251,000,000$ miles)

49. (5) The total volume of the statue can be measured only if the entire statue is under water when Step 3 is carried out.

50. (2) Only choice (2) would lead to an error in measuring the volume of clay. If the statue is hollow, the volume of clay may be much less than the volume of the statue itself.

Evaluation Chart

The chart below indicates the distribution of questions that will be on the official GED Science Test. Contemporary's Science Pretest matches the official GED distribution. The Pretest question numbers are placed in the chart according to the organization of the GED Test.

Circle the number of any question you missed. If you missed fewer than 10 questions, you might consider doing the **Short Course in Science** discussed on page xiii. However, even if you do very well on the Pretest, we recommend that you study as much of this book as your time permits. This will ensure that you are thoroughly prepared for the GED Test and that you have rounded out your knowledge of science—an important step as you continue your education.

Subject Area / Themes	Life Science (45%) (pages 157–254)	Physical Science (35%) (pages 255–336)	Earth and Space Science (20%) (pages 337–385)
Fundamental Understandings	12 questions 5, 6, 14, 15, 16, 20, 26, 40, 44, 45, 46, 47	7 questions 3, 18, 30, 31, 41, 42, 49	6 questions 10, 11, 21, 22, 28, 48
Unifying Concepts and Processes (pages 27–48)	1 question 35	1 question 43	0 questions
Science as Inquiry (pages 49–94)	3 questions 4, 7, 8	3 questions 17, 19, 50	1 question 23
Science and Technology (pages 95–114)	1 question 34	1 question 24	1 question 33
Science in Personal and Social Perspectives (pages 115–138)	5 questions 1, 2, 13, 27, 37	2 questions 9, 32	2 questions 12, 38
History and Nature of Science (pages 139–155)	1 question 36	2 questions 25, 39	1 question 29

CHAPTER 1

Concepts and Processes in Science

One thing I have learned in a long life: that all our science, measured against reality, is primitive and childlike—and yet it is the most precious thing we have.

~ Albert Einstein

For human beings today, the world is a place of amazing discoveries. Earth is our laboratory, and our imagination knows few boundaries. We have discovered an incredible amount about planet Earth, the life forms on Earth, the solar system, and the universe as a whole. And, most of our knowledge has come to us in a very short time. In fact, if the time human beings have been on Earth could be condensed to one day, then it would be true to say that 99 percent of our present knowledge has been discovered in the final seconds of the final minute of the final hour. How have we accomplished this? The answer has to do with widespread education and the increasingly careful use of the following methods of science:

- Observing
- Identifying
- Describing
- Experimenting
- Explaining
- Communicating

These methods are used in all fields of science and are the basis of many practice exercises in this book. You may want to make these methods part of your daily life.

Today we look at Earth as a home to be understood and taken care of. Many problems face us to be sure, but we believe that science can and will provide answers to our most serious challenges. We have faith in the future, and we have faith in ourselves.

Did you know that people have not always felt this way? For much of human history, people thought of Earth as a fearful place, a place ruled by an assortment of gods, giants, and demons. Storms, volcanoes, earthquakes, and even the Sun itself were not features of Earth to study and understand. They were warnings and punishments to be feared. Human and animal sacrifices often were used as a form of communication and peacemaking between human beings and their gods.

- In the valley of Mexico before the arrival of Spanish conquerors in the sixteenth century, the Aztecs offered human sacrifices to the Sun.

- In western Africa centuries ago, one tribe of Aborigines believed that the jungle was the hair of a giant. They thought that creatures in the jungle were lice in the giant's hair and that earthquakes came from the giant shaking his head.

- In ancient Iceland, Norsemen believed that earthquakes resulted from quarrels among their gods.

- Ancient Polynesian islanders believed that the goddess Pele and her sister Namakaokahai battled across the Pacific Ocean and that a scar of each battle created each of the Hawaiian Islands.

- The ancient Chinese made human and animal offerings to the spirits of ancestors and to a variety of gods.

- Ancient Europeans believed that Iceland's most active volcano, Hekla, was Hell's Gate and that the lava that shot out of its crater contained the souls of the damned.

The beliefs of ancient peoples seem strange to us today. This is because we live at a time in which scientific explanation has replaced fear-based explanation. Today, scientific knowledge is based on logic, observation, and experimentation. While explanations of natural processes have changed over the centuries, one thing hasn't changed. People have always tried to explain, in the most meaningful way they can, those things that they observe and those things that are most important to them.

Thinking About Science

Directions: Below are two beliefs that were falsely held in the sixteenth century. Why may people have drawn each of these conclusions? Write a possible reason for each conclusion on the lines below.

1. Frogs fall from the sky during a rainstorm.

   _____

   _____

2. Maggots (the larval stage of flies) form from the rotting remains of meat.

   _____

   _____

Answers are on page 433.

GED PRACTICE

Directions: Choose the <u>one best answer</u> to each question.

Questions 1 and 2 refer to the following passage.

About 2,600 years ago, the Greek philosopher Thales was one of the first scholars to try to understand natural phenomena in a scientific way. Thales taught that Earth was a flat disk floating on the universal element, water.

1. What did Thales most likely see that led him to conclude that Earth is a flat disk?

   (1) the shape of the full moon
   (2) the shape of the coastline of Greece
   (3) the shape of mountains in Greece
   (4) the shape of the sea near Greece
   (5) the numerous rivers in Greece

2. Suppose Thales wondered about why the moon appeared to change shape during the days of each month. Which of the following scientific steps would Thales not have been able to do?

   (1) observe the shape of the moon each night for a month
   (2) describe how the shape changed from night to night
   (3) experiment in order to determine the distance of the Moon from Earth
   (4) explain what he observed to the best of his ability
   (5) communicate his beliefs to other Greek scholars

Answers are on page 433.

Systems, Order, and Organization

To begin the study of science, we will first look at some unifying ideas in science—ideas that are the bedrock upon which modern scientific understanding is based.

Systems

Because the world is a complex place, scientists choose to investigate small units for better understanding. Each unit of investigation is called a **system.** A system is an organized group of related objects or components that form a whole.

- A system can be a whole living organism or a part of an organism. Example: The human body can be thought of as a single system or a group of smaller systems working together. Among these systems are the circulatory system, the digestive system, the nervous system, the muscular system, and the skeletal system.

- A system can be the whole Earth or part of Earth. Example: A river valley is made up of a river, a valley, and surrounding mountains.

- A system can encompass more than what the eye can see. Example: The solar system contains the Sun, planets, and all other objects that revolve around the Sun.

- A system can be smaller than the unaided eye can see. Example: A colony of bacteria can be seen only with a microscope.

- A system can be something that people have made. Example: A computer system may contain a computer, a viewing terminal, a keyboard, a printer, speakers, and other components.

Systems are not independent. The well-being of one system often involves other systems. When you have a fever, it makes little sense to say that your digestive system has a fever. Your whole body has a fever. When an automobile is involved in an accident, you would not say that the electrical system of the car got rear-ended.

A computer system

The human circulatory system

Order

Fortunately, the world has **order**—properties and behavior that are predictable. Our personal sense of this order is based on personal experience. Much of this experience we learn as children growing up. As babies we have a very limited sense of order. Without order in nature, we would find the world very confusing. Here are some examples of what life might be like in a world without order:

- Suppose the Sun rose only one day each week, but what's worse, suppose you never knew in advance which day that would be! Because sleep depends on predictable patterns of daylight and darkness, your sleep would be very disrupted and you undoubtedly would be tired much of the time.

- Suppose that an ice cube did not always melt when placed in a glass of water. What if on some days the ice would melt and cool the water and on some days it wouldn't. You would never be able to count on using ice to cool water. You would only know that it might cool water.

- Suppose that a dropped rock didn't always fall to the ground. What if on some days the rock would rise into the sky? This would bring new meaning to the signs that read Watch Out for Falling Rocks.

- Suppose you were driving a car. What if sometimes you hit the accelerator and the car slowly sped up and other times the car would speed up rapidly. How would you know how much force you needed to apply to the accelerator?

Your experience tells you what happens in our real world. The sun rises each day. Ice always melts in room-temperature water. Rocks always fall to the ground. The more force you use on the accelerator, the more quickly the car speeds up. Personal experience gives you a sense of the order that is a property of our world.

Order gives meaning to our lives. Order enables us to structure our time. Order gives us things that we can rely on. Experience also teaches us that order in nature does not change from day to day nor from place to place. Order enables us to predict events based on the probability that they will or won't occur.

Because of order, scientists know that experiments done today in their laboratories will give the same results as experiments done at another time in another place. These results can be trusted and can be used to better understand and help human life on Earth. Order makes scientific progress possible.

Organization

Scientists often describe systems by how they are organized. There seems to be a natural organization to most things, living and nonliving, that are objects of scientific study.

- Stars are organized into grouped clusters called galaxies.

- Galaxies are organized into star systems that include stars, planets, moons, and asteroids.

- Organisms are organized at several levels. At the lowest level are cells. Groups of cells organize to form tissues. Groups of tissues organize to form organs. Groups of organs organize to form organ systems. The group of all organ systems comprises the organism.

- Chemicals that make up all parts of cells are made up of organized molecules.

- Molecules are made up of organized atoms.

- Atoms are made up of electrons surrounding a central nucleus that contains protons and neutrons.

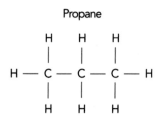

Propane

A propane molecule is organized as eight atoms of hydrogen and three atoms of carbon.

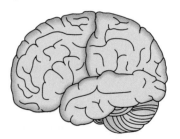

The human brain, a specialized organ that is the center of thought and emotions, is an organization of many types of tissues.

Scientists often classify, or organize, systems to better show their similarities and differences.

- Stars are classified by size, shape, age, and composition.

- Organisms are classified by structure and function.

- Elements are classified by number of electrons.

- Elements are organized in a list called the periodic table.

Thinking About Science

Directions: Answer each question below.

1. What is a system?

   _____

2. What do scientists mean by *order?*

   _____

3. What are three parts of the human digestive system—the system involved in eating and digesting food?

   _____

4. What would happen if you dropped several ice cubes into a heated pan sitting on a red-hot burner on a stove?

   _____

Answers are on page 433.

GED PRACTICE

Directions: Choose the <u>one best answer</u> to each question.

Questions 1 and 2 refer to the reading selection on pages 30–32.

1. Which of the following statements about systems is true?

   (1) Every system is visible to the eye.
   (2) Every system is a living thing.
   (3) Every system is a nonliving thing.
   (4) A system may be a living or a nonliving thing.
   (5) All systems are organized in the same way.

2. Which of the following is an inborn skill that a baby can do without needing to learn from experience?

   (1) read
   (2) walk
   (3) cry
   (4) write
   (5) crawl

Answers are on page 433.

Evidence, Models, and Explanation

Evidence

Scientists base scientific explanation on **evidence**—observations and data that come from experiments. As an example, a chemist may believe that a fuel additive will increase a car's gasoline mileage. But, his belief itself is not a scientific fact. The chemist must base his belief on evidence. To do this, the chemist tests the car with the fuel additive placed in the gasoline. If the mileage does improve, the chemist has evidence to support his belief. What the chemist thinks will happen is not as important as what actually does happen. It is this reliance on evidence that is characteristic of scientific investigation.

Models

Models are ideas, drawings, or objects that stand for real things. Models help scientists picture the way things are. A model can take many forms, including a mental image, a drawing, a physical object, a mathematical equation, and a computer simulation. Scientists often use models to illustrate written explanations, as shown below.

For example, sound travels through air as a compression wave. If you could look at a sound wave from the side, you would see alternating groups of compressed air molecules and rarefied (widely spaced) air molecules. The distance between two similar groups is called the wavelength.

A sound wave can be represented by a drawing or by a physical object (such as a spring).

DRAWING REPRESENTING A SOUND WAVE

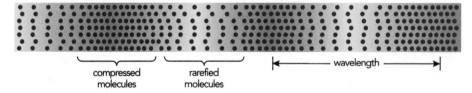

compressed molecules   rarefied molecules   wavelength

PHYSICAL MODEL OF A SOUND WAVE

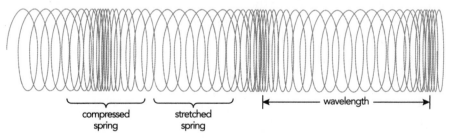

compressed spring   stretched spring   wavelength

Explanation

Scientific **explanation** starts with scientific facts that are already known. To these facts, scientists add newly acquired evidence that comes from observation, experiments, and models. In the search for better explanations, scientists must carefully distinguish between scientific facts, hypotheses, and opinions.

- A **scientific fact** is a conclusion, based on evidence, that scientists agree on. For example, it is a scientific fact, based on geological evidence, that dinosaurs became extinct about 70 million years ago.

- A **hypothesis** is a reasonable explanation of evidence or a prediction based on evidence. Some scientists hypothesize that dinosaurs became extinct because of the sudden occurrence of an ice age most likely brought about by an asteroid crashing into Earth.

- An **opinion** is a personal belief that is often based on a person's own value system. A person may have the opinion that the study of dinosaurs is a waste of taxpayers' money.

Thinking About Science

Directions: Write *F, H,* or *O* on the line preceding each statement below to classify the statement as a fact, hypothesis, or opinion.

_____ 1. The reason that human beings and chimpanzees show genetic similarities may be that each evolved from a common ancestor millions of years ago.

_____ 2. Although any person can lose his or her hair, baldness is much more common in men than in women.

_____ 3. Because of superior intelligence, human beings are the most important animals that have ever lived.

_____ 4. During winter months, tree roots store food that is used by the plant as it grows new leaves and stems in the spring.

_____ 5. The reason that Moon rocks are so similar to Earth rocks may be that the Moon and Earth once were part of the same cloud of matter in space.

Answers are on page 433.

Directions: Choose the <u>one best answer</u> to each question.

Questions 1–3 refer to the following passage.

While hiking, Jerry and DeShawn had a strange encounter with bees. On the way up the mountain, several bees buzzed around Jerry but not around DeShawn. To see what would happen, Jerry and DeShawn traded shirts for the walk back down. Jerry gave his orange shirt to DeShawn, and Jerry wore DeShawn's brown shirt. On the way down the mountain, several bees now buzzed around DeShawn but not around Jerry. Jerry and DeShawn are now trying to explain what they have observed.

1. Which fact is the most important evidence for Jerry and DeShawn?

    (1) Jerry is taller than DeShawn.
    (2) DeShawn is older than Jerry.
    (3) The shirts are different colors.
    (4) The shirts are the same size.
    (5) Both shirts have long sleeves.

2. Which additional information would Jerry and DeShawn need to know before they can explain the bee activity?

    (1) whether bees have a sense of smell
    (2) whether bees have color vision
    (3) whether bees have a sense of taste
    (4) what time of day bees seek food
    (5) in what way bees tell direction

3. Which of Jerry's statements below is best called a hypothesis?

    (1) The buzzing sounds of bees are made by their wings.
    (2) Bees build hives in which they lay their eggs.
    (3) Bees produce honey.
    (4) Bees are an annoyance.
    (5) Bees would be attracted to anything that has a flower color.

Question 4 refers to the following passage and drawing.

The *wavelength* of a sound wave decreases as the frequency of the wave, or pitch of the sound, increases. For example, the wavelength of the sound of a bass drum is much longer than the wavelength of a high note played on a flute.

Shown below are picture models of five frequencies.

4. Which picture represents the sound with the highest frequency?

    (1) A
    (2) B
    (3) C
    (4) D
    (5) E

Answers are on page 433.

Change, Constancy, and Measurement

Change

Change, perhaps more than any other property, characterizes our world. Many things around you are in the process of change: children grow, leaves fall from trees, rivers slowly carve canyons along their paths, and so on. Change is even a property of simple activities, such as kicking a soccer ball.

KICKING A SOCCER BALL	
Things That Are Changing	**Things That Are Not Changing**
speed of the ball	shape of the ball
position of the ball on the field	weight of the ball
dirt on the ball	material the ball is made from
temperature of the ball	air contained within the ball

Scientists study every type of change. Some changes, such as the kicked soccer ball, occur just once unless the ball is kicked again. Other types of changes occur in a cyclical way, over and over without human intervention. Cyclical changes are of great interest to scientists. Here are a few examples:

- Daily changes, such as ocean tides coming in and going out on a predictable time schedule

- Seasonal changes, such as the falling of leaves in autumn and new growth in spring

- Yearly changes, such as the migration of whales and birds

Constancy

Scientists also study **constancy,** or the tendency for things to remain unchanged. A kicked soccer ball maintains its shape and weight. The material it is made from does not change, nor does the air inside the ball.

Scientists take a special interest in some things that remain constant.

- **Laws of Nature:** A law of nature is a property of nature that does not change. Laws of nature are discovered, not invented, and can often be written as mathematical formulas. The law of gravity is an example of a law of nature. The law of gravity states that all objects are pulled toward each other by gravitational force and that this force decreases as the distance between objects increases.

  Gravity pulls objects to Earth's surface. No one is sure why there is gravity. Experience, though, tells us that gravity exists and that it does not change. Scientists believe that gravity has existed from the time the universe began. Scientists also believe that the law of gravity is constant and is the same throughout the universe.

- **Biological Processes:** A biological process is a fundamental property that is common to all living organisms. One example of a biological process is the property that each species passes on its own traits to its offspring through a genetic process. Both physical characteristics and behavior patterns can be passed from one generation to the next.

- **Laws of Chance:** A law of chance describes the probability of something happening. When you flip a penny, about half of the time the penny lands heads up and half of the time it lands tails up. Experience tells us that the laws of chance don't change. Today, you have a 50 percent chance of a flipped penny landing heads up. Ten years ago, you had the same chance. Ten years from now, you will have the same chance.

The constancy of the laws of chance is the basis of modern statistics. Insurance rates, for example, are determined after consideration of the laws of chance.

There is order in the world even though most things are in a state of change. There is order because most changes can be understood and fairly well predicted. Even laws of chance are in a state of order. Laws of chance are a predictable uncertainty.

Measurement

Units of measurement don't change. Because of this, numbers can be assigned to things that change and comparisons can be made. For example, a child's height can be measured with a ruler and compared to previous measurements. Likewise, a change in a child's weight can be measured on a scale, and a change in a child's age can be measured with a calendar.

Measurement is an important part of scientific study because units of measurement remain constant through time and place. They are the same in different locations and at different times. An inch in Seattle is the same length today as it was ten years ago. Also, an inch in Seattle is the same length as an inch in New York. The fact that units of measurement don't change is an example of order. A ruler does not change length from time to time or from place to place.

The United States uses two systems of measurement: the more familiar U.S. customary system and the metric system. Canada and most of the other industrialized nations of the world use the metric system.

- Familiar units in the U.S. customary system are inches, feet, yards, miles, fluid ounces, cups, quarts, gallons, pounds, and tons.

- Familiar units in the metric system are centimeters, meters, kilometers, milliliters, liters, grams, and kilograms.

See the Science Almanac on page 457 for more information on systems of measurement.

 **Thinking About Science**

Directions: For each action described below, mention two things that change and two things that remain constant.

1. A helium-filled balloon is released into the air.
   a. Change: _____

   b. Remain constant: _____

2. A glass of water, sitting on a counter, slowly loses water due to evaporation.
   a. Change: _____

   b. Remain constant: _____

3. Write each list of measures below in order from least to greatest. See the Science Almanac on page 457 if you need help.
   a. centimeters, kilometers, millimeters, meters:

   _____   _____

   _____   _____

   b. fluid ounces, tablespoons, gallons, quarts:

   _____   _____

   _____   _____

Answers are on page 433.

 Go to **www.GEDScience.com** for additional practice and instruction!

Directions: Choose the <u>one best answer</u> to each question.

Question 1 refers to the information on pages 37–39.

1. Which of the following would be classified as a cyclical change?

   (1) the growth of a child
   (2) new concrete hardening
   (3) a raging forest fire
   (4) a radio playing
   (5) the phases of the Moon

Question 2 refers to the following passage.

One general scientific law that you may be familiar with is the principle that objects expand when they are heated and contract when they are cooled. A rock will expand when heated to high temperatures and will contract in low temperatures. In fact, it is this expansion and contraction of rocks that cause many large rocks to crack and break apart.

2. Which of the following is <u>not</u> an application of the principle of expansion/contraction?

   (1) A sidewalk is made in sections with a small space between the sections.
   (2) A metal screen door shuts more easily on a cold day than on a warm day.
   (3) Wearing a white shirt on a hot sunny day keeps you cooler than wearing a dark-colored shirt.
   (4) A stuck jar of jam can be more easily opened if hot water is first run over the lid.
   (5) A metal pipe is measured to be slightly longer on a hot day than on a cold day.

Questions 3 and 4 refer to the passage below.

Inherited traits are characteristics that are passed on from parents to children. Hair color is an inherited trait. Two black-haired parents will have a black-haired child.

Traits that are a result of changes you make yourself cannot be passed on. For example, if two black-haired parents dye their hair blonde and then mate, their child will still have black hair.

Genetic characteristics cannot be changed by changes that the parents make. These characteristics are part of the parents' genetic codes.

3. Which of the following characteristics is not an inherited trait?

   (1) weak eyesight
   (2) bone structure
   (3) height
   (4) pierced ears
   (5) baldness

4. Which of the following characteristics is a person most likely to be able to change?

   (1) poor hearing
   (2) leg strength
   (3) height
   (4) eye color
   (5) pain sensitivity

Answers are on page 433.

Evolution, Equilibrium, and Entropy

Evolution

Evolution is a series of changes that occur over time. Evolution can refer to changes taking place in the universe as a whole, to Earth itself, or to organisms on Earth.

- The universe is slowly changing as stars die and new stars are born. Scientists are just beginning to learn of the complex nature of the universe and of the forces at work in it.

- Earth evolves by natural processes such as earthquakes, volcanoes, wind erosion, and water erosion. Scientists have recently discovered that the actions of humans can affect air quality and possibly influence weather patterns and the evolution of Earth itself.

- Organisms evolve over time in response to changes in their natural environment. It is believed that organisms evolve in order to increase survival chances for their species. According to the modern theory of evolution, many differing types of organisms evolved from common ancestors that existed long ago but do not exist today.

Equilibrium

Equilibrium is a condition in which change takes place but not in an obvious way. In a state of equilibrium, change takes place in equal and opposite ways.

Suppose you place several tablespoons of salt in a glass of water. After a while, some salt has dissolved in the water and some has settled to the bottom of the glass. It appears that no further change takes place. However, salt is constantly condensing from the water and settling on the bottom, and the salt on the bottom is constantly dissolving and entering the water. In this state of equilibrium, exactly the same amount of salt is condensing as is dissolving. It looks like nothing is happening, but change is continually taking place.

Entropy

Entropy is the tendency of certain organized systems to become randomly disorganized.

On a pool table, for example, balls very quickly become randomly distributed around the table after the first few shots.

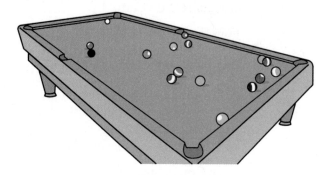

The tendency toward randomness is characteristic of systems in our world.

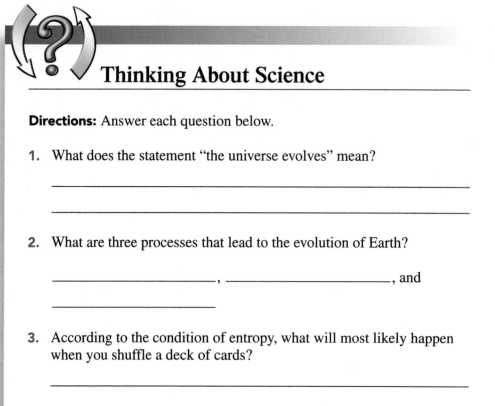

Thinking About Science

Directions: Answer each question below.

1. What does the statement "the universe evolves" mean?

   _____

   _____

2. What are three processes that lead to the evolution of Earth?

   _____ , _____ , and

   _____

3. According to the condition of entropy, what will most likely happen when you shuffle a deck of cards?

   _____

Answers are on page 433.

Directions: Choose the <u>one best answer</u> to each question.

Questions 1 and 2 refer to the following passage.

Homeostasis is a term used to describe the tendency of a biological system to maintain a state of equilibrium. Homeostasis is an organism's way of maintaining a stable internal environment that best aids in the organism's own chances for survival. One example of homeostasis in human beings is the body's tendency to try to maintain a stable amount of sugar in the blood.

1. Which of the following is an example of homeostasis occurring in a human being?

   (1) a toothache
   (2) sweating
   (3) a nosebleed
   (4) running
   (5) forgetting

2. Which of the following is least likely to help a young girl keep warm on a very cold day when she is outside?

   (1) rubbing her hands together
   (2) shivering
   (3) jumping up and down
   (4) running back and forth
   (5) sitting still

Question 3 refers to the following diagram.

Shown below, out of order, are three pictures of a glass of water and a sugar cube.

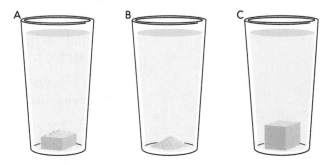

3. In which order should these three pictures be placed if a physical process is being shown?

   (1) C, B, A
   (2) B, A, C
   (3) A, B, C
   (4) C, A, B
   (5) B, C, A

Answers are on page 434.

Form and Function

In nature there is a strong relationship between the form, or physical characteristics, of an organism and the function served by that form.

- A shark is shaped in a way that allows it to swim through water most quickly.

- A seagull has large wings that enable it to glide over ocean beaches in search of food.

- A giraffe has a long neck that enables it to reach high into trees for leaves that other animals cannot reach.

Animals that are closely related may have slightly different body structures. The differing structures are most likely related to the special needs of each animal. The forms differ slightly to better serve slightly differing functions.

What is the main difference between the African elephant (found in Africa) and the Asian elephant (found in Asia) pictured below?

AFRICAN ELEPHANT   **ASIAN ELEPHANT**

The ears on the African elephant are much larger than those on the Asian elephant. Why is this so? The answer has to do with cooling. Both elephants have large ears that are used for cooling. Ear lobes are full of blood vessels and as an elephant flaps its ears the blood within the lobes is cooled. The cooled blood circulates through the elephant and helps cool the whole animal.

The difference in ear size is related to the fact that the African elephant lives in a much hotter climate than the Asian elephant. The cooling needs of the African elephant are greater than those of the Asian elephant.

Sometimes, related animals have developed quite different uses for very similar body parts. The penguin, like a seagull, is a bird. The penguin has wings but does not fly. A penguin uses its wings only as flippers for swimming. A seagull uses its wings for flying and gliding. While the structures of wings on penguins and seagulls are very similar, the function they serve is very different. The seagull and the penguin use their wings in a way most useful to each. There is great flexibility in nature's design.

Learning from Nature

Nature often helps us understand how form and function are best related. Think about the similarities in shape between the two largest objects in the ocean: whales and submarines. Also notice the similarities in shape between airplanes and birds. Animals, it seems, have evolved in a way that makes the best use of form and function.

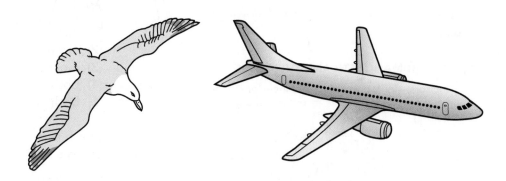

The shape of a bird is the model for the shape of an airplane.

Thinking About Science

Directions: Name a function served by each body part listed below.

1. the tail of a cow: _____

2. the trunk of an elephant: _____

3. the tail of a fish: _____

Answers are on page 434.

GED PRACTICE

Directions: Choose the <u>one best answer</u> to each question.

Questions 1 and 2 refer to the following diagram.

HUMAN TEETH AND THEIR USES

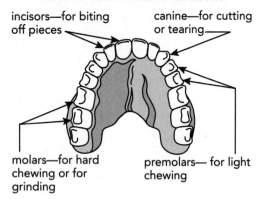

1. Which teeth would you most likely use for chewing a cut piece of steak before swallowing?

   (1) incisors
   (2) canines
   (3) molars
   (4) both incisors and canines
   (5) both incisors and premolars

2. Which teeth are you most likely to use for biting a string in half?

   (1) incisors
   (2) canines
   (3) premolars
   (4) molars
   (5) both premolars and molars

Answers are on page 434.

Concepts and Processes in Science Review

Directions: Choose the <u>one best answer</u> to each question.

Questions 1 and 2 refer to the following passage.

The study of the development of different species of animals raises many fascinating questions. One of the most interesting questions concerns the discovery of vestigial organs. A *vestigial organ* is an organ that is small or imperfectly developed and seems to have no use. What is the purpose of a vestigial organ? So far, scientists have not found a purpose.

An example of a vestigial organ is the presence of leg bones in a snake. These small bones are absolutely useless to snakes that exist at the present time. One explanation of vestigial organs is that present-day animals evolved from ancestors who needed these organs. According to this explanation, snakes inherited the genes that produce leg bones from an ancestral relative among ancient reptiles that did have legs.

1. Which of the following is a fact that is given in the reading passage?

   (1) Vestigial organs are not very large and are easily identified.
   (2) Vestigial organs are present in all reptiles alive today.
   (3) A vestigial organ is not inherited.
   (4) A vestigial organ may have more than one use in an organism.
   (5) A vestigial organ has no known use in an organism.

2. Which of the following is a hypothesis?

   (1) Vestigial organs evolved from useful organs.
   (2) Vestigial organs are present only in snakes.
   (3) Snakes have vestigial leg bones.
   (4) Snakes inherited genes from previous generations of reptiles.
   (5) Vestigial organs have no known purpose.

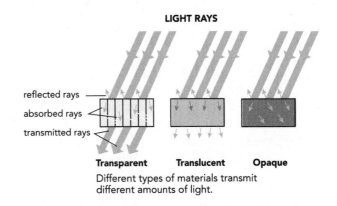

LIGHT RAYS

reflected rays
absorbed rays
transmitted rays

Transparent Translucent Opaque

Different types of materials transmit different amounts of light.

Questions 3–5 refer to the drawing above.

3. What process does the drawing represent?

   (1) how energy is carried by light
   (2) how sunlight is composed of a rainbow of colors
   (3) how light intensity varies with different light sources
   (4) how light acts when it strikes different surfaces
   (5) how light reflects off of metal surfaces

4. Which type of material would make the best clear window glass?

   (1) transparent glass
   (2) translucent glass
   (3) opaque glass
   (4) either transparent or opaque glass
   (5) either translucent or opaque glass

5. What feature is used as a basis for classifying the three types of materials pictured?

   (1) color change when struck by light
   (2) light transmitting properties
   (3) temperature change due to absorption of light
   (4) weight change due to absorption of light
   (5) tendency to crack when heated by light

Questions 6 and 7 refer to the following passage.

According to the scientific principle of stimulus-response, an organism will respond when acted on by a stimulus (something that can be felt, seen, heard, or smelled). An organism tries to respond to each stimulus in a way that best ensures its own well-being.

6. A young boy throws a handful of crackers into a pond. Which of the following is the best example of a response to this stimulus?

    (1) The crackers dissolve in the water.
    (2) Fish in the pond pay no attention.
    (3) A nearby frog catches a mosquito.
    (4) Ducks swim toward the crackers.
    (5) The boy walks towards his parents.

7. Which of the following is true about a stimulus-response reaction?

    (1) The response and the stimulus occur exactly at the same time.
    (2) The response always occurs before the stimulus.
    (3) The stimulus always occurs before the response.
    (4) The purpose of a stimulus is to help ensure an organism's survival.
    (5) The purpose of a response is to attract attention.

Questions 8 and 9 refer to the following illustrations.

BEAK STRUCTURES OF NORTH AMERICAN BIRDS

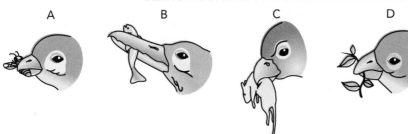

A	B	C	D	E
eating insects	capturing fish	tearing	eating seeds	sieving (taking tiny food particles from water)

8. Which two illustrations show beaks designed for getting food from rivers, lakes, and oceans?

    (1) A and C
    (2) B and D
    (3) C and E
    (4) B and E
    (5) D and E

9. Which illustration shows the beak structure found on birds that are least dependent on keen eyesight for food gathering?

    (1) A
    (2) B
    (3) C
    (4) D
    (5) E

Answers are on page 434.

CHAPTER 2

Comprehending and Applying Science

Knowledge for itself alone seeks answers to such questions as "How high is the sky?" or "Why does a stone fall?" This is sheer curiosity . . . Yet there have always been people who ask such apparently useless questions and try to answer them out of the sheer desire to know . . .

~ Isaac Asimov

As a first step in investigation, scientists often read material written by other scientists. Scientists need to comprehend, or understand, what they read so they can determine how the information applies to their investigation.

The GED Science Test will test your critical thinking skills in scientific inquiry. Two very important skills include being able to comprehend science materials and to apply science concepts. You will be tested on reading passages and graphics: drawings, diagrams, and graphs. In this chapter you will practice each of these skills.

Comprehending Science Materials

Comprehension refers to three main skills:

- Summarizing the main idea

- Restating information

- Identifying implications and inferences

Summarizing the Main Idea

To **summarize** the main idea means to briefly express a writer's key thought. You may be asked to summarize (or find) the main idea of a single paragraph or of several paragraphs. For example, a reading passage may consist of several paragraphs on research done on vaccines for common wintertime respiratory infections. You may determine that each paragraph and its many details support one main idea: There is still no way to prevent the common cold.

In the following paragraph on page 50, the main idea is stated in the first sentence. The other sentences in the paragraph provide details to support the main idea. Notice how the first sentence draws the reader's immediate attention to the point the writer is trying to make.

The action of ocean waves can change the shape of a shoreline. Waves can erode the shore, breaking up land masses near the water. Waves can also move the eroded dirt and rocks great distances down the shoreline. Beaches are formed when waves move more rock fragments toward the shore rather than away from it. Cliffs are formed when waves move more rock fragments away from the shore than toward it.

The changing shape of a shoreline is the writer's main idea. Each of the other sentences gives an example of how this change takes place. Each example is a detail that supports the main idea.

In the next paragraph the main idea is stated in the final sentence. Notice how the last sentence summarizes the information given in the sentences that lead to it.

Imagine taking a microscope and looking at the edge of a piece of paper in the hope of seeing a single atom! Using the world's most powerful microscope, you still could not see one atom. In fact, if you could see one, you would find that it takes about one million atoms, placed side by side, to cross a distance as short as the thickness of the edge of the paper. Atoms are so small that scientists must be content with studying large numbers of them at the same time.

In some passages a main idea may not be expressed in a single sentence. In this case, you can usually express the main idea as a summary of several points made by the writer.

The first action your body takes when you eat food is to begin the process of digestion. Digestion takes place in the mouth, stomach, and intestines. During digestion, food is broken down into small molecules. These molecules pass into the bloodstream when they reach the intestines. The step following digestion is called absorption. During absorption, food molecules leave your blood and enter your cells. The final step, assimilation, takes place within the cells themselves. During assimilation, cells use the food molecules for body growth and maintenance.

The main idea of this paragraph is not stated in a single sentence. If you were to summarize this information, you might write: *Digestion, absorption, and assimilation are the three steps used by the body in making use of the food you eat.*

A main idea may also be taken from a graphic. The use of a graphic makes it possible for a writer to convey much information in a compact way. Also, a graphic is easy to read and summarize.

The circle graph below shows the breakdown of Earth's surface. Each segment has a label and a percent value. For example, the graph shows that the Pacific Ocean covers 33 percent (about one-third) of Earth's surface.

The main idea of this graph is that *the surface of Earth is covered mainly by water.* Supporting details tell the percent of the surface covered with land and the percents covered by each of the four major oceans and other seas.

EARTH'S SURFACE

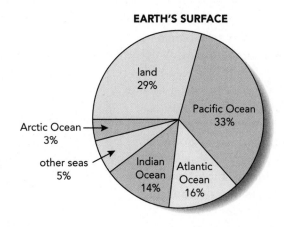

 **Thinking About Science**

Directions: Answer each question below.

1. How do beaches form?

   _____

   _____

   _____

   _____

2. What happens during the absorption of food molecules?

   _____

   _____

   _____

   _____

Answers are on page 434.

Directions: Choose the <u>one best answer</u> to each question.

Question 1 refers to the following passage.

Chimpanzees are highly intelligent members of the ape family and are genetically very similar to human beings. Because of the similarity with humans, chimpanzees are used as subjects in medical experiments. Researchers purposely infect chimpanzees with various diseases to study the effects of new drugs and to learn and practice new types of surgery. For example, chimpanzees purposely infected with the AIDS virus do not become sick and die as do many human AIDS patients. By studying the properties of the chimpanzee's blood and immune system, researchers hope to develop new types of medicines that can provide protection against the devastating effects of AIDS.

1. What is the main idea expressed in this passage?

   (1) Chimpanzees get many human diseases because they are genetically similar to human beings.
   (2) Chimpanzees are intelligent apes that do not differ much from human beings.
   (3) Chimpanzees are not harmed when experiments are performed on them.
   (4) Chimpanzees are used in medical research because they are genetically similar to human beings.
   (5) Chimpanzees are not exposed to the AIDS virus as long as they are living in their natural habitat.

Questions 2 and 3 refer to the circle graph below.

SOLID WASTE DISPOSAL IN THE UNITED STATES

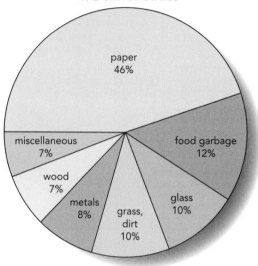

2. According to the graph, what material is the largest component of garbage in the United States?

   (1) glass
   (2) paper
   (3) food garbage
   (4) metals
   (5) wood

3. An author used this graph in an article about the value of recycling paper, metal, and glass products. Which of the following statements best summarizes a key point made by the graph?

   (1) The United States produces more garbage than any other country on Earth.
   (2) Garbage can be conveniently classified in seven broad categories.
   (3) Sixty-four percent of American garbage is material that could be recycled.
   (4) Recycling efforts are failing because too much garbage is being recycled.
   (5) Because of the amount of dirt in garbage, most things that are thrown away cannot be recycled.

Question 4 refers to the line graph below.

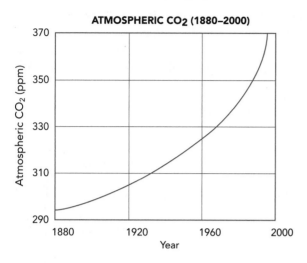

ATMOSPHERIC CO₂ (1880–2000)

* CO₂ is carbon dioxide gas.

* ppm means "parts per million."

4. The graph above recently appeared in an article that discussed the *greenhouse effect* (the warming of Earth's atmosphere as a result of an increase in atmospheric CO_2) on Earth. What main point do you think the author wanted to make by using this graph?

   (1) Atmospheric CO_2 increased steadily between 1880 and 2000.
   (2) No measurements of atmospheric CO_2 were made after 2000.
   (3) Atmospheric CO_2 was not considered a problem before 1880.
   (4) All atmospheric CO_2 should be considered harmful to human health.
   (5) Atmospheric CO_2 levels are now less than they were in 2000.

Question 5 refers to the following passage.

Using specially designed radio telescopes, astronomers can study the sky above us every minute of each day and night. These radio telescopes monitor millions of channels at the same time as they search for clues of life on planets of faraway stars.

No one can predict if or when Earth will ever receive a message sent by intelligent beings from elsewhere in the universe. But one thing is sure. If we do receive such a message, we will be hearing thoughts from the past! Any incoming message would have been sent millions of years ago. This is because it takes radio waves that long to travel the incredible distances that separate our solar system from other star systems.

5. What is the main idea expressed in the final paragraph?

   (1) Intelligent beings probably live on other planets.
   (2) A message received from space would have been sent long ago.
   (3) Large distances separate Earth from other planets.
   (4) Scientists are studying the possibility of life on other planets.
   (5) Earth may someday receive messages from space.

Answers are on page 434.

Go to **www.GEDScience.com** for additional practice and instruction!

Restating Information

To **restate** information is to use different words and phrases to express the same idea. A restatement may not sound quite the same as the original statement, but it has the same meaning. Most often, you restate information to put it into words that are familiar to you—words that make it easier for you to understand and remember what you are reading.

Here are two examples of restated information.

Original
Excess fat and carbohydrate consumption can lead to obesity.

Rocks from the surface of the Moon show features characteristic of rocks found on Earth.

Restatement
You will get fat if you eat too many fats and carbohydrates.

Moon rocks are very similar to Earth rocks.

Notice that each restatement provides information in a way that is more like the way you talk or think. Yet, in the original and in the restatement, the information given is really about the same.

 **Thinking About Science**

Directions: Using your own words, restate each sentence

1. Light reflecting from the lunar surface indicates the spherical shape of our nearest neighbor.

   _____

2. Touching an exposed electric wire, Miguel's finger sensed the passage of electric current and demonstrated a quick reflex.

   _____

3. When Carlina slightly lacerated her finger, the exposed blood reacted with oxygen and formed fibrin, a fibrous substance. As a result, further bleeding was prevented.

   _____

Answers are on page 434.

GED PRACTICE

Directions: Choose the <u>one best answer</u> to each question.

Questions 1–3 refer to the following passage.

The success of modern agriculture is due in large part to our successful fight against crop diseases. To aid in the fight against diseases caused by insects, chemists have developed special types of insect poisons called pesticides.

When pesticides were first used, they were believed to be safe and effective. Although a few pesticides are still safe enough to use, many of them are now known to cause both air and water pollution and to be harmful to human health. One example is DDT, a once widely used pesticide that is now known to be so dangerous to animal and human life that its use has been banned in the United States.

Pesticides can be inhaled directly from the air by animals and people living in areas where air spraying takes place. Because of this potential danger to humans, the spraying of many types of pesticides is now prohibited or strictly controlled near residential areas. Pesticides also get into animal and human foods. For example, insect-eating animals (including game animals) absorb pesticides when they eat contaminated insects. Contaminated game animals can pose a serious threat to human health. In addition, when cows eat grass that has been sprayed with pesticides, both milk and beef become contaminated. Still another problem occurs when pesticides are sprayed over crop fields. These pesticides soak into the ground and can be washed by rain into groundwater and local streams. The pesticides are then eaten by fish and other aquatic animals.

1. What is DDT supposed to protect crops from?

   (1) cold weather
   (2) pollution
   (3) insect diseases
   (4) game animals
   (5) contamination

2. According to the passage, which of the following is true about DDT?

   (1) DDT are the initials of three people who invented a pesticide.
   (2) DDT is the most dangerous pesticide ever used in the United States.
   (3) DDT is still used in many European countries.
   (4) DDT is a pesticide that is now banned in the United States.
   (5) DDT has been found in samples of tuna and other ocean fish.

3. According to the passage, what is one way that pesticides get into groundwater?

   (1) Birds carry pesticides to rivers when they go to drink.
   (2) Contaminated fish bring pesticides to rivers in which they swim.
   (3) Rainwater washes pesticides present in soil into groundwater.
   (4) Wind carries sprayed pesticides into groundwater reservoirs.
   (5) Sprayed insects contaminate groundwater reservoirs.

Questions 4–6 refer to the following diagram.

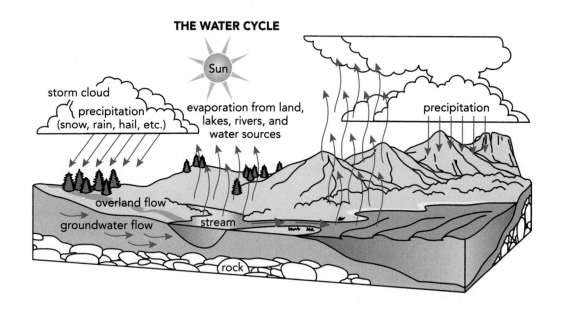

THE WATER CYCLE

4. According to the diagram, which of the following would be the best definition of the label *precipitation*?

   (1) the gases that surround Earth
   (2) moisture that evaporates into the sky
   (3) the seeping of water into Earth
   (4) moisture that falls to Earth
   (5) the flow of water over land

5. What label on this diagram means the same as "moisture that rises into the atmosphere from all land and water sources"?

   (1) stream
   (2) overland flow
   (3) groundwater flow
   (4) precipitation
   (5) evaporation

6. What is the diagram mainly attempting to show?

   (1) the removal of fresh water from land by the actions of both runoff and the growth of vegetation
   (2) the evaporation of water from land and streams due to energy
   (3) the back-and-forth movement of water between Earth's surface and atmosphere
   (4) the formation of storm clouds over a stream and land at the same time
   (5) the changing of fresh water found in clouds to salt water found in oceans

   Answers are on page 434.

Identifying Implications and Inferences

To **imply** means to suggest. An **implication** is a point of view that another person presents to you. For example, someone may write, "Scientists invented nuclear weapons, but I sure don't want them to work on arms control!" This writer implies that he does not have a lot of faith in the political ability of scientists.

To **infer** means to guess at what is not stated directly. An **inference** is a point of view that you arrive at because of what you read, hear, or see. Quite often, you infer what the other person implies.

For an example of both an implication and an inference, read the following:

> With today's gas prices at an all time high, many homes and businesses have switched from gas heat and have installed Emerald solar heating units. Our solar heating unit captures the Sun's energy and uses this energy to heat your residence or office. Happy customers are those who choose Emerald as their solar energy specialist.

The writer implies that heating by solar energy costs less than heating by gas energy. The writer also implies that all of Emerald's customers are happy they switched to solar energy. This writer would like you to infer each of these same points, whether they are true or not.

There is one thing you can infer from this passage: the writer wants you to make Emerald your solar energy specialist!

 **Thinking About Science**

Directions: Read the following passage and answer the questions that follow.

One of the great inventions of the twentieth century is the robot. With its tiny electronic brain humming along, it can be programmed to do just about anything. Since the installation of several robots in our factory, business has really picked up and we have saved a ton of money.

A robot is a great investment. Robots don't take rest breaks, and they don't get sick. They don't require a lunchroom or a smoking area. You don't need to give them medical coverage or retirement benefits. What's more, each robot can do the work of several employees, and it doesn't complain about working 24 hours each day.

1. How would you describe the writer's attitude toward robots?

_____

_____

Answers are on page **435.**

Directions: Choose the <u>one best answer</u> to each question.

Questions 1 and 2 refer to the passage below.

Extinction is the disappearance of a species from Earth. Some species become extinct because of a natural occurrence, such as an ice age. Most likely this is what happened to dinosaurs 70 million years ago. Other species become extinct because of human actions. The passenger pigeon was hunted to extinction during the 1800s. During that same century, the buffalo was almost hunted to extinction.

Today, certain species of whales are in danger of being hunted to extinction. The panda is in danger of becoming extinct in the wild because its main source of food, the bamboo forests of Asia, is being cut down. Thousands of species of small animals, insects, and plants are in danger of extinction because of the burning of Earth's tropical rain forests. Many of these forests are being cleared for the mining of gold and for the grazing of livestock.

Scientists believe that all organisms are on Earth for a limited time, after which better-adapted organisms take their place. This may also apply to human beings.

1. What is the writer's main implication in this passage?

   (1) Humans have no ability to control natural disasters.
   (2) Human actions can either help cause or help prevent extinction.
   (3) Extinct life forms are gone forever.
   (4) Extinction takes place mainly in tropical rain forests.
   (5) Dinosaurs are the largest animals that have become extinct.

2. To which group do you infer that the writer most probably belongs?

   (1) a mining company
   (2) a group protesting higher taxes
   (3) a hunting club
   (4) a group protesting "big government"
   (5) an environmental protection group

Questions 3–5 refer to the following line graph.

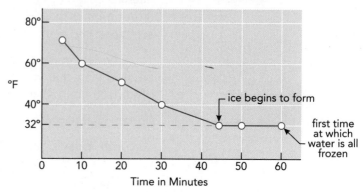

TRAY OF WATER PLACED IN FREEZER

3. About what temperature is the water after 20 minutes have passed?

   (1) 52°F
   (2) 41°F
   (3) 35°F
   (4) 24°F
   (5) 15°F

4. About how long does it take the tray of water to reach a temperature of 32°F?

   (1) 10 minutes
   (2) 20 minutes
   (3) 28 minutes
   (4) 44 minutes
   (5) 55 minutes

5. What can you infer that the tray most likely will contain after being in the freezer for 50 minutes?

   (1) all water at a temperature slightly above 32°F
   (2) all water at a temperature slightly below 32°F
   (3) partly water and partly ice, all at a temperature of 32°F
   (4) all ice at a temperature of 32°F
   (5) all ice at a temperature slightly above 32°F

Answers are on page 435.

Applying Science Concepts

On the GED Science Test, you will be asked to apply scientific concepts to new situations. This application is a measure of two abilities:

- Applying given ideas in a new context

- Applying prior knowledge in a new context

Applying Given Ideas

Many principles in science apply to a lot of different contexts, or situations. One important principle is the following:

> Energy can be changed from one form to another with no energy being lost in the process.

For example, when you turn on a light switch, electrical energy is changed into both light energy and heat energy. The heat energy that is produced is due to the inefficiency of the bulb itself. A 100 percent efficient lightbulb would produce no heat energy.

What types of energy changes are taking place below?

> Naoka lies in the sun at the beach.

> Carlita flips a switch to turn on her portable radio.

In the first sentence, energy from the Sun is being changed into heat energy that warms Naoka. Also, sun energy is being changed into chemical energy to give Naoka a suntan. In the second sentence, electrical energy from the radio's batteries is being changed into sound energy.

 Thinking About Science

Directions: Describe the energy changes taking place in each example below.

1. A solar-powered calculator begins to work when a flashlight is shined on it.

   _____

2. A candle burns after being lit with a match.

   _____

Answers are on page 435.

Directions: Choose the <u>one best answer</u> to each question.

Questions 1–3 are based on the following passage.

A sound wave causes the atoms of a substance to vibrate. The vibrating atoms cause nearby atoms to vibrate at the same rate, or frequency. In this way, a sound wave moves from atom to atom throughout the entire substance. Sound waves cannot travel through any space that does not contain air or other matter.

As a general rule, the speed of sound depends on the density and temperature of the material through which the sound passes. Substances such as iron have tightly packed atoms that transmit sound at a higher speed than substances such as air that have loosely packed atoms.

Sound travels more rapidly in a substance as its temperature is raised. The speed of sound in iron increases as the iron is heated.

1. In which substance would you expect the speed of sound to be the greatest?

    (1) warm water at 112°F
    (2) iron at 212°F
    (3) boiling water at 212°F
    (4) wood at 212°F
    (5) iron at 150°F

2. Two equal-size bars of metal were tested. The researcher found that sound travels more rapidly in lead than in aluminum. What can you infer from this discovery?

    (1) The lead bar was tested first.
    (2) The bars were not the same shape.
    (3) Lead is denser than aluminum.
    (4) Aluminum is heavier than lead.
    (5) Lead and aluminum are equal in weight.

3. Through which of the following is it <u>not</u> possible to transmit sound waves?

    (1) a glass window
    (2) a wire carrying electricity
    (3) cold air over Antarctica
    (4) an ice cube
    (5) the vacuum space in a thermos

Questions 4–6 are based on the following diagram.

PRINCIPLE OF REFLECTION

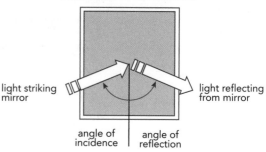

When light strikes a smooth reflective surface such as a mirror, much of the light is reflected. The reflected light leaves the mirror at the same angle that it struck the mirror. Said another way, the angle of incidence equals the angle of reflection.

4. Suppose a light beam strikes a mirror at a 45 degree angle. What is the angle of reflection?

    (1) 30 degrees
    (2) 45 degrees
    (3) 54 degrees
    (4) 90 degrees
    (5) 145 degrees

5. In which study is knowledge of the principle of reflection <u>least</u> likely to be important?

    (1) design of eyeglasses
    (2) design of telescopes
    (3) design of radios
    (4) design of television sets
    (5) design of microscopes

6. In which example does the principle of reflection <u>least</u> apply?

    (1) car headlights shining on a wet highway
    (2) a flashlight shining on a pond
    (3) light from a computer screen shining on a person's eyeglasses
    (4) a lamp shining on a roughly textured ceiling
    (5) an overhead kitchen light shining on a flat piece of aluminum foil

Answers are on page 435.

Scientific Classification

One special way to apply given ideas is scientific classification. As an example, the passage below describes classes of relationships between organisms.

When animals and plants live together in the same environment, such as a forest or a lake, special nutritional relationships develop among many of the different organisms. These relationships can be classified as follows:

- *predator-prey relationship*—One organism kills and eats a second organism. (Example: A lion kills and eats a gazelle.)

- *saprophytic relationship*—An organism takes nutrients from the remains of dead organisms that it finds. (Example: A vulture eats the remains of a dead mouse.)

- *parasitic relationship*—One organism takes nutrients from the living body of another organism and, in doing so, may harm but not kill the other organism. (Example: A flea lives on and takes nutrients from a dog.)

- *mutualistic relationship*—Organisms live together in a way that nutritionally benefits all of the organisms. (Example: A lichen is formed by a mutual relationship between a certain type of algae and fungus.)

- *commensal relationship*—One organism nutritionally benefits from a second organism, while the second organism neither benefits nor is harmed. (Example: A man-of-war fish lives among the poisonous tentacles of a jellyfish in order to escape being eaten by larger fish.)

Thinking About Science

Directions: Compare the following relationships with the preceding definitions.

1. In a freshwater lake, bass live by eating minnows and small crustaceans. What is the nutritional relationship of bass to minnows and small crustaceans?

   _____

2. Many tiny lice can live on the body of a bird by slowly eating its feathers. Although lice damage the feathers, they do not kill the bird. However, the bird does not benefit in any way from this relationship. What is the relationship of the lice to the bird?

   _____

Answers are on page 435.

Directions: Choose the <u>one best answer</u> to each question.

Questions 1–5 refer to the information on page 61.

1. As uninvited guests, small beetles often live in the nest of an ant colony, helping themselves to food supplies built up by the ants. During a prosperous season, the portion of food taken by the beetles is not missed. How would you classify this relationship?

   (1) predator-prey
   (2) saprophytic
   (3) parasitic
   (4) mutualistic
   (5) commensal

2. A fungus causes the disease chestnut blight in the native American chestnut tree. This fungus takes nutrients from the tree and damages plant tissue on any part of the tree on which it grows. Fortunately, chestnut trees usually do not die from this disease. How do you classify the relationship of the chestnut-blight fungus to the chestnut tree?

   (1) predator-prey
   (2) saprophytic
   (3) parasitic
   (4) mutualistic
   (5) commensal

3. Decay bacteria play an important role in bringing nitrogen, needed for plant growth, back into the soil. These bacteria take nutrients from plant and animal remains, break down the proteins, and release ammonia into the soil. How do you classify the relationship of decay bacteria to dead plants and animals?

   (1) predator-prey
   (2) saprophytic
   (3) parasitic
   (4) mutualistic
   (5) commensal

4. While a herd of gazelles graze close by, a solitary lioness lies quietly in the grass. With a powerful but graceful lunge, the lioness brings down a gazelle that strays too far from the herd. The gazelle provides needed meat for the lioness and its cubs. How do you classify the relationship of lioness to the gazelle?

   (1) predator-prey
   (2) saprophytic
   (3) parasitic
   (4) mutualistic
   (5) commensal

5. Some algae live in such close association with a fungus that the two plants together are given the name *lichen*. In a lichen, the fungus captures moisture for the algae and provides protective skin-like covering. The algae produce the food necessary to support the life of both plants. How do you classify the relationship of the fungus to the algae in a lichen?

   (1) predator-prey
   (2) saprophytic
   (3) parasitic
   (4) mutualistic
   (5) commensal

Answers are on page 435.

Applying Remembered Ideas

Some of the questions on the GED Science Test will draw on knowledge you might already have. Below is an example of this type of question. Read it carefully and choose the most reasonable answer.

How might an animal's color be related to its needs?

(1) to allow for absorption of sunlight

(2) to serve as protection from predators

(3) to allow for easy identification

You are correct if you chose (2) *to serve as protection from predators* as your answer. A general principle of science is that animals adapt to their environment in a way that gives them the best chance of survival. If an animal's coloring matches its environment, the animal is less likely to be seen by a predator.

Both in this book and on the GED Science Test, you sometimes may not be familiar with the principle mentioned in a question. If you see a question on the GED Test that you are not able to answer, make the most reasonable guess you can and then move on to the next question.

Thinking About Science

Directions: Answer each question below by applying a remembered idea.

1. In the autumn of each year, ducks and geese gather in huge flocks and begin a long journey to a warmer climate before winter begins. Why do ducks and geese make this annual journey?

   _____

   _____

2. Erosion is the wearing away of land formations by the actions of nature. What might be a cause of erosion of the Rocky Mountains?

   _____

   _____

Answers are on page 435.

Directions: Choose the <u>one best answer</u> to each question.

Questions 1–4 refer to the information on page 63.

1. Which of the following is <u>not</u> an effort to reduce the amount of air pollution to which the general public is exposed?

    (1) developing fuel-efficient car engines
    (2) improving emission-control devices used on truck engines
    (3) restricting the daily use of wood stoves
    (4) reducing money spent researching the problem of acid rain
    (5) limiting the spraying of pesticides near residential areas

2. Which of the following devices is designed to change chemical energy into electrical energy?

    (1) a microwave oven
    (2) a television set
    (3) a car battery
    (4) a hot-air balloon
    (5) an electric fan

3. Viruses that cause the common cold can survive several hours outside the human body. Which of the following is <u>not</u> directly related to your preventing the spread of a cold when you have one?

    (1) covering your mouth when you cough
    (2) dressing extra warmly
    (3) sneezing into a tissue
    (4) washing your hands often
    (5) avoiding close contact with others

4. Suppose a person accidentally swallows liquid from a bottle marked *Harmful if Swallowed*. Which of the following would a doctor be <u>least</u> interested in?

    (1) the amount of liquid swallowed
    (2) the type of liquid that was swallowed
    (3) the time the liquid was swallowed
    (4) the last time the victim ate
    (5) the place the liquid was purchased

Questions 5–6 refer to the following diagram.

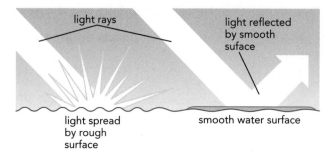

5. In which case are you most likely to see sunlight reflecting off a smooth water surface?

    (1) taking a bath
    (2) sitting by a calm wading pool
    (3) hiking on a mountain trail
    (4) walking in the rain
    (5) swimming in the ocean

6. What is another substance with reflective properties similar to a smooth water surface?

    (1) sandpaper
    (2) drying house paint
    (3) laundry soap
    (4) furniture polish
    (5) candle wax

7. Suppose you want a room to reflect as much light as possible in all directions equally. What is the best finishing texture to apply to the ceiling?

    (1) a smooth white finish
    (2) a smooth dark finish
    (3) a rough white finish
    (4) a rough dark finish
    (5) a smooth finish, white in the center and dark near the walls

Answers are on page 435.

Comprehending and Applying Science Review

Directions: Choose the <u>one best answer</u> to each question.

Questions 1 and 2 refer to the following passage.

Heat always flows from an object of higher temperature to an object of lower temperature. For an object to feel cool to the touch, heat must flow from your hand to the object. When heat leaves your skin, your skin feels cool.

Heat will flow from your hand only if the object you touch is at a lower temperature than your body temperature (about 98.6°F). Also, heat will flow from your hand more easily if the object you touch conducts, or transmits, heat easily. For example, room-temperature metal is a good conductor of heat and feels cool to the touch. Room-temperature cloth is a poor conductor of heat and usually feels neither hot nor cold.

1. Which of the following best summarizes a main point in the passage above?

   (1) Hard objects tend to feel cooler to the touch than soft objects do.
   (2) The sensation of coolness occurs when heat leaves your body.
   (3) An object that is at a lower temperature than 98.6°F cannot burn you.
   (4) Your hands are the part of your body most sensitive to hot and cold.
   (5) Objects at room temperature are usually good conductors of heat.

2. From information given in the passage, which of the following can you infer?

   (1) When metal and cloth touch, heat flows from the metal to the cloth.
   (2) Any object at a temperature below 98.6°F feels cool to the touch.
   (3) Regardless of its temperature, metal always feels cool to the touch.
   (4) Metal at a temperature above 98.6°F feels warm to the touch.
   (5) Any object at a temperature above 98.6°F feels warm to the touch.

Questions 3–5 refer to the following passage.

Many factors affect the survival chances of each organism in an ecosystem. These factors may be *biotic*—other living or once-living organisms, or *abiotic*—nonliving conditions or substances.

The availability of food resources is a biotic factor that helps an organism's chances for survival. A natural predator is a biotic factor that decreases an organism's chances for survival.

The quality of air and water are abiotic factors that directly affect the growth and health of all organisms in an ecosystem.

3. Which of the following best summarizes the information given in the passage?

   (1) Only biotic factors affect an organism.
   (2) Both biotic and abiotic factors affect an organism.
   (3) Only abiotic factors affect an organism.
   (4) Abiotic factors are more important than biotic factors.
   (5) Biotic factors are more important than abiotic factors.

4. Which of the following is an abiotic factor for a fish living in a pond?

   (1) fish-eating birds swimming in the pond
   (2) a log rotting in the pond
   (3) algae, poisonous to the fish, in the pond
   (4) pesticides in the pond water
   (5) a lack of food resources in the pond

5. In which of the following are both abiotic and biotic factors most likely to be controlled so as to best ensure the survival of all organisms?

   (1) a zoo
   (2) a national park
   (3) a forest preserve
   (4) a backyard
   (5) a sheltered bay

Questions 6 and 7 refer to the following diagrams.

DAYTIME AIR CONDITIONS

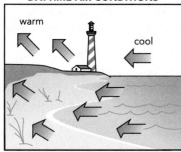

NIGHTTIME AIR CONDITIONS

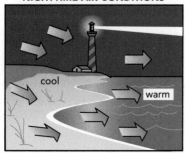

6. From the diagrams what can you infer must occur if there is no wind at a beach?

   (1) The air above land is cool.
   (2) The air above water is warm.
   (3) The air above land is the same temperature as the air above water.
   (4) The sun is either rising or setting.
   (5) Rain is falling over both land and water at the same time.

7. Which of the following could cause a reversal in the direction of a normal daytime breeze?

   (1) unusually cold ocean water
   (2) unusually choppy ocean waves
   (3) thick, early-morning fog over both land and ocean
   (4) unusually warm daytime air over the land but not the ocean
   (5) unusually cold daytime air over the land but not the ocean

Questions 8 and 9 refer to the illustrations below.

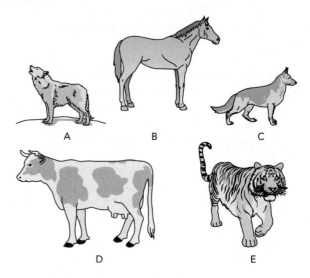

8. Which pair of animals most likely evolved from the most closely-related common ancestor?

   (1) A and B
   (2) A and C
   (3) B and D
   (4) B and E
   (5) C and E

9. Which animal is most closely related to a buffalo?

   (1) A
   (2) B
   (3) C
   (4) D
   (5) E

Answers are on page 436.

CHAPTER 3

Analyzing and Evaluating Science

Science advances but slowly, with halting steps. But does not therein lie her eternal fascination? And would we not soon tire of her if she were to reveal her ultimate truths too easily?

~ Karl von Frisch

Above all else, science is about inquiry—asking questions about our world. Part of the challenge faced by scientists is to analyze and evaluate new information that adds to or changes our understanding of the world around us.

Analyzing Science Materials

On the GED Science Test you may be tested on your ability to analyze a passage or graphic in any of four ways:

- Distinguishing facts from hypotheses and opinions
- Recognizing unstated assumptions
- Identifying cause-and-effect relationships
- Distinguishing a conclusion from supporting statements

Distinguishing Facts from Hypotheses and Opinions

You may recall the brief discussion of this skill in the section on scientific explanation on page 35. Because this skill is so important in scientific analysis, we'll briefly review the differences between scientific facts, hypotheses, and opinions.

- A **scientific fact** is a conclusion based on evidence that scientists agree on.

- A **hypothesis** is a reasonable explanation of evidence or a prediction based on evidence.

- An **opinion** is a personal belief that is often based on a person's own value system.

Thinking about Science

Directions: Classify each statement as a fact, hypothesis, or opinion. Write *F, H,* or *O* on the line before each statement.

_____ **1.** Because many people are frightened by snakes, no effort should be made to save endangered snakes.

_____ **2.** Moonlight is light from the Sun that reflects off the Moon's surface.

_____ **3.** The valleys on Mars are most likely a result of ancient rivers on the Martian surface.

_____ **4.** Air pollution is a negative byproduct of the Industrial Revolution.

_____ **5.** Regardless of medical research, vitamins produced in a laboratory can't possibly be as healthful as vitamins found naturally in food.

_____ **6.** The reason that one person is often so strongly attracted to a second person may be smell rather than personality.

_____ **7.** It is certain that somewhere else in the universe intelligent beings live on planets not unlike Earth.

_____ **8.** More scientific knowledge has been learned in the last century than in all the rest of recorded history.

_____ **9.** Intelligence has possibly evolved in human beings to help them survive in a very dangerous world.

_____ **10.** Genetically changing food products is against natural law and should be legally banned.

_____ **11.** The changing weather patterns we are seeing at the beginning of the twenty-first century may be a consequence of global warming.

_____ **12.** The clearing of rain forests is bringing humans into contact with viruses, such as Ebola, for which humans presently have no defense.

_____ **13.** The Grand Canyon is the most beautiful of all the natural wonders of the world.

_____ **14.** At the present rate of research, many genetic diseases will be curable within the next 20 years.

Answers are on page 436.

Directions: Choose the <u>one best answer</u> to each question.

Questions 1–3 refer to the following passage.

Before the year 2025 biologists and chemists may develop vaccines that can eliminate many diseases that we now have. A vaccine helps to prevent a disease, not to cure it. A vaccine is a dose of a germ that is enough to trigger your immune system into action but not enough to make you sick. For example, a flu vaccine consists of a small dose of flu virus. Once this vaccine is taken, your body responds by making antibodies, a form of protein that acts as a virus fighter. These antibodies prevent more of the same flu virus from entering and attacking cells in your body.

Vaccines that have been very successful are the DPT vaccine, which has all but eliminated the three long-feared childhood diseases of diphtheria, tetanus, and pertussis (commonly known as whooping cough), and the vaccines for pneumonia, influenza, polio, measles, mumps, German measles, and smallpox. The effectiveness of vaccines is most obvious when parents fail to have their children immunized at proper times. When this happens, the number of children stricken with polio and other diseases once again rises.

Although vaccines are usually safe, there is an element of risk. A small number of people who take a vaccine actually get the disease itself. For example, it is estimated that one child in 310,000 who takes the DPT vaccine will become ill and suffer brain damage. Yet, without the DPT vaccine, it is claimed that the incidence of death due to whooping cough would be nineteen times higher than it is now and the incidence of brain damage would be four times as high. Because of the potential danger of vaccines, medical research in studies of vaccine safety is continuing. Parents are advised to check with their own doctor or with a local health clinic to see which vaccines are appropriate for their children.

1. Which of the following is a fact that the author could prove by citing scientific evidence?

   (1) Someday, most diseases caused by viruses will be curable by vaccines.
   (2) By the year 2025 scientists will discover a vaccine that will prevent all cancers.
   (3) The beneficial effect of a vaccine occurs because of the production of a person's own antibodies.
   (4) A vaccine is made up of antibodies designed to fight viruses and bacteria.
   (5) A flu virus prevents a person who has the flu from being able to infect other people.

2. Which of the following is a hypothesis based on the passage?

   (1) A vaccine is a dose of a germ that triggers your immune system into action.
   (2) Someday vaccines may prevent all diseases that afflict human beings.
   (3) About one child in every 310,000 that takes the DPT vaccine is made ill by it.
   (4) Without vaccines, civilization could not survive another 1,000 years.
   (5) The decrease in childhood diseases during this century has most likely resulted from the use of vaccines.

3. Which of the following is an opinion that can neither be proved nor disproved with evidence?

   (1) Vaccines have been very successful in preventing many diseases caused by viruses and bacteria.
   (2) Because of the risk, all vaccinations should be halted until vaccines can be perfected.
   (3) Many cancers are believed to be caused by viruses, and work is being done on possible types of cancer vaccines.
   (4) The success of vaccines has been due to the work of chemists involved in medical research.
   (5) By failing to get their children vaccinated as directed by their doctor, parents risk the health of their children.

Questions 4–6 refer to the following graph.

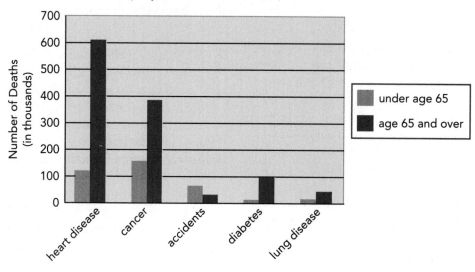

FIVE LEADING CAUSES OF DEATH
(per year in the United States)

4. Which of the following is a fact that is supported by information given in the graph?

   (1) For people under age 65, accidents are the leading cause of death.
   (2) Cancer is the second-leading single cause of death in people age 65 and older.
   (3) Diabetes is responsible for more deaths in all age groups than is lung disease.
   (4) Most people suffering from cancer are hospitalized unnecessarily.
   (5) More money is spent on heart disease research than on any other area of medical study.

5. Which of the following is an opinion?

   (1) Cancer is the most feared of all diseases.
   (2) The average hospital stay for a cancer patient is longer than the average hospital stay for one with heart disease.
   (3) The cost of heart transplant operations is now being covered by some insurance companies.
   (4) Many terminally ill patients are encouraged to spend their remaining time at home with family members when possible.
   (5) In schools where there is accident prevention instruction, accidental student deaths have been reduced.

6. Which of the following is a hypothesis?

   (1) The cure rate for certain types of cancer has increased by more than 50 percent during the last twenty-five years.
   (2) Recent evidence suggests that heart disease is on the decrease.
   (3) Drunk drivers are responsible for more than half of all highway accident deaths.
   (4) The American diet, high in fat and sugar, is very possibly the main reason why so many Americans die from heart problems.
   (5) Workplace accidents have decreased in the United States during the last century.

Answers are on page 436.

Unstated Assumptions

When you make an **assumption,** you take something as being true without checking the validity of the statement. For example, when a light goes out in a room, you might assume that the lightbulb has burned out because this is the most frequent cause of a light failure. The problem, however, could be elsewhere. A wire in the wall switch may have popped loose, or the light socket itself may be broken.

When you read a science passage, it is important to be aware of the writer's unstated assumptions. An unstated assumption is something the writer takes for granted. The unstated assumption may be an idea the writer didn't think of, or it may be a point of view that the writer wants you to take. This is a technique used by salespeople, politicians, and others who want you to believe and act a certain way.

See if you can spot the unstated assumption in the statement below.

When the world's supply of oil runs out, automobile use will decrease drastically.

What unstated assumption is the writer making? The writer is assuming that scientists will not find an alternate energy source for automobiles.

Thinking About Science

Directions: Read each passage below, and answer the question that follows.

1. When life is discovered on another planet, its form will be much different from any of the life forms on Earth.

   What is the writer assuming? _____

   _____

2. An astronaut stated, "Manned space travel is absolutely necessary if we are to learn about the planets outside of our own solar system."

   What assumption is the astronaut making? _____

   _____

3. To make ice in her freezer as quickly as possible, Rhoda first ran the tap water until it was as cold as she could get it. She then placed a tray full of this cold tap water into the freezer.

   What assumption is Rhoda making? _____

   _____

Answers are on page 436.

Directions: Choose the <u>one best answer</u> to each question.

Questions 1–3 refer to the following passage.

When scientists first developed nuclear power, it was hailed as the energy source of the future. People saw only the positive side of its use: an inexpensive, almost inexhaustible source of energy. Little was said about the radioactive waste that nuclear power plants produce.

Today, the nuclear waste issue is one of the most serious issues of our time. Scientists still know of no way to safely dispose of radioactive waste. In fact, radioactive waste cannot be disposed of at all; it can only be stored. If the stored waste gets into the air or drinking water, it can cause cancer, genetic mutations, and death.

Nuclear waste, once created, must be stored for the thousands of years that it remains harmful to life. Many communities have resisted the building of nuclear-waste storage sites near their towns and even in their states. Because of concern over safety and of the unexpected high costs of nuclear power plant construction, many nuclear power plants have been closed during the last decade. However, a growing concern about power needs is once again bringing the nuclear power question to the forefront.

1. Which of the following is an unstated assumption made by those who favor more nuclear power plants?

   (1) The demand for electrical energy will decrease in the future due to more efficient consumer products.
   (2) Nuclear power companies are more concerned about radioactive waste than is the general public.
   (3) Scientists will someday invent safe methods of disposal or storage of radioactive waste.
   (4) Nuclear power plants do not produce radioactive waste.
   (5) There is a shortage of scientists who are trained to run nuclear power plants.

2. Which of the following was most likely true when nuclear power was first developed?

   (1) Scientists believed they had developed an effective plan for storing radioactive waste.
   (2) Scientists did not know that radioactive waste was dangerous to human life.
   (3) Scientists did not know that nuclear power plants would create radioactive waste.
   (4) Scientists believed that no one would discover the danger of the radioactive waste.
   (5) Scientists believed that safe storage facilities would be created before the public found out about the dangers of radioactive waste.

3. Which assumption(s) is (are) most likely made by those who favor shutting down all nuclear power plants in the United States?

   A. Shutting down nuclear power plants will permanently put thousands of people out of work.
   B. Public officials will act to shut down nuclear power plants if enough people demand it.
   C. Nuclear power provides only a small part of the energy used in the United States.

   (1) A only
   (2) B only
   (3) C only
   (4) A and C only
   (5) B and C only

Answers are on page 436.

Identifying Cause and Effect

Imagine that on the evening news, you hear that an earthquake in southern California caused extensive damage to nearby cities and towns. During the next few weeks, you hear that frightened residents now demand that earthquake-proof buildings be built to replace those destroyed by the quake.

The earthquake and the later demands by the citizens are a good example of a cause-and-effect relationship. In this type of relationship, you can identify an event (the **effect**) with the condition that made the event occur (the **cause**). In the example above, the cause is the earthquake and the effect is the action taken by the citizens.

In many cases, one cause leads to an effect that then itself becomes the cause of a second effect, and so on. This is called a chain of causes and effects. Below is listed a chain of causes and effects that might be started by an earthquake.

CAUSE	EFFECT
Earthquake	Damaged buildings
Damaged buildings	Action taken by citizens
Action taken by citizens	New building codes
New building codes	Safer buildings

What is a likely effect that might result from the construction of safer buildings? Several answers are possible. Here are two of them: (1) *citizens feel safer,* and (2) *the new buildings don't get destroyed in the next earthquake.*

In any chain of events, a cause always occurs before the effect. It is important to remember this because a passage may mention the effect first.

Look at this sentence:

Jimmy had several fillings before he was six years old because he did not brush his teeth daily.

The cause—Jimmy's failure to brush his teeth—is the second part of the sentence. The effect— Jimmy's teeth got cavities and needed fillings—is listed first.

Thinking About Science

Directions: Read the following passage and list of causes and effects. Match each effect listed in the column on the right with its cause listed on the left. Write the correct letter in the space before each number.

During times of unexpected stress or fright, the human body reacts in a most protective, amazing way. First, the adrenal glands give off into your bloodstream two hormones: adrenaline and noradrenaline. These adrenal hormones give you extra strength and endurance. When you get a "rush of adrenaline," you might experience some or all of these changes:

- Your heart beats faster.

- The pupils of your eyes dilate (become wider).

- Your liver releases stored sugar, increasing the energy supply to your muscles.

- Digestive processes slow down.

- The blood vessels near the surface of your skin constrict (become more narrow), slowing the bleeding of any surface wounds and causing a greater flow of blood to the muscles, brain, and heart.

- The bronchial tubes in your lungs dilate, increasing the rate at which you're able to absorb oxygen.

Because your adrenal glands have this effect, they are often called the glands of "fight or flight." This refers to the fact that a surprised, scared animal will usually flee if given the chance but will fight if it has no choice. The adrenal hormones prepare the animal for either course of action.

Cause	Effect
_____ **1.** unexpected stress or fright	(a) increased muscle energy
_____ **2.** adrenal hormones in blood	(b) increased absorption of oxygen
_____ **3.** dilation of bronchial tubes	(c) the adrenal glands give off two adrenal hormones
_____ **4.** release of stored sugar by liver	(d) increased blood flow to the heart
_____ **5.** constriction of surface blood vessels	(e) increased heart rate

Answers are on page 436.

Directions: Choose the <u>one best answer</u> to each question.

Questions 1–4 refer to the following passage.

The Mesozoic era, called the Age of the Reptiles, began about 225 million years ago. During this era, the giant reptiles called dinosaurs—from the Greek words *deinos* and *sauros*, meaning "terrifying lizard"—roamed Earth. For more than 150 million years, these wondrous and feared creatures dominated all other life forms. Then, about 70 million years ago, the dinosaurs suddenly disappeared. In fact, the only reptiles that survived this period were the ones we know today as snakes, lizards, turtles, and crocodiles.

The reason for the dinosaurs' extinction remains one of the strangest mysteries in science. According to one popular theory, a large asteroid or comet from space crashed into Earth. This collision kicked a tremendous amount of dirt into the atmosphere. With only little sunlight getting through a darkened atmosphere, the temperature of Earth's surface rapidly decreased. Within one or two months, Earth froze and a devastating ice age began. Tropical forests quickly died, as did all animals, including the dinosaurs, that depended on the lush vegetation for their survival.

With the disappearance of the dinosaurs, another animal form became dominant. This next era, called the Age of the Mammals, is the one we are still in.

1. According to the passage, which of the following is an effect of the ice age?

   (1) the beginning of the Mesozoic era
   (2) a drop in temperature at Earth's surface
   (3) a collision between Earth and a comet
   (4) the dominance of another species
   (5) the death of tropical forests

2. According to the passage, what event coincided with the end of the Mesozoic era?

   (1) the emergence of dinosaurs as the dominant life form
   (2) the sudden occurrence of an ice age
   (3) the survival of snakes, lizards, and turtles
   (4) the emergence of mammals as the dominant life form
   (5) the death of tropical forests

3. What is given as the cause of the possible ice age that occurred 70 million years ago?

   (1) the presence of asteroids in the solar system
   (2) the passage of 150 million years
   (3) the blockage of sunlight by dirt in the atmosphere
   (4) the disappearance of the dinosaurs
   (5) the death of tropical forests

4. If the theory presented in the passage is correct, what directly caused the extinction of dinosaurs?

   (1) the collision of a small object from space with Earth
   (2) the disappearance of their food supply
   (3) the beginning of an ice age in which the dinosaurs froze
   (4) the emergence of mammals
   (5) a lack of sunlight by which to see

Questions 5–8 refer to the following diagram.

SOLAR HEATING SYSTEM

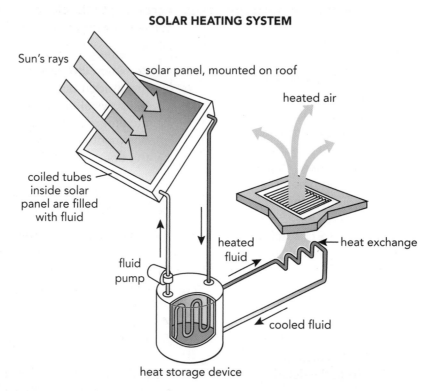

Sun's rays

solar panel, mounted on roof

heated air

coiled tubes inside solar panel are filled with fluid

fluid pump

heated fluid

heat exchange

cooled fluid

heat storage device

5. Which statement best describes what takes place in a solar heating system?

(1) Heat exchangers produce heat that is used to heat a house and a solar panel.
(2) A heat storage device is used to heat a solar panel.
(3) Energy from the sun warms a fluid that is circulating in the heating system.
(4) Pumps heat a fluid that circulates through both a solar panel and several heat exchangers.
(5) The solar panel acts as an air conditioner by removing heated air from a house.

6. What would be a likely cause of a slowdown of fluid circulating through the system?

(1) a lack of sunshine
(2) a faulty pump
(3) a closed air vent
(4) the presence of another heat source
(5) a cold heat storage device

7. What is the purpose of the heat exchanger?

(1) to warm the house by transferring heat from the fluid to the air around the heat exchanges
(2) to circulate the fluid through the heating system
(3) to capture the sun's energy and heat the circulating fluid
(4) to store heat for later use
(5) to measure the temperature in the house

8. What is the most likely purpose of the heat storage device?

(1) to store heat in case the system breaks down
(2) to remove excess heat from the fluid so the house does not get too hot
(3) to provide a source of heat to warm the fluid at night
(4) to provide a source of heat during winter months when the sun doesn't shine
(5) to serve as a source of extra fluid in case the system develops a leak

Answers are on page 437.

Drawing Conclusions

You may know that the directions on a map, read clockwise, are north, east, south, and west. If a map is oriented so that the top is pointing toward north, what direction will be to the left side?

If you answered west, you correctly drew this conclusion from the detail that tells you north is at the top of the map. You could also conclude that south is at the bottom of the map and east is at the right.

Answering the above question is an example of drawing a conclusion from details. When you **draw a conclusion**, you express an unstated idea that is logically connected to the information you are given.

Read the following passage:

> Fossils are the hardened remains or traces of any plant or animal that lived in previous times. Many fossils have been found in the layers of sedimentary rock that make up the cliff faces of the Grand Canyon. The 200-million-year-old rocks contain predominantly fossils of reptiles; the 400-million-year-old rocks contain mainly fossils of fishlike animals; and even older rocks contain only the fossils of worms.

Which of the following three statements is a conclusion that can be drawn from the details given in the passage?

(1) Ancient fishlike animals fed on worms and were themselves devoured by reptiles.

(2) Each geological time period is characterized by the types of life forms that predominated during that period.

(3) Only the remains of small animals are preserved in fossils.

Only statement (2) is a conclusion you can draw from this passage. Fossil evidence allows you to conclude that different types of animals predominated during widely separated time periods. However, this evidence does not allow you to conclude that either statement (1) or statement (3) is true.

Statement (1) is an interesting hypothesis but not a conclusion that can be drawn. The passage doesn't give any information about the diets of different animal forms.

Statement (3) is not true and could not be concluded from the passage. The passage does not describe the sizes of the fossils.

Thinking About Science

Directions: The Beaufort scale below is used to measure wind force. Answer each question by circling the correct choice.

Type of Wind	Wind Speed (miles per hour)	What Happens
no wind	0	Smoke rises straight up.
light breeze	1–12	Leaves and twigs move.
moderate breeze	13–24	Small trees sway.
strong breeze	25–36	Wind is hard to walk against.
gale	37–48	Branches break on trees. Store windows break.
strong gale	49–72	Trees are uprooted.
hurricane	above 73	Buildings are greatly damaged.

1. What kind of wind would be considered safe for children to play in? *(moderate breeze, gale, strong gale)*

2. For which type of predicted wind would it be wise to cover the windows of your house if you live in a wooded area? *(moderate breeze, strong breeze, gale)*

3. If 60-mile-per-hour winds are expected, what type of wind is being predicted? *(strong breeze, strong gale, hurricane)*

Answers are on page 437.

Go to **www.GEDScience.com** for additional practice and instruction!

Directions: Choose the <u>one best answer</u> to each question.

Question 1 refers to the passage below.

For any substance to burn in air, oxygen gas must be present. Without oxygen, a flame will simply go out. For example, when Erin's science class placed a burning candle in a jar and then placed a lid on the jar, the candle burned for only thirty-five seconds before the flame died out.

1. What is a reasonable conclusion that Erin can make from the observation?

   (1) An open jar contains less oxygen than a closed jar.
   (2) If the space above a candle flame is blocked, the candle cannot burn for more than thirty-five seconds.
   (3) A shorter candle would burn for more than thirty-five seconds before going out.
   (4) A candle will not stay lit in a jar either open or closed.
   (5) In thirty-five seconds, a candle flame uses up all the oxygen in the jar.

Questions 2 and 3 refer to the following illustration.

DIFFERENCES IN THE PRODUCTION OF DRONE AND WORKER HONEYBEES

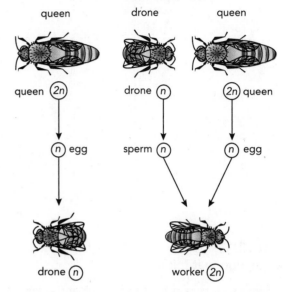

Relative chromosome number is indicated inside circles.
n = number of chromosomes

2. Which of the following best summarizes the information presented in the illustration?

   (1) Both the drone and worker honeybees develop from eggs laid by the queen.
   (2) The queen is the most important type of honeybee in the hive.
   (3) The worker honeybee is not able to reproduce.
   (4) Of the three types of honeybees in a hive, only the queen lays eggs.
   (5) The worker honeybee develops from a fertilized egg while the drone develops from an unfertilized egg.

3. As a general rule, two animals can mate only if both have the same number of chromosomes. From the drawing, which type(s) of honeybee can you conclude is an exception to this rule?

   (1) two queen honeybees
   (2) two drone honeybees
   (3) two worker honeybees
   (4) a queen honeybee and a drone honeybee
   (5) a queen honeybee and a worker honeybee

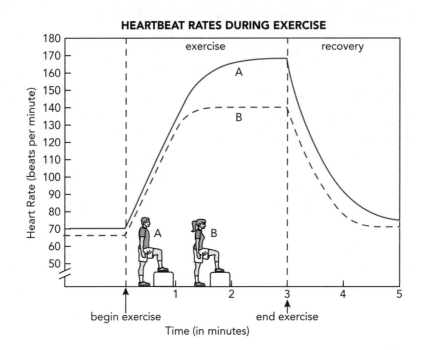

HEARTBEAT RATES DURING EXERCISE

Questions 4–8 refer to the line graph above and the passage that follows.

Two students (indicated as student A and student B) are doing a step exercise as part of a conditioning class. Their heartbeat rates before, during, and after the exercise are shown on the line graph above.

4. How long did the step exercise last?

    (1) less than one minute
    (2) exactly one minute
    (3) more than one but less than three minutes
    (4) exactly three minutes
    (5) more than three minutes

5. At what point does the greatest difference between the heartbeat rates of student A and student B occur?

    (1) just before beginning the step exercise
    (2) just after beginning the step exercise
    (3) just before stopping the step exercise
    (4) just after stopping the step exercise
    (5) after recovery is complete

6. Suppose the step exercise continued for five minutes. What would student A's heart rate most likely be at the 5-minute point?

    (1) 70 beats per minute
    (2) 90 beats per minute
    (3) 120 beats per minute
    (4) 150 beats per minute
    (5) 170 beats per minute

7. What heart rate will student A most likely have one hour after quitting the step exercise?

    (1) 70 beats per minute
    (2) 90 beats per minute
    (3) 120 beats per minute
    (4) 150 beats per minute
    (5) 170 beats per minute

8. What must you assume if you want to compare the physical condition of student A with that of student B?

    (1) Both students are the same sex.
    (2) Both students are the same height.
    (3) Both students are the same age.
    (4) Both students are exercising at the same rate.
    (5) Both students are exercising at the same time.

Answers are on page 437.

Evaluating Science Materials

According to a tobacco company spokesperson, "There is no convincing medical evidence that smoking causes ill health." Do you agree with this person? Before you can intelligently answer this question, you should ask for more information.

First, you may want to know what medical evidence is available. (**Evidence,** as used here, is any information that either supports or opposes the stated point of view.) For example, you may want to know about any medical evidence that links smoking to respiratory diseases and to lung cancer. You also may want to know whether the tobacco company has any evidence that disagrees with or questions the medical findings. Only then, after you've considered both points of view, will you be ready to give an informed opinion yourself.

When you hear or read something, don't assume that it is true. Too often, people base their opinions on half-truths, emotions, and the biased opinions of others instead of on the facts. It is important in decision making to evaluate, or judge, the validity of evidence objectively.

On the GED Science Test, evaluation questions measure your ability to make judgments about information that's presented to you. On the pages ahead, you'll learn to evaluate information in three ways. Then you'll see how a scientist uses the same skills to do experiments. This section is divided into the following four parts:

- Judging the value of information

- Judging the adequacy of information

- Recognizing the influence of values

- Using the scientific method

Judging the Value of Information

Before making a decision or drawing a conclusion, you must judge the value of all available information. Most often this means distinguishing relevant information from irrelevant information.

- **Relevant information** includes any facts that directly affect your decision.

- **Irrelevant information** includes any facts that do not affect your decision.

For example, suppose you want to know if a small garden will grow on a plot of land near your home. Relevant information will include any facts that answer questions about whether a garden will grow, as in the following question:

Is the soil on the land a fertile, garden-type soil?

Irrelevant information includes facts that answer any questions that do not tell you whether or not a garden will grow, such as in the following question:

Would I rather plant corn or beans if space is limited?

Which of the following questions are relevant to whether you would be able to grow the garden?

(1) Is there a nearby source of water for the proposed garden?

(2) How much snow does this land get during the winter?

(3) Should I put a fence around the garden?

(4) Does the plot receive adequate daily sunshine?

(5) Which store has the best buy on garden supplies?

Only questions (1) and (4) are relevant. Water and sunlight are both needed for crops to grow. Questions (2), (3), and (5) are not relevant to the needs of crops.

Thinking About Science

Directions: Place a check next to each question that asks for relevant information about the topics below.

1. the health risks associated with smoking

   _____ a. What is the cost of a pack of cigarettes?

   _____ b. Is there evidence that links lung cancer to smoking?

   _____ c. How many different brands of tobacco are on the market today?

   _____ d. Is smoking a socially acceptable activity?

   _____ e. Does the risk of a heart attack increase if a person smokes?

2. the safety of space travel

   _____ a. What is the cost of sending the space shuttle into space?

   _____ b. During takeoff, is the space shuttle protected from lightning?

   _____ c. How expensive are the space suits worn by astronauts?

   _____ d. For how long can astronauts remain healthy in zero-gravity conditions?

   _____ e. Are astronauts at risk for being hit by small meteors?

Answers are on page 437.

Directions: Choose the <u>one best answer</u> to each question.

Questions 1 and 2 refer to the following passage.

Alcohol is a chemical that interferes with the normal functioning of the human body. Its effects can range from loss of coordination to unconsciousness to death. As the following story shows, alcohol does not mix well with driving.

After having five beers during the first hour at a party, Larry got mad at the hostess and left. Even though he was an alcoholic who had received medical treatment for drinking problems, Larry felt he could "hold his booze." While driving home, he was stopped by a police officer who had noticed that a car with one headlight burned out was weaving down the highway. The officer gave Larry a Breathalyzer test that showed his blood-alcohol level to be at 0.15 percent, 0.05 percent greater than 0.10 percent (the level at which a person is legally considered to be too drunk to drive).

1. Which of the following facts would be *most* relevant to the officer when he has to decide whether Larry is legally too drunk to drive?

   (1) Larry is an alcoholic.
   (2) Larry had consumed five drinks.
   (3) Larry's blood-alcohol level was above 0.10 percent.
   (4) Larry had previously received medical treatment.
   (5) Larry's car was weaving down the highway.

2. Which of the following facts is probably *not* related to Larry's drunk driving?

   (1) Larry was unable to drive his car in a straight line.
   (2) Larry took a Breathalyzer test.
   (3) Larry's blood-alcohol level was above 0.10 percent.
   (4) Larry's car had a burned-out headlight.
   (5) Larry was stopped by a police officer.

Question 3 refers to the following passage.

Although both light and sound are forms of wave energy, the speed of light is much greater than the speed of sound. Light travels at about 186,000 miles per second. Sound travels at only about 1,100 feet per second. One way to see the difference between the speeds of light and sound is to watch a lightning storm.

Lightning is caused by separated electrical charges rushing together in the atmosphere. At the instant the charges come together, both a flash of light and a loud sound are created. Although the flash of lightning reaches your eyes almost at once, the thunder may not reach your ears until several seconds later.

You can use the relative speeds of light and sound to find out how far away the lightning is. When you see a flash of lightning, start counting slowly, spacing your counts one second apart.

For each five seconds you count before you hear the thunder, you know that the lightning is about one mile away. (In five seconds, sound travels a distance of about 5,500 feet, which is just a little farther than one mile—5,280 feet.) If you see a flash and count to ten before hearing thunder, the lightning flash occurred about two miles from you.

3. Assume you know that both light and sound are created at the instant that lightning occurs but that you do not know either the speed of light or the speed of sound. From which fact below can you deduce that light travels faster than sound?

   (1) As you move farther away from a lightning storm, the sound of thunder becomes fainter.
   (2) You always see a lightning flash before you hear the thunder that is created with it.
   (3) The speed of sound is about 1,100 feet per second.
   (4) Light and sound are both forms of wave energy.
   (5) One mile is a distance of exactly 5,280 feet.

Answers are on page 437.

Judging the Adequacy of Information

In the previous section, you read about distinguishing between relevant and irrelevant information. A closely related skill is the ability to determine if there is enough information to support a conclusion. For example, suppose that during a storm the power goes off in your house just a second after you plugged in an old toaster. What can you conclude? Nothing, really! Perhaps the trouble is with the power lines because of the storm, or your own house power may have switched off because of a faulty toaster. Until you have more information, you can't be sure what the trouble is.

Read the passage below:

> A tide is the alternate rising and falling of the surface of the ocean. At any point along a coast, a rising tide occurs at a regular interval and is later followed by a falling tide. A rising tide is called a *flood tide*, and a falling tide is called an *ebb tide*. Oceanographers often keep tide tables to tell you when tides occur.

Which detail below do you need before you can know which tide will next occur in Depoe Bay?

(1) how long it's been since the last tide

(2) whether the previous tide was an ebb tide or a flood tide

(3) the highest water level of the last flood tide

According to the passage, an ebb tide follows a flood tide, and vice versa. Thus, answer (2) is the information you need. If, for example, the previous tide was an ebb tide, then the next tide will be a flood tide. Answers (1) and (3) refer to the tide but do not help you determine what type of tide the next one will be.

 **Thinking About Science**

Directions: Check your skill at identifying missing information. Read the passage below and then answer the question that follows.

Competition for food determines where animals can live in a forest. When two different animals eat the same foods, each animal may have to find its own region of the forest where it has sole access to that particular food supply.

Which information below would you need to know in order to decide whether owls and hawks can live in the same part of the forest?

(1) whether owls and hawks use the same hunting methods

(2) whether owls and hawks eat the same daily amount of food

(3) whether owls and hawks eat the same sources of food

Answers are on page 437.

Directions: Choose the <u>one best answer</u> to each question.

Question 1 refers to the following passage.

Scientists have discovered that pollutants that enter the human body are stored in human fat cells. One way of reducing pollutants in our bodies is by loosing excess weight.

Scientists have also discovered that pollutants in food sources increase as you move up the food pyramid. Root vegetables contain the least, followed by grains, legumes, fruits, and vegetables. The most polluted foods are meat, fish, poultry, and dairy products. High-fat diets increase both the amount and the storage of ingested pollutants.

1. Which fact enables you to conclude that you should reduce your consumption of fish and fatty beef and pork?

    (1) Many chemical pollutants cause no known harmful effects.
    (2) An increased cancer risk is related to a body's concentration of pollutants.
    (3) Organically grown foods contain very low levels of chemical pollutants.
    (4) Cooking destroys many types of chemical pollutants found in meat.
    (5) Shellfish contain higher levels of chemical pollutants than other fish.

Question 2 refers to the following diagram.

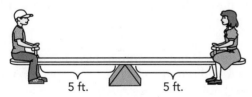

5 ft.   5 ft.

2. Assume that the teeter-totter in the diagram is moving. What do you need to know in order to determine whether the teeter-totter will balance when the children stop it?

    (1) the sum of the weights of the children
    (2) the height of each child
    (3) the average weight of the children
    (4) the weight of the teeter-totter
    (5) the weight of each child

Questions 3 and 4 refer to the following passage.

The density (weight per unit volume) of one liquid can often be compared with the density of a second liquid by combining the liquids in the same container. When two liquids are combined, either one liquid will float on the other, or the liquids will mix freely. When one liquid floats on the other, you know that the liquid on top has the lesser density. As an example, because oil floats on water, you can conclude that oil is less dense than water.

Liquids that freely mix together are said to be *miscible*. When two liquids are miscible, simply combining them won't give you any information about which liquid has the lesser (or greater) density. For example, water and alcohol are miscible in all proportions. Mixing them reveals nothing about whether alcohol is more dense than water, or vice versa.

3. Which of the following facts would enable you to conclude that the density of water is greater than the density of gasoline?

    (1) Gasoline and alcohol are miscible.
    (2) Gasoline and oil are miscible.
    (3) Water that condenses in a car's gas tank can prevent the car from starting.
    (4) Gasoline floats on water.
    (5) Water will not put out a gasoline fire.

4. Which additional fact would you need to know in order to determine whether alcohol will float on oil?

    A. if oil and alcohol are miscible
    B. if the density of alcohol is less than the density of water
    C. if the density of alcohol is less than the density of oil

    (1) A only
    (2) B only
    (3) C only
    (4) A and B only
    (5) A and C only

Answers are on page 437.

Recognizing Values

A **value** is a principle or a quality that a person believes is important. Values help people to make decisions. People often express their values when they write letters to newspapers, when they vote for certain political candidates, or when they donate money or time to organizations that have values similar to their own. For example, many people donate money and time for a special interest, such as having a clean and enjoyable recreation area in a neighborhood.

Values affect the way each of us makes decisions. Sometimes a conflict between values occurs, such as when a personal belief does not agree with the scientific facts that we believe. A good example is the question of evolution. Though scientific evidence strongly supports the basic principles of evolution, many religious groups oppose these ideas on the ground that evolution does not agree with religious teachings. A conflict between values often forces a person to choose one value over another and to make decisions based on that choice.

The passage below describes a situation. What two competing values are in conflict in this situation?

> Reggie is nineteen and has a job at a factory. The men he works with all chew tobacco. To "feel like the other men," Reggie started to chew tobacco about three weeks ago. Last night, for the first time, Reggie heard about medical evidence that strongly indicates that chewing tobacco can cause cancer of the mouth. Because Reggie is concerned about his health, he finds himself having to make an uncomfortable choice.

Reggie is in a very common situation. He is faced with choosing between the value he places on wanting to feel accepted by the group he works with and the value he places on his health.

 Thinking About Science

Directions: For each situation described below, express the values you believe are in conflict.

1. Betty's religious beliefs say she is not allowed to have a medical operation. Recently, Betty found out that she needs an operation if she wants to give birth to a child, a lifelong dream.

   _____

2. Jay, a physicist, has just found out that the company he works for wants him to do work in nuclear weapons research. Jay strongly opposes nuclear weapons.

   _____

Answers are on page 437.

Directions: Choose the <u>one best answer</u> to each question.

Questions 1 and 2 refer to the following cartoon.

"Dangerous? No, our work is simply with plants!"

1. How do you think the artist feels about genetic engineering?

   (1) excited about each new discovery
   (2) looking forward to practical applications
   (3) concerned about monetary cost
   (4) concerned about unforeseen results
   (5) happy about the humorous side of research

2. What message do you think the artist is trying to get across by using humor?

   (1) Genetic engineering has great potential in the development of new species.
   (2) Genetic engineering can have serious consequences to human health and safety.
   (3) Genetic engineering will be a gold mine for many pharmaceutical companies.
   (4) Genetic engineering can help unlock the mysteries of many human diseases.
   (5) Genetic engineering should be banned because it is unnatural.

Answers are on page 438.

Using the Scientific Method

Scientists must objectively evaluate evidence. In fact, they have developed a special research method for collecting, organizing, and evaluating evidence. The **scientific method** is a logical way to do experiments and to draw conclusions that are supported by all available evidence.

Step 1: Ask Questions to Clearly Identify a Problem

The first step of the scientific method is to observe a situation and to identify a problem. Most often, the problem is presented as a question. Here's an example.

Lauren, a science teacher, is studying the growth of food plants. She recently noticed that one group of tomato plants in her classroom is growing much more quickly than the other group of tomato plants.

Lauren asks the following question:

"Why is one group of tomato plants growing more quickly than the other group of tomato plants?"

Group of quick-growing Plants   Group of normal plants

Step 2: Collect Information

After identifying the problem, Lauren wants to collect information that might help answer the question. Part of Lauren's role as a scientist is to determine which information is important.

Lauren checks the lab records to make sure the quick-growing plants received a normal amount of water and light. Lauren then asks her students if anything unusual has happened to the plants. One of her students tells Lauren that she gave one group of plants a little extra plant food that she brought from home. Lauren asks to see the bottle.

Lauren collects the following information:

- The plants received a normal amount of water and light.
- The plants were given a plant growth hormone contained in the bottle of plant nutrients.

Step 3: Form a Hypothesis

After collecting information, it is time to form a **hypothesis**—a possible explanation for why something is happening. Lauren's hypothesis will try to explain the unusual growth rate in the group of quick-growing plants.

Lauren develops the following hypothesis based on the information she collected:

> The added plant-growth hormone is causing the increased growth rate.

Step 4: Test the Hypothesis by Designing an Experiment

The next step is to test the hypothesis to determine whether it gives a reasonable answer to the question. The best way to test a hypothesis is to design and carry out an **experiment.**

Here is the experiment Lauren develops to test her hypothesis:

> Lauren will grow two new groups of tomato plants. Each group of plants will be grown in its own planter. The growth rates of the two new groups of plants will be compared with each other and with the growth rate of the first group of rapidly growing plants she has been observing.
>
> - One group, the experimental group, will be treated with the growth hormone.
> - The second group, the control group, will not be treated with the hormone.
>
> Both the experimental group and the control group will be given equal amounts of water and light. The purpose of the control group is to let Lauren know what would happen to the plants if they did not receive growth hormones. By comparing the growth rates of the two groups of plants, Lauren can determine the effect of the growth hormone. On a weekly basis, Lauren will measure and graph the height of each plant in both the control and experimental groups.

Step 5: Analyze Results and Draw Conclusions

After completing the experiment, the next step is to analyze the results and to draw conclusions. The two new groups of plants are shown below after several weeks of growth.

Here are the results of Lauren's experiment:

Experimental group   *Control group*

After several weeks, the plants in the experimental group are taller than the plants in the control group. Lauren finds that the growth rate of the experimental group is identical to the growth rate of the quick-growing plants that she first observed.

Based on these results, Lauren draws the following conclusion:

The growth hormone increases the rate at which tomato plants grow.

Thinking About Science

Directions: Answer each question below.

1. Why did Lauren grow both a control group of plants as well as an experimental group of plants?

    _____

2. Why is it better that Lauren grew several plants in each container, rather than one?

    _____

Answers are on page 438.

Directions: Choose the <u>one best answer</u> to each question.

Questions 1 and 2 refer to the following passage and table.

Wanda knows that the force of gravity pulls all objects toward the surface of Earth. She now wants to determine whether heavier objects fall more quickly than lighter objects.

To find out, Wanda tries three experiments. In these experiments she will use a three-pound brick, a one-pound rock, and a paper clip. In each experiment, Wanda drops two objects side by side from a height of three feet. As she completes the three experiments, Wanda records the results shown in the table.

Experiment	Objects Dropped	Observed Results
1	3-lb brick and 1-lb rock	Both brick and rock reached the ground at the same time. Both fell at the same rate.
2	3-lb brick and paper clip	Both brick and paper clip reached the ground at the same time. Both fell at the same rate.
3	1-lb rock and paper clip	Both rock and paper clip reached the ground at the same time. Both fell at the same rate.

1. From the results of her experiments, which of the following can Wanda most reasonably conclude?

    (1) Heavy objects fall more quickly than light objects.
    (2) Metal objects fall more quickly than bricks.
    (3) Heavy and light objects fall at the same rate.
    (4) Heavy objects fall more slowly than light objects.
    (5) Objects made of different substances fall at different rates.

2. Which of the following could most affect the results of Wanda's three experiments?

    (1) a light rain
    (2) high air temperature
    (3) wet ground
    (4) a strong wind
    (5) nearby traffic noise

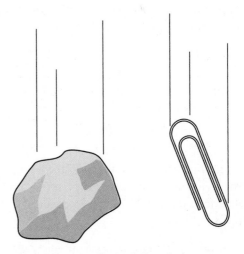

The rock and the paper clip fall at the same rate.

Question 3 refers to the following passage.

Wanda now does a fourth experiment. She drops a paper clip and a leaf side by side. She discovers that, even though the paper clip and leaf are about the same weight, they do not fall at the same rate. The paper clip falls much more quickly than the leaf.

3. From this observation, which of the following can Wanda most reasonably conclude?

    (1) Light objects fall at the same rate.
    (2) The rate at which a light object falls depends on what it is made of.
    (3) Man-made objects fall more quickly than objects from nature.
    (4) The rate at which a light object falls depends on the size of its surface.
    (5) The rate at which a heavy object falls depends on the size of its surface.

Questions 4 and 5 refer to the following passage.

Noticing that a paper clip falls much more quickly than a leaf, Wanda forms her first hypothesis:

Light objects fall at different rates because of the effects of air resistance.

Wanda believes that air resistance slows lightweight objects by different amounts. A light object with a large surface, such as a leaf, is slowed much more than a light object with a small surface, such as a paper clip.

4. To test her first hypothesis, Wanda plans to drop two more objects and observe which falls more quickly. Which two objects should Wanda choose?

    (1) a safety pin and a small sewing needle
    (2) an envelope and a small plastic spoon
    (3) a paper plate and a napkin
    (4) a green leaf and a brown leaf
    (5) a piece of typing paper and a small paper bag

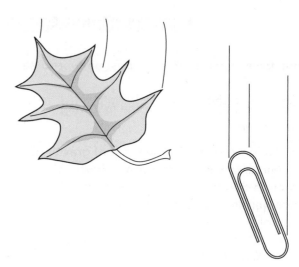

A paper clip drops more quickly than a leaf.

5. Wanda conducts her fifth experiment and then writes a second hypothesis:

    Without air friction, all objects fall at the same rate.

    Which of the following would be the most ideal place to test Wanda's second hypothesis?

    (1) in the pressurized passenger cabin of an airplane flying at 35,000 feet
    (2) standing underwater on the bottom of a swimming pool
    (3) in the "weightless" condition of an orbiting space shuttle
    (4) on a simulated surface of the Moon, which has gravity but no air
    (5) in a very still room where the windows are closed and there is no air movement

Answers are on page 438.

Analyzing and Evaluating Science Review

Directions: Choose the <u>one best answer</u> to each question.

Questions 1 and 2 refer to the following passage.

Natural mimicry is the resemblance that one organism has to another. *Protective mimicry* improves the imitator's chances for survival. For example, a defenseless animal may be protected from predators because of its resemblance to an animal that predators tend to avoid.

An example is the viceroy butterfly, which resembles a monarch butterfly. Because the monarch butterfly has an unpleasant taste, birds do not like to eat it. As a result, birds also avoid the viceroy, even though scientists have discovered in laboratory experiments that birds do enjoy the taste of the viceroys. It seems that, in the wild, birds are not willing to take a chance of accidentally mistaking a monarch for a viceroy.

1. Which statement is a valid hypothesis that may be difficult to prove?

    (1) Birds have a difficult time distinguishing between viceroys and monarchs.
    (2) Birds experience taste in a way similar to how humans experience taste.
    (3) Viceroy and monarch butterflies have very similar eating habits.
    (4) A viceroy looks similar to a monarch.
    (5) There are chemical differences between monarchs and viceroys.

2. The robber fly looks much like a bumblebee. Knowing that robber flies eat bumblebees, which statement below is most likely true?

    (1) Robber flies are attracted to flowers where they lay eggs.
    (2) Robber flies share their food supply with other robber flies.
    (3) Robber flies are not attacked by other insects as they look for bumblebees.
    (4) Robber flies are mistaken for bumblebees and are not feared by bumblebees.
    (5) Robber flies are not eaten by birds.

Questions 3–5 refer to the following information.

Fernando, a psychologist, wants to determine if mice suffer from anxiety when they are forced to live in crowded conditions.

3. Which of the following experimental conditions will provide the best evidence on which Fernando can base a conclusion?

    (1) Place six mice in each of two identical small cages.
    (2) Place six mice in each of two identical large cages.
    (3) Place twelve mice in one small cage.
    (4) Place twelve mice in one large cage.
    (5) Place six mice in a small cage and six mice in a large cage.

4. Suppose Fernando finds that crowded mice show an increased level of anxiety. Which of the following types of research would provide the best evidence to support Fernando's belief that human beings may suffer in a similar way?

    (1) research on the anxiety and depression levels of people living in crowded conditions in an inner-city neighborhood
    (2) research on the rate of teenage pregnancies in large cities
    (3) research on the anxiety levels of farmers struggling to exist during low-income years
    (4) research on the anxiety levels of people living in a small midwestern town
    (5) research on the rate of crime in large cities where there is a high rate of drug use

5. In addition to believing that crowded conditions lead to anxiety in human beings, Fernando also believes that anxiety from crowding may result in panic in an emergency. If Fernando is correct, in which location would panic most likely occur if a fire breaks out?

    (1) a nearly empty restaurant
    (2) a golf course during a tournament
    (3) a movie theater during the showing of a popular movie
    (4) a football stadium two hours after a game
    (5) a grocery store at midnight

Questions 6–9 refer to the following table.

Name of Planet	Distance from Sun (in miles)	Diameter (in miles)	Length of Year* (in Earth days)	Length of Day** (in Earth days)	Main Elements of Which Planet Is Composed
Mercury	36,187,500	3,050	88	59	nickel, iron, silicon
Venus	67,625,000	7,560	225	243	nickel, iron, silicon
Earth	93,500,000	7,973	365	(1 day = 24 hr.)	nickel, iron, silicon
Mars	142,120,000	4,273	687	1	iron, silicon
Jupiter	486,120,000	89,500	4,329	(10 hr.)	hydrogen
Saturn	891,875,000	75,000	10,585	(10 hr.)	hydrogen
Uranus	1,793,750,000	32,375	30,660	(16 hr.)	hydrogen, helium
Neptune	2,810,625,000	30,937	60,225	(19 hr.)	hydrogen, helium
Pluto	3,687,500,000	1,875	103,660	9	unknown

* A year is the length of time it takes a planet to make one complete orbit around the sun. This time is also called the period of revolution.

** A day is the length of time it takes a planet to make one complete turn on its own axis. This time is also called the period of rotation.

6. Which planet is closest in size to Earth?

    (1) Mercury
    (2) Venus
    (3) Mars
    (4) Jupiter
    (5) Pluto

7. From the information shown in the table, which of the following can you conclude to be true?

    (1) Earth is one of the three largest planets in the solar system.
    (2) Most elements found on Earth are not found on any other planet.
    (3) Earth is the largest of the five smallest planets in the solar system.
    (4) Earth is the closest planet to the Sun.
    (5) Earth is the farthest planet from the Sun.

8. Excluding the Sun, the largest planets contain most of the matter in the solar system. Which two elements make up most of this matter?

    (1) iron and silicon
    (2) iron and hydrogen
    (3) silicon and helium
    (4) nickel and iron
    (5) hydrogen and helium

9. Which two planets can you conclude rotate (spin on their axes) most slowly?

    (1) Mercury and Venus
    (2) Uranus and Neptune
    (3) Earth and Mars
    (4) Jupiter and Saturn
    (5) Pluto and Mercury

Answers are on page 438.

CHAPTER 4

Science and Technology

Why bother building a robot that's capable of getting from here to there, if once it gets there it can't tell the difference between a table and a cup of coffee?

~ Marvin Minsky

The Nature of Technology

Technology is the use of knowledge, materials, and tools to solve human problems and to provide for human needs and wishes.

Technology gives us many types of products:

- Consumer products, from groceries and the clothes we wear, to automobiles, compact discs, and cellular telephones

- Scientific-research products, from microscopes and telescopes, to the space shuttle and orbiting satellites

- Multipurpose products, such as the computer, that are popular with consumers but that also have many other uses in science and industry

Distinguishing Between Science and Technology

Science and technology are like two sides of the same coin. On the science side is understanding; on the technology side is application. Like the two sides of a coin, each side seems incomplete without the other. Understanding often seems too aloof and independent of application. Application, on the other hand, often seems to move ahead more quickly than the knowledge needed to properly inform and safeguard the public.

Science seeks understanding of the natural world, of the whole universe. The goal of science is to understand, not necessarily to use that knowledge in any practical way. The study of life on Earth is just one part of science. Much scientific research is done in other parts of science that have no immediate practical benefits for human beings.

Technology uses scientific knowledge to build practical devices. The goal of technology is to improve human life. Because of this, technology has a more direct impact on human life than does science.

Here are two other differences between science and technology:

- Science often challenges peoples' understandings and personal beliefs. Technology changes the way people live, from entertainment to travel.

- Scientific findings are always communicated to the public through announcements and scientific publications. Scientific findings are available for public use. Technological knowledge is usually not available for public use. In fact, most technological advances are protected from public use by patents. A patent gives the inventor sole rights to the use of new technology for a period of years.

Yet, even with their differences, science and technology depend on one another. New technology allows scientists to do experiments that might otherwise not be able to be done. And, quite often, solving technological problems results in advances in scientific knowledge.

 **Thinking About Science**

Directions: Answer each question below.

1. What is the goal of science?

   _____

2. What is the goal of technology?

   _____

Answers are on page 438.

GED PRACTICE

Directions: Choose the <u>one best answer</u> to each question.

Questions 1 and 2 refer to the information on pages 95 and 96.

1. What is the purpose of a patent?

   (1) to advance scientific knowledge
   (2) to improve technological products
   (3) to deny public use of inventions
   (4) to keep inventions a secret
   (5) to keep scientific discoveries a secret

2. Which of the following is a goal of science but may not be a goal of technology?

   (1) to develop faster computers
   (2) to improve the sound of the speaker's voice on cellular phones
   (3) to improve the quality of medicinal drugs
   (4) to build higher quality automobiles
   (5) to determine if there is life on Mars

Answers are on page 438.

Milestones in Technology

A **milestone** is a turning point, a point at which everything changes. A milestone in technology is an invention that changes all human life that follows. As this definition implies, many years may pass before we know if an invention changes human life in a substantial way.

There have been many important inventions over the centuries, but not all of these are milestones. A few of the early milestones are discussed below. As you'll see, many milestones are things we simply take for granted. But imagine for a second what life would be like without them in your life.

Fire

Learning to control fire was a great leap forward for human beings. By striking pieces of flint (volcanic rock) against other rocks, people essentially invented the first match. The sparks that flew off were used to ignite dry brush and twigs. With controlled fire, people had a source of heat and light. Fire also could be used as a weapon of protection against animal predators. And, equally important, fire was the key to making clay cooking pots. With cooking pots, grains came into the human diet, an event that helped lead to agriculture. As metal ores were discovered and began to be hammered into shape, people learned that fire could be used to keep hammered metal from cracking. This process, called annealing—alternately heating and hammering metal—made possible the invention of sickles and other tools for farming, spears for hunting, and swords for protection.

The Wheel

With the invention of the wheel came human mobility—the ability to move humans, food sources, and personal belongings over long distances. The oldest known wheels date back about 5,500 years ago. The invention of wheels quickly led to the invention of wheeled carts, the first land vehicles. With the domestication of oxen and water buffaloes, wheeled carts could be used to move people and goods great distances over land.

The City

About the time the wheel was invented, cities began to develop. You may not think of a city as a product of technology, but it is. In fact, a city is a technological system. Not surprisingly, the first symbol for a city was a circle containing a network of crossing lines. These lines most likely represented transportation and communication systems. The rise of cities meant a concentrated population engaged in a common goal: mutual survival. The sharing of interests led to a division of labor and skills. The success of the city resulted in a concentrated abundance of food and material wealth. Along with cities came the construction of both temples and tombs. The designers of these structures are considered the first engineers.

The Clock

The first mechanical clock was invented in the thirteenth century. The clock gave people a way of keeping track of time that didn't depend on the position of the Sun. The clock also became a great navigational aid and helped lead to transoceanic navigation. Also, the precise measurement of time is a cornerstone of modern science today.

The Cotton Gin

The invention of the cotton gin in 1793 by Eli Whitney made it possible for cotton to become a common source of clothing fabric. Before the use of cotton, most articles of clothing were wool, and wool was known to be scratchy, often soggy and fungus-filled.

The Steam Engine

The invention and development of the steam engine over a period of time from 1698 to 1769 changed the way physical work would be done forever. With the invention of this engine, tasks that used to be done by hand could now be done with the harnessed use of energy. In a steam engine, wood or coal is burned to produce heat that causes water to boil. The high pressure steam is used to produce mechanical energy that can power everything from a cotton gin to a train engine.

The Internal Combustion Engine

The internal combustion engine is a machine that obtains mechanical energy from the burning of fuel in a combustion chamber. The internal combustion engine was invented in the 1870s and is today a key component of cars, trucks, trains, ships, and airplanes. The three most common types of combustion engines are the gasoline engine, the diesel engine, and the jet engine. The internal combustion engine replaced the steam engine in being the principal power plant in transportation vehicles.

Electricity

Practical uses of electricity are too numerous to mention. The invention of the telephone in 1876, the lightbulb in 1879, the electric motor in 1892, the electrocardiograph in 1903, and the radio receiver in 1913 are just a few of the early devices that have proven to be milestones in technology.

There is room here to mention only these few of the hundreds of inventions that are truly technological milestones. Think about your life and try to identify other milestones—those inventions that you just can't seem to live without!

Thinking About Science

Directions: Answer each question below.

1. What is meant by *technological milestone*?

   _____

2. Name four machines that use internal combustion engines.

   _____ , _____ , _____ ,

   _____

   Answers are on page 438.

GED PRACTICE

Directions: Choose the <u>one best answer</u> for each question.

Questions 1–3 refer to the following passage.

Like many inventions before it, the typewriter is declining in use. Invented in 1868, the typewriter offered people an alternative to handwriting. By printing or impressing type characters on paper, the typewriter produced text more quickly and far more legibly than written words.

With the invention of the electric typewriter by 1920, typewriters became easier to use, and professional-looking documents became the norm. Electric typewriters set the standard for document production until the 1970s.

With the invention of personal computers in the 1970s, everything changed. The typewriter began to give way to electronic word processors whereby documents can be electronically created and stored, sent electronically over telephone lines as e-mail, or printed in multiple copies on a printer. Electronic word processing is a standard feature on today's personal computers.

1. What led to the reduced use of typewriters in the workplace?

   (1) the invention of electric typewriters
   (2) the rising cost of production
   (3) the high price of computers
   (4) the invention of electronic word processors
   (5) the increased use of telephones

2. What is meant by *word processing*?

   (1) learning faster typing techniques
   (2) creating, editing, storing, and printing documents
   (3) paying a professional to produce typed documents
   (4) using smaller-size type to enable putting more text on a single page
   (5) recycling used typing paper

3. What does e-mail most likely stand for?

   (1) electronic mail
   (2) erasable mail
   (3) everyday mail
   (4) exact mail
   (5) edited mail

Questions 4–7 refer to the following passage and diagram.

A diagram of one cylinder of an internal combustion engine is shown below. The operation of the cylinder takes place in four strokes.

Stroke 1: During the intake stroke, the piston moves down the cylinder and draws a gasoline-air mixture into the cylinder. The mixture enters the cylinder through the intake valve.

Stroke 2: During the *compression stroke*, the piston moves up and compresses the gasoline-air mixture.

Stroke 3: During the *power stroke*, the piston reaches the top, and the spark plug fires and ignites the mixture. The ignited gasoline-air mixture rapidly expands due to heat caused by the burning gasoline. The expanding gas forces the piston back down the cylinder. It is this mechanical energy that powers the car.

Stroke 4: During the *exhaust stroke*, the piston rises up again in the piston and pushes exhaust gas out of the cylinder and through the exhaust valve.

ACTION OF PISTONS

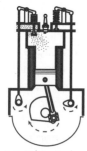
1. Intake stroke

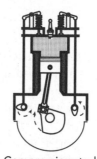
2. Compression stroke

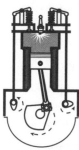
3. Power stroke

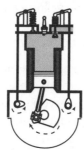
4. Exhaust stroke

4. What is the purpose of the intake valve?

   (1) to ignite the spark plug
   (2) to admit gasoline and air into the cylinder
   (3) to start the engine
   (4) to emit exhaust gases from the cylinder
   (5) to compress the gasoline-air mixture

5. What principle involving gases does the internal combustion engine rely on?

   (1) Air is a mixture of gases.
   (2) Gases freely mix with one another.
   (3) All types of gases burn when put in the presence of a spark.
   (4) Gases contract when heated.
   (5) Gases expand when heated.

6. Which sentence best describes the conversion of energy that takes place in an internal combustion energy?

   (1) Electrical energy is converted to mechanical energy.
   (2) Mechanical energy is converted to chemical energy.
   (3) Chemical energy is converted to mechanical energy.
   (4) Mechanical energy is converted to electrical energy.
   (5) Chemical energy is converted to electrical energy.

Answers are on page 438.

How Technology Influences Science

Technology is often referred to as applied science. This definition of technology, however, is far too limiting. Technology not only applies science, but it also provides scientists with research tools with which to probe deeper into science questions.

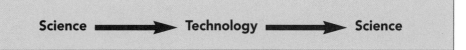

Science ➡ Technology ➡ Science

Discoveries of science are crucial to the development of new technology. New technology enables scientists to probe deeper into the questions of science.

For examples of how technology influences science, let's briefly look at how technology has aided scientists both in looking inward at life processes and outward at our solar system.

A Changing View of Cells

In 1665 a British scientist named Robert Hooke built a microscope and took a look at a thin slice of cork. Cork is a soft plant tissue found in the bark of cork oak trees. Hooke was surprised to see a honeycomb structure of little boxes. He called these little boxes *cells,* which means "little rooms" in Latin. Hooke is generally credited with being the first scientist to see the division of living tissue in smaller units.

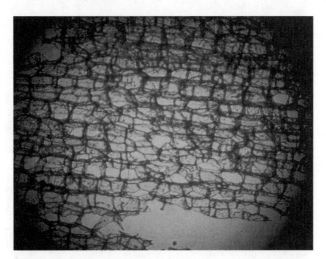

Hooke saw hundreds of cells when he looked at a piece of cork under a microscope.

Microscope technology has come a long way since the time of Robert Hooke. Optical microscopes, similar to Hooke's, are much improved and still very much in use. Electron microscopes, which use beams of electrons instead of visible light, are used when high magnification is needed.

- The optical microscope uses visible light to create a magnified image of an object. A high-powered optical microscope can magnify an object up to 2,000 times its normal size.

- A scanning electron microscope (SEM) bounces a beam of electrons off the surface of an object being viewed. The SEM produces an image of the surface of the object. An SEM can magnify the surface of an object 100,000 times its actual size.

- A transmission electron microscope (TEM) shoots a beam of electrons through an object. This beam of electrons produces a magnified image of the object being viewed. A TEM microscope can magnify an object 1,000,000 times its actual size.

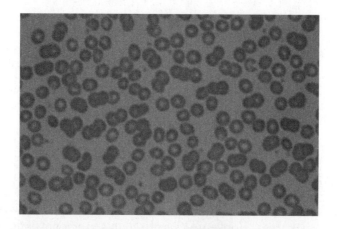

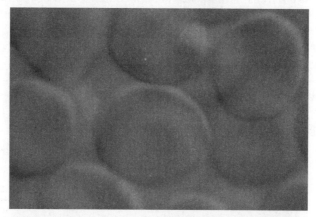

Red blood cells at three different magnifications. The higher the magnification, the more detailed the image.

A Changing View of Mars

Seen through a telescope, Mars appears as a red and orange disk. White ice caps can be seen at the north and south poles. Blowing dust gives the impression of color changes and changing surface features. Before spacecraft, this was the limit of our understanding of Mars.

Early in the twentieth century, astronomers believed they saw canals on the surface of Mars. One American astronomer, Percival Lowell, believed that these canals were built by an advanced civilization on Mars, and he wrote books expounding this belief. Lowell believed that Martian canals carried water from wet polar regions to dry equatorial deserts.

Unfortunately, perhaps—and certainly less exciting—telescope improvements and spacecraft visits to the red planet have shown that no canals exist on Mars. And so far, no forms of life of any kind have been found on our neighboring planet.

Pathfinder sent this picture to Earth from the surface of Mars on July 4, 1997.

Thinking About Science

Directions: Answer each question below.

1. How does technology influence science?_____

   _____

2. Why did Percival Lowell believe that there was life on Mars?

   _____

   _____

3. What have advancements in technology allowed scientists to discover about Mars? _____

   _____

Answers are on page 439.

Directions: Choose the <u>one best answer</u> to each question.

Questions 1 and 2 are based on the following illustrations.

UNIVAC 1 (1951)

ENIAC (1955)

iMac (1999)

1. Which of the following advantages of a modern computer over the first computers cannot be inferred from the photographs?

   (1) smaller dimensions
   (2) speed of operation
   (3) less weight
   (4) easier to use
   (5) easier to move

2. What does a modern computer contain that the first computers did not contain?

   (1) electric wires
   (2) metal parts
   (3) logic circuits
   (4) microchips
   (5) a power source

   Answers are on page 439.

Go to **www.GEDScience.com** for additional practice and instruction!

Technology and Values

During the mid- to late-twentieth century, technology advanced more rapidly than ever before. As a result, things became possible that once were imagined only in science fiction. Along with scientific understanding came technology that may have conflicted with values you hold dear. A few of these new technologies are mentioned below. Which, if any, of these technologies conflict with your personal values?

Genetically Altered Food

A gene is a piece of genetic material that determines the characteristics of every organism. Scientists have learned how to alter the properties of an organism by injecting it with genes from a second organism. For example, suppose tomato producers want tomatoes that grow more quickly than natural tomatoes. The producers may hire scientists to genetically alter the tomatoes. The scientists inject the genes from a fast-growing vegetable into the tomatoes. The tomatoes then grow faster, thus increasing food production and company profit.

When you eat a genetically altered food, you are eating a food that nature did not create. Whether genetically altered foods have risks associated with them is a question that has not been answered to everyone's satisfaction.

Surrogate Parenting

A surrogate mother is a woman who, on behalf of another person, carries a fetus throughout pregnancy and birth. Following delivery, the surrogate mother gives the newborn child to the other person. The surrogate mother may play this role as a favor to a friend who is unable to become pregnant herself, or she may do it for the other person's convenience. In this latter case, the surrogate mother may be paid for her services.

A surrogate mother may provide her own egg and thus actually be the biological mother of the newborn. Or, she may instead have a fertilized egg placed within her uterus. In this case, she is not biologically related to the fetus she is carrying. She is simply allowing her uterus to be used for the gestation period.

Sex Selection of Children

It is now possible for parents-to-be to select the sex of the child they wish to have. This is based on the scientific fact that the male sperm cell determines the sex of a child. Some male sperm cells produce male children, and some produce female children. The two types of sperm can be separated outside of the body.

Suppose a couple wants a female child. An egg from the mother-to-be would be combined with a male sperm cell that will produce a female offspring. In the same way, a couple could arrange to produce a male offspring.

Cloning

Cloning is a process in which identical-twin animals are produced. One cloning method is known as embryo splitting. An embryo that is in the early stages of development is split into two parts. Each part is then placed in a separate uterus. Both mice and sheep have been cloned by embryo splitting. A more surprising, and controversial, cloning method was developed in which a single cell taken from an adult sheep was chemically and electrically stimulated to begin cell division. The cloned sheep, named Dolly, is an identical twin of its adult mother. Dolly now appears to be a healthy growing sheep, normal in all ways. Dolly is the first clone to be made from the nucleus of an adult cell.

Cloning presents a whole list of controversial possibilities. The most frequently asked question is, "Will it be possible to clone a human being, using just a single cell of an adult?" In other words, could a scientist make a carbon copy of himself or herself? Scientists cannot say for sure if this will ever be possible, but some scientists are likely to experiment with single-cell human cloning.

Harvesting of Organs

Along with cloning whole organisms, genetic engineering may lead to the possibility of cloning individual organs. Suppose, for example, a cell taken from your heart could be used to grow an identical heart in a laboratory. If you were to develop heart disease, the cloned healthy heart could be placed in your body, and your diseased heart would be discarded.

The harvesting of personal organs may someday be a possibility. Scientists are on the forefront of research in this field.

Genetic Testing of a Human Fetus

Scientists can now run extensive medical tests on a human fetus. If the test results show that the fetus has a genetic disorder, doctors may be able to treat the fetus before birth. In fact, certain types of surgery have already been successfully performed on fetuses.

Fetal testing may also lead to a challenge of the decision-making right of a pregnant woman. If a fetal test shows serious mental or physical problems, should a woman be able to decide whether to continue the pregnancy or to terminate it?

Nuclear Weapons

To end World War II, the United States dropped atomic bombs on Japan in 1945. More than 100,000 people were killed instantly. These bombs were the first of a terrible new kind of weapon. Since that time, even more powerful nuclear weapons have been developed. When a nuclear bomb explodes, matter is converted to pure energy in processes similar to those that occur in the Sun. These thermonuclear reactions unleash energy unlike anything ever seen before in history. A single nuclear bomb can destroy an entire city the size of Chicago.

It goes without saying that the use of these weapons must be prevented if human life, or possibly any life, is to survive on Earth. The potential use of nuclear weapons is perhaps the greatest threat yet to the survival of the human species.

Thinking About Science

Directions: The questions below arise from emerging technologies. These questions deal with personal values, and you may not want to answer every question. Write answers and supporting reasons only for those questions with which you are comfortable.

1. Should food labels identify genetically altered food? (This question arose in 2000 when a food manufacturer did not label its genetically altered foods. After much public protest, the food was recalled.)

   _____

   _____

2. Should a woman be allowed, for a fee, to serve as a surrogate mother for a woman who doesn't want pregnancy to interfere with her career goals?

   _____

   _____

3. For what reason might a couple want to choose the sex of their child?

   _____

   _____

4. Do you think research and experimentation for the cloning of human beings should be allowed to continue?

   _____

   _____

5. Would you like a laboratory to have an exact copy of each of your major organs, waiting for the day you may need one?

   _____

   _____

6. Under what conditions do you think tests should be run on a human fetus? What limits, if any, do you think should be placed on the decision-making rights of the pregnant woman?

   _____

   _____

Answers are on page 439.

Questions 1 and 2 refer to the information on pages 105–107.

1. Which of the following is likely to be the most controversial aspect of surrogate parenting?

   (1) the age of the surrogate mother
   (2) the sex of the developing fetus
   (3) the health of the biological father
   (4) a fee paid for pregnancy services
   (5) the method of childbirth used

2. What would be the least controversial reason to run potentially dangerous tests on a human fetus?

   (1) to identify eye color
   (2) to identify the biological father
   (3) to identify the biological mother
   (4) to identify a genetic disease that can possibly be treated before birth.
   (5) to identify blood type

Questions 3 and 4 refer to the information on pages 105–106 and to the following passage.

The process of embryo splitting to produce identical twins occurs naturally in mammals. An embryo is a fertilized egg cell that consists of a female egg together with a male sperm. An embryo contains genes from each parent.

For unknown reasons, an embryo of just a few cells may split into two identical twin embryos. If one of these two embryos splits again, identical triplets develop. The process of embryo splitting two or more times occurs in humans as well as in other mammals.

3. The cloned sheep Dolly is also a type of identical twin. At the time of her birth, what did Dolly have in common with her twin?

   (1) length
   (2) age
   (3) weight
   (4) gender
   (5) diet

4. What does Dolly not have that twins who form from embryo splitting do have?

   (1) genes from two parents
   (2) genes from her mother
   (3) complete organs
   (4) normal growth
   (5) an immune system

Questions 5 and 6 refer to the following passage.

Tamara bought a box of cereal at a local grocery store. After finishing the box, she heard on a news report that this cereal is made from genetically altered grain. Tamara never would have bought the cereal had she known this fact.

Tamara is careful to read the list of ingredients on all prepared food products that she buys. There was no information on the box to indicate that genetically altered foods were present.

5. Which of the following most likely does <u>not</u> describe the way Tamara felt when she heard the news report?

   (1) concerned
   (2) betrayed
   (3) happy
   (4) upset
   (5) unhappy

6. Which person or organization is <u>most</u> responsible for informing the public about the ingredients of prepared food products?

   (1) the grocery clerk
   (2) an environmental group
   (3) a government agency
   (4) the store manager
   (5) the manufacturer

   Answers are on page 439.

Concerns and Limits of Technology

Concerns of Technology

The rapid advance of technology during the twentieth century brought with it special concerns. With the development of atomic and nuclear weapons, battleships, chemical warfare, and other weaponry, concern over the safety of civilization itself became an issue. Perhaps for the first time, people became aware that all life on Earth was endangered by an emerging technology.

In the latter part of the twentieth century, scientists drew attention to other products of technology that threaten civilization. Among these were pesticides and industrial chemicals that poison our drinking water and the fish we eat; automobile exhausts and factory discharges that poison the atmosphere; and wastes from nuclear weapons production and nuclear power plants that remain poisonous for thousands of years.

Along with threats to physical health, new technology also threatens mental health. With the beginning of the computer age has come a threatened invasion of privacy. The computer age also brings with it the threat of increasing levels of unemployment as factories switch from human workers to industrial robots.

History teaches us that every technology has both valuable and harmful aspects.

- On the one hand, technology gives us products that benefit people in some way.

- On the other hand, production uses energy and materials and creates waste. Waste includes industrial chemicals and materials left over from production. Waste also includes the new products themselves at the time consumers no longer want them.

Balancing the benefits of each new product with its real social costs is a challenge for consumers and government agencies, such as the Environmental Protection Agency. This challenge is ongoing and may become more critical in coming years.

Limits of Technology

In 1899 Charles H. Duell of the U.S. Patent Office wrote a letter to President William McKinley urging him to close the patent office. His reason: "Everything that can be invented has been invented." Do you wonder what Mr. Duell would think today?

In 1948 a group of distinguished scientists published a paper in which they discussed the possibility of space travel. They concluded that humans would never leave Earth for a trip to the Moon. The rocket fuel would be so heavy, they believed, that the burning fuel would not be able to lift itself off Earth. Some of those scientists lived to see the United States land men on the Moon in 1969.

The history of science is full of predictions that later turned out to be in error. Because of this, scientists are now much more hesitant to predict limits to technology. Many scientists feel there are amazing technologies yet to be invented. The question is no longer *if*, but *when* these technologies will be invented.

Here are a few questions regarding future technology:

- Will future technology prevent all major diseases?
- Will future technology allow average people to travel to other planets?
- Will future technology enable average people to live as long as they want?
- Will future technology make war a thing of the past?

These questions and many more may have occurred to you already. Only the future can bring the answers. Now, as you think about the role technology plays in your life, realize that not all problems are addressable by scientific and technological advancement.

Here are several questions that may never be answered:

- Why are we here?
- What is the best way to live?
- What existed before the universe?
- What exists besides the universe we see?

These questions have been asked for centuries, but it will be difficult to find their answers, because these questions are out of the realm of science. Science depends on experiments for information, and no experiments can be designed that address these issues. Answers, if they are sought, must be found in personal philosophy or religious beliefs.

Thinking About Science

Directions: Answer each question below. Give a reason for each answer.

1. Suppose a company knowingly discharges dangerous levels of air pollutants into the atmosphere. Do you think company officials should be held criminally liable for such actions? (Criminal liability means possible jail time if convicted.)

   _____

   _____

2. When a company replaces workers with industrial robots, do you think the company has any obligation toward employees who are laid off?

   _____

   _____

3. Do you think that human beings will ever land on Mars? (Because of the distance involved, the trip is estimated to take about 6 months each way.)

   _____

   _____

Answers are on page 439.

Directions: Choose the <u>one best answer</u> to each question.

Questions 1–3 refer to the following passage.

In spite of safety features in nuclear power plants, there have been major accidents. The most serious accident occurred in 1986 at Chernobyl in what was then part of the USSR. One of four nuclear reactors exploded and burned. Radioactive material blanketed the countryside, and dangerous levels of radioactive gas were detected over Scandinavia and northern Europe. At least 30 people died on the spot. More than 130,000 residents of Chernobyl were evacuated. In the years that have followed, thousands more people have become sick with various cancers and other illnesses caused by radiation poisoning. The exact death toll attributable to the Chernobyl accident may never be known.

1. What was the immediate danger to the public following the Chernobyl accident?

   (1) stored radioactive gas at the plant
   (2) radioactive material in the atmosphere
   (3) heat produced by the plant
   (4) loss of electric power
   (5) cost of repairing the plant

2. Which of the following can you conclude from information given in the passage?

   (1) Nuclear accidents always cause immediate deaths.
   (2) Nuclear accidents cannot be prevented.
   (3) Nuclear accidents are seldom serious.
   (4) Radiation sickness may take years to develop.
   (5) Radiation sickness is never fatal.

3. Which sentence best states the lesson that we need to learn from Chernobyl?

   (1) Accidents happen to everyone.
   (2) When mistakes are made, move on.
   (3) Safety must be the first concern.
   (4) All technology presents risk.
   (5) Older technologies are not reliable.

Questions 4 and 5 refer to the following passage.

A catalytic converter is a device that is placed on the exhaust system of an automobile to reduce pollutants in exhaust gas. Small beads in the converter react with the carbon monoxide gas and hydrocarbon gases that the engine emits. These dangerous gases are converted to carbon dioxide gas and water. Since 1980 all cars sold in the United States have been equipped with catalytic converters.

4. On which of the following does a catalytic converter have an effect?

   (1) engine electric current
   (2) engine intake gas
   (3) engine exhaust gas
   (4) headlight beams
   (5) air conditioning gases

5. For what purpose was the catalytic converter invented?

   (1) to reduce pollutant gases in the atmosphere
   (2) to increase pollutant gases in the atmosphere
   (3) to reduce the level of carbon dioxide gas in the atmosphere
   (4) to increase the level of water vapor in the atmosphere
   (5) to decrease the level of pollutants in engine oil

Answers are on page 439.

Science and Technology Review

Directions: Choose the <u>one best answer</u> to each question.

Questions 1 and 2 refer to the following passage.

The time in which we live is often referred to as the *information age*. This phrase is a recognition of the importance that information (words and numbers) plays in modern life. In fact, a growing number of employees spend full workdays dealing solely with the flow of information. Examples include everyone from office workers, who spend their days at a computer, to journalists, who spend their time obtaining and publishing information, to teachers, who spend all day in classrooms sharing information with students.

The information age may be a direct result of the invention of the modern computer, the primary use of which is to create, store, and process information. Or, it may be claimed that the computer was invented to handle the needs of the coming information age. This is a "chicken and egg" question that may never be answered.

1. Which of the following jobs is least likely to be considered information-age employment?

    (1) radio announcer
    (2) pharmacist
    (3) lawyer
    (4) pilot
    (5) telephone operator

2. Which of the following inventions is <u>not</u> mainly used for creating, storing, or processing information?

    (1) microwave oven
    (2) electronic organizer
    (3) CD burner
    (4) laptop computer
    (5) video camera

Questions 3 and 4 refer to the following passage.

Asteroid is the name given to any of the small celestial bodies that orbit the Sun primarily between the orbits of Mars and Jupiter. Scientists believe that as many as 1,500 large asteroids may be in orbits that cross Earth's orbit, although only about 200 have actually been spotted. If any of these large asteroids collided with Earth, a global catastrophe, perhaps extinction of all life on Earth, could result. Yet, even with the large number of asteroids believed to exist, chances are that a major collision takes place only once every 300,000 years. The extinction of dinosaurs 70 million years ago was believed to have resulted from the collision of Earth and a large asteroid.

If astronomers spotted a large asteroid on a collision course with Earth, the collision could take place in just a few years, or it may not occur for decades or centuries. Scientists argue that we need to develop a new technology specifically for dealing with the asteroid threat. At present, we simply are not prepared to deal with this threat.

3. What is the greatest threat posed by a collision of an asteroid with Earth?

    (1) the changing of Earth's atmosphere
    (2) the destruction of Earth's surface
    (3) the death of all life on Earth
    (4) the changing of Earth's orbit
    (5) the raising of Earth's temperature

4. At present time, what is the one thing in our favor regarding large asteroids?

    (1) knowledge of asteroid positions
    (2) technological preparedness
    (3) Earth's orbit around the Sun
    (4) distance of the asteroids from Earth
    (5) low probability of collision

Questions 5–8 refer to the following cartoons.

"You won't feel the benefit, Gak"

Andy Davey. Used by permission of www.CartoonStock.com.

"We saw a light on so we dropped in."

Philip Berkin. Used by permission of www.CartoonStock.com.

5. In what way are the two light sources shown above similar?

   (1) Each can be easily turned off.
   (2) Each gives off both light and heat.
   (3) Each uses wood as a fuel.
   (4) Each costs money for the people using it.
   (5) Each puts out a constant amount of light.

6. What discovery made possible the invention of the lightbulb?

   (1) solar energy
   (2) magnetism
   (3) gravitation
   (4) electricity
   (5) sound waves

7. What is a typical problem with the pictured technology that the lighthouse-keeper most likely experiences?

   (1) high cost of lightbulbs
   (2) availability of lightbulbs
   (3) lightbulbs burning out
   (4) inadequate lighting
   (5) danger from falling lightbulbs

8. What is a common activity today by which people can escape technological progress and return to simpler times?

   (1) golfing
   (2) typing
   (3) bowling
   (4) reading
   (5) camping

Answers are on page 439.

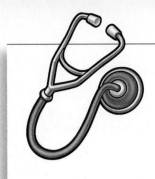

CHAPTER 5

Science in Personal and Social Perspectives

We already know enough to begin to cope with all the major problems that are now threatening human life and much of the rest of life on Earth. Our crisis is not a crisis of information; it is a crisis of decision, of policy and action.

~ George Wald

Personal and Community Health

Children learn many lessons as they grow up. One lesson is that life brings with it the possibility of injury, illness, disability, and death. An equally important lesson is that we can do much to reduce risk in our lives. Our lifestyle has much to do with both health and safety. In fact, as humans, we have a variety of mechanisms that help us to modify and prevent hazards. These mechanisms are of sensory, motor, emotional, social, and technological natures. On the next few pages, we'll review a few things that scientists have discovered about health and safety.

Disease: An Attack on the Body

Diseases are classified into two broad groups: infectious and noninfectious.

Infectious diseases spread from one person to another. These diseases, such as the common cold, are caused by **pathogens**—harmful bacteria, viruses, and fungi that invade the body.

Pathogens are often spread by direct contact. They leave the infected person through body openings, mucous membranes, blood, and other body fluids. For example, the common cold virus is spread by moisture droplets that accompany coughing or sneezing. This virus can be spread by touch—hand to hand, hand to doorknob, etc.—or from transmission through the air. Bacteria and viruses that cause many sexual diseases are transmitted by sexual contact. The virus causing AIDS is spread through contact with infected blood and also through sexual contact.

Noninfectious diseases do not spread from person to person. Common examples are heart disease and cancer, neither of which is caused by an infectious organism or virus. Perhaps surprisingly, these diseases are the leading causes of death in the United States. The risk of these diseases can be minimized by the following behavior:

- Don't smoke.

- Don't drink excessively.

- Eat a nutritious diet.

- Keep body weight at a recommended level.

- Exercise regularly.

- Reduce stress as much as possible.

- Live an emotionally rich life.

Every disease has characteristic symptoms. The most common symptoms of disease are fever, swelling, tiredness, nausea, pain, coughing, breathing difficulty, and rashes. Doctors rely on symptoms to help in the diagnosis of common ailments. For some diseases, doctors must rely on extensive medical tests, including blood tests and X rays.

Age-Related Diseases

Some diseases such as arthritis, Parkinson's disease, and Alzheimer's are more likely to occur as patients get older. These degenerative diseases involve the progressive breakdown of body tissues. Joints may become sore and stiff. Bones become brittle and may easily break. Blood vessels become constricted, and blood circulation is impeded.

Hereditary Diseases

Hereditary diseases, such as hemophilia and sickle-cell anemia, are caused by hereditary genetic disorders. Other diseases, such as diabetes and high blood pressure, tend to run in families and may be partly genetic. Recent research is leading many medical experts to believe that alcoholism, drug addiction, and obesity are, in part, genetic diseases.

Environmental Diseases

Many noninfectious diseases are caused by environmental factors. Excessive exposure to carbon monoxide gas can affect heart functions and vision and even lead to death. Exposure to coal dust, cotton dust, and asbestos can lead to a multitude of lung diseases.

Repetitive Stress Diseases

In recent years, a new class of disease has been identified: repetitive stress disease. This disease results from repeating certain motions over and over. Permanent nerve damage can be caused to fingers, wrists, elbows, knees, and other joints.

Immune System: The Body's Natural Defenses

In response to the onset of disease, humans (and most other animals) have a defense system called an **immune system**. An immune system is composed of molecules, cells, and organs that work together to defend the body against pathogens.

The degree to which a person is affected by a disease varies widely. Young people with healthy immune systems usually recover quickly from a cold, the flu, or even pneumonia. For people with a weakened immune system, pneumonia can be fatal.

An **epidemic** is the rapid spread of a disease—either infectious or noninfectious—through a group of people or through an entire population. Epidemics can be devastating. In 1918 a worldwide epidemic of influenza (a type of flu) killed between 20 and 40 million people. About 500,000 Americans died in this epidemic, more than were killed in World War I, World War II, and the Vietnam War combined.

The fight against epidemics is ongoing. Some infectious diseases that caused epidemics in the past, such as smallpox and diphtheria, have been almost eliminated from Earth. Others, such as acquired immune deficiency syndrome (AIDS) and hantavirus, are epidemics that have been discovered since 1970 and are presently a worldwide threat.

Some noninfectious epidemic diseases, such as alcohol addiction, drug addition, and obesity, are widespread in many cultures. These diseases are often referred to as diseases of choice because many medical experts believe that they are behavior related. These experts claim that diseases of choice can be controlled by changes in behavior: better eating habits, exercise, and good medical care. As mentioned, recent research shows, however, that genetics may play a role in individual susceptibility to each of these diseases. The extent to which these diseases are diseases of choice is still a very controversial issue.

Medical Defenses Against Disease

During the late-nineteenth and all of the twentieth century, much scientific progress was made toward understanding, preventing, and curing disease. A few notable discoveries are listed here:

- First and foremost, the importance of sanitation and cleanliness was recognized in preventing the spread of disease and for improving cure and survival rates in hospitals.

- The invention and use of vaccines for disease prevention became standard practice.

- The importance of a nutritious diet, rich in vitamins and minerals, was recognized.

- The use of antibiotics to fight bacterial diseases was invented.

- Organ transplantation was developed as a way of replacing severely damaged organs.

- Gene therapy is a newly developing technique for dealing with diseases caused by genetic disorders.

Many scientists believe that the medical fight against disease is in its infancy. Through advances in molecular biology, gene therapy, medicinal drugs, and public health awareness, scientists look forward to the day when today's diseases are just topics in medical history.

Public Health

Most diseases are more easily prevented than treated. This is true in developed countries such as the United States and in developing countries in Africa. The role of public health officials is to bring modern medical knowledge and medicines to all those who need it. This is an ongoing struggle. In developed countries, lifestyle choices often interfere with individual health and safety. In developing countries, internal politics and social policy often interfere with the safety and health of citizens.

Thinking About Science

Directions: Answer each question below.

1. What is a pathogen? _____
   _____

2. Name three types of infectious disease.

   _____, _____,

   _____

3. Name three noninfectious diseases that are thought to be hereditary.

   _____, _____,

   _____

4. Antibiotics are helpful in curing which types of diseases?

   _____
   _____

Answers are on page 439.

Directions: Choose the <u>one best answer</u> to each question.

Questions 1 and 2 refer to the following passage.

The human body has two types of immunity designed to protect you from invading pathogens (harmful bacteria, viruses, and fungi).

• *Innate immunity* is the body's first defense against invading pathogens. Innate immunity defenses help prevent pathogens from entering the body. These defenses include skin, tears, mucus, and saliva.

• *Adaptive immunity* comes into action when pathogens get through the innate immunity defenses. Adaptive immunity is provided by cells, molecules, and organs of the immune system. These body systems attack only specific invaders and do not attack normal body cells. What's more, the adaptive immune system has a memory. It responds better to later exposures of the same invader, even if several years pass between exposures.

1. Carlita touches a doorknob on which the common cold virus is present. What is Carlita's first line of defense against this virus.

    (1) nasal membranes
    (2) antibodies in her blood
    (3) healthy skin
    (4) white blood cells
    (5) tears from her eyes

2. Which of the following is <u>not</u> a property of adaptive immunity?

    (1) responds to a pathogen
    (2) involves body tissue
    (3) does not attack normal cells
    (4) only occurs during a fever
    (5) has a memory

Question 3 refers to the following passage.

Cancer is a noninfectious disease that affects more than on million new patients each year in the United States. More than 500,000 people die each year from cancer in the United States alone.

Cancer is the uncontrolled growth of abnormal cells that invade and destroy tissue. Cancer cells can originate in any body tissue and can spread to other types of body tissue. As cancer cells multiply, they often form a mass of cells called a *tumor*. A tumor may continue to enlarge without regard to the function of the tissue of which it is a part.

Evidence indicates that most cancers are more related to environmental conditions than to heredity. Avoiding environmental contaminants, not smoking, following a nutritious diet, and engaging in regular exercise can help prevent cancer. Also, knowing the seven main warning signs of cancer may someday save your life or the life of a loved one.

EARLY WARNING SIGNS FOR CANCER

• Unusual bleeding or discharge
• A lump or thickening in the breast or elsewhere
• A sore that does not heal
• Change in bowel or bladder habits
• Hoarseness or cough that continues
• Indigestion or difficulty in swallowing
• Change in size or color of a wart or mole

---

3. What can you infer to be true from the passage?

    (1) Cancer is primarily a hereditary disease and lifestyle has little to do with it.
    (2) A tumor is an indication that cancer cells are localized and not spreading.
    (3) Cancer is the leading cause of death in the United States.
    (4) There are many lifestyle choices you can make that reduce your risk of cancer.
    (5) There are only seven warning signs for cancer.

Answers are on page 440.

Natural Resources

Human well-being also depends on the resources that are available to support life. An important part of these are **natural resources**, resources provided by nature. The most common natural resources are water, air, topsoil, energy, and biodiversity—the wide variety of plant and animal life on Earth. Natural resources are often classified in two broad categories: renewable and nonrenewable.

- **Renewable resources** are resources, such as trees, that can be used and then replaced over a relatively short period of time. Solar energy is the one renewable resource that is considered to be in unlimited supply.

- **Nonrenewable resources** are those that cannot be replaced or take hundreds or thousands of years to replace. Practically speaking, all nonrenewable resources can run out. Most minerals and fossil fuels are nonrenewable resources. Large tropical rainforests and species of animals and plants that are in danger of extinction are also considered nonrenewable resources.

Some resources were once thought to be renewable but are now considered nonrenewable. Fertile topsoil is an example. A few inches of rich topsoil may take thousands of years to create but can be washed away in less than a year. Scientists estimate that since 1945 human activities alone have caused more than 50 percent of Earth's topsoil to become degraded. About half of this degraded topsoil is no longer capable of sustaining agriculture.

Worldwide, water is the natural resource in shortest supply. Water is essential for the growing of all crops, yet more than 40 countries lack sufficient water for agriculture. Half of these countries are in Africa and the Middle East, where water scarcity can last for months or years. Severe food shortages result, followed by mass starvation and death. If current population trends continue, it is estimated that by the year 2025, 75 percent of Africans will live in regions of severe food shortage due to lack of water.

Energy resources are also in short supply. Most of the energy of industrialized societies today is provided by **fossil fuels**, such as petroleum, coal, and natural gas. Petroleum provides gasoline for cars and heating oil for homes. Coal is used to power electrical power plants. Natural gas is used in hot-water heaters, stoves, and heating furnaces.

Fossil fuels are being used more quickly than they are being produced. Fossil fuels will someday run out, but when each fuel will run out can only be estimated. Based on known reserves, scientists estimate that petroleum may run out within the next 100 years, natural gas within the next 500 years, and coal within the next 200 years.

Several factors make these predictions uncertain: increasing efficiency in energy production and use, new discoveries of unknown fossil fuel deposits, and worldwide social and political factors over which we have little control.

Conservation

Conservation is the controlled use and preservation of natural resources. To conserve natural resources means using fewer of them. Here are a few examples of conservation.

- Walking or riding a bicycle short distances instead of driving a car: This method of conservation saves fuel, prevents air pollution, and saves wear on automobiles, buses, and highways. Also, the exercise improves the health of all participants.

- Using organic compost, such as household food waste, on a home garden: This method of conservation reduces the number of chemicals needed for making fertilizer. Also, organic compost is not a source of soil and water pollution, which commercially prepared fertilizers often are.

To conserve means to use fewer natural resources. Using less resources creates less waste and fewer pollutants in our air, water, and soil.

Recycling

One recycling technique enables consumer products to be reused for their original purpose. When a child has outgrown its crib, for example, the crib can be given or sold to another family with small children. Recycling beverage containers is another example of this technique. Reusing products in this way conserves natural resources.

When products cannot be reused in their original form, another technique, call **resource recovery,** may be possible. Resource recovery involves the breaking down of waste (trash) in order to regain material for human use. The parts that are unrecoverable are then burned to create electricity. If a child's crib is beyond repair, for example, it may be possible to recycle the wood, metal, and plastic parts and to burn the unrecoverable parts for electricity. If the unrecoverable trash collected in the United States were efficiently burned, the amount of electricity produced would equal that produced by 15 nuclear power plants.

Interest in recycling is growing in the United States. Yet, at the present time, the United States recycles only about 10 percent of its trash. Compare this with Japan, which recycles 50 percent of its trash, and Europe, which recycles 30 percent.

Much of solid waste can be recycled. Plastic, paper, cans, glass, and cardboard are examples.

- Every week, one million trees are used in the production of newspapers. The recycling of newspapers alone can save more than half of these trees.

- Recycling aluminum cans can save 90 percent of the energy needed to change bauxite ore into aluminum.

- Glass, which now makes up almost 10 percent of American trash, can be recycled.

- Lead batteries can be recycled into new batteries.

Protecting Biodiversity

Biodiversity (or species diversity) creates a healthy variety of plant and animal species that coexist in an environment and make the environment more stable. Protecting biodiversity is important for human life. Biodiversity provides food, clean air and water, and fertile soil. Also, biodiversity provides products for human use. Today, about 40 percent of medicinal drugs are obtained from plant and animal sources. Also, biodiversity provides natural pest control and natural beauty.

Extinction—the dying off of an entire plant or animal species—threatens biodiversity. At present, about 20,000 plant species and 5,000 animal species have been identified as endangered and are possibly headed for extinction. There are many potential causes of extinction:

- Natural extinction

- Destruction of habitat

- Air and water pollution

- Hunting for sport or for trade in body parts

Natural extinction occurs as a normal part of evolution. Changes in climate, food resources, the number of competitors for resources, and the number of natural predators can lead to natural extinction. There are perhaps millions of species of plants and animals that have become extinct throughout history without our even knowing of their existence. Newly discovered fossil evidence (any trace of an extinct organism) continually reminds us of many life forms that long ago vanished from Earth.

During the last few centuries, the human appetite for resource consumption has caused the rate of extinction to increase rapidly. Humans interfere with natural habitats and kill endangered species at an alarming rate. Estimates are that as many as 20,000 species are becoming extinct each year. Many of these species have not even been identified. They simply disappear as tropical forests are burned and cleared. Many scientists believe that humans are causing the greatest mass extinction since the time of the dinosaur extinction 70 million years ago.

Thinking About Science

Directions: Match each word on the left with the best description on the right. Write the correct letter on the line.

_____ **1.** renewable resources

_____ **2.** biodiversity

_____ **3.** nonrenewable resources

_____ **4.** conservation

_____ **5.** fossil fuels

(a) the controlled use and preservation of natural resources

(b) resources that can be used and then replaced over a short period of time

(c) a major energy source for industrialized societies

(d) the coexistence of a variety of plant and animal species

(e) resources that cannot be replaced

Answers are on page 440.

GED PRACTICE

Directions: Choose the one best answer to each question.

Question 1 refers to the following passage.

To protect biodiversity, it is necessary to protect individual species. In the United States, the Endangered Species Act of 1973 is an attempt to do just that. According to this act, no federal project can destroy or interfere with the habitat of any endangered species. Two degrees of endangerment are identified:

• *endangered species:* any species, such as the tiger, that is in immediate risk of extinction

• *threatened species:* any species, such as the bald eagle, that is not in immediate risk of extinction but could become so if something isn't done to protect it

1. Which of the following conclusions can you draw from the Endangered Species Act?

   (1) The United States is concerned about endangered animals that are native to the country.
   (2) The United States is concerned about endangered animals worldwide.
   (3) The United States has no concern about endangered animals.
   (4) European countries are more concerned about endangered animals than the United States.
   (5) There are no endangered animals in the United States.

Answers are on page 440.

Population Growth

In 1798 Thomas Malthus, an English clergyman and economist, wrote *An Essay on the Principle of Population.* In this essay, Malthus said that food production cannot keep up with a rapidly growing population. According to Malthus, the only way to prevent world **famine** (widespread starvation) is to limit population growth. Family planning—limiting the number of children—is necessary if famine is to be avoided. Malthus pointed out that, besides family planning, the only alternatives to starvation are epidemic diseases and war.

Malthus's essay was the first scholarly discussion of food shortages and rapidly growing populations. At that time, though, few readers took Malthus's concerns seriously. Since 1798 the world population has grown at an ever-increasing rate, which has led to new concerns about population growth.

- In 1804 the world population reached 1 billion.

- By 1960 the world population had risen to 3 billion.

- By 2000 the world population reached 6 billion.

- By 2050 the world population is projected to reach 9 billion.

Notice that between 1804 and 1960, a period of nearly 150 years, the world population tripled. Between 1960 and 2050, a period of only 90 years, the world population is expected to more than triple. Unless the growth rate slows, the population may triple again by 2060!

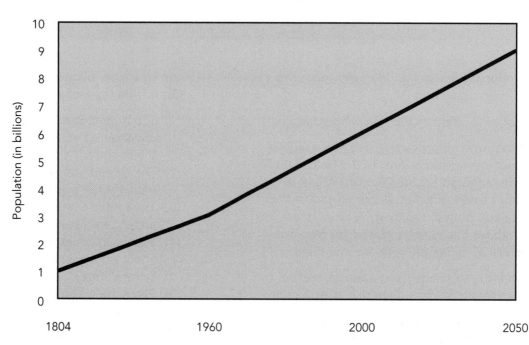

HUMAN POPULATION GROWTH

For a population to grow at an increasing rate, the number of births must exceed the number of deaths. This happens when life expectancy increases and early deaths from disease decrease. These conditions are occurring worldwide as the average standard of living is slowly getting better.

Beginning in about 1950, advanced countries—primarily the United States and European countries—brought low-cost vaccines, antibiotics, insecticides, and agricultural resources to less-developed countries. Water supplies were improved, sewage-disposal systems were built, transportation systems were modernized, and productive agricultural practices were begun. As a result, general health increased, food resources increased, infant mortality rates dropped, and deaths at all ages from disease decreased. Life expectancy in developing countries rose from about 35 years in 1950 to about 60 years in 1990.

The graph below shows the increase in life expectancy of men and women living in the United States during the twentieth century. The reason for the rise in life expectancy is better medical care, better nutrition, a decreasing rate of death due to disease, and a decreasing rate of death due to occupational injury.

LIFE EXPECTANCY OF U.S. MEN AND WOMEN IN THE 20TH CENTURY

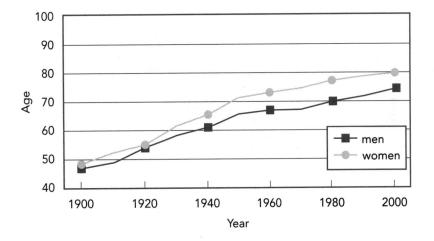

Consequences of a Large Population

There are many consequences to a rapidly growing population. Food shortage is a concern, but, so far, food production in most developed countries has kept up with population needs. Better land use, better fertilizers, and better crops have resulted in adequate food production. At some point in the future, however, sufficient food supplies may no longer be possible.

In some developing countries, even a low population growth rate does not guarantee an adequate food supply. Haiti, for example, has a very low growth rate, but more than two out of three Haitians are undernourished. China, the world's most populous country, is actually declining in population, but one out of six Chinese are undernourished. In both Haiti and China, food shortages are caused by extreme poverty, a condition that must be solved by social and economic policies.

One negative consequence of a large population in a developed country such as the United States is the ever-increasing number of consumer products. Consumer products use natural resources, contribute to increasing levels of air and water pollution, result in an increasing amount of trash, and often add to noise pollution—annoying levels of noise found in and around large population centers.

Controlling Population Growth

Ironically, the great success of science and technology in the areas of medicine, agriculture, water purification, and sewage disposal has helped create the worldwide population explosion. However, science and technology have also provided a number of safe, reliable family planning options. These options include a number of pregnancy prevention methods and pregnancy termination options.

Controlling population growth is now more a matter of education and social policy than a matter of science. As a result, many countries in the world have national policies regarding population planning.

- Japan was the first developed country to begin a birth-control program. In 1948 the Japanese government began a policy to limit family size through the use of contraception and abortion.

- In 1952 India adopted an official policy to slow its population growth. Although methods of family planning are being widely taught, little progress has been made in slowing India's huge population.

- China, the world's most populated country, has successfully reduced its population growth. The official government position is that families will limit themselves to one child or suffer economic consequences. The goal of China is to reduce the country's growth rate to zero during the first decade of the twenty-first century.

- The United States has no official policy on population control. In 1972 a President's Commission on Population Growth on the American Future proposed that the government take strong measures to move the United States to zero population growth. President Richard M. Nixon rejected the recommendation because it advocated education on family planning and promoted the wide availability of contraception and abortion services.

- By 1979 more than 90 percent of the governments of developing countries supported family planning methods of one form or another. In general, these efforts take into account the health of the mother and the right of parents to choose when to have their children.

In many parts of the world today, as in the United States, family planning is not as much a scientific question as a social-policy question. Politicians, political parties, religious leaders, and religious organizations have a lot to do with influencing beliefs regarding methods of population control in their own countries. All would agree, however, that population growth remains one of the great challenges of the twenty-first century.

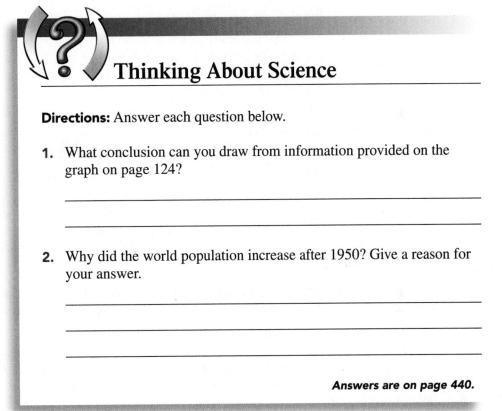

Thinking About Science

Directions: Answer each question below.

1. What conclusion can you draw from information provided on the graph on page 124?

   _____

   _____

2. Why did the world population increase after 1950? Give a reason for your answer.

   _____

   _____

   _____

Answers are on page 440.

Directions: Choose the <u>one best answer</u> to each question.

Questions 1–4 refer to the information on pages 124–127 and to the graph below.

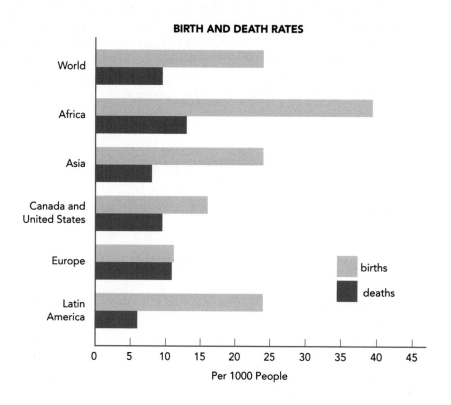

BIRTH AND DEATH RATES

1. For the world as a whole, how does the birthrate compare to the death rate?

   (1) The birthrate is about one-fourth the death rate.
   (2) The birthrate is a little less than half of the death rate.
   (3) The birthrate is equal to the death rate.
   (4) The birthrate is a little more than twice the death rate.
   (5) The birthrate is about four times the death rate.

2. In which region are the birth and death rates most nearly equal to the proportion of those of the world as a whole?

   (1) Africa
   (2) Asia
   (3) Canada and United States
   (4) Europe
   (5) Latin America

3. Which region of the world has the greatest ratio of birth to death rate?

   (1) Africa
   (2) Asia
   (3) Canada and United States
   (4) Europe
   (5) Latin America

4. Which region of the world has the lowest population growth?

   (1) Africa
   (2) Asia
   (3) Canada and United States
   (4) Europe
   (5) Latin America

Answers are on page 440.

Environmental Quality

So far in this chapter several factors affecting the quality of human life have been discussed: diseases, depletion of natural resources, and overpopulation. Now we will look at the role that pollution plays in affecting environmental quality. **Pollution** is any form of contamination (introduction of harmful substances into the environment) that affects the quality of life. Pollution control is another of the great challenges of the twenty-first century.

Pollution affects all life on Earth, from human beings to birds to whales. Some pollution, such as that caused by a volcanic eruption, has a natural cause. Most pollution, though, is caused by the actions of human beings.

Air Pollution

Air pollution is the presence of **contaminants** (substances that harm the environment) in the air. Air pollution in and around cities is called smog. Smog is a smoky mixture of carbon monoxide and hydrocarbon gases formed by the incomplete burning of fossil fuels. Smog comes from two main sources: automobile exhaust and industrial smokestacks.

When the gases in smog react with water vapor and oxygen in the atmosphere, sulfuric acid and other organic acids form. These chemicals fall to the ground in the form of acid rain. Smog, a major health hazard in many cities in the twentieth century, has brought many cities a new phenomenon: smog alerts, when residents are advised to stay inside and not breathe outside air.

Water Pollution

The main causes of water pollution are untreated sewage (human and animal body wastes), industrial chemicals, fertilizers, and pesticides. In many parts of developing countries, almost all human waste enters rivers and lakes as untreated sewage. In the United States, pollution from chemical waste, not human waste is a problem. Today, about one of every three rivers and lakes in the United States is too polluted to use for fishing or swimming.

The oceans, as large as they are, can also become seriously polluted. Oceanic pollution and the threat it brings to sea life is particularly threatening to the 15 percent of people worldwide who depend on fish as their major source of protein. Waste disposal in the oceans, contaminated river water, and oil spills from oil tankers all contribute to oceanic pollution. In 1989 the oil tanker *Exxon Valdez* spilled 260,000 barrels of oil in Alaska's Prince William Sound. The environmental damage caused by this oil is likely to take decades to undo. In 1992 alone there were 8,800 reported oil spills in and around U.S. waters.

Soil Pollution

Clean soil is essential for the growth of food crops. Soil pollution occurs when toxic chemicals, disease-causing organisms, or radioactive wastes get into the soil.

Treating soil with fertilizers, pesticides, and fungicides poses two risks: chemical residues in the soil are both absorbed into food crops and washed by rainwater into drinking-water aquifers. As an example, farmers in California put methyl bromide in the soil to kill organisms that harm young strawberry plants. Methyl bromide is poisonous for human consumption.

Solid Waste Disposal

Solid wastes are unwanted materials such as household garbage, paper, plastics, metals, and woods. The United States produces about 200 million tons of solid wastes in its cities alone each year. The typical American consumer produces about four pounds of solid waste each day. Citizens in developing countries produce much less solid waste per person than citizens of the United States. And, the solid waste produced in developing countries contains far less synthetic materials—materials that take longer to decompose.

Solid-waste disposal is a major problem worldwide. There are several methods of solid-waste disposal:

- A **landfill** is a place where solid wastes are buried. Landfills are the most common form of waste disposal, but they do have problems. Landfills quickly become overfilled, and they are often a source of air, water, and soil pollution.

- **Incineration** is the burning of solid wastes. Incineration produces wastes in the forms of smoke and ash. This smoke and ash can be a dangerous form of air pollution, because it may contain toxic compounds.

- **Composting** is the using of natural biological processes to aid in the decomposition of organic materials, such as grass, leaves, twigs, and household food wastes. Composting is inexpensive and works well for organic waste. Composted waste makes excellent natural fertilizer. Composting does not work with inorganic wastes such as chemicals, plastics, and metals.

- **Recycling**, as discussed on page 121, is the breaking down of trash into its component substances and reusing them in new products. Recycling is beginning to play a major role in solid-waste disposal in developed countries. About 20 percent of solid waste produced in cities in the United States is now recycled.

Hazardous-Waste Disposal

Hazardous waste is waste that is harmful or deadly to people and that does not naturally break down into nontoxic substances. Even brief exposure to some types of hazardous waste can cause cancer, birth defects, nervous system disorders, and death. Included are agricultural wastes (fertilizers and pesticides), industrial chemicals, medical wastes (leftover medicines, body tissue, and contaminated blood), household wastes (paints and solvents), and radioactive wastes (from nuclear power plants).

The safe disposal of hazardous waste is an ongoing concern. Many companies have negligently contaminated sites and later abandoned those sites without cleaning them up. These hazardous-waste sites have not received the attention that is needed. At present the United States has about 10,000 abandoned hazardous-waste sites that need to be cleaned up. Environmental scientists estimate that, if work started today, it could take 50 years to clean up these sites and cost $100 billion.

The disposal of radioactive nuclear waste is an even worse nightmare. There is no scientifically known way to dispose of these deadly products, many of which will remain radioactive for thousands of years. All we can do is store them, keeping them from the public, for many centuries to come.

A radiation warning symbol

A Closer Look at Plastic Trash

With the invention of polymers (long chains of carbon atoms), chemists gave us plastic, an almost ideal material. Plastic is strong, versatile, and durable. It does not substantially degrade under heat and pressure and can be subjected to total submersion in water (even ocean water) without being broken down. Plastic, if left outside, remains almost as good as new, despite the weather. Unlike most other materials, plastic doesn't naturally decay.

For useful consumer products, this remarkable durability is a blessing. Plastic bottles are light and unbreakable. Plastic bags don't easily leak or tear. Along with this blessing, though, is an environmental nightmare. When plastic items are ready for the garbage, what do you do with them? Unfortunately, many people just throw them away. Now, millions of tons of plastic trash litter our highways and beaches.

Plastic trash can be devastating to ocean life. According to the National Academy of Sciences, more than 600,000 plastic containers and bags are tossed into the oceans every day. Fishermen lose or discard an estimated 150,000 tons of plastic fishing gear each year. At least forty-two species of seabirds are known to snack on plastic, a habit that is often fatal. In addition, tens of thousands of seals, sea lions, and turtles die each year after becoming entangled in bits of fish netting.

What should we do with the hundreds of millions of tons of plastic and other polymer products that end up in the garbage each year? We could burn it. However, burning plastic creates a thick, black smoke that is both intolerable to see and dangerous to breathe. We could bury it, but landfills have their own pollution problems. Too often, plastic trash in landfills does not stay buried and becomes a health hazard for birds and other animals. What's more, highly populated countries with limited space may find that land is far too valuable to use as a landfill. Then, dumping at sea may become the alternative.

Scientists do not have a solution to the plastic trash problem. **Biodegradable** plastics (plastics that naturally decompose) may be the ultimate answer. For now, individuals can help by recycling as many plastic products as possible. Also, reusing plastic bags rather than throwing them away would help. Some people choose not to buy plastic products when the same item is available in paper or glass. Of course, these are only small steps, but they are perhaps part of the solution.

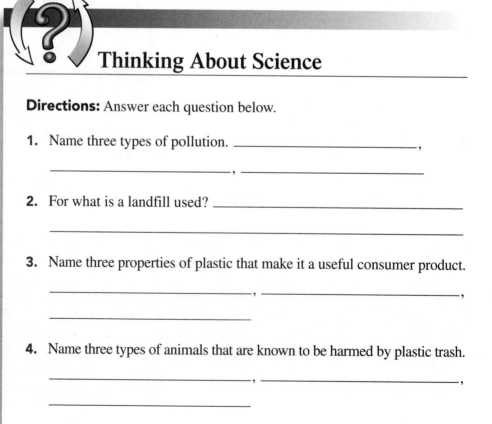

Thinking About Science

Directions: Answer each question below.

1. Name three types of pollution. _____,
    _____, _____

2. For what is a landfill used? _____
    _____

3. Name three properties of plastic that make it a useful consumer product.
    _____, _____,
    _____

4. Name three types of animals that are known to be harmed by plastic trash.
    _____, _____,
    _____

Answers are on page 440.

Directions: Choose the <u>one best answer</u> to each question.

Questions 1 and 2 refer to the information on pages 129–132.

1. The following are four methods of disposing of plastic trash:

    A. dumping it in the ocean, miles from shore

    B. recycling (reusing) polymer consumer products

    C. burning polymer trash on disposal ships far out at sea

    D. burying polymer trash in a properly designed and carefully regulated solid-waste dump

    Which of the above methods are harmful to the environment?

    (1) B and C only
    (2) C and D only
    (3) A and C only
    (4) A, B, and D only
    (5) A, C, and D only

2. What is the main property of plastic that makes it such an environmental concern?

    (1) the ease with which it can be broken
    (2) its use in such a wide range of consumer products
    (3) the fact that it can be manufactured anywhere in the world
    (4) its resistance to weathering or to decay
    (5) its light weight compared to steel

3. What is the main risk of treating soil with pesticides?

    (1) polluting food crops
    (2) killing valuable insects
    (3) changing the weather pattern
    (4) reducing crop growth
    (5) reducing water flow

Questions 4–6 refer to the following passage.

In a process called *bioremediation*, bacteria or other microorganisms are used to remove some types of polluting substances from air, water, and soil. Bioremediation works best on organic compounds—carbon-based substances such as gasoline and toluene. Bioremediation was used to help clean up Alaskan beaches contaminated with oil from the *Exxon Valdez*. Also, bioremediation is used in tanks or lagoons to help clean some forms of industrial waste.

4. What is bioremediation?

    (1) the use of microorganisms in the process of digestion.
    (2) the use of microorganisms to aid in pollution control.
    (3) the killing of microorganisms using organic compounds.
    (4) the removal of carbon from organic compounds.
    (5) the cleaning of industrial waste by the use of organic compounds.

5. How does an organic compound differ from an inorganic compound (a compound that is not organic)?

    (1) by weight
    (2) by color
    (3) by odor
    (4) by chemical content
    (5) by the presence of contaminants

6. Which of the following can you infer from information given in the passage?

    (1) Bioremediation works for all hazardous wastes.
    (2) Bioremediation does not work for any hazardous wastes.
    (3) All industrial wastes are organic compounds.
    (4) Oil is not an organic compound.
    (5) Oil is an organic compound.

Answers are on page 440.

The Greenhouse Effect and Global Warming

Life on Earth is made possible by a delicate balance of many factors. If this balance is upset, extinction can result. One factor is a temperature range that supports life. Earth's present mild surface temperature results from the heating effect of sunlight together with the insulating and warming properties of the atmosphere—known as the **greenhouse effect.**

There is a type of air pollution that can cause the greenhouse effect to overheat Earth's surface, a result called **global warming.** This air pollution is mainly excess carbon dioxide gas and to a lesser extent several other gases. Collectively these gases are referred to as greenhouse gases.

Our close neighbor, the planet Venus, has experienced such a temperature increase. Like Earth, Venus has a solid surface of minerals and an atmosphere. You might think Venus is a place where organisms could develop and grow. Not so. The surface temperature of Venus is about 900°F—too hot for any form of life that we know about.

Venus is so hot because of its carbon dioxide-rich atmosphere. Venus can't cool as Earth cools: by sending excess heat energy back into space. On Venus, heat energy radiating from the surface is absorbed by excess carbon dioxide gas in the atmosphere.

The greenhouse effect gets its name from the glass-sided buildings used for plant nurseries. Sunlight passes through the glass and warms the nursery. The glass prevents heat from leaving. Overheating is prevented by opening windows. On Venus, dense carbon dioxide gas in the atmosphere traps heat energy and prevents its escape into space. Overheating cannot be prevented.

The current level of carbon dioxide gas in Earth's atmosphere traps some heat and lets much heat escape into space. However, the burning of wood, coal, oil, and other fossil fuels is adding an abnormal amount of carbon dioxide to the atmosphere. The result is that the level of carbon dioxide gas in Earth's atmosphere is increasing. Slow global warming may be the result.

CONSTANT CO$_2$ IN ATMOSPHERE　　　　**INCREASED CO$_2$ IN ATMOSPHERE**

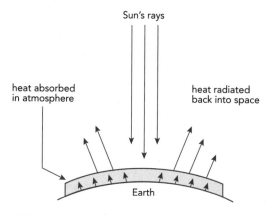

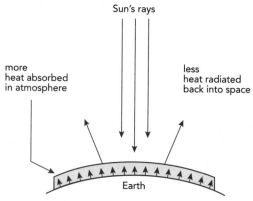

With a constant level of carbon dioxide in the atmosphere, Earth cools by radiating excess heat back into space.

As the high level of carbon dioxide in the atmosphere increases, Earth's average temperature also increases.

Measurements show that the amount of carbon dioxide gas in Earth's atmosphere has increased 28 percent in the last hundred years. At this rate, the level could rise another 40 percent by the end of the twenty-first century. If this increase happens, several things may occur:

- The average surface temperature of Earth will increase, perhaps by as much as 3.6°F.

- Glacial ice will melt and the oceans will rise by several feet. Coastal cities, such as San Francisco and New York, will be partially underwater.

- World rainfall patterns will change. The United States, now the breadbasket of the world, may become an arid, parched wasteland.

Scientists are not sure how serious global warming is becoming. However, one thing is sure: Everyone on Earth lives under a shared atmosphere. Proper care of this atmosphere is a must if Earth's environment is to remain capable of sustaining life.

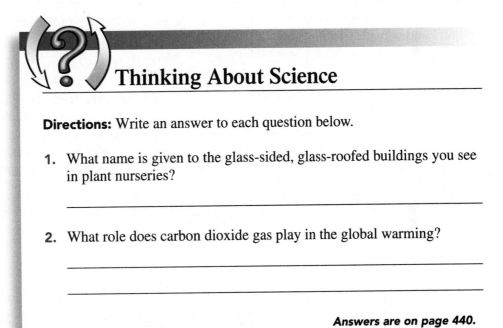

Thinking About Science

Directions: Write an answer to each question below.

1. What name is given to the glass-sided, glass-roofed buildings you see in plant nurseries?

   _____

2. What role does carbon dioxide gas play in the global warming?

   _____

   _____

   Answers are on page 440.

Directions: Choose the <u>one best answer</u> to each question.

Questions 1–4 refer to the information on pages 134 and 135.

1. Which of the following is most similar to the heating that takes place inside a nursery greenhouse?

   (1) warming yourself by standing in front of a fireplace in a closed room
   (2) being warmed by sunlight while sitting inside a car with all the windows closed
   (3) becoming suntanned while lying on the beach on a warm summer day
   (4) warming yourself after a shower by standing under a sunlamp
   (5) keeping warm on a cold day by wearing a wool sweater and a heavy overcoat

2. Which of the following is a direct cause of global warming on Earth?

   (1) a slow melting of polar ice caps
   (2) the success of the Industrial Revolution
   (3) the fact that a single atmosphere covers Earth
   (4) the slow rising of Earth's ocean levels
   (5) the increasing levels of carbon dioxide in Earth's atmosphere

3. Which of the following items would be of <u>least</u> importance to someone studying global warming?

   (1) any change in the average thickness of the polar ice caps
   (2) any change in the average air temperature off the coast of Alaska
   (3) the success of efforts designed to protect Arctic polar bears from extinction
   (4) a comparison of summer and winter conditions on Venus
   (5) any change in the average levels of high and low tides in San Francisco Bay

4. Which of the following would be the <u>most</u> effective solution for the potential problem known as global warming?

   (1) reducing our dependence on all forms of fossil fuels
   (2) placing restrictions on wood stoves
   (3) developing cars that get high mileage
   (4) managing forests in order to prevent lightning fires
   (5) placing high taxes on fossil fuels

   Answers are on page 440.

Go to **www.GEDScience.com** for additional practice and instruction!

Science in Personal and Social Perspectives Review

Directions: Choose the one best answer to each question.

Questions 1 and 2 are based on the following passage.

One of the possible devastating consequences of overpopulation is famine—severe shortage of food. Besides overpopulation, famine can be caused by droughts, floods, earthquakes, insect plagues, and deliberate military action or government policy.

Famine results in widespread hunger and malnutrition. The affected population suffers weight loss in adults and retarded physical growth and mental development in children. Death often follows, usually beginning with older adults and then young children.

Death from famine is due both to starvation and to a decreased ability to fight infection. Malnutrition severely weakens the body's immune system. Regions suffering famine today often have epidemics of diarrhea, measles, and tuberculosis.

1. Which of the following is not mentioned as resulting from famine?

    (1) weight loss
    (2) premature aging
    (3) retarded mental development
    (4) increased chance for disease
    (5) hunger

2. Which of the following causes of famine does a population have the most control over?

    (1) overpopulation
    (2) drought
    (3) floods
    (4) earthquakes
    (5) insect plagues

Questions 3 and 4 refer to the following passage.

Changes in society can have profound effects on public health. One such effect occurs from the increase in air travel. People infected with a virus normally found on one part of Earth can carry that virus to another part in only a few hours time. International trade by ships, trucks, and airplanes also makes it possible for local viruses to move quickly to other countries.

In 1985 larva of the Asian tiger mosquito traveled to Texas on tires imported from Asia. The Asian tiger mosquito carries dengue fever and other tropical diseases.

Human movement into tropical rain forests brings humans in contact with deadly viruses once found only in forest animals. The Ebola virus, first identified in Africa, is a much feared example. Symptoms of the Ebola virus are massive bleeding and the destruction of internal organs.

3. Which of the following is not mentioned as a method of how viruses travel from one country to another?

    (1) contaminated ocean currents
    (2) international travelers
    (3) movement of consumer goods
    (4) movement of food products
    (5) human movement into rain forests

4. Which of the following can be inferred from the passage?

    (1) Forest animals are affected by viruses just as humans are.
    (2) Forest animals have viruses that can be transferred to humans.
    (3) Forest animals are not made sick by viruses.
    (4) All forest animals carry viruses that are harmful to humans.
    (5) Humans have viruses that can be transferred to forest animals.

Questions 5–7 refer to the following passage.

The rosy periwinkle is a small plant found in Madagascar, an island off the southeast coast of Africa. This rare plant produces chemicals that are used in the fight against two deadly cancers, Hodgkin's disease and leukemia. Unfortunately, the forest habitat of the rosy periwinkle is being cut down. The cut wood is being used as firewood by the poor people of the island while the cleared land is being converted to farmland. Other plant species that are exclusive to Madagascar similarly face extinction.

5. What makes rosy periwinkle a valuable natural resource?

   (1) location of habitat
   (2) beauty
   (3) aroma
   (4) chemical properties
   (5) decorative value

6. What is threatening the survival of the species known as rosy periwinkle?

   (1) poverty of local citizens
   (2) tropical climate changes
   (3) destruction of habitat
   (4) lack of farmland
   (5) other plant species

7. Who is most likely to suffer from the extinction of rosy periwinkle?

   (1) cancer patients everywhere
   (2) medicinal drug companies
   (3) government of the United States
   (4) government of Madagascar
   (5) farmers of Madagascar

Questions 8 and 9 refer to the following circle graph.

SOLID-WASTE DISPOSAL IN THE UNITED STATES

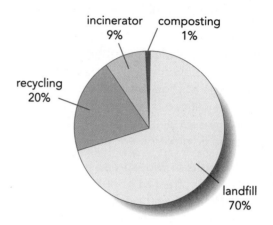

8. According to the graph, what is the most common way of disposing of trash in the United States?

   (1) burning in an incinerator
   (2) dumping at sea
   (3) using a landfill
   (4) composting
   (5) recycling and composting

9. Out of every 100 pounds of solid waste produced in the United States, how many pounds end up in a landfill?

   (1) 70 pounds
   (2) 50 pounds
   (3) 30 pounds
   (4) 9 pounds
   (5) 1 pound

Answers are on page 440.

CHAPTER 6

History and Nature of Science

Science investigates; religion interprets. Science gives man knowledge, which is power; religion gives man wisdom, which is control.

~ Martin Luther King, Jr.

Science as a Human Endeavor

Characteristics of Scientists

How do scientists differ from the rest of us? This is an interesting question. The answer may be that scientists simply spend more time doing science than most people. That fact is certainly true. But do scientists have interests that differ very much from most people's interests?

Here are some characteristics of scientists:

- Scientists tend to be curious about the world.

- Some scientists prefer to work alone. Others prefer to work with other people, sometimes in groups of several hundred people.

- Scientists take pride in their work.

- Scientists like to tell other people about their work.

- Scientists are influenced by their own personal beliefs, values, and religion.

- The work of scientists is often influenced by the needs of society.

- The work of scientists is often limited by a lack of funding (money).

Do these characteristics sound familiar? If so, you may be more of a scientist than you think! Do you wonder why the sky is blue, why birds sing, or what walking on the Moon feels like? Do you think of yourself as an idea person or as an inventor? If you answer yes to any of these questions, you are thinking like a scientist. Remember, being a scientist does not mean you must do science for a living. Plenty of people consider science as a hobby instead of a career.

Science is truly a human endeavor. Science involves people like you: people who ask questions; people who want to know. The following statements were made by renowned scientists regarding their desire to know more about the natural world:

> I can live with doubt and uncertainty. I think it's much more interesting to live not knowing than to have answers that might be wrong.
>
> ~ Richard Feynman (1918–1988), Recipient of the 1965 Nobel Prize in physics

> My goal is simple. It is a complete understanding of the universe, why it is as it is and why it exists at all.
>
> ~ Stephen Hawking (1942–), British theoretical physicist and mathematician

> The world of learning is so broad, and the human soul is so limited in power! We reach forth and strain every nerve, but we seize only a bit of the curtain that hides the infinite from us.
>
> ~ Maria Mitchell (1818–1889), American astronomer

The Hopes and Dreams of Scientists

Over the centuries, scientists have had very high hopes for science. But the search for knowledge has often ended sadly, with the discoveries of science being used for destructive purposes. Over the years, many scientists have spoken directly of both their hopes for and their disappointments regarding science.

> Science is triumphant with far-reaching success, but its triumph is somehow clouded by growing difficulties in providing for the simple necessities of human life on Earth.
>
> ~ Barry Commoner (1917–), American biologist, ecologist, and educator

> Why does this magnificent applied science, which saves work and makes life easier, bring us so little happiness? The simple answer runs: Because we have not yet learned to make sensible use of it.
>
> ~ Albert Einstein (1879–1955), German-born American physicist and Nobel prize-winner

In recent times, modern science has developed to give mankind, for the first time in the history of the human race, a way of securing a more abundant life, which does not simply consist in taking away from someone else.

~ Karl Taylor Compton (1887–1954), American physicist

Science knows no country, because knowledge belongs to humanity, and is the torch which illuminates the world. Science is the highest personification of a nation because that nation will remain the first which carries further the works of thought and intelligence.

~ Louis Pasteur (1822–1895), French chemist, biologist, and founder of microbiology

Perhaps the hope of all scientists for a better future is best expressed in the words of Dimitry Mendeleyev (1834–1907), a Russian chemist, who said:

There will come a time, when the world will be filled with one science, one truth, one industry, one brotherhood, one friendship with nature. . . . This is my belief.

Albert Einstein

Louis Pasteur

Dimitry Mendeleyev

Thinking About Science

Directions: Look at the following cartoon and answer each question below.

1. What point do you think the cartoonist is trying to make about modern conveniences provided by advances in science and technology?

   _____

   _____

2. Name two modern consumer products that you wish had not been invented. Give a brief reason why you do not like these products

   _____

   _____

   _____

Answers are on page 441.

Directions: Choose the <u>one best answer</u> to each question.

Questions 1–3 refer to the information on pages 139–141.

1. Which of the following words or phrases does <u>not</u> describe the personality of a good scientist?

   (1) curious
   (2) proud of his or her work
   (3) willing to share ideas
   (4) secretive
   (5) honest

2. Which of the following types of scientific research is a result of the sad reality of modern life?

   (1) medical research
   (2) research on the intelligence of apes
   (3) weapons research
   (4) research on physical activity
   (5) research on nutrition

3. What is one thing scientists have very little control over?

   (1) the number of hours they work
   (2) the type of work they do
   (3) how they choose to share information with other scientists
   (4) how they report scientific discoveries to the general public
   (5) how scientific discoveries are used by society

Questions 4 and 5 refer to the following warning label.

SURGEON GENERAL'S WARNING:

Quitting Smoking Now Greatly Reduces Serious Risks to Your Health

4. A scientist supports placing this warning label on all tobacco products. What concern is this scientist responding to?

   (1) house fire danger
   (2) restrictions on personal freedom
   (3) level of government taxation
   (4) tobacco company profits
   (5) community health

5. A scientist claims that there is no medical evidence to support this label. Which concern probably plays no role in this scientist's thinking?

   (1) scientific accuracy
   (2) job security
   (3) tobacco company profits
   (4) tobacco company image
   (5) maintaining a variety of popular tobacco brands

Answers are on page 441.

Historical Perspectives

The Science of Primitive People

As used here, primitive people are those who lived between 100,000 years ago and about 5,000 years ago. These are people who did not leave a written record of their lives or thoughts. What we know about how primitive people interpreted the world comes from cave drawings and legends that passed from generation to generation.

Most likely, primitive people questioned their world much as we question ours. They are likely to have answered those questions in ways that were meaningful to them, much as we do today. The difference between their interpretation of the world and ours is this: primitive people most likely formed beliefs based on a range of emotions rather than on a detailed study of the natural world. Some of those beliefs are listed below:

- The belief that spirits or souls were the givers and maintainers of life

- The belief that fire had a religious importance and may have been a divine gift

- The belief that demons caused natural disasters, such as violent storms, forest fires, earthquakes, and volcanic eruptions

- The belief that evil spirits caused disease

Primitive people did not separate the properties of the world from the personalities of spiritual beings. In this way of thinking, causes and effects were simply a demonstration of the will of spiritual beings.

As you can see, the science of primitive people was very unlike our science today. While primitive people may have feared or worshipped a full moon, we flew to that moon, walked on it, and brought part of it to Earth.

The Science of Aristotle

Between 600–200 B.C., the country of Greece rose as the center of learning of Western civilization. One of the great thinkers of this period was Aristotle (384–322 B.C.), whose science dominated Western thinking for 1,800 years, until the beginning of the Renaissance in the fourteenth century.

Aristotle helped organize an accumulating body of observations. He believed these observations held the key to understanding the processes of Earth and its life forms. Aristotle believed in cause and effect. He believed that to understand an effect you must first understand its causes and the purposes of those causes. With this belief as a starting point, Aristotle proposed the following scientific theories:

- The world is composed of individuals occurring in a fixed number.

- Each individual grows according to a pattern.

- Each individual seeks self-realization (maturity) as a goal.

- Earth is the center of the universe.

- All things are made of the same four elements: earth, air, fire, and water.

- Life forms do not change over time. (Evolution does not occur.)

- All thinking and all knowledge come from experience.

- All motion of objects on Earth is in a straight line. Objects in motion move downward, toward the center of Earth. The purpose of their movement is to go to their natural resting place.

- Fire moves upward, toward its natural resting place in heaven.

- The heavens move in a circle around Earth.

Unlike the science of primitive people, the science of Aristotle was based on a detailed study of the natural world. Aristotle did not turn to spiritual beings to account for all things that happen. Instead, he tried to logically connect those things that he saw. The science of Aristotle is truly the infant of modern science today.

The Science of the Renaissance

The Renaissance is a period of great intellectual growth and achievement that began in the fourteenth century and extended into the seventeenth century. Between the time of Aristotle and the beginning of the Renaissance, little progress was made in scientific thinking. This was soon to change. The Renaissance brought with it a spirit of curiosity and experimentation unseen since the time of Aristotle.

One of the first great achievements of the Renaissance was to move away from the idea that the universe centers on human beings. In the Renaissance way of thinking, humans were part of a universe that included Earth.

A second important change in thinking also occurred. Renaissance scientists rejected the idea that there was a hidden purpose behind everything. A rock didn't fall to the ground to move toward its natural resting place. A rock fell to the ground because of gravity. People of the Renaissance understood that gravity is a property of matter, that it is a force between two objects. Today, we can measure the effects of gravity, and we can make predictions based on our discoveries. But for the people of the Renaissance to realize that Earth and its life forms have properties that can be studied and understood is arguably the single greatest achievement of the Renaissance.

The following are a few important discoveries from the Renaissance that totally changed the way scientists viewed the world:

- Andreas Vesalius (1514–1564), a Belgian doctor, did detailed studies of the human body by cutting open corpses. His work corrected misconceptions that had prevailed since the time of Aristotle. The work of Vesalius began the modern study of anatomy.

- Christopher Columbus (1451–1506), an Italian sailor for Spain, made use of inventions and discoveries about navigation and sailed west from Spain on a quest to sail to Asia. Columbus paved the way for navigators to discover that Earth is not flat.

- Johannes Gutenberg (1390–1468), a German printer, is credited with inventing the first movable-type printing press in 1450. Movable type led to printed books and the spreading of knowledge.

- Nicolaus Copernicus (1473–1543), a Polish astronomer, proposed that the Sun is at the center of the universe and that Earth rotates once daily on its axis. (This was a revolutionary idea at that time. Today we know that the Sun is at the center of our solar system, not the center of the universe.)

- Galileo Galilei (1564–1642), an Italian physicist and astronomer, first pointed a telescope toward the heavens and made many remarkable discoveries: mountains and valleys on the Moon, dark spots on the Sun, and moons circling the planet Jupiter.

- Leonardo da Vinci (1452–1519), an Italian artist and scientist, did studies in optics, anatomy, and hydraulics that led to modern studies in each of these fields. He invented an underwater diving suit and drew pictures of "flying devices," anticipating the later invention of airplanes.

The work of Renaissance scientists paved the way for the discoveries and inventions that followed. The Renaissance, as its name means, was a rebirth, a revival of the human intellect.

The Science of Today

Between the Renaissance and today, science has come an incredible distance. Along with discoveries and inventions has come the scientific method. One main feature of the scientific method is the following: scientists attempt to look at the natural world objectively. This means that scientists try to see things as they are, without letting values or beliefs cloud their view. This is quite unlike the science of primitive people and even the science of the Renaissance.

Scientific knowledge today is based on explanations that are affirmed by experiments. The goal of science is to answer questions about our world by creating the best possible explanation that agrees with experimental results.

For an explanation to be considered scientific, the explanation must fulfill the following requirements:

- Be logically consistent with known facts

- Be capable of being confirmed by experiment and observation

- Be a basis from which accurate predictions can be made

- Be open to criticism and revision as more information becomes available

To make findings available to others, scientists report all experimental results and the procedures used to acquire those results. In this way, other scientists can redo experiments to see if they get the same results. Scientists often check the work of other scientists in this way.

The Role of Personal Beliefs

From the time of primitive people to the present, personal beliefs, particularly religious beliefs, have played a role in science. When science was in its infancy, scientific discoveries often were in disagreement with religious teachings. When that happened, religious beliefs were usually considered correct and further scientific inquiry was stopped.

Today, science and religion have come a long way from those earlier times. Now the questions of science do not overlap questions of faith.

- Science deals with questions of the natural world, questions for which experiments can be performed. For example, "Is there life on Mars?"

- Faith deals primarily with questions of values, questions for which science cannot give answers. For example, "Should we do medical experiments on chimpanzees?"

As we begin the twenty-first century, we need to realize that the most difficult questions ahead of us will be questions of values, not science. Each of us must accept a personal challenge and ask ourselves, "What do I want the human race to become as a species?" Science will give us many possible choices, but it will not provide an answer to this question.

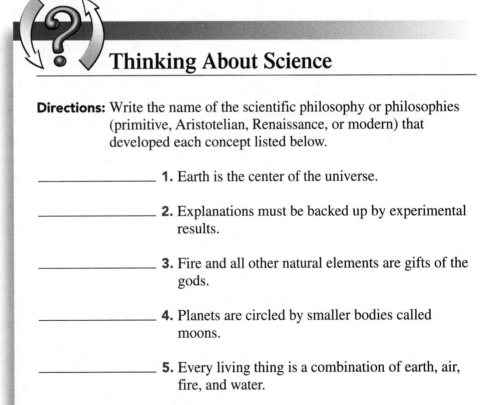

Thinking About Science

Directions: Write the name of the scientific philosophy or philosophies (primitive, Aristotelian, Renaissance, or modern) that developed each concept listed below.

_____ **1.** Earth is the center of the universe.

_____ **2.** Explanations must be backed up by experimental results.

_____ **3.** Fire and all other natural elements are gifts of the gods.

_____ **4.** Planets are circled by smaller bodies called moons.

_____ **5.** Every living thing is a combination of earth, air, fire, and water.

Answers are on page 441.

Directions: Choose the <u>one best answer</u> to each question.

Questions 1 and 2 refer to the information on pages 145–147.

1. Seen from Earth, what is the main difference most likely noticed by early observers of the Moon and the Sun?

    (1) The Sun looks much larger than the full Moon.
    (2) The Sun is not the same color as the bright part of the Moon.
    (3) The Sun is at a greater distance from Earth than is the Moon.
    (4) The Sun has a higher temperature than the Moon has.
    (5) The Moon goes through phases while the Sun does not.

2. Before the rise of modern science, what was the main objection to the idea that Earth is not the center of the universe?

    (1) an objection based on scientific theory
    (2) an objection based on economics
    (3) an objection based on a poll of voters
    (4) an objection based on religion
    (5) an objection based on evidence

Questions 3–5 refer to the following passage.

Thales, a sixth century B.C. Greek philosopher, is often given credit as being the father of scientific thought. Thales taught that water is the original principle of all things. Thales said that everything comes from water and everything returns to water.

Before the time of Thales, explanations of the universe were based on myths. Thales was the first philosopher who based explanations on physical properties of Earth that were observable.

3. What feature of Thales's approach to science became a major part of the modern scientific method ?

    (1) the importance of mathematics
    (2) the importance of patience
    (3) the importance of sharing ideas
    (4) the importance of reproducibility
    (5) the importance of observation

4. Which of the following is the <u>least</u> likely reason that Thales chose water as the original principle?

    (1) Deep water appears blue, like the sky.
    (2) Water quenches human thirst.
    (3) Water is needed to grow crops.
    (4) Water is involved in childbirth.
    (5) Water can be used to both cool a fever and warm a chilled person.

5. Which additional fact, unknown to Thales, could he have used to support his theory that water is the original principle?

    (1) Mountains and valleys are found along the ocean floor.
    (2) Fresh water can be formed by evaporating ocean water.
    (3) Many ocean fish cannot live in fresh water.
    (4) Between 50 and 90 percent of the weight of all living organisms is water.
    (5) The boiling temperature of water decreases as altitude increases.

Answers are on page 441.

Milestones in Modern Science

Scientific understanding usually proceeds in little bits and pieces, much like a huge jigsaw puzzle being put together. Yet, every once in a while, an idea occurs or a discovery is made that gives us a huge jump in our understanding. Many such milestones in science have occurred during the last two hundred years. Here we will briefly mention a few of these major discoveries. You will learn more about them in the remaining chapters of this book.

Evolution of Earth

For most of recorded history, Earth was believed to be the center of the universe, perfect in its creation and unchanging.

Modern science changed that view. Earth is now understood to be just one of many similar planets circling one of hundreds of billions of stars. Earth is not the center of anything; Earth is not perfect; and Earth is not unchanging. Earth is a cooling ball of fiery liquid that once looked similar to the Sun.

Not far below Earth's surface is an ocean of hot metal. Floating on this liquid core are tectonic plates—individual pieces of land that make up Earth's surface. Volcanoes are points where this fiery liquid gushes up through the surface of the tectonic plates. Earthquakes result when the tectonic plates rub against each other.

The movement of tectonic plates constantly changes the features of Earth's surface. At one time, 100 million years ago or so, all the continents likely sat side by side and formed a single large landmass.

Evolution of Species

The publication in 1859 of the book *On the Origin of Species by Means of Natural Selection* by Charles Darwin was truly a turning point in scientific understanding. This book is often called "the book that shook the world."

Charles Darwin proposed a theory that stands today as a central principle in life science. Darwin proposed that species, or particular types of life forms, evolve, or change over time. Each species undergoes slight variations that can be passed on to offspring. Furthermore, Darwin said that all similar organisms that exist today may have descended from a common ancestor.

Darwin suggested that humans today may not look like humans did thousands of years ago. He also suggested that humans and monkeys may have evolved from a common ancestor. Both of these ideas shocked his readers, especially religious leaders. Such a theory, they argued, would rob human beings of their special place in the story of creation. In Darwin's theory, humans are just one of many animals in a constant struggle for survival.

Even scientists had trouble accepting Darwin's theory. The scientists of his day did not see how variations could occur in any species. And, even if variations did occur, there was no way for a variation to be passed to offspring. These scientific objections to Darwin's theory were answered and supported by the theory of genetics a few years later.

Structure of Matter

For thousands of years, people have wondered about the structure of matter. Often, the following question, or one like it, would be asked:

> Suppose you take a piece of gold and divide it into smaller and smaller pieces. What does the smallest possible piece of gold look like?

Experiments performed in the nineteenth and twentieth centuries finally answered this question. Scientists discovered that all matter, including all life forms, is made of about one hundred different elements. Some substances, such as gold, are made of a single element. Other substances, such as water, are made of more than one element. Water is made of two elements: hydrogen and oxygen.

The smallest piece of an element that has properties of that element is an atom. An atom is very, very small. It would take many billions of atoms placed side by side to cross this page. The smallest possible piece of gold is a single gold atom. The smallest piece of water is a single water molecule. A water molecule contains two hydrogen atoms and one oxygen atom. If a water molecule were broken down into the two elements that make it up, the water molecule would disappear. In its place would be separated hydrogen and oxygen atoms.

Living organisms are made of the same elements that make up Earth itself. A living organism is mainly made of three elements: hydrogen, oxygen, and carbon.

The Molecular Basis of Heredity

Following the publication of Darwin's theory came increased interest in biological inheritance. How are physical, biochemical, and behavioral traits passed from parent to offspring? Furthermore, how do individual cells of an organism know what to be?

While earlier scientists discovered the basic laws of heredity, the molecular structure of genes and chromosomes was not discovered until the early 1950s. According to the laws of heredity, every organism has a set of coded instructions. These instructions can be passed to offspring. A newborn whale's set of instructions, for example, contains a code that causes the whale to look like its parents. The code also tells the whale how to swim at the moment of birth. The whale isn't taught to swim. The whale's coded instructions make swimming part of its nature.

A complete set of coded instructions is in every cell of every organism. These instructions are contained in special molecules called DNA, or deoxyribonucleic acid. Each cell in an organism has the same DNA found in each other cell. A human skin cell contains a complete set of instructions for that person. So does a heart cell, a blood cell, and a muscle cell. Instructions in an individual cell also tell the cell its function.

DNA

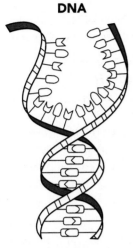

DNA is a molecule organized in a double helix shape. When a cell divides, its DNA splits into two parts, each part then forming a new DNA molecule that is identical to the original.

Organisms differ from other organisms because of chemical and structural differences in DNA. Human DNA is different from frog DNA and from monkey DNA. However, human DNA is more closely related to monkey DNA than to frog DNA.

Physical or behavioral variations in an organism are due to mutations, or changes, occurring in the DNA contained in a reproductive cell. A variation in this DNA can be passed along to offspring.

The theory of the molecular basis of heredity explains how both physical characteristics and behavior patterns are inherited. Also, an understanding of DNA is giving scientists a better understanding of how cells work. This understanding is showing great promise in the fight against inherited diseases such as sickle-cell anemia.

Thinking About Science

Directions: Briefly describe what is meant by each phrase below.

1. evolution of Earth: _____

_____

_____

2. evolution of species: _____

_____

_____

3. atomic theory of matter: _____

_____

_____

4. molecular basis of heredity: _____

_____

_____

Answers are on page 441.

Directions: Choose the <u>one best answer</u> to each question.

Question 1 refers to the following passage.

Before Darwin published his theory of evolution, Jean Lamarck, a French biologist, proposed a different theory on how species evolved. According to Lamarck, an individual organism could acquire certain traits by its own efforts. Lamarck believed that these traits would then be inherited by all of the organism's future offspring.

Lamarck's most famous example was a giraffe. He claimed that giraffes once had short legs and short necks. But then, as they strained to reach leaves high in trees, giraffes stretched their necks and legs a little bit at a time. In this way the bodies of giraffes changed shape. When each "stretched" giraffe reproduced, its offspring were born with long necks and long legs!

Scientists today do not accept Lamarck's theory. Although organisms can adapt their own bodies to their environment, they cannot pass these changes to offspring.

1. According to Lamarck, which of the following factors most influenced a change in shape in giraffes?

   (1) a lack of natural predators
   (2) an abundance of vegetation close to the ground
   (3) the great depth of rivers during frequent floods
   (4) a lack of vegetation close to the ground
   (5) the need to be larger than natural predators

2. Which example supports Lamarck's theory but would not be considered an inherited trait by modern geneticists?

   (1) a tree frog passed on its green color to its offspring
   (2) a sheep passed on its thick wool to its offspring
   (3) a mother dyed her brown hair red and passed this trait onto her child
   (4) a bird passed on its ability to fly to its offspring
   (5) a polar bear passed on its white fur to its offspring

Answers are on page 441.

Go to **www.GEDScience.com** for additional practice and instruction!

History and Nature of Science Review

Directions: Choose the <u>one best answer</u> to each question.

Questions 1 and 2 refer to the following passage.

Before Darwin published his theory of evolution, most scientists believed that Earth had experienced several separate creations of animal and plant life. Each creation followed a sudden catastrophe that destroyed much or all life on Earth. Many scientists believed that the most recent catastrophe was Noah's flood, spoken of in the Christian Bible. In the view of scientists who believed the *catastrophe theory of species change*, species were created individually. Then, once created, a species did not change.

According to the catastrophe theory, fossils are the only reminder of any species that is now extinct.

1. Which idea would be rejected by scientists who believed the catastrophe theory of species change?

    (1) Natural catastrophes can eliminate many species from Earth.
    (2) A worldwide flood could be a major natural catastrophe.
    (3) Fossils are traces of organisms that may now be extinct.
    (4) Living species do not change characteristics over time.
    (5) Living species are related to species that are now extinct.

2. In the biblical story, Noah takes a certain number of species on a boat (ark) to protect them from the flood. According to the catastrophe theory, what happened to the species on Noah's ark?

    (1) Each species evolved into a new species.
    (2) Their descendants are unchanged today.
    (3) Their descendants live only on islands.
    (4) Their descendants live only in the ocean.
    (5) Each species became extinct.

Questions 3 and 4 refer to the following passage.

Following publication of Darwin's theory of evolution, a search took place for a fossil that could prove the existence of an evolutionary ancestor of both humans and apes. No one knew if this ancestor, called the *missing link*, even existed.

Then, in 1912 near Piltdown, England, an ape-like fossil was found that seemed to confirm the existence of the missing link. The scientific community was astounded. Charles Dawson, an amateur naturalist gained instant fame from his discovery.

It wasn't until 1953 that Piltdown man, as the fossil came to be known, was proved to be a fake. Dating techniques, which only became available in 1953, showed the skull bones to be only several hundred years old rather than the million or more years that a genuine missing-link fossil would be.

The fossil was made of the cranium of a human and the jaw of an ape. The pieces of skull had been stained and sanded to give them a very aged appearance.

3. What is meant by the words *missing link*?

    (1) an ape's skull with human features
    (2) a common ancestor of all apes
    (3) a common ancestor of humans and apes
    (4) a fossil of a human that is more than one million years old
    (5) a fossil of a human that is older than any known fossil of an ape

4. For what reason did the Piltdown man hoax go undiscovered for many years?

    (1) inadequate dating techniques
    (2) lack of confirming evidence
    (3) lack of interest by scientists
    (4) secrecy regarding the discovery
    (5) existence of confirming evidence

Questions 5 and 6 refer to the following passage.

Albert Einstein (1879–1955), a German-born American physicist, is one of the most famous scientists of all time. In 1905 Einstein published his *theory of relativity*. Einstein concluded that mass is a form of energy and that there is an equivalence between mass and energy. This relationship is expressed by what is perhaps the most well-known equation: $E = mc^2$ (energy = mass times the square of the speed of light).

Einstein's equation states that mass (matter) and energy can be changed into one another. For the first time, it was realized that atoms themselves can be turned into pure energy. This is very unlike chemical energy in which matter changes from one form to another but is not destroyed in the process. The idea that matter can disappear in a burst of energy was an astonishing discovery.

The amount of energy released by matter is far greater than energy released by any other energy source. Einstein's insight made possible the understanding of energy processes on our Sun and on stars, and led to the development of atomic bombs and of nuclear power plants.

5. How does a nuclear power plant differ from a fossil-fuel plant?

   (1) how energy is released
   (2) production of electricity
   (3) cost of energy produced
   (4) need for safety regulations
   (5) use of human workers

6. Which of the following can you conclude from information given in the passage?

   (1) Solar energy is decreasing each year.
   (2) Solar energy in unlimited.
   (3) The mass of the Sun remains constant.
   (4) The mass of the Sun is decreasing.
   (5) The mass of the Sun is increasing.

Questions 7 and 8 refer to the following diagram.

Thomas Malthus (1766–1834) proposed a theory that is represented by the graph below.

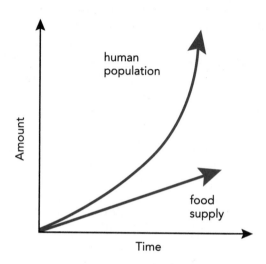

7. What is the best summary of the theory proposed by Malthus?

   (1) Human population increases less rapidly than the available food supply.
   (2) Human population increases more rapidly than the available food supply.
   (3) Human population growth and food supply are not related to one another.
   (4) An increase in human population growth leads to an increase in food supply.
   (5) An increase in food supply leads to an increase in human population growth.

8. What does the graph imply will eventually occur in countries that have a very high growth rate?

   (1) a high rate of disease
   (2) overcrowding in major cities
   (3) mass starvation
   (4) air pollution in urban areas
   (5) extinction of the human race

Questions 9 and 10 refer to the following diagram.

THREE MODELS OF THE EARTH, MOON, AND SUN

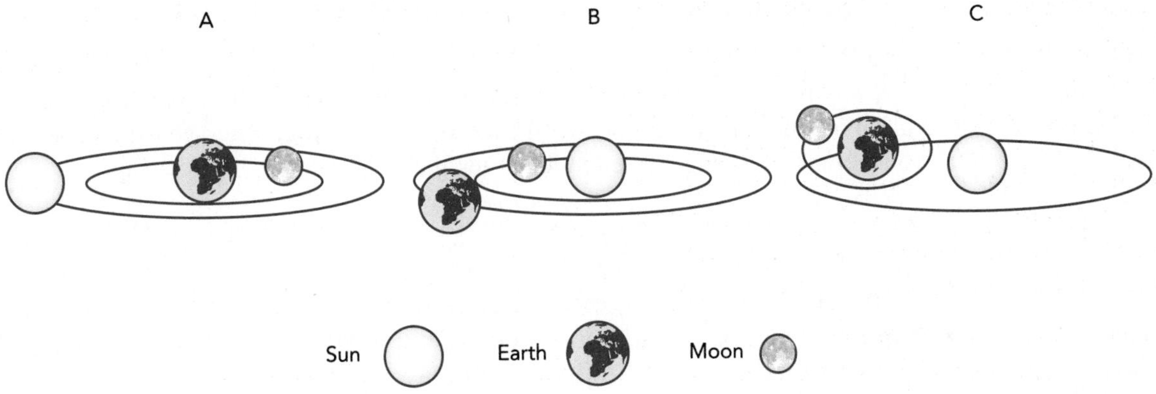

9. Which model of the Earth, Moon, and Sun would Aristotle and other scientists of his time most likely have thought correct?

    (1) A
    (2) B
    (3) C
    (4) either A or B
    (5) either B or C

10. Which model of the Earth, Moon, and Sun do scientists today believe to be correct?

    (1) A
    (2) B
    (3) C
    (4) both A and B
    (5) both B and C

    Answers are on page 441.

Themes in Science Writing Activities

The following topics will give you extra practice in thinking and writing about themes in science.

Directions: Choose one of the topics below and write a well-developed essay (approximately 250 words). You may wish to plan your essay before you write. Pay attention to your organization, development, and control of sentence structure, punctuation, grammar, word choice, and spelling. After you finish writing your essay, reread what you have written and make any changes that will improve your essay.

TOPIC 1

New developments in science often lead to new developments in technology and vice versa. Sometimes these developments in technology can have a major impact on human life. In your opinion what is the single greatest technological milestone of the last century?

In your essay describe what you believe to be the greatest technological milestone. Give examples to support your belief.

TOPIC 2

Albert Einstein once said, "The problems that exist in the world today cannot be solved by the level of thinking that created them." Do you think that scientific advancement has created more problems that it has solved?

In your essay state whether you believe science has created more problems than it has solved. Give specific reasons to support your belief.

TOPIC 3

Within the next five to ten years, the cloning of valued animals, such as livestock, endangered species, and domestic pets, may be a common occurrence. In fact, some companies are now preserving genetic material from these animals for future use. Would you ever consider cloning a valued animal?

In your essay present your views regarding the cloning of valued animals. Give specific examples to support your opinion.

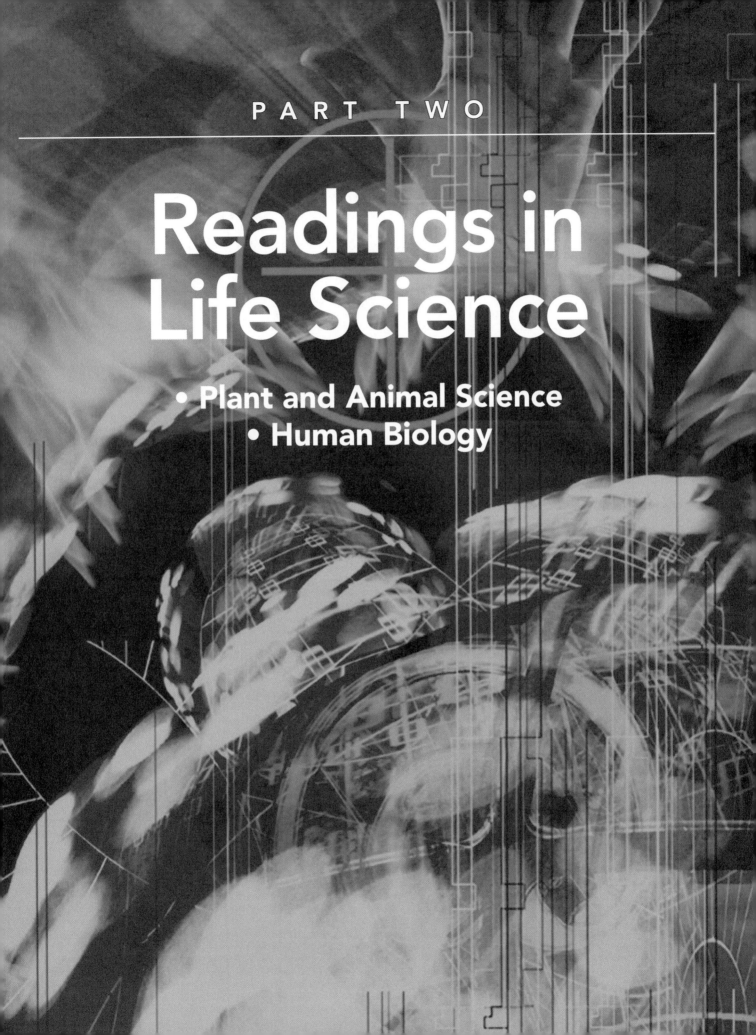

PART TWO

Readings in Life Science

- **Plant and Animal Science**
- **Human Biology**

CHAPTER 7

Plant and Animal Science

In a purely technical sense, each species of higher organism is richer in information than a Caravaggio painting, Bach fugue, or any other great work of art.

~ Edward O. Wilson

Imagine for a moment what it's like to sleep in a meadow. Until you fall asleep, you listen to the chirping of crickets, the croaking of frogs, and the occasional buzzing of a bothersome mosquito. Unless you're used to these sounds, you're probably surprised at how much of a racket these little creatures can make!

But you soon grow used to the noise, and the next thing you know you're awakening to the first rays of sunlight. Your sleeping bag and the grass around you are moist with morning dew—but at least the crickets and frogs are quiet! The only sounds you hear now are those of insects busily starting their day. Small bees hover above the flowers, looking for blossoms from which to take sweet nectar for making honey. A butterfly alights on a dandelion a few feet away. Beyond the butterfly, spring buttercups slowly open their golden petals toward the morning light. And just beyond the buttercups, a robin pulls a worm from the grass and flies off to feed its young. Sitting up and starting to feel hungry yourself, you are amazed at the variety of life and activity around you.

Sleeping in a meadow is quite an educational experience. It gives you a glimpse into the world of plants and animals—some big, some small, but all living out their lives in their own ways while sharing Earth together.

Life science (also called **biology**) is the study of all these living things, from plants and animals too small to be seen by the human eye to huge redwood trees, elephants, and whales. The interests of life scientists are almost as numerous as the 1.5 million types of **organisms** (living things) known to be on Earth. Much of this interest focuses on the study of plant and animal structures and on life cycles.

Of recent interest is the field of **ecology,** the study of the relationship of organisms to their environment. An **environment** is all the living and nonliving things that affect an organism's life in some way.

The study of life science began thousands of years ago when people first attempted to understand living things. The word *biology* itself comes from two Greek words—*bios*, meaning "life," and *logos,* meaning "study of."

Even though the study of life has been ongoing since that time, the important principle called **biogenesis** is only about 150 years old. According to biogenesis, life comes only from life. Each organism comes from the reproduction of other organisms. This principle may not surprise you, but before the mid-1800s, many people believed that insects and worms came from rotting soil. People also believed that frogs formed in clouds and fell to Earth during rainstorms!

Today, life scientists know a great deal about the types of organisms that inhabit Earth. Many of these organisms have been identified and studied, and they are broadly classified into five groups. Two of the more familiar classifications are plants and animals. The study of plants is called **botany,** and the study of animals is called **zoology.** This chapter will focus on many of the characteristics of life that are common to all living things.

Thinking About Science

Directions: Match each word on the left with the best description on the right. Write the correct letter on the line.

_____ **1.** botany	(a) the study of all living things
_____ **2.** ecology	(b) the study of animals
_____ **3.** biology	(c) the study of the relationship of organisms to their surroundings
_____ **4.** environment	(d) the study of plants
_____ **5.** zoology	(e) all things that affect an organism

Answers are on page 442.

GED PRACTICE

Directions: Choose the <u>one best answer</u> to each question.

Questions 1 and 2 refer to the information on pages 159 and 160.

1. Which of the following best summarizes the first two paragraphs on page 159?

   (1) A meadow is a cold damp place at night.
   (2) In a meadow you can hear firsthand how much noise small animals can make.
   (3) A meadow is filled with a variety of life forms, each going about an activity that is part of its life cycle.
   (4) Some animals eat plants, and some animals eat other animals.
   (5) Many baby animals, such as small robins, depend on their parents for food.

2. Which of the following statements is an opinion, not a fact?

   (1) Frogs eat insects, a fact that makes frogs more important to humans than worms are.
   (2) Certain types of animals hunt for food mainly at night, and other animals hunt mainly during the day.
   (3) The study of an organism includes the way in which it interacts with other organisms.
   (4) Many flowers respond to the sun by opening their petals.
   (5) Both plants and animals exhibit behavior that helps ensure their survival.

Questions 3–5 refer to the following passage and illustrations.

In a famous experiment in the seventeenth century, Francesco Redi wanted to disprove the common belief that meat left to rot would change into maggots. (A maggot is the newly hatched, crawling stage of a fly.) Redi believed that living things, such as maggots, did not come from nonliving matter, such as meat; he believed that maggots came only through the reproduction of parent flies. To prove this hypothesis, Redi placed a piece of meat to rot in each of two jars. The control jar was covered with a piece of cloth. Although air could pass through the cloth, flies couldn't. The experimental jar was left uncovered.

EXPERIMENT BEGINS

control jar   experimental jar

As the experiment begins, no maggots are on the meat in either jar. Flies can lay eggs only in the experimental jar.

SEVERAL WEEKS LATER

control jar   experimental jar

Several weeks later, maggots cover the meat in the experimental jar. No maggots have appeared on meat in the control jar.

3. For what purpose did Redi place cloth over the control jar?

   (1) to keep dirt off the meat in the control jar
   (2) to keep the smell of rotting meat from leaving the control jar
   (3) to keep fresh air from circulating in the control jar
   (4) to encourage flies to lay eggs on the cloth
   (5) to prevent flies from laying eggs on the meat in the control jar

4. What is the most reasonable conclusion that can be drawn from these results?

   (1) Rotting meat turns into maggots only in the presence of fresh air.
   (2) Maggots turn into flies only when they get nutrients from rotting meat.
   (3) The cloth slows down the rotting process.
   (4) Maggots appear on rotten meat only after hatching from fly eggs.
   (5) Flies reproduce only in the presence of rotting meat.

5. Which of the following factors should Redi have been most careful about when he began the experiment?

   (1) that both jars were exactly the same size
   (2) that both pieces of meat were free of fly eggs
   (3) that the temperature of each jar would be kept constant
   (4) that both pieces of meat were exactly the same size
   (5) that no flies would be allowed to enter either jar

Answers are on page 442.

Characteristics of Living Things

Seeing a squirrel or dog is an experience that's easily taken for granted. Too often we forget just how unique and remarkable life is. Perhaps it is a good idea from time to time to remember that of all the planets in the solar system (and possibly of all the planets in the universe), Earth is the only one that contains life. This means that Earth is a very special place. Earth has just the right combination of chemical elements and climatic conditions needed to produce and sustain a variety of living things.

What Is a Living Thing?

Life science is the study of **organisms,** or living things. To begin this study, let's review some of the characteristics of living things, such as plants and animals.

Living Things Have a Life Cycle of Five Stages

All living things go through a **life cycle** that can be divided into five stages:

- During the beginning stage, an organism takes shape. For animals, the beginning stage is the time preceding birth.

- Growth is the period when an organism grows to its mature, or adult, size and develops the ability to reproduce, or create another living thing.

- During maturity, an organism uses energy mainly for the maintenance of life.

- During decline, an organism is not as able to keep itself in top shape, possibly causing the organism to become less active.

- At death, an organism stops living.

Living Things Depend on a Source of Energy

Living things need energy in order to carry out their life cycles. In your own life, hunger is your body's way of telling you that it needs energy. You satisfy this need by eating food. Your body digests the food and releases energy stored in the food. All other organisms also need energy to carry out daily activities.

Living Things Reproduce

Living things reproduce—that is, they create another living thing. **Reproduction** makes it possible for each type of organism to continue to exist by producing future generations of its own kind.

Living Things Respond to Stimuli

Living things respond to stimuli, or anything in their environment that causes a change in behavior. A **stimulus** may be something seen, heard, felt, smelled, or tasted. A living thing tends to respond to a stimulus in a way that helps it to survive. For example, when a deer hears a mountain lion growl, the deer dashes away. The big cat's growl is the stimulus. The deer's reaction—running away—is the **response.**

Living Things Are Comprised of Cells

Living things are made of basic units called **cells.** Cells carry out important life activities throughout each stage of an organism's life. Some tiny organisms are made of only one cell; other organisms, such as ourselves, are made of trillions of cells.

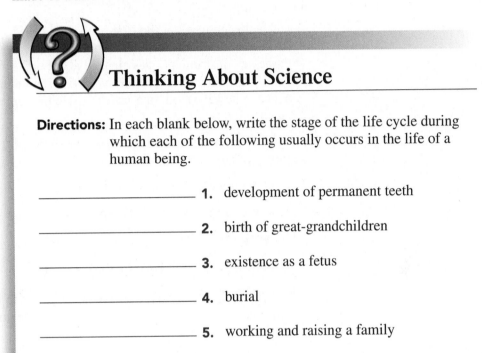

Thinking About Science

Directions: In each blank below, write the stage of the life cycle during which each of the following usually occurs in the life of a human being.

_____ **1.** development of permanent teeth

_____ **2.** birth of great-grandchildren

_____ **3.** existence as a fetus

_____ **4.** burial

_____ **5.** working and raising a family

Answers are on page 442.

GED PRACTICE

Directions: Choose the <u>one best answer</u> to each question.

Questions 1 and 2 refer to the information on pages 162 and 163.

1. What is the most likely result for a mouse that responds more slowly to a cat's hissing than most other mice do?

   (1) The mouse will have a slower-than-average growth rate.
   (2) The mouse will have a shorter-than-average life span.
   (3) The mouse will use less than an average amount of energy for its daily activities.
   (4) The mouse will be rejected by other mice.
   (5) The mouse will have a longer-than-average life span.

2. Nonliving things also change when their environment changes. For example, a puddle of water freezes when the water temperature drops below 32°F. Which statement illustrates the main difference between a puddle freezing and an animal's response to freezing temperature?

   (1) An animal responds more slowly.
   (2) An animal does not freeze because it is not made of pure water.
   (3) An animal does not freeze as quickly.
   (4) An animal responds to freezing temperatures in a way that best ensures its own survival.
   (5) An animal freezes solid at a different temperature from that of a puddle.

   Answers are on page 442.

The Cell

The Structure of Plant and Animal Cells

The invention of the microscope was a great leap forward for biologists in the seventeenth century. For the first time, they could see beyond the limits of the human eye. The British scientist Robert Hooke, after looking at slices of cork with the new instrument, was amazed at the tiny boxlike cavities out of which the cork was made. Because these cavities reminded him of cells (rooms) in a monastery, he gave the name *cells* to these tiny units of cork.

Today, biologists know that cells are the basic building blocks of both plants and animals. A cell is the smallest living unit that carries on the activities of an organism.

The cell theory of life is stated in three parts:

- The cell is the basic unit of life.

- All organisms are made of one or more cells.

- All cells come from existing cells.

Shown below are examples of plant and animal cells:

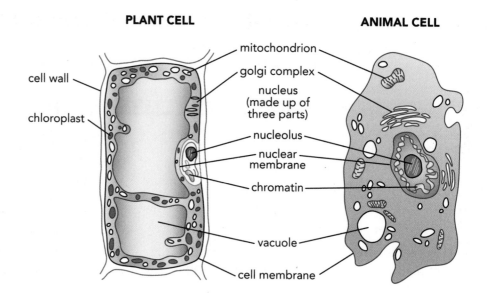

Although the cells of plants and animals differ in some ways, they do have several common characteristics.

Cell Membrane

Every cell has a **cell membrane,** a soft and flexible covering. This membrane holds the cell together and separates the cell from other cells. The cell membrane is permeable, allowing substances to enter and leave the cell. Food molecules, needed to provide energy, enter a cell through the cell membrane. Waste products produced within the cell are released from the cell through the cell membrane.

Nucleus

Every plant and animal cell contains a single large oval or round body called a **nucleus.** The nucleus controls the activities of the cell. Also, the nucleus stores hereditary information in genetic material called **chromatin.** A smaller round body within the nucleus, called the **nucleolus,** is responsible for making protein that is used in new cell growth.

Cytoplasm

Outside the nucleus of every cell is the **cytoplasm,** a jellylike fluid of water, salt, minerals, and many types of **organic** (carbon-carrying) molecules that are essential to all life processes. Within the cytoplasm are specialized structures that carry on the work of the cell.

Organelles

Organelles are any of the specialized structures within the cytoplasm of a cell. Each organelle performs a special life activity of the cell. The nucleus is the most prominent organelle in most cells.

Plant Cells

A plant cell has two special structures not found in an animal cell.

- A **cell wall** surrounds the cell membrane of most plant cells. This wall both supports and protects the cell. In many plants the cell wall is tough but flexible. Cell walls are what make vegetables like celery crunchy to bite and chew. In plants such as trees, cell walls are thick and rigid, which enables them to provide the tree with great strength.

- **Chloroplasts** are organelles that contain **chlorophyll,** the green substance that is used to capture light energy. The plant uses this energy from the Sun to produce glucose, a simple sugar that the plant uses as its food.

Thinking About Science

Directions: Match each term on the left with the best description on the right. Write the correct letter on the line.

_____ 1. cell wall   (a) the name given to the fluid and structures outside the nucleus of a cell

_____ 2. nucleus   (b) the surface layer of a cell through which certain substances can pass

_____ 3. organelle   (c) the rigid outer layer of a plant cell

_____ 4. cytoplasm   (d) any of a number of specialized structures within a cell

_____ 5. cell membrane   (e) the structure that controls the activities of a cell

Answers are on page 442.

GED PRACTICE

Directions: Choose the <u>one best answer</u> to each question.

Questions 1–4 refer to the information on pages 164 and 165.

1. Which of the following is found in plant cells but not in animal cells?

   (1) cytoplasm
   (2) nucleus
   (3) cell membrane
   (4) organelle
   (5) cell wall

2. Mushrooms, like other fungi, do not use sun energy to produce glucose. Instead, they obtain their nutrients by absorbing them from other living or dead organisms. Knowing this, which of the following bodies would you *not* expect to find in a mushroom cell?

   (1) cytoplasm
   (2) cell wall
   (3) chloroplast
   (4) nucleus
   (5) cell membrane

3. Some unicellular, or one-celled, organisms reproduce by simply dividing into two equal parts. Which structure in the original cell contains the hereditary information that is passed on to the two newly forming cells?

   (1) nucleus
   (2) cell wall
   (3) cell membrane
   (4) cytoplasm
   (5) chloroplast

4. Which of the following makes a raw carrot crunchy to eat?

   (1) nucleus
   (2) cell wall
   (3) cell membrane
   (4) cytoplasm
   (5) chloroplast

Questions 5–7 refer to the following diagram and passage.

THE T4 PHAGE VIRUS

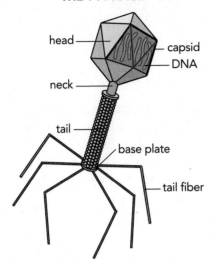

A *virus* is an infectious agent that is found in all living things. A virus is not a cell, does not have the properties of a cell, and cannot live if left on its own. A virus exists only inside a living cell. A virus does not have a nucleus, cytoplasm, or cell membrane. It consists only of genetic material surrounded by a protective coating of protein. Viruses tend to be very small, ranging from 0.05 to 0.1 microns. This is 20,000 to 100,000 times smaller than a millimeter!

Although a virus seeks to reproduce itself, a virus cannot do so unless it invades a living cell. The virus can take control of the living cell and use it to produce more of the virus. Some diseases caused by viruses are the common cold, chicken pox, mumps, measles, foot-and-mouth disease (in livestock), some types of cancers, and AIDS.

There are currently no medicines that cure viral disease, though treatments to alleviate symptoms do exist. One reason for the difficulty in developing cures for viral disease is that many variants (different forms) of a virus can cause the same disease, making it difficult for scientists to create a specialized drug. Also, medicines that might destroy a virus often destroy healthy cells.

Research on viruses is an ongoing activity in medical centers. The study of viruses has led to many discoveries that have proved important to overall human health.

5. In what way is a virus like a cell?

   (1) A virus is similar in size to a cell.
   (2) A virus is similar in shape to a cell.
   (3) A virus contains cytoplasm.
   (4) A virus contains genetic material.
   (5) A virus can live on its own.

6. For what reason does a virus invade a cell?

   (1) to destroy the cell
   (2) to reproduce
   (3) to absorb energy
   (4) to change into a cell
   (5) to become part of the cell

7. Which of the following can you infer from the reading selection on viruses?

   (1) Viruses evolved before plant and animal cells evolved.
   (2) The human body has no natural defenses against viruses.
   (3) Antibiotics that work against bacterial infections do not work against viruses.
   (4) Viruses always cause fatal diseases.
   (5) Viruses never cause fatal diseases.

   Answers are on page 442.

Specialized Functions of Organelles

To stay alive, a cell carries out a variety of activities. A cell must take in food and use it as a source of energy. A cell must keep a certain amount of organic substances in its cytoplasm, construct proteins and other organic molecules as needed, store organic substances for later use, and expel waste products. A cell must move organic substances into and out of the cell. All of these activities involve chemical reactions and are carried out by a cell's organelles.

Energy Production

Once food molecules are absorbed inside a cell, bean-shaped structures called **mitochondria** break down the chemical bonds of the food molecules to release energy. This energy is stored for later use in a compound called **ATP.** Mitochondria can do their work only if they have a source of oxygen. This is why you breathe—to supply mitochondria in your cells with oxygen.

In the chloroplasts of plant cells, a green substance called chlorophyll absorbs sunlight and converts it to food in a process known as **photosynthesis.** During photosynthesis, a plant changes sunlight, carbon dioxide gas, and water into **glucose,** a simple sugar. The plant's mitochondria use this sugar to produce energy for the plant.

Animals, which do not produce their own food, must obtain food energy from plants. Animals obtain this food energy by either eating the plants themselves or eating other animals that eat plants.

Protein Creation

Organisms need **proteins** for growth and repair and sometimes as a source of energy. The cytoplasm of cells contains organic molecules called **amino acids,** the building blocks of proteins. Also in the cytoplasm are tiny organelles called **ribosomes** on which the amino acids combine to make proteins. A cell contains numerous ribosomes to meet its need for protein production.

Delivery System

A folded structure called the **endoplasmic reticulum** produces **lipids** (energy-storing fat), breaks down chemicals that could damage the cell, and transports proteins for delivery to all parts of the cell. The endoplasmic reticulum also may transport proteins to the cell membrane so they can be expelled from the cell.

Shipping System

The **Golgi complex** receives proteins from the endoplasmic reticulum and modifies these proteins for different functions. The Golgi complex then encloses the final product in a membrane and moves the material to other places within the cell or outside the cell.

Storage Center

A **vesicle** is a membrane-covered compartment near the cell membrane that stores proteins and other organic substances, often for immediate ingestion. In a plant cell, a larger compartment, called a **vacuole,** stores water and other liquids that help support cellular life.

Waste Disposal

Animal cells have special organelles called **lysosomes.** A lysosome is a special kind of vesicle that contains particular proteins called **enzymes**, which break down organic molecules. Lysosomes get rid of waste materials, protect the cell from foreign invaders, and destroy worn-out or damaged organelles.

Cell Specialization

Some of the simplest organisms are **unicellular organisms** that consist of a single cell and yet live on their own. Most familiar organisms, however, are **multicellular organisms** consisting of more than one cell. Multicellular organisms such as roses, trees, frogs, giraffes, and more simple organisms are similar in that each begins life as a single cell. The single cell divides into two cells, then each of these cells divides into two more cells. This growth process continues until a recognizable organism forms.

From the first cell to the recognizable organism, a remarkable thing happens. Newly forming cells develop in ways different from the parent cell. Cells begin to specialize in shape, structure, and function. This is the beginning of **cell specialization**, which leads to the very complex life forms we see around us.

Tissue

As cells divide, groups of cells retain similar characteristics and functions. A collection of similar cells is called a **tissue.** A group of nerve cells in a frog's brain is one example of a tissue. The skin of a tomato is another.

Organs

A complex multicellular organism also shows a high degree of organization not found in more simple organisms. Not only do cells work together to form tissue, but groups of different types of tissue may work together and form an **organ.** A frog's brain is an organ that is made of nerve tissue, fat tissue, and vascular (blood-carrying) tissue. Other examples of a frog's organs are its eyes, heart, lungs, and stomach.

Organ Systems

Several organs working together are called an **organ system.** The digestive system of a frog is an organ system that provides the frog with a way of getting energy from food sources. The digestive system includes the mouth, stomach, small and large intestines, and other organs. Other systems common to most animals are the respiratory system (used for breathing), the circulatory system (used for moving blood), the nervous system (used for transmitting messages to and from the brain), the reproductive system (used for reproduction), and the excretory system (used for the elimination of wastes).

Thinking About Science

Directions: Answer each question below.

1. Match each item on the left with the best description on the right. Write the correct letter on the line.

   _____ 1. mitochondrion   (a) transports proteins throughout the cell

   _____ 2. ribosome   (b) gets rid of waste materials

   _____ 3. endoplasmic reticulum   (c) engaged in the creation of proteins

   _____ 4. Golgi complex   (d) modifies proteins for different functions

   _____ 5. vesicle   (e) releases energy from food substances

   _____ 6. lysosome   (f) stores proteins and other organic substances

2. Circle *T* for each statement below that is true and *F* for each statement that is false.

   T   F   a. Groups of organs that work together are called a tissue.

   T   F   b. Both plants and animals have specialized cells.

   T   F   c. Unicellular organisms have tissue.

   T   F   d. An elephant begins life as a single cell.

   Answers are on page 442.

GED PRACTICE

Directions: Choose the <u>one best answer</u> to each question.

Questions 1–4 refer to the information on pages 168 and 169.

1. Which structure in an orange most likely holds the orange juice?

   (1) vacuole
   (2) Golgi complex
   (3) ribosome
   (4) endoplasmic reticulum
   (5) lysosome

2. In what way does a plant cell differ from an animal cell?

   (1) A plant cell does not have protein.
   (2) A plant cell uses energy.
   (3) A plant cell contains water.
   (4) A plant cell has organelles.
   (5) A plant cell produces sugar.

3. What is one similarity between unicellular and multicellular organisms?

   (1) Each is made up of only one cell.
   (2) Each is made up of more than one cell.
   (3) Each contains tissue.
   (4) Each starts life as a single cell.
   (5) Each develops organ systems.

4. What would a life scientist need to know to determine the function of a tissue sample?

   (1) the weight of the sample
   (2) the length and width of the sample
   (3) the number of cells in the sample
   (4) the organ the sample was taken from
   (5) the type of cells in the sample

   Answers are on page 443.

Heredity

Questions about how one generation of an organism determines characteristics of the next generation puzzled life scientists for a long time. How does a newly produced cell know what it is supposed to do? Why does a daughter look partly like her mother, partly like her father, and partly like one of her grandparents? During the last two centuries, the study of **genetics** has found that the answer to the second question is very much related to the answer to the first.

Cell Division

How does an organism grow? And how are traits, such as color, size, shape, and sex, passed from a parent to its offspring? Life scientists have found the answers to these questions. They have discovered that the nucleus of a cell contains a substance called DNA, which controls the cell's activities. **DNA** is a large, complex molecule formed by chains of chemical compounds. Each DNA molecule forms a single **chromosome** that is composed of a series of **genes.** The information for specific functions or traits are carried in the genes.

Scientists have also discovered that an organism grows when a cell divides and produces more cells. This process of cell division is called **mitosis.** Before mitosis occurs, however, the cell makes a duplicate copy of the DNA in its chromosomes. Then mitosis begins. The dividing cell, called the parent cell, splits into two new cells called daughter cells. Each daughter cell receives a set of the parent cell's chromosomes. In this way, the daughter cells each have the same set of activity-controlling genes as the original parent cell had.

FIVE STEPS OF MITOSIS

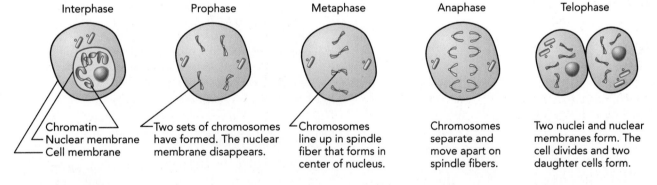

Interphase	Prophase	Metaphase	Anaphase	Telophase
Chromatin Nuclear membrane Cell membrane	Two sets of chromosomes have formed. The nuclear membrane disappears.	Chromosomes line up in spindle fiber that forms in center of nucleus.	Chromosomes separate and move apart on spindle fibers.	Two nuclei and nuclear membranes form. The cell divides and two daughter cells form.

Sometimes exposure to radiation and certain kinds of chemicals can cause an error when a cell duplicates its chromosomes before mitosis. This error results in a change in a gene that is passed on to new cells. This change in the genes or chromosomes of a cell is called a **mutation.** Some mutations are minor and have no visible effect. Other mutations, however, are major and cause loss of function or other harm to the organism. Inherited mutations cause such conditions as muscular dystrophy, hemophilia, and sickle-cell anemia.

Reproduction and Heredity

Organisms that have the same number of chromosomes look alike and are said to be in the same **species.** In most cases members of the same species can mate and produce fertile offspring (offspring capable of reproducing). When a male and a female mate, chromosomes from a male sex cell combine with chromosomes from a female sex cell. Together, they form the chromosomes of the fertilized egg—the one-celled first stage of the offspring. In this way, an offspring receives an equal number of chromosomes from each parent.

The genes carried in the chromosomes determine the traits of the offspring. Some of the genes come from the male parent and some from the female parent. Thus, an offspring has genes representing characteristics of both parents.

- Examples of inheritable characteristics in animals are eye color, hair color, ear shape, and overall body structure.

- Examples of inheritable characteristics in plants are flower color, leaf shape, and height.

When male and female organisms mate, their offspring always receives two genes for each inheritable trait. One gene for each trait comes from each parent. For example, each parent in the following diagram has two eye-color genes, labeled *Br* for brown and *Bl* for blue. The female parent has one *Bl* gene and one *Br* gene. The male parent has two *Bl* genes. An offspring of this union will inherit one eye-color gene from each parent. The offspring may receive any of the four possible combinations of genes shown in the boxes below.

Female Parent

		Br	Bl
Male Parent	Bl	Br Bl brown offspring	Bl Bl blue offspring
	Bl	Br Bl brown offspring	Bl Bl blue offspring

Dominant and Recessive Genes

Eye color, like every other inheritable trait, depends on the presence or absence of a **dominant gene.** A dominant gene is one gene in a gene pair that determines the effect of the gene pair. For example, a *Br* gene is dominant over a *Bl* gene. *Bl* genes are said to be recessive. A **recessive gene** has no effect if a dominant gene is present. Because of this, an offspring that has either one or two *Br* genes will have brown eyes. An offspring will have blue eyes only if it has two *Bl* genes.

In the example above, the female parent has brown eyes and the male parent has blue eyes. The offspring's eyes will be brown if it inherits a *Br* gene. Two of the four possible gene combinations result in an offspring inheriting a *Br* gene, and two do not. Therefore, the offspring is equally likely to be born with brown eyes or blue eyes.

Thinking About Science

Directions: Complete each sentence by filling in the blanks with the correct word(s).

1. _____ is the passing of traits, through genes, from parents to offspring.

2. Chromosomes are composed of _____ found in a cell's _____ .

3. A _____ contains instructions for a specific function or trait.

4. An offspring receives _____ gene(s) for each inheritable trait. (number)

5. Each member of a species has the same number of _____ .

Answers are on page 443.

GED PRACTICE

Directions: Choose the <u>one best answer</u> to each question.

Questions 1 and 2 are based on the information on pages 171 and 172.

1. Which statement best summarizes the role played by genes in heredity?

   (1) A gene may be either dominant or recessive.
   (2) An organism receives genes from each of the parent organisms.
   (3) The number of an organism's genes determines which two organisms are able to mate.
   (4) Genes carry the hereditary information that determines an organism's traits.
   (5) Genes always occur in pairs and determine the number of an organism's chromosomes.

2. In which pair of animals is the difference in genes most likely to be greatest?

   (1) pheasants and turkeys
   (2) gorillas and horses
   (3) bees and wasps
   (4) alligators and crocodiles
   (5) robins and sparrows

Questions 3 and 4 refer to the following passage and diagram.

Each parent organism contains two genes for every inheritable trait. One or both genes may be the dominant gene for that trait. Remember that during reproduction each parent passes on to its offspring only one gene from each pair of its own genes.

Below are two parent pea plants, A and B. Plant A *(TT)* has two tall-plant genes, whereas plant B *(tt)* has two short-plant genes. The first-generation offspring are all *Tt*, inheriting one gene from each parent. (Notice that all first-generation plants will inherit a *T* from plant A and a *t* from plant B.) Assume that plants C and D are the first-generation offspring that produced the four second-generation offspring.

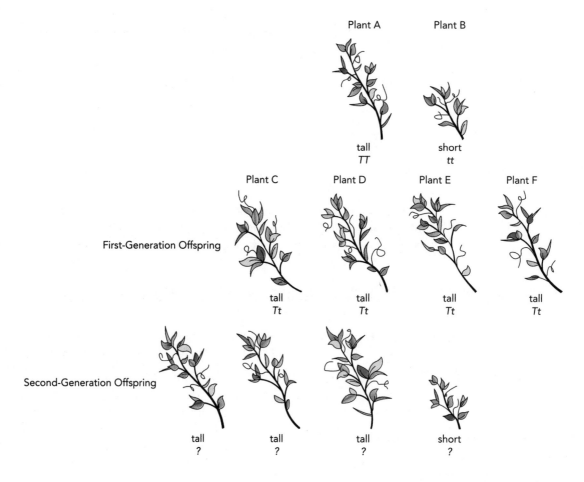

3. From looking at the diagram, what can you conclude?

   (1) Both plants A and B have a dominant gene for tallness.
   (2) Neither plant A nor plant B has a dominant gene for tallness.
   (3) Each first-generation offspring plant has two dominant genes.
   (4) The *T* gene is dominant, while the *t* gene is recessive.
   (5) The *t* gene is dominant, while the *T* gene is recessive.

4. Which of the following correctly labels the gene combinations that are possible in the second-generation plants produced by crossing (mating) plants C and D?

   (1) *TT, TT, TT, tt*
   (2) *TT, TT, tt, tt*
   (3) *TT, tt, tt, tt*
   (4) *TT, Tt, Tt, tt*
   (5) *Tt, Tt, Tt, Tt*

   Answers are on page 443.

Characteristics of Simple Organisms

Think of the many types of organisms you encounter in your daily life—a dog walking down the street, flowers in your garden, or even mildew on the bathroom wall. How do scientists keep track of the diverse population of living things?

While a dog, flowers, and mildew display the same characteristics of living things, they are all very different in physical appearance. Life scientists use different physical traits to group organisms into five main classifications, called **kingdoms.** Some important distinguishing traits of an organism are its number of cells, structural organization, and methods of reproduction and nutrition.

The five kingdoms of living things are listed below:

- *Monera*
- *Protista*
- *Fungi*
- *Plantae*
- *Animalia*

Organisms in the kingdoms *Monera* and *Protista* are primarily unicellular, while organisms in the kingdoms *Fungi, Plantae,* and *Animalia* are multicellular—ranging in structure from simple to very complex.

Unicellular Organisms

In the late seventeenth century, Antonie van Leeuwenhoek—famous for making improvements in microscope design—looked through one of his instruments at a sample of pond water. Surprised at what he saw, he used the word *beasties* to describe the tiny creatures he watched scurrying about in the drop of water.

This was the first time that humans saw a world never before imagined—a world populated by an uncountable number of tiny creatures scampering about and carrying on life activities much like our own. While our bodies contain trillions of cells, each tiny creature seen by van Leeuwenhoek was made up of just a single cell.

The beasties of van Leeuwenhoek are known today as unicellular organisms. Most of these organisms are too small to be seen without the aid of a microscope. Although they do not grow larger, these tiny unicellular organisms are complete living things, carrying on all of life's essential activities.

There are two types of unicellular organisms:

- **Prokaryotes** are organisms whose cells do not contain a nucleus and other specialized cell structures. Organisms in the kingdom *Monera* are unicellular prokaryotes.

- **Eukaryotes** are organisms composed of one or more cells containing a nucleus and organelles. Organisms in the kingdoms *Protista, Fungi, Plantae,* and *Animalia* are multicellular eukaryotes.

Monerans

Monerans, or organisms from the kingdom *Monera*, are among the simplest and smallest living things. Bacteria, the most common type of moneran, are so small that hundreds of thousands can fit on the head of a pin. Normally when you see bacteria, you see a colony containing hundreds of millions of bacteria cells. The mildew on your shower wall is actually a colony of bacteria.

Bacteria do not have a nucleus, but they do contain genetic material scattered throughout the cell. Bacteria reproduce through a process called **binary fission.** They simply divide into two identical cells—two identical organisms.

Bacteria play a large part in our daily lives. They aid in the decay of plants and animals and thereby add nutrients to the soil. Foods such as cheese and yogurt depend on bacterial action. Bacteria help produce new medicines through genetic engineering. But bacteria can also be harmful, causing diseases such as strep throat and tuberculosis.

BACTERIUM

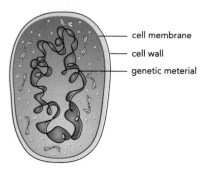

- cell membrane
- cell wall
- genetic meterial

A bacterium is a unicellular prokaryote.

Protists

Protists, organisms from the kingdom *Protista*, are single-celled eukaryotes that can display the traits of fungi, plants, or animals. Like the monerans, protists reproduce by splitting into two equal parts.

Amoebas, a type of animal-like protist, live in water, on aquatic plants, or in moist soil. Some amoebas live in other animals. One form of amoeba lives in human beings and causes amebiasis and dysentery. These diseases often occur in areas where raw sewage gets into the drinking water.

Algae are plant-like protists that carry out photosynthesis. While many forms are unicellular, some forms are multicellular. Like amoebas, algae live in water or on very wet surfaces. Some forms, such as diatoms, are an essential part of the food chain of aquatic animals. Pond scum and seaweed are other forms of algae.

AMOEBA

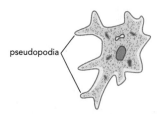

pseudopodia

An amoeba is a unicellular eukaryote that moves by extending cytoplasm outward to form pseudopodia (false feet).

DIATOM

silica cell wall

A diatom is a unicellular alga with a cell wall made of silica.

Thinking About Science

Directions: Write a brief definition for each term below.

1. unicellular organism: _____

2. prokaryote: _____

3. eukaryote: _____

4. binary fission: _____

5. moneran: _____

6. protist: _____

Answers are on page 443.

GED PRACTICE

Directions: Choose the <u>one best answer</u> to each question.

Questions 1 and 2 refer to the information on pages 175 and 176.

1. Which statement below is true about both bacteria and amoebas?

   (1) Both are protists.
   (2) Both are monerans.
   (3) Both are used in cheese production.
   (4) Both can cause disease.
   (5) Both live primarily in a water environment.

2. Before the seventeenth century, what did people lack that kept them from becoming aware of unicellular organisms?

   (1) scientific curiosity
   (2) education system
   (3) adequate microscopes
   (4) contaminated pond water
   (5) knowledge of amoebas

Questions 3 and 4 refer to the following passage.

In the mid-1800s, Louis Pasteur, a French scientist, was doing research on the making of wine. Pasteur wanted to prevent wine from going sour. He solved the problem by showing that soured wine contained bacteria not found in good wine. Pasteur then showed that this bacteria could be eliminated during the making of the wine by heating the starting sugar solutions to a high temperature.

Pasteur also looked at the problem of the souring of milk, and he proposed a similar solution. Today, when you buy milk, it has been heated to a high temperature before being placed in containers. This process of destroying bacteria naturally found in milk is called *pasteurization.*

Many fruit and vegetable drinks are also pasteurized to help prevent the spread of bacterial diseases.

3. What is the best definition of pasteurization?

   (1) identifying harmful bacteria in perishable food products
   (2) using heat to destroy harmful bacteria in perishable food products
   (3) using alcohol to destroy harmful bacteria in perishable food products
   (4) using heat to destroy bacteria found in substances containing alcohol
   (5) preventing the spread of disease by the use of heated alcohol

4. What is a good policy to follow before drinking water from a freshwater lake?

   (1) Let it sit in the sun for several minutes.
   (2) Mix it with a pasteurized product.
   (3) Shake it thoroughly.
   (4) Boil it for several minutes.
   (5) Add sugar to it.

Questions 5 and 6 refer to the following passage.

Louis Pasteur also believed that many diseases are caused by bacteria invading the host organism, in a manner similar to the way bacteria invades milk and causes it to spoil. The idea that small microscopic organisms can cause disease came to be called the germ theory of disease. Pasteur was one of the first scientists to believe in the germ theory.

Many scientists of his day thought that Pasteur was wrong. They did not believe that organisms as small as bacteria could attack and kill much larger organisms.

Pasteur was able to prove that anthrax, a fatal disease of cattle and sheep, was caused by bacteria. Moreover, Pasteur showed that a weakened form of the disease could be given to the sheep to protect them from the disease itself. Pasteur not only proved the germ theory of disease, but he developed vaccines for several diseases.

5. What did Pasteur discover that led to the germ theory of disease?

   (1) Bacteria are capable of causing disease in other organisms.
   (2) Cattle and sheep get a fatal disease called anthrax.
   (3) Anthrax is caused by the same bacteria that causes milk to spoil.
   (4) Milk can be protected from spoiling by being vaccinated.
   (5) Bacteria are present in all organisms.

6. What is the best description of a vaccine?

   (1) a bacterium that causes fatal disease
   (2) a weakened form of anthrax
   (3) a germ theory of health
   (4) a weakened large organism
   (5) a weakened form of bacteria

Answers are on page 443.

Simple Multicellular Organisms

Unicellular organisms are the simplest and most primitive life forms on Earth. The evolution of more complex organisms began with simple multicellular organisms such as fungi, moss, and ferns. (Some fungi are unicellular, but here we will discuss multicellular fungi.)

In multicellular organisms, cells may differ in shape and in function. Cells specialize to meet the needs of the organism. In the multicellular organisms described here, we see the most simple forms of cell specialization.

Fungi

Fungi (organisms in the kingdom *Fungi*) resemble plants in physical appearance. Unlike most plants however, fungi do not use photosynthesis to create food. Fungi obtain needed nutrients by directly absorbing them through their cell walls. Like plants, fungi are rooted in one place. They feed on plants and animals in whose decaying remains the fungi are growing. Fungi reproduce by growing new cells or by releasing tiny reproductive cells, called **spores.** The most common fungi are mildew, mold, mushrooms, and yeast.

Fungi have many uses to humans. Many mushrooms are a food, although some are poisonous. Yeast is used in the making of bread. Some species of fungi have medicinal uses, such as with the antibiotic penicillin. Fungi can cause many diseases that affect humans. One common fungal disease is athlete's foot.

MUSHROOM

Cap

Gills

Stem

A mushroom is a common type of fungus.

Simple Plants

Moss

All organisms from kingdom *Plantae* are divided into two types—vascular and nonvascular. Mosses are the main type of **nonvascular plant**—a plant that has no specialized tissue to transport water and nutrients to its parts. Most nonvascular plants live in water or moist areas. This allows nutrients and water to move directly into the cells of the plants. The water and nutrients then pass from one cell to another inside the plants.

Moss plants are very small, consisting mainly of small stalks and leaves. True mosses have two stages in their reproductive cycle. In the first stage, both male and female cells are produced on a leafy plant. In moist conditions, the cells meet and form a fertilized egg. This first stage, in which two different sex cells meet and produce an offspring, is called **sexual reproduction.**

In the second stage, the fertilized egg grows into a spore-bearing plant. Spores are spread in the wind or by animals brushing up against the moss. When the spores land on fertile wet ground, they grow into new sexual plants and the cycle repeats. This second stage, in which an organism is produced from a spore, is called **asexual reproduction.**

Ferns

Ferns are the simplest of the **vascular plants**—plants that have specialized tissue for transporting water and nutrients to their parts. Ferns have roots, stems, and leaves, but ferns do not produce flowers. Most ferns live in damp, shady places, although some species grow on dry ground, soil, or rocks.

Unlike most vascular plants, ferns do not produce seeds. Instead, ferns are similar to mosses in that they go through both an asexual and a sexual form of reproduction. During asexual reproduction, spore cases form on the underside of the fern's leaves. When the spore cases dry out, they break open and spores spread out to the ground. In the right conditions of heat and moisture, the spores germinate and form a sexual fern plant.

The sexual fern plant contains both female and male parts, which produce fertilized eggs that give rise to a new asexual plant. As the asexual plant starts to grow, the parent sexual plant dies.

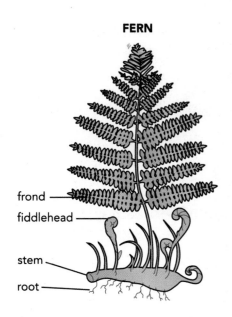

MOSS

— costa

— rhizoids

Moss plants are found all over the world.

FERN

frond —

fiddlehead —

stem —

root —

Ferns are among the world's oldest plants.

Thinking About Science

Directions: Circle *T* for each statement below that is true and *F* for each statement that is false.

T F   1. Nonvascular plants contain roots, stems, and leaves.

T F   2. Fungi carry on photosynthesis.

T F   3. Both mosses and ferns go through asexual and sexual reproduction.

T F   4. Ferns produce seeds as part of their sexual reproductive stage.

T F   5. Penicillin is made from a type of fungus.

Answers are on page 443.

GED PRACTICE

Directions: Choose the <u>one best answer</u> to each question.

Questions 1 and 2 refer to the information on pages 179 and 180.

1. What is the function of a spore?

   (1) to unite with a male sex cell
   (2) to carry a fertilized egg cell
   (3) to absorb nutrients from the ground
   (4) to become a vascular cell
   (5) to form a vascular plant

2. Which of the following best illustrates the reproductive cycle of a moss plant?

   (1) growth of sexual plant; production of spore-bearing plant; production of male and female cells; scattering of spores; growth of sexual plant
   (2) production of seeds; scattering of spores; growth of sexual plant; production of spore-bearing plant
   (3) production of male and female cells; production of spore-bearing plant; scattering of spores; growth of sexual plant
   (4) growth of bud; production of spore-bearing plant
   (5) scattering of spores; production of spore-bearing plant; division of male and female cells

Answers are on page 443.

Characteristics of Flowering Plants

Besides being delicious and nutritious, what do oranges, apples, strawberries, tomatoes, avocados, grapes, and hickory nuts all have in common? They all are produced by flowering plants. Spring flowers on these plants give way to summer fruit. What do broccoli, cabbage, and cauliflower have in common? This answer may surprise you—the parts of them that we eat are their flowers!

Flowering plants are complex multicellular organisms that play a special role in our lives. They provide us with fruits, nuts, vegetables, and, of course, flowers. Because flowering plants are so important, scientists have learned much about their structure and behavior.

Like all other plants, flowering plants have basic survival needs. They need a source of energy, a source of water and minerals, and a means of reproduction. The parts of a flowering plant are shown below.

FLOWERING PLANT

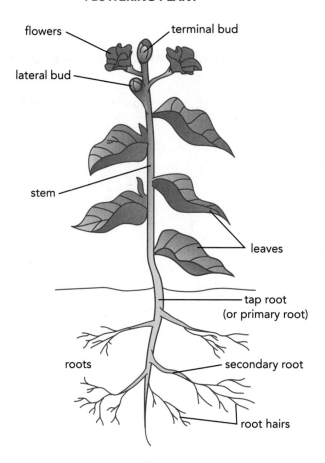

Structure of Flowering Plants

Roots

Unlike animals, most plants have roots and spend their entire lives in one spot. **Roots** anchor a plant in the ground and absorb water and minerals from the soil. Plants such as grass have a system of small branching roots. Most larger flowering plants have a single large root, called a tap root or primary root, and numerous smaller secondary roots. The long extensions of the secondary root are called **root hairs**, which are the main point of entrance for water into the root.

Stems

Growing above the ground are the stem and leaves. The **stem** holds the leaves up toward sunlight and transports water and minerals from the roots to the leaves. Some stems, such as those on small wildflowers, may be shorter than an inch. Other stems, such as the trunks of some trees, may be hundreds of feet tall. Some noticeable features of stems are their **buds,** the parts where new growth takes place. On the top of the stem is a terminal bud from which the plant grows taller. Along the sides of the stem are lateral buds that develop into branches, leaves, or flowers. In some plants, such as onions and tulips, parts of the stem, called bulbs, grow underground and serve as a storage place for food.

Leaves

The **leaves** are the food production factories of a plant. Photosynthesis takes place only in the presence of chlorophyll, the green pigment of leaves. Photosynthesis is the process during which food is produced from sunlight, water, and carbon dioxide gas. Leaves also contain **stomata,** tiny openings that allow gases to enter and exit the leaves. The larger a plant grows, the more leaves it usually has. In many plants, leaves and stems form as a single structure. The prickly stem of a desert cactus is an example.

Reproduction of Flowering Plants

Flowers are the parts of plants in which reproduction occurs. Inside the petals—the large brightly colored parts of an open flower—are the stamens and the pistil. **Stamens** are the male reproductive structures. The **pistil** is the female reproductive structure.

Flowering plants reproduce by **pollination.** During pollination, **pollen**—a grain that contains the male sex cell—leaves the stamen and is deposited on a **stigma,** the sticky top part of a pistil.

From the stigma, pollen moves through a long tube, called a **style,** to the ovary, where the female sex cells are located. In the ovary, male and female cells join to form a fertilized egg. The fertilized egg develops into a seed from which a new plant grows.

PARTS OF A FLOWER

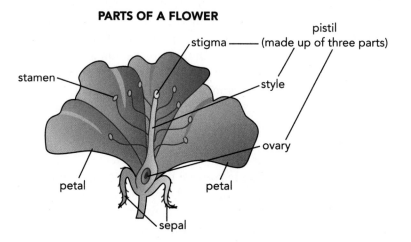

Many plants self-pollinate. Pollen from a plant fertilizes the same plant's eggs to produce seeds. Other types of plants must be fertilized by pollen from a second plant. Since plants cannot search for mates, they must rely on nature to carry pollen to them. Pollen is carried by wind, water, and animals. Bees, butterflies, and hummingbirds are the best-known pollinators.

Thinking About Science

Directions: Answer each question below.

1. What purpose is served by each part of a plant listed below?

   a. roots: _____

   b. stems: _____

   c. leaves: _____

   d. flowers: _____

2. What role does each of the following parts of a flower play in reproduction?

   a. stamen: _____

   b. stigma: _____

   c. style: _____

   d. pollen: _____

3. What are two animals that carry pollen from one flower to another?

   a. _____ b. _____

4. Read each statement below. Circle *T* if the statement is true or *F* if the statement is false.

   T F a. Photosynthesis is the production of food by means of the sun's energy.

   T F b. A plant's stem is the main organ that absorbs water and minerals from the soil.

   T F c. A flowering plant contains only female reproductive parts.

   T F d. All flowering plants can pollinate themselves.

Answers are on page 443.

Directions: Choose the <u>one best answer</u> to each question.

Questions 1–5 refer to the following information.

Plants respond to stimuli in various ways. Below are five types of plant responses to stimuli.

phototropism—the bending (or growth) of a plant toward a source of light

touch response—the movement of leaves or other parts of a plant in response to being touched

positive geotropism—the downward growth of a plant root in the direction of gravity

negative geotropism—the upward growth of a plant stem, directly away from the direction of gravity

circadian rhythm—a natural pattern of plant activity that takes place in a twenty-four-hour cycle

1. When an insect enters the open leaves of a Venus flytrap, the plant's leaves snap shut and trap the insect. What type of response is the plant's reaction?

   (1) phototropism
   (2) touch response
   (3) positive geotropism
   (4) negative geotropism
   (5) circadian rhythm

2. Morning glories open their petals each morning, even if the day is cloudy or overcast. What type of response is this?

   (1) phototropism
   (2) touch response
   (3) positive geotropism
   (4) negative geotropism
   (5) circadian rhythm

3. When Trinh planted flowers in the spring, she accidentally planted her tulip bulbs upside down. Later, Trinh dug up a bulb and found that the root had sprouted from the top but was now growing downward. The root was moving deeper into the soil and passing along the side of the bulb. What type of response is the root showing?

   (1) phototropism
   (2) touch response
   (3) positive geotropism
   (4) negative geotropism
   (5) circadian rhythm

4. On clear days the large yellow-rayed flowers of mature sunflower plants slowly follow the Sun across the sky. How is this plant movement best classified?

   (1) phototropism
   (2) touch response
   (3) positive geotropism
   (4) negative geotropism
   (5) circadian rhythm

5. A small corn plant was accidentally uprooted and buried upside down. A few days later the stem of the plant had broken through the surface of the ground and was growing upward. What is this response called?

   (1) phototropism
   (2) touch response
   (3) positive geotropism
   (4) negative geotropism
   (5) circadian rhythm

Answers are on page 444.

Characteristics of Animals

Simple Invertebrates

The study of animals (from kingdom *Animalia*) begins with the study of **invertebrates**—animals without backbones or skulls. More than 95 percent of all known animal species are insects, snails, jellyfish, and other invertebrates. We'll begin with the study of the simplest invertebrate, sponges.

Sponges

Sponges, once thought to be plants, are now known to be animals because they cannot make their own food. Sponges eat other organisms.

Sponges are unlike other animals in several ways. They have no head, no arms or legs, no nerves, and no central digestive pathway. Instead, sponges have a central cavity lined with collar cells. Collar cells filter particles of food from the water and digest them. No other animal has cells anything like collar cells.

All sponges live in water, mostly in the ocean. A sponge pumps water through its body through pores found in its outer covering. The water flows through a central cavity and out a hole at the top called an osculum.

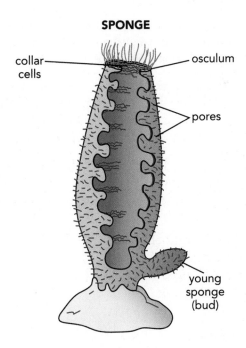

SPONGE

collar cells

osculum

pores

young sponge (bud)

Jellyfish

A jellyfish is a more complex animal than a sponge. A jellyfish has a digestive cavity and a nervous system. It also has long tentacles covered with special stinging cells. When a fish or other prey comes within contact of a jellyfish, hundreds of these stinging cells can fire into the organism and paralyze it. Close relatives of the jellyfish are hydra and sea anemones.

JELLYFISH

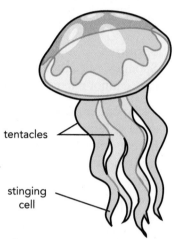

tentacles

stinging
cell

Complex Invertebrates

Worms

Worms are the simplest of the complex animals. There are many types of worms, but the most familiar is probably the earthworm. Earthworms are among the most advanced worms.

Earthworms have a segmented body. They have a mouth at one end, a digestive tract from one end of the body to the other, and an anus for removing waste from the body. Earthworms have a nervous system that responds to both light and sound, even though earthworms do not have eyes or ears.

Unlike almost all other animals, earthworms have both male and female reproductive organs. However, most earthworms mate in pairs. The sperm of one worm fertilizes the eggs of the other worm.

EARTHWORM

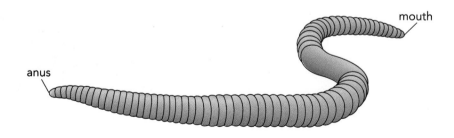

mouth

anus

Mollusks

Next in order of complexity are mollusks. Most mollusks have a soft body covered by a protective shell. Familiar mollusks are clams, snails, and oysters. Some familiar mollusks that do not have a protective shell are slugs, squids, and octopuses.

Mollusks have centers of nerve activity called ganglia. In most mollusks, these ganglia are scattered throughout the body. The most complex mollusks are octopuses and squids. These animals have a brain. Octopuses are known to have advanced learning capabilities. Research has shown that they can learn to make their way through a maze and can also tell the difference between various shapes and colors.

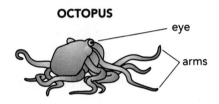

OCTOPUS

Arthropods

Arthropods are animals that have jointed limbs. The most common arthropods are insects, spiders, crabs, and centipedes. Arthropods make up about 75 percent of all animal species. All arthropods have the following four characteristics:

- a segmented body

- jointed leglike structures

- an exoskeleton (a hard outer covering)

- a complex nervous system

The material that forms the exoskeleton is not living tissue and does not grow with the rest of the organism. Because of this, arthropods must periodically shed their exoskeleton to grow. The shedding of the exoskeleton is called **molting.** During molting, the old exoskeleton splits open and the animal crawls out. After a short period of time, a new exoskeleton forms.

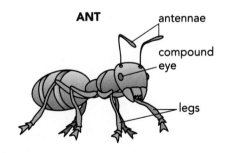

ANT

Insect Life Stages

Insects live out their lives in three or four stages. This process is called **metamorphosis.** All insects begin as eggs.

- Insects that go through three life stages hatch from eggs into **nymphs.** The nymphs look similar to adults, but they are smaller. They have no wings and their reproductive systems are incomplete. The nymph goes through several moltings. With each molting, the nymph grows and looks more like the adult. The three-stage life cycle is called **incomplete metamorphosis.**

- Insects that go through four life stages hatch into wormlike creatures called **larvae.** After the larva stage, the insect goes into a resting stage and becomes a **pupa.** In the pupa stage, the insect wraps itself in a cocoon. Within the cocoon the tissues of the larva change into the tissues of an adult. The insect emerges from the cocoon as an adult. The four-stage life cycle is called **complete metamorphosis.**

COMPLETE METAMORPHOSIS   **INCOMPLETE METAMORPHOSIS**

egg

larva

pupa

adult

egg

nymph

adult

 **Thinking About Science**

Directions: Match each invertebrate on the left with its description on the right. Write the correct letter on the line.

_____ 1. sponge

_____ 2. jellyfish

_____ 3. earthworm

_____ 4. mollusk

_____ 5. arthropod

(a) has a body covered by a shell

(b) contains both male and female sexual organs

(c) once believed to be a plant

(d) undergoes periodic molting

(e) characterized by tentacles with stinging cells

Answers are on page 444.

GED PRACTICE

Directions: Choose the one best answer to each question.

Questions 1 and 2 are based on the information on pages 187–190.

1. What characteristic do all invertebrates share?

   (1) lack of legs in the adult
   (2) lack of a backbone
   (3) lack of a centralized brain
   (4) presence of a centralized brain
   (5) a segmented body

2. Which description is not common to both complete and incomplete metamorphosis?

   (1) a several stage life cycle
   (2) the development of wings only in the adult stage
   (3) a final life stage as an adult
   (4) a resting stage in which tissue changes take place
   (5) a beginning life stage as an egg

   Answers are on page 444.

Vertebrates

A **vertebrate** is an animal with a **backbone**—a segmented column of bones called vertebrae. Vertebrates also have a **skull**—a bone that protects the brain and other organs in the head. The skull and vertebrae are made of either bone or cartilage. **Cartilage** is a tough, flexible material that covers bones and joints. In humans it is the tough, flexible part of the ears and nose.

All vertebrate **embryos,** or organisms in the early stage of development, contain cartilage but no bone. As most vertebrates grow, nearly all of the cartilage is replaced by bone.

Cold-Blooded Vertebrates

Vertebrates may be either warm-blooded or cold-blooded. **Cold-blooded** vertebrates cannot control their own internal body temperature. The body temperature goes up or down depending on the outside air temperature. Nearly all fish, amphibians, and reptiles are cold-blooded.

Fish

Fish were the first vertebrates to appear on Earth. Today, there are more species of fish than any other vertebrate. More than 25,000 species of fish inhabit the bodies of water on Earth, from oceans to freshwater streams to underground caverns.

Some fish eat other fish, while other fish eat only plants. Fish are cold-blooded animals with a well-developed nervous system and brain. Unlike land animals that breath oxygen through lungs, fish have special organs called **gills** to take oxygen out of water. Oxygen passes from the gills through a thin membrane and into the fish's blood.

Most fish reproduce by external fertilization. The female lays her unfertilized eggs in the water and the male places his sperm upon them. Some fish reproduce by internal fertilization. In this case, the male deposits sperm inside the female who then lays fertilized eggs.

Fish are divided into three major types:

- *Cartilaginous fish*—fish whose skeletons are cartilage and not bone. Cartilaginous fish are heavier than water and must swim continuously or they sink to the bottom. Sharks and rays are two well-known examples.

- *Bony fish*—fish that have skeletons made of bone. Bony fish also have a swim bladder—a balloon-like organ that the fish fills with oxygen. A swim bladder enables a fish to float in water without sinking. Most common fish are bony fish. Examples are salmon, trout, and halibut.

- *Jawless fish*—fish that do not have a jaw. Descended from the first type of fish, jawless fish today have skeletons made of cartilage. Examples include lampreys and hagfish.

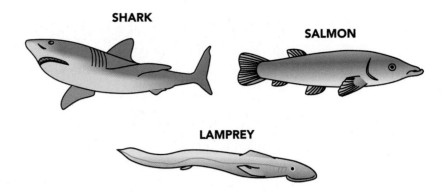

Amphibians

Most amphibians have two quite different stages to their lives. Amphibians go through a process of metamorphosis similar to that of insects. In the first stage, a tadpole hatches from a waterborne egg. A tadpole has a tail and gills and lives in water. In the second stage, the tadpole loses its tail and gills, develops legs and lungs, and lives on land. Even as adults, however, amphibians must stay close to water.

Amphibians are cold-blooded and have smooth, moist skin. Unlike other types of animals, adult amphibians can breathe through their lungs or they can breathe by directly absorbing oxygen through their skin. Because the skin of amphibians is very thin, they can lose water through the skin and easily become dehydrated. This is why amphibians must live near water and keep their skin moist.

The most familiar amphibians are frogs and salamanders.

AMPHIBIAN LIFE CYCLE

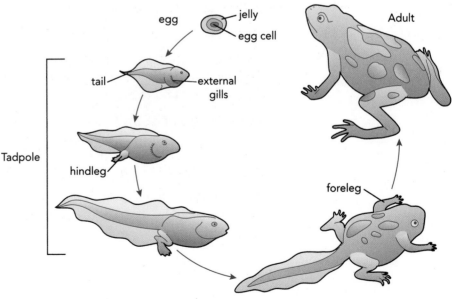

Metamorphosis in the frog

Reptiles

Reptiles are cold-blooded animals with thick, dry skin. Scales are a familiar feature of reptile skin. Although reptiles are adapted to living on land, many species spend much of their time in or near water. Some reptiles, however, live in very dry climates. Familiar reptiles include snakes, turtles, alligators, and lizards.

One of the most interesting characteristics of reptiles is their **amniotic egg.** When reproducing, a male fertilizes the female egg internally. A hard shell forms around the egg and the female lays the egg in soil or sand. The amniotic egg protects the developing embryo from predators, bacterial infection, dehydration, and extreme weather conditions. The amniotic egg also feeds the reptile embryo as it grows and develops.

Unlike amphibians, reptiles have no tadpole stage and they do not go through metamorphosis. Reptiles have lungs throughout their lifetime.

AMNIOTIC EGG

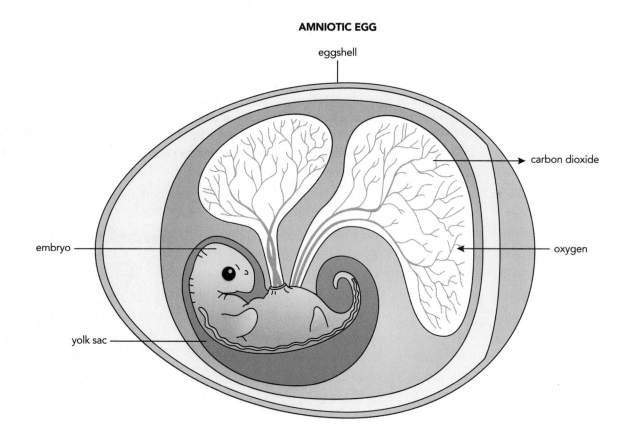

Thinking About Science

Directions: Answer each question below.

1. Write a brief definition for the following terms.

   a. vertebrate: _____

   b. cold-blooded: _____

   c. gills: _____

   d. cartilaginous: _____

2. Match each term on the left with the best description on the right. Write the correct letter on the line.

   _____ 1. fish   (a) can breathe by absorbing oxygen through its skin

   _____ 2. shark   (b) a fish that does not have a jaw

   _____ 3. reptile   (c) the first vertebrate to inhabit Earth

   _____ 4. amphibian   (d) lays an amniotic egg

   _____ 5. lamprey   (e) a fish that does not have bones

Answers are on page 444.

GED PRACTICE

Directions: Choose the <u>one best answer</u> to each question.

Questions 1–4 refer to the information on pages 192–194.

1. What do fish, reptiles, and amphibians have in common?

   (1) They are warm-blooded.
   (2) They are cold-blooded.
   (3) They spend all of their lives in water.
   (4) They eat only plant life.
   (5) They eat only animals.

2. Which of the following is <u>not</u> one of the purposes served by an amniotic egg?

   (1) protection of the parent from infection
   (2) prevention of the embryo from dehydration
   (3) protection of the embryo from weather
   (4) nourishment for the developing embryo
   (5) protection of the embryo from predators

3. Which of the following do insects and amphibians have in common?

   (1) Both have the same reproductive process.
   (2) Both have the same number of legs.
   (3) Both go through metamorphosis.
   (4) Both live their entire lives on land.
   (5) Both live part of their lives in water.

4. Which of the following organs makes it possible for a frog to live out of water?

   (1) tail
   (2) large eyes
   (3) lungs
   (4) legs
   (5) gills

Answers are on page 444.

Warm-Blooded Vertebrates

Warm-blooded vertebrates control their own internal body temperature. They do this by capturing the heat released from chemical reactions within their body cells. Birds and mammals are warm-blooded vertebrates. Because they are warm-blooded, birds and mammals are able to live in very cold climates.

Birds

Most birds fly. That fact makes us think that birds are very different from other vertebrates. Life scientists, however, have discovered more similarities than differences between birds and vertebrates that do not fly.

- Bird wings are structurally similar to the front limbs of other vertebrates.

- Bird feathers are a modified version of a reptile's scales.

- Bird fertilization is internal, similar to that of reptiles.

- Birds lay amniotic eggs, similar to those of reptiles. Unlike reptiles, though, birds must keep their eggs warm in order for the embryo to develop fully.

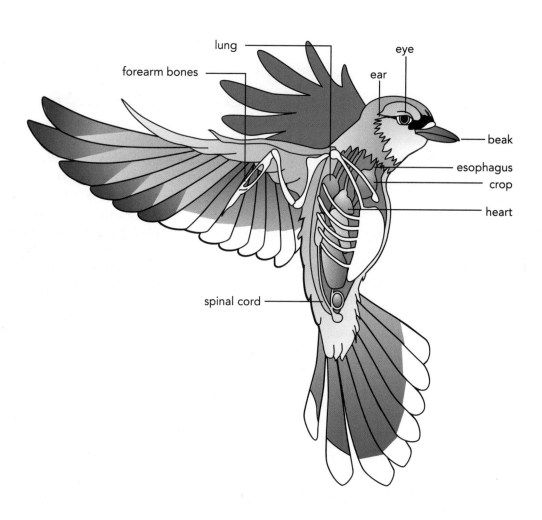

BIRD

Mammals

Mammals, the classification of warm-blooded vertebrates that contains human beings, is not a large category. Although there are nearly 10,000 species of birds, there are only about 4,500 species of mammals. Mammals do, though, come in a wide variety of shapes and sizes. The tiniest mammals include bats, mice, and shrews; the largest are blue whales. Some mammals fly, some swim, and some live entirely on land.

What do dolphins, whales, bats, dogs, cats, elephants, and human beings all have in common? They all share the common traits of mammals.

- All female mammals have mammary glands that secrete milk to nourish the young.

- All mammals are warm-blooded and maintain a relatively constant body temperature.

- Mammals have specialized teeth. In each species of mammals, teeth are adapted to the diet of that species.

- Mammals have lungs and a large muscle called a diaphragm to help draw air into the lungs.

- Mammals rely on five senses: sight, hearing, smell, touch, and taste.

- Mammals reproduce sexually by internal fertilization.

- Mammals are protective of their young.

- Mammals have complex nervous systems and large, active brains. Many mammals are capable of complex thinking and problem solving.

Mammals are divided into three classes.

MONOTREMES

Monotremes are mammals that lay eggs. Like bird eggs, monotreme eggs must be kept warm in order for the embryo to develop. On Earth today, monotremes are found only in Australia and New Guinea. The egg-laying mammals are the echidna, or spiny anteater, and the duck-billed platypus.

MARSUPIALS

Marsupials are mammals with pouches in which newly hatched infants develop. The most well-known marsupials are kangaroos, koalas, and opossums. Unlike monotremes, marsupials are born alive but not fully developed. Soon after birth, a marsupial baby finds its way to its mother's pouch where it develops while being nourished on its mother's milk.

PLACENTALS

The embryo of a placental mammal stays in its mother's body while it develops. The embryo develops in a special organ called a **uterus.** Only female placentals have a uterus. While in the uterus, the embryo receives nourishment from the mother through a special tissue called the **placenta**. The placenta also removes waste from the embryo.

More than 90 percent of all mammals are placental mammals. The most familiar types of placentals are listed in the following chart.

COMMON PLACENTAL FAMILIES

Toothless Mammals mammals that have small teeth or no teeth at all	anteaters armadillos ➡ aardvarks	
Insect Eaters mammals that have small brains, few specialized teeth, and long pointed noses	moles shrews hedgehogs ➡	
Rodents mammals that have sharp front teeth used for chewing and gnawing	mice squirrels ➡ porcupines beavers	
Lagomorphs mammals that have powerful, long legs used for jumping	rabbits ➡ hares	
Flying Mammals mammals that fly	bats ➡	
Carnivores mammals that eat other animals, having teeth specialized to do so	bears lions ➡ raccoons wolves	
Hoofed Mammals mammals that have thick hooves, adapted for swift running	cows deer horses ➡	
Trunk-Nosed Mammals mammals that have a long trunk	elephants ➡	
Cetaceans mammals that live in water	whales dolphins ➡ porpoises	
Primates mammals that have eyes facing forward and grasping fingers and thumbs	monkeys apes ➡ human beings	

Thinking About Science

Directions: Fill in each blank with a word from the reading passage.

1. The two types of warm-blooded vertebrates are _____ and _____ .

2. Feathers are to a bird as _____ are to a reptile.

3. The five senses that all mammals have are _____ _____ , _____ , _____ , and _____ .

4. The three classes of mammals are _____ , _____ , and _____ .

Answers are on page 444.

GED PRACTICE

Directions: Choose the <u>one best answer</u> to each question.

Questions 1–4 refer to the information on pages 196–198.

1. What characteristic makes it possible for penguins to live on Antarctica?

   (1) Penguins are birds.
   (2) Penguins are unable to fly.
   (3) Penguins are warm-blooded.
   (4) Penguins use their wings for swimming.
   (5) Penguins eat fish.

2. In what way are birds similar to reptiles?

   (1) They both lay an amniotic egg.
   (2) They both have rough skin.
   (3) They both are vegetarians.
   (4) They both give birth to live young.
   (5) They both are warm-blooded.

3. What purpose is served by the diaphragm, a large muscle found only in mammals?

   (1) It helps in climbing.
   (2) It helps in running.
   (3) It helps in talking.
   (4) It helps in breathing.
   (5) It helps in eating.

4. Which class of mammals is characterized by forward-facing eyes?

   (1) rodents
   (2) primates
   (3) cetaceans
   (4) lagomorphs
   (5) insect eaters

Answers are on page 444.

Animal Behavior

If living things are to survive, they must adapt to conditions in their **environment,** or surroundings. A seagull, for example, is well suited for life along the coast. A seagull has long, angled wings that help it glide in coastal air currents as it hunts for food. These wings are well oiled in order to deflect ocean water as the gull picks its prey from the surf. The gull's webbed feet enable it to walk on the sand and paddle on the water's surface.

Animal Senses

As shown by the seagull, traits that help an animal survive tend to be more complex than those of plants. Animal traits involve not only body shape, size, and color but also patterns of **behavior**—actions or reactions to the environment. Complex animals have five senses: sight, hearing, smell, taste, and touch. These senses give animals a wide range of experiences unknown to plants. Also, animals can move around in ways that plants cannot. Animals can swim, fly, walk, dig, crawl, and burrow. Although no one animal can do all of these, many animals can do two or more.

The complex behavior patterns of most animals are often connected with the constant struggle to survive and reproduce. The types of animals alive on Earth today are those that have been successful in this struggle. Although many animals die young, enough usually survive and reproduce to ensure that their species does not become **extinct,** or disappear from Earth.

Biological Time Keeping

Many animals have a **biological clock,** an internal control of natural behavioral cycles. Some biological clocks signal activities that occur over a short period of time, such as sleeping or eating; others signal activities that occur over longer periods of time, such as growth and sexual maturation. Biological clocks that control daily activity are called **circadian clocks.** For example, most animals of a particular species wake up at about the same time each day. They also go to sleep at about the same time.

Navigation

When animals **migrate**—move from one place to another—how do they know the way? For some trips, animals may rely on landmarks—things in the environment that they recognize. Birds, for example, use mountains and bodies of water to help them find their way. Some animals use the position of the Sun and stars as guides. Other animals can sense Earth's magnetic field and use it to guide their movement.

Animal Defenses

The behavior exhibited by animals varies greatly. Many animals are **predators,** or hunters of other animals. Predators such as sharks and lions are powerfully built, have keen senses of smell and taste, can move rapidly, and have teeth designed to rip **prey** (a hunted animal) apart. The bodies of these animals are ideally suited for the aggressive behavior needed by successful hunters. Other animals are not hunters; they are simply the hunted. For these animals, survival depends on one or more types of animal defenses.

Running Away
One type of animal defense is the ability to move quickly. Animals such as antelopes and gazelles rely on alertness, speed, and endurance to outrun lions or other predators.

Protective Coloring
An animal's coloring can be a defense. One type of protective coloring is called **camouflage**—a coloring pattern that enables an animal to blend into its surroundings and not be seen by predators. For example, snakes and frogs have green skin if they live in green weeds. Rabbits and weasels have earth-colored fur in the summer and white fur in the winter.

For some animals, being very visible is actually an advantage. An animal's distinctive coloring may be a defense, warning predators of previous bad experiences. The black and white stripes of a skunk, for example, serve as a reminder to predators of the horrible smell that this animal will emit if it is provoked.

Protective Outer Layer
Some animals rely on a strong or menacing outer layer for protection. The armadillo has a covering of tough, bony plates that predators cannot grasp. Clams and snails have shells in which they can hide. The North American porcupine has sharp fishhook-like quills that cover its body. If touched, these quills come out and cause painful wounds. Similarly, the porcupine fish has sharp spines that stick out of its body like thorns.

Fighting Back
For many animals, the best defense is simply to fight back. Some animals fight back by biting, kicking, or ramming. The baboon fights with sharp teeth and powerful jaws. Elk and deer fight by kicking with sharp feet and by ramming a predator with their antlers. Other animals resist their attackers with chemical weapons. Ants and bees use stingers to inject poison, while many snakes and spiders inject poison with fangs.

Playing Dead
Finally, some animals play dead when attacked. For example, when an opossum is attacked, it closes its eyes and goes limp. Many predators, including many types of bears, will usually not bother an animal that appears dead.

Social Behavior

Most animals live with other animals of their own type. The behavior of animals of the same type as they live together is called **social behavior.** Some animals live alone but near other animals of their own type. Other animals live in groups with animals of the same type.

Communication

When animals communicate, they send a signal from one animal to another. For true communication to take place, the animal receiving the signal must respond in some way. Animals communicate in order to signal one another, find food, avoid enemies, and protect their homes.

Courtship

Animals have courtship rituals. Courtship is a special type of communication that leads to mating. Courting animals may sing, dance, wrestle, stare, bite, and fight as part of courtship.

Playing

Many animals engage in playful activity. Playing is a natural expression of mutual acceptance and comfort. Familiar animals that play are dogs, cats, monkeys, and apes.

Living in a Group

There are many advantages to living in a group. First, living in a group provides safety because a group of animals cooperates to spot and to protect themselves from predators. Some animals, such as lions, hunt as a group and can kill animals larger than themselves.

Toolmaking

Scientists for a long time believed that toolmaking was a skill that separated human beings from other animals. However, research during the last few decades has shown that many other animals are also able to make tools. One of the most interesting discoveries concerns chimpanzees. Scientists now believe that chimpanzees make and use tools in ways that perhaps are similar to the toolmaking of the earliest known human cultures.

Through observation, scientists have discovered that chimpanzees in the wild use broken branches to attack predators. They also use stones to crack nuts, and they have learned to wad a bunch of leaves into a sort of sponge to hold drinking water.

Warm-Blooded Vertebrates

Warm-blooded vertebrates control their own internal body temperature. They do this by capturing the heat released from chemical reactions within their body cells. Birds and mammals are warm-blooded vertebrates. Because they are warm-blooded, birds and mammals are able to live in very cold climates.

Birds

Most birds fly. That fact makes us think that birds are very different from other vertebrates. Life scientists, however, have discovered more similarities than differences between birds and vertebrates that do not fly.

• Bird wings are structurally similar to the front limbs of other vertebrates.

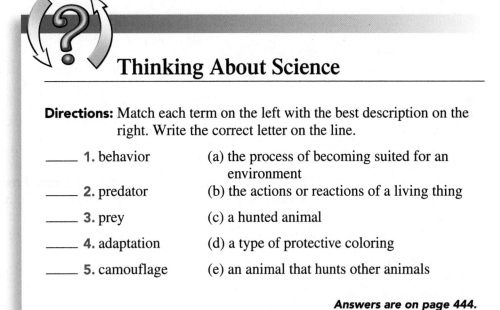

Thinking About Science

Directions: Match each term on the left with the best description on the right. Write the correct letter on the line.

_____ **1.** behavior   (a) the process of becoming suited for an environment

_____ **2.** predator   (b) the actions or reactions of a living thing

_____ **3.** prey   (c) a hunted animal

_____ **4.** adaptation   (d) a type of protective coloring

_____ **5.** camouflage   (e) an animal that hunts other animals

Answers are on page 444.

Go to **www.GEDScience.com** for additional practice and instruction!

Directions: Choose the <u>one best answer</u> to each question.

Questions 1–5 refer to the information on pages 200–203.

1. What purpose does the shell of a turtle most likely serve?

   (1) warmth
   (2) weight
   (3) protection
   (4) biological clock
   (5) nutrition

2. Which sense do animals that live only underground rely on least?

   (1) hearing
   (2) sight
   (3) touch
   (4) smell
   (5) taste

3. Sharks have a very keen sense of smell but poor vision. For what purpose do sharks most likely rely on their sense of smell?

   (1) courting
   (2) playing
   (3) communicating
   (4) eating
   (5) breathing

4. Which of the following best summarizes research on the toolmaking ability of chimpanzees?

   (1) Chimpanzees are as intelligent as humans.
   (2) Chimpanzees are not strict vegetarians because they eat termites and ants.
   (3) People in primitive cultures were no more intelligent than chimpanzees.
   (4) Chimpanzees have developed a skill once thought possible only of human beings.
   (5) Chimpanzees may have many skills that we don't yet know about.

5. Until the 1960s, many scientists believed that animals in the wild were not able to make or use tools. Which of the following most likely changed this opinion?

   (1) pride in human accomplishments
   (2) knowledge available at that time about animal intelligence
   (3) improvement in zoo design
   (4) observations of animals in captivity
   (5) observations of animals in the wild

Questions 6–8 refer to the terms below.

Below are five types of behavior shown by vertebrates.

Inborn behaviors:

reflex—an automatic response to a stimulus

instinct—a complex, unlearned response that is not dependent on experience

self-preservation—a reaction for the purpose of escaping life-threatening danger

Learned behaviors:

conditioned response—learning that connects an unusual stimulus with a desired response

intelligent behavior—a complex response that uses past learning in new situations

6. When it saw a cat, the mouse ran for its life. What type of behavior was the mouse exhibiting?

    (1) reflex
    (2) instinct
    (3) self-preservation
    (4) conditioned response
    (5) intelligent behavior

7. During mating, the Adelie penguin of Antarctica builds a nest out of pebbles and the bones of its ancestors. What type of behavior is the Adelie penguin exhibiting?

    (1) reflex
    (2) instinct
    (3) self-preservation
    (4) conditioned response
    (5) intelligent behavior

8. Each time Jenny claps her hands, Scruffy rolls over and barks. What type of behavior is Scruffy exhibiting?

    (1) reflex
    (2) instinct
    (3) self-preservation
    (4) conditioned response
    (5) intelligent behavior

Answers are on page 444.

Communities of Living Things

Ecosystems

Many different kinds of animals and plants live in and around a pond. The survival of each organism depends on the others. Many animals eat plants. Plants, in turn, depend on animals for waste products that provide nutrients. Along the shore, insects eat plants, frogs eat insects, snakes eat frogs, and birds eat snakes. Within the pond, small fish feed on plankton—tiny plant and animal life that floats in the water. Large fish and ducks eat the smaller fish. Through this interdependence, called a **food chain,** each organism plays a role in the ongoing life in and around the pond.

A pond is a **habitat,** or home, for a community of organisms. All of the organisms of one type are called a **population.** For example, we are part of the human population. Other habitats that contain numerous populations are forests, grasslands, deserts, mountains, rivers, and oceans. A community of populations of organisms, together with the habitats and the natural resources that affect the community, is called an **ecosystem.** Some natural resources that are important in an ecosystem are adequate sunshine, clean water, and clean air.

Food Webs

Many relationships exist among organisms in an ecosystem. A nutritional relationship among organisms leads to food chains. In every food chain, organisms either produce their own food or obtain food by eating other organisms. Algae and green plants create food through photosynthesis, their primary source of energy, and obtain nutrients from water and soil. Mushrooms and other fungi cannot make food, so they take nutrients from trees and other plants. Animals do not make their own food either, so they obtain it by eating plants and other animals that are parts of other food chains.

The many different food chains that are linked in this more complex relationship are called a **food web.** In a food web, organisms that are part of one food chain may also be part of another food chain. As nutrients move through a food web, they are reused and recycled. For example, think of a pond in which water lilies are growing. The leaves of the lilies are eaten by a snail that, in turn, is eaten by a small fish. The fish lives for a while before it is swallowed by a duck. Circling over the duck's head is a hawk, looking for prey. The hawk eats the duck and, at some time in the future, dies near the pond where bacteria feed on its decomposing body. The bacteria return nutrients to the soil. The nutrients in the soil are washed into the pond where they are used by water lilies to grow new leaves.

Competition for Limited Resources

A second relationship among organisms in an ecosystem is based on competition for limited resources. For example, in a pond both bass and ducks eat small fish. The greater the number of fish eaten by ducks, the less food there is for the bass. Each animal has other sources of food, so this competition is not likely to lead to either animal starving. However, competition among members of the same species can be much more intense. Because each is after the exact same resources, the members of a species directly compete, with starvation waiting for the poorest competitors. Besides food, animals might also compete for mating partners and space in the habitat.

In a stable ecosystem, each population of an organism stays about constant. The number of each species that die is balanced by the number of newborns that survive.

Dependence on a Stable Ecosystem

Disruptive changes can easily upset the stability of an ecosystem.

- A forest fire can destroy all plant and animal life in a forest, along a river, and around the shore of a pond. A fire can also pollute a pond with ash.

- A flood or mudslide can wipe out the side of a mountain, flood the banks of a river, and dump tons of sediment into a pond, destroying life on the side of the mountain, along the shore, and within the pond as well.

- Pollution from human activities can also affect an ecosystem. For example, a chemical spill or pesticides sprayed overhead can kill all plant and animal life that comes in contact with the chemicals.

- A housing development along the bank of a river or on the shore of a pond can bring both garbage and noise pollution, in addition to direct physical destruction of these habitats.

Thinking About Science

Directions: Match each term on the left with the best description on the right. Write the correct letter on the line.

_____ **1.** resource 　　　(a) a place in which organisms live

_____ **2.** population 　　(b) a habitat and all the organisms in it

_____ **3.** ecosystem 　　(c) clean water

_____ **4.** habitat 　　　(d) the complex food links between plants and animals in an ecosystem

_____ **5.** food web 　　(e) the group of all frogs living next to a lake

Answers are on page 444.

Directions: Choose the <u>one best answer</u> to each question.

Questions 1 and 2 refer to the information on pages 206 and 207.

1. In order for the population of an organism in a habitat to increase, which of the following must be true?

   (1) The population's reproduction time must be short compared to the reproduction time of its predators' populations.
   (2) The population must have no predators.
   (3) The population's birthrate must be equal to its death rate.
   (4) The population's birthrate must be greater than its death rate.
   (5) The population's birthrate must be less than its death rate.

2. At present there are no bass in Waldo Lake, a mountain fishing lake that doesn't freeze during winter. Richard, a wildlife biologist who works for the forest service, is going to start a bass population in the lake by releasing 10,000 baby bass during the warm month of June.

   Which of the following will be the *least* relevant factor in determining the eventual size of a stable bass population in Waldo Lake?

   (1) the availability of food sources in Waldo Lake for bass
   (2) the average number of fishermen who will fish for bass in Waldo Lake during the coming summers
   (3) the health of the insect populations in and around Waldo Lake during the coming years
   (4) the number of other fish that presently live in Waldo Lake
   (5) the types of plants that live on the shore of Waldo Lake

Hawk (eats snake)

Snake (eats frog)

Droppings (bacteria and fungi break down droppings and dead organisms into nutrients)

Sun

Frog (eats grasshopper)

Grasshopper (eats grass and leaves)

Nutrients (water, phosphorus, nitrogen, calcium...)

Plant Life (nourishes self through photosynthesis; needs nutrients in order to grow)

Question 3 refers to the diagram at left.

3. Based on the diagram, what most likely would happen to the animal populations after chemical spraying kills most of the region's mosquitoes and gnats, both of which are sources of food for frogs?

   (1) a decrease of both frogs and snakes
   (2) a decrease in frogs and an increase in grasshoppers
   (3) an increase in both frogs and snakes
   (4) a decrease in snakes and an increase in hawks
   (5) an increase in both snakes and hawks

Answers are on page 445.

The Theory of Evolution

To account for the wide varieties of organisms on Earth, scientists have proposed a theory of biological **evolution.** According to this theory, organisms evolve (change) over time. The net result is that organisms today are much better suited for their environment than they were in the distant past. A species alive today may have looked much different from the way it looked a million years ago. Scientists estimate that the variety of organisms that exist on present-day Earth is the result of over 3.5 billion years of evolution. While speculations about evolution have been going on since the early nineteenth century, the modern theory of evolution began with the work of Charles Darwin.

Darwin's Discoveries

In 1832, a twenty-four-year-old naturalist named Charles Darwin sailed from England aboard a British naval ship, the HMS *Beagle.* During the next three years, Darwin explored the rain forests of South America and hiked throughout the Galápagos Islands, located off that continent's western shore. These explorations revealed things to Darwin that forever changed his ideas about the nature of life on Earth.

On the Galápagos Islands, Darwin saw creatures that existed nowhere else. He saw land tortoises that seemed to be the same as the small land tortoises of South America. However, the tortoises on the island were huge—large enough to ride. He saw finches (small birds) similar to the finches found on the continent, only they weren't quite the same. The island finches had beak shapes and eating habits that were different from those of the South American variety.

Darwin saw how similar yet different the island animals and the continent animals were. After much thought, Darwin concluded that each island species had originally come from the continent, perhaps thousands of years ago. At that distant time, each island species must have been exactly like its mainland relatives.

Darwin believed that, once on the islands, each species became isolated from the mainland. Then, because the island environment was much harsher than the mainland environment, the island species slowly changed through many generations. The island species changed in both appearance and behavior from their South American relatives. The island species became much better suited (or fit) for the island environment. Darwin used the word *evolution* to refer to this process of gradual change.

Darwin theorized that evolution is a process that occurs in all organisms. As generation follows generation, adaptive changes slowly occur. These changes include variations in structure and behavior. Each change makes an organism better suited for its environment. Darwin saw evolution as a process that links the millions of different species of plants, animals, and microorganisms that live on Earth today with those of the past.

Darwin's Theory of Evolution

Darwin's theory can be summarized as follows:

- There are genetic variations among the members of every species. Many of these variations, called favorable traits, aid in the struggle for survival. For example, a hawk with long claws kills prey more easily than a hawk with short claws.

- An ecosystem can support only a certain number of organisms of any one species. Competition for food and water, predators, and disease limit the population of each species. Only a certain number of hawks can live at one time in an ecosystem.

- Members of a species most likely to survive are those with favorable traits. During a time of limited prey, hawks with long claws are more likely to capture prey than are hawks with short claws. By surviving, long-claw hawks will pass on this favorable trait to offspring. Short-claw hawks will most likely starve to death and not reproduce. The unfavorable trait of short claws will slowly be eliminated in this species of hawk.

Natural Selection

The idea that individuals with favorable traits are the most likely members of a species to survive, reproduce, and pass on those traits is known as **natural selection.** Because of natural selection, only favorable traits are likely to be passed on to future generations. Darwin realized that natural selection, operating over thousands of years or more, would lead to the type of world he saw: a world in which organisms were superbly adapted to their environments.

Mutations

Evolution can occur because of mistakes in an organism's DNA. Most genetic errors harm the organism. Others have little impact. Occasionally, a genetic mistake benefits an organism. Then the trait may be passed on to the next generation.

A **mutation** is a change in the genetic information within a cell. In most cases, mutations occur when chromosomes are damaged. Pieces that contain some genes can be lost or changed in structure. This situation describes a chromosome mutation. Another type of mutation is a gene mutation, which can be caused by X rays, nuclear radiation, or chemicals. The result of mutation is that the offspring differ from their parents because the cells have received new genetic instructions.

Punctuated Equilibrium

Scientists today believe that Darwin's ideas are essentially correct. Evolution takes place as species gradually become better adapted to a slowly changing environment. But evidence that was not available to Darwin suggests that another type of evolution also is taking place. This is a rapid evolution called **punctuated equilibrium.** Study of fossil records shows that many species suddenly have disappeared from Earth. Dinosaurs, for example, once ruled Earth and then suddenly became extinct about 70 million years ago. Similarly, the fossil record shows that many new species have suddenly appeared on Earth.

Current thinking is that punctuated equilibrium is brought about by unusual catastrophic events. Suggested causes of punctuated equilibrium include an asteroid colliding with Earth and rapid genetic mutation caused by disease or unusually high doses of radiation from space.

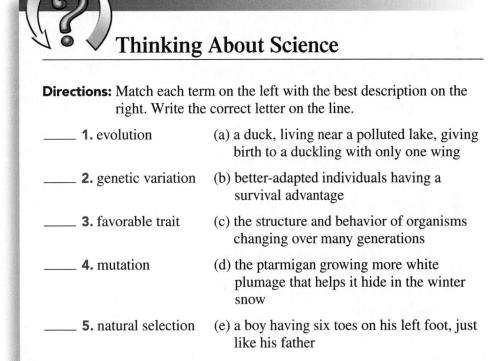

Thinking About Science

Directions: Match each term on the left with the best description on the right. Write the correct letter on the line.

_____ **1.** evolution

(a) a duck, living near a polluted lake, giving birth to a duckling with only one wing

_____ **2.** genetic variation

(b) better-adapted individuals having a survival advantage

_____ **3.** favorable trait

(c) the structure and behavior of organisms changing over many generations

_____ **4.** mutation

(d) the ptarmigan growing more white plumage that helps it hide in the winter snow

_____ **5.** natural selection

(e) a boy having six toes on his left foot, just like his father

Answers are on page 445.

Directions: Choose the one best answer to each question.

Questions 1–4 are based on the information on pages 209–211.

1. Which of the following best summarizes Darwin's theory of evolution?

   (1) Organisms purposely change in order to adapt to environmental conditions.
   (2) Organisms change over time, and those that are the most fit have the best chance of surviving and passing on their own genetic characteristics.
   (3) Although many life forms are now extinct, living organisms have not changed since the beginning of life on Earth.
   (4) Genetic traits are passed from one generation of an organism to the next generation.
   (5) All organisms have an equal opportunity to learn to adapt to changing environmental conditions.

2. What is the most important factor in determining what shape of beak would be the most favorable trait for a bird?

   (1) the types of food sources in the bird's habitat
   (2) the bird's average life expectancy
   (3) the type of predator that hunts the bird
   (4) the bird's nesting habits
   (5) the times during the day or night that the bird hunts

3. Which trait would be most useful for birds on a small island that is hit periodically by severe storms that kill most of the island's land animals?

   (1) longer claws, useful for carrying twigs
   (2) a high-pitched cry, useful for mating
   (3) darker tail feathers, useful for camouflage
   (4) a wider beak, useful for capturing fish
   (5) sharper claws, useful for killing rodents

4. Which of the following observations best supports Darwin's theory of evolution?

   (1) Offspring of organisms tend to behave in ways similar to the way their parents behave.
   (2) Dinosaurs were once the dominant life form on Earth, but they are now extinct.
   (3) Polar bears would become extinct because of hunters if the bears were not a protected species.
   (4) Certain genetic diseases such as sickle-cell anemia can be inherited.
   (5) Fossils show that many of today's organisms are similar to, but not identical to, organisms that are now extinct.

Answers are on page 445.

The Fossil Record

A **fossil** is the preserved remains or traces of an ancient living thing. Fossils provide evidence of organisms that once lived on Earth but which are now extinct. By studying fossils, scientists also find clues as to how today's organisms evolved from extinct ancestors. Scientists have used fossils to confirm that slow evolution does seem to take place as proposed by Darwin. Fossils also indicate that punctuated equilibrium is an important part of the evolutionary process.

Evidence from Fossils

Fossils can tell us many things about extinct organisms:

- when an organism first appeared on Earth

- how an organism differed from ancestor organisms from which it evolved

- characteristics of the organism's life

- how long an organism was on Earth before becoming extinct

- what caused an organism to become extinct

Scientists believe that life originated in water and that most early life forms were simple water animals and plants. The earliest fossils show that single-celled bacteria, called blue-green algae, lived on Earth 3.5 billion years ago. Apparently, this algae evolved very little, if at all, during the next 3 billion years. Jellyfish and worms, the first complex organisms, began appearing about 680 million years ago. The first animals with backbones (vertebrates) appeared about 570 million years ago. By 500 million years ago, the oceans contained a variety of plant and animal life forms.

Then, about 400 million years ago, living organisms began migrating to land. First came plants and then simple amphibians, perhaps ancestors of today's frogs and salamanders. Reptiles such as lizards, snakes, and dinosaurs began appearing about 300 million years ago. The first mammals appeared about 100 million years ago. Mammals, though, would not come to be a dominant land species until the extinction of dinosaurs about 65 million years ago. Flowering plants, which first started appearing about 120 million years ago, also did not become abundant until after the extinction of dinosaurs.

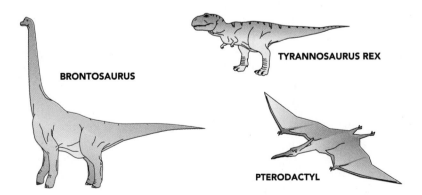

BRONTOSAURUS

TYRANNOSAURUS REX

PTERODACTYL

The extinction of dinosaurs made possible the rise of mammals as the dominant life form.

Earth's Time Periods

Scientists have used the fossil record to divide Earth's history into time periods based on life forms. The earliest time period is known as the Precambrian era. The Precambrian era was a time when Earth was populated by soft-bodied organisms whose remains are not well preserved. The shortest and most recent period, the Cenozoic era, is the period during which most modern plants and animals came into being.

EVOLUTION OF LIFE FORMS

Eras	Years Before Present	Life Forms
Cenozoic		
	65,000,000	
Mesozoic		
	240,000,000	
Paleozoic		
	600,000,000	
Precambrian		

Two well-known examples of extinct animals are the saber-toothed tiger and the mammoth (often called the woolly mammoth).

Saber-toothed tigers roamed Earth for about 35 million years. The last saber-toothed tiger died about 1 million years ago. Though this animal is called a tiger, it has many characteristics that are very unlike tigers today. The most striking feature was their upper canine teeth. Also, the saber-toothed tiger walked flat-footed, very similar to the way bears walk today. Many scientists question whether the saber-toothed tiger is more closely related to today's cat family or bear family.

Mammoths roamed Earth for a million years or so, with the last mammoth dying during the Ice Age, which ended about 20,000 years ago. The mammoth is a distant relative of today's elephant. Mammoths had long, curving tusks and a shaggy covering of thick hair. An almost complete frozen baby mammoth was found in Siberia in 1977.

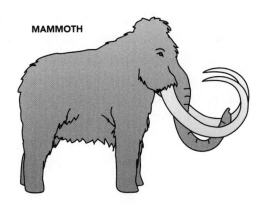

MAMMOTH

SABER-TOOTHED TIGER

Thinking About Science

Directions: Answer each question below.

1. When do scientists believe that life first began on Earth?

   _____

2. What was the first organism for which there is a fossil record?

   _____

3. What happened that led to the rise of mammals as Earth's dominant life form?

   _____

Answers are on page 445.

Directions: Choose the <u>one best answer</u> to each question.

Questions 1 and 2 refer to the information on pages 213–215.

1. Which of the following is information about an extinct animal for which fossils do not provide evidence?

   (1) the animal's diet
   (2) the animal's evolutionary ancestors
   (3) when the animal first appeared
   (4) the animal's sleeping pattern
   (5) when the animal became extinct

2. Which of the following animals is <u>least</u> likely to be related to the saber-toothed tiger?

   (1) buffalo
   (2) polar bear
   (3) house cat
   (4) black bear
   (5) lion

Questions 3 and 4 refer to the passage below.

Sometimes fossils are formed when the remains of a dead organism are completely altered by chemical changes. The cells of the organism start to dissolve and are slowly replaced by minerals from the surrounding rocks and soil. Over time the minerals harden, often creating a fossil that shows the fine details of the original organism. This process is called *petrifaction*.

Scientists believe that petrifaction takes place molecule by molecule over a long period of time. The minerals most commonly involved in petrifaction are silica (a glassy mineral that is found in sand), calcite (a mineral found in both limestone and marble), and pyrite (a mineral made up of iron and sulfur).

A petrified fossil may look almost identical to the original organism. The detailed cell structure of the original tissues may even be apparent. Perhaps the most familiar petrified fossil is petrified wood. This hard glassy mineral substance clearly shows growth rings and other tissue features of the ancient tree from which it was produced.

3. What role do minerals play in petrifaction?

   (1) Minerals surround and preserve a fossil.
   (2) Minerals cause a fossil's remains to harden into a rocklike substance.
   (3) Minerals replace a fossil's original cell materials.
   (4) Minerals change the size of a fossil.
   (5) Minerals change the shape of a fossil.

4. What might a person be able to determine by looking at a petrified tree trunk?

   (1) the height of the tree when it died
   (2) the length of time in which petrifaction took place
   (3) the location of the tree when it died
   (4) the date that the tree died
   (5) the age of the tree when it died

Answers are on page 445.

Plant and Animal Science Review

Directions: Choose the <u>one best answer</u> to each question.

Questions 1–4 refer to the following diagram and passage.

OPARIN'S THEORY OF THE ORIGIN OF LIFE

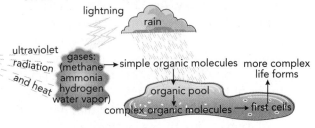

In 1922 a Russian scientist named Aleksandr Oparin extended Darwin's theory of evolution back in time to explain how organic molecules developed naturally from gases in Earth's atmosphere. Oparin proposed that before life began, Earth's atmosphere contained four main gases: methane (made of carbon and hydrogen), ammonia (made of nitrogen and hydrogen), water vapor (made of oxygen and hydrogen), and pure hydrogen.

According to Oparin, sunlight or lightning provided the energy that split these gases into their basic elements. Instead of recombining into the gases they had been originally, however, these elements recombined in new ways. The molecules that were created were organic molecules, molecules made mainly of carbon, hydrogen, and oxygen. Organic molecules are now known to be the basic building blocks of all living organisms.

Oparin believed that large numbers of organic molecules were then washed from the atmosphere by rain and that they collected in shallow "organic pools." Next, the molecules in the organic pools combined to form more complex molecules. Then, he believed, these complex molecules eventually organized into the first living cells.

1. Before life began, what most likely was the main element in Earth's atmosphere?

   (1) oxygen
   (2) hydrogen
   (3) carbon
   (4) iron
   (5) nitrogen

2. According to Oparin's theory, which of the following would have had to come first?

   (1) rocks containing carbon
   (2) a multicellular organism
   (3) an atmosphere containing methane
   (4) the first living cell
   (5) a pool containing organic material

3. Which of the following does Oparin's theory *not* attempt to explain?

   (1) the formation of the first organic molecules
   (2) how atmospheric gases might be split apart
   (3) how sunlight and lightning played a part in the development of the first living cells
   (4) differences between plant and animal cells
   (5) the formation of shallow organic pools

4. The principle of biogenesis asserts that a living organism can come only from another living organism. Which statement is true about Oparin's theory?

   (1) Oparin's theory is not consistent with biogenesis.
   (2) Oparin's theory supports biogenesis.
   (3) Oparin's theory proves that biogenesis is not correct.
   (4) Oparin's theory proves that biogenesis is correct.
   (5) Oparin's theory supports the theory of evolution.

Questions 5 and 6 refer to the following passage.

SEA HORSE

The sea horse is one of the most interesting of all fish. Sea horses live in warm ocean waters and have long snouts and long tails. They eat mainly a diet of crustaceans (small aquatic organisms such as shrimp).

When sea horses breed, the female deposits her eggs in a brood pouch beneath the tail of the male. The eggs attach themselves to the wall of the male and obtain nourishment from the male's blood. After about two weeks, the pouch ruptures and young sea horses emerge.

5. What is the most likely reason that the sea horse is known by this name?

(1) its size
(2) its looks
(3) its breeding habits
(4) its diet
(5) its habitat

6. What characteristic of sea horses is a kangaroo-like feature?

(1) water habitat
(2) crustacean diet
(3) brood pouch
(4) young nourished by male parent
(5) shape of features

Question 7 refers to the passage below.

Convergent evolution occurs when populations of different organisms living in similar environments or having similar ways of life evolve similar characteristics.

Convergent evolution explains the similarity in body features between ichthyosaurs, which became extinct about 65 million years ago, and dolphins of today. An ichthyosaur was an ocean reptile that had a streamlined body and a pointed snout. The need for survival in the ocean environment caused the dolphin to evolve body features that are very similar to those of the extinct ichthyosaur. A dolphin, however, is an ocean mammal that has no direct evolutionary link to the ichthyosaur.

7. What function is served by the shape of the ichthyosaur and the dolphin?

(1) holding captured fish
(2) quick breathing
(3) deep diving
(4) protective camouflage
(5) efficient swimming

Questions 8 and 9 refer to the following graph.

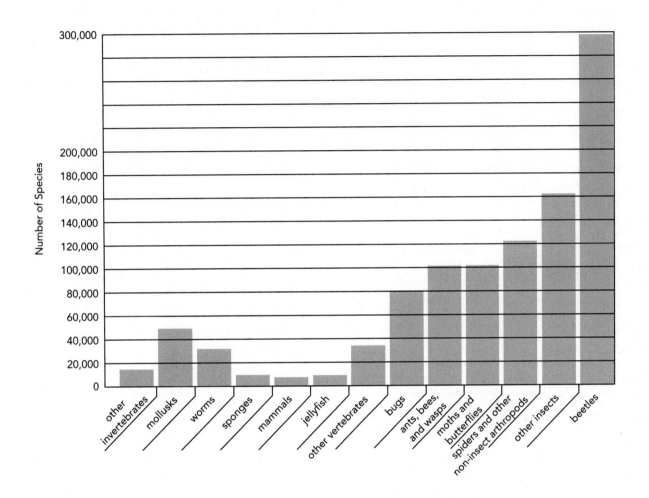

8. Approximately one-fourth of all animal species are what type of animal?

   (1) moths and butterflies
   (2) mollusks
   (3) beetles
   (4) mammals
   (5) jellyfish

9. Which type of animal has the fewest species?

   (1) bugs
   (2) jellyfish
   (3) worms
   (4) sponges
   (5) mammals

Questions 10–12 refer to the following passage.

Many animals live with their own kind for the purposes of feeding, reproducing, and migrating and for mutual protection. Fish swim together in schools, elephants roam together in herds, wolves hunt together in packs, and ducks migrate together in flocks. The most complex living arrangement, though, occurs with the social insects: ants, bees, wasps, and termites. Social insects form groups in which the needs of the group are more important than the needs of any particular member. Each individual is specially adapted to perform a function for the group, not for itself. In fact, the group's survival often depends on individuals giving up their own lives

Social insects are characterized by several kinds of group behavior. They live together, forming a colony or hive; they care for their young; they often feed each other as well as their young; and they usually stem from the same female parent who is the lone queen of the colony or hive.

Each social-insect group survives through a division of labor among its members. For example, a honeybee hive consists of a single queen bee, many worker bees (underdeveloped female bees), and many drones (male bees). The sole job of the queen, the largest honeybee, is to lay the eggs. A worker's job is more varied: She must gather nectar, feed and care for the queen and drones, and keep the hive clean and cool. She must also protect the hive from invaders. A drone's only task is to fertilize the queen bee when she is aloft in the "marriage flight." After the drone performs this single task, he dies.

10. Which of the following best summarizes the key points made in the passage on social insects?

   (1) Social insects work together, each member of a group playing a role to aid in the survival of the group.
   (2) Social insects form loose but cooperative group living associations.
   (3) Social-insect groups place low value on the lives of those members designated as workers.
   (4) Social-insect groups are inefficient because many members do little or no work.
   (5) Members of social-insect groups must sacrifice their own lives.

11. Which of the following *best* explains the presence of many dead worker bees on the ground around a beehive?

   (1) The hive was hit by a falling branch.
   (2) The worker bees accidentally gathered poison nectar.
   (3) The worker bees had mated with the drones.
   (4) The hive was disturbed by a bear looking for honey.
   (5) The drones killed the worker bees to make more room in the crowded hive for newly developing bees.

12. In what important way does a social-insect group differ from a human social group?

   (1) Social insects join together to better accomplish a group purpose.
   (2) Social insects share the group's labor in an orderly way.
   (3) Some members of a social-insect group give up their lives as a natural result of performing their role for the group.
   (4) Social insects care for and feed the young members of the group.
   (5) Each member of a social-insect group specializes in a certain type of work.

Answers are on page 445.

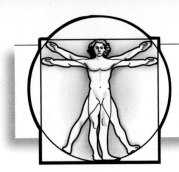

CHAPTER 8

Human Biology

We must, however, acknowledge, as it seems to me, that man with all his noble qualities . . . still bears in his bodily frame the indelible stamp of his lowly origin.

~ Charles Darwin

Animals, as a rule, stay in the environment for which they're best adapted for survival. You may find penguins living near the coast of Antarctica, but you'd be surprised to see even one in the Sahara Desert! Likewise, while you expect to see camels in the Sahara Desert, you wouldn't expect one to live near Antarctica. Penguins and camels, like almost all other animals on Earth, show no desire or ability to venture away from their home environment. Even animals that migrate spend their lives in only two homes for which they're specially adapted.

The one exception to the rule is human beings. By nature, humans—naked and without thick skin or a coat of fur—are adapted only to life on land where the temperature is mild. Compared to most other animals, we are not very fit for survival even there. We are not very strong, we cannot run very fast, we cannot fly, and we cannot fight very well. By inventing clothes, forms of shelter, weapons for hunting, and other survival aids, however, we have done things that no other animal, no matter how well adapted, has ever done. We have made homes on all the continents and islands of Earth. We have lowered ourselves to the bottom of the ocean. We have flown to the top of the atmosphere and to the Moon. Perhaps most important, we have produced a culture where even the least fit have an opportunity to survive and prosper. These are remarkable achievements.

What makes human beings unique? Most certainly it is the power of the human mind. Although our survival needs are similar to those of other animals, our means of meeting those needs are more complex. We anticipate and plan for the future, we learn from experience, and we have free choice. Other animals do not have these abilities. While an ant can build an anthill, we can build a skyscraper, a school, a church, or a sports stadium. While other animals constantly search for food, we engage in fulfilling work and meaningful recreational lives.

Although human beings are different from other organisms, the study of human biology is also about the similarities that are found in all life forms. We know we differ from other animals, but in what ways are we the same?

Biologists have discovered that human beings may be biologically related to many different species. Similarities in body structure suggest that humans and other animals have similar genetic codes for the formation of many different structures and organs. The arm bones of a human, for example, are very similar to the leg bones of a dog as well as to the forelimb bones of a bird.

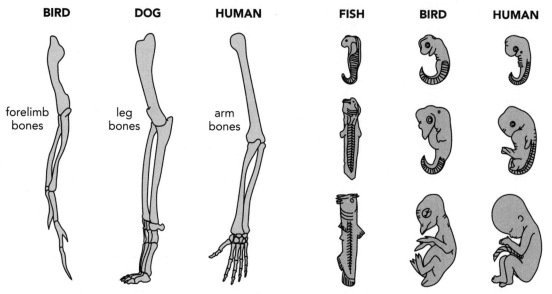

BIRD **DOG** **HUMAN** **FISH** **BIRD** **HUMAN**

forelimb bones   leg bones   arm bones

Similar bone structure indicates that many different species of animals may be biologically related. Similarities shown in the stages of embryonic development may be an indication of a common biological history.

A surprising similarity also exists between organisms at the embryo stage—the early stage of development of a new individual from a fertilized egg. For example, embryos of many vertebrates (animals with backbones) are so similar that it is difficult for an untrained person to tell a fish embryo from a bird embryo or from a human embryo. Many scientists think that embryonic similarity is a sign of common biological history.

Biologists have also discovered that the chemical makeup of a human is much like that of other animals. For example, the proteins in the human body differ in structure by less than 1 percent from the proteins in the body of a chimpanzee.

Because of these structural and chemical similarities, biologists think that human beings may share many more characteristics with other organisms. Biologists hope to use this information to help them understand the biological origin of human life as well as the origin of other forms of life.

Biologists classify animals according to body structure and function. Different species that look very much alike tend to be placed in the same classification group. For example, cattle and sheep are classified in a group that does not include chickens or salmon. Human beings are classified in the group *mammals* and are given the biological name *Homo sapiens*. Human beings are also placed in a small subgroup called *primates*—mammals with eyes facing forward, grasping fingers and a thumb, and the ability to walk on two legs. This subgroup includes human beings, apes, and monkeys.

Thinking About Science

Directions: Answer each question below.

1. Name two types of evidence that suggest that human beings are biologically related to other animals.

   a. _____

   b. _____

2. Complete each sentence by filling in the blank(s) with the correct word(s).

   a. Biologists classify animals according to their

   _____ and _____.

   b. _____ is the biological name given to the animal species better known as human beings.

   Answers are on page 445.

GED PRACTICE

Directions: Choose the <u>one best answer</u> to each question.

Questions 1–3 refer to the information on pages 221 and 222.

1. According to the reading selection, human beings are classified in a subgroup of mammals called primates. Which of the following animals is also a primate?

   (1) goat
   (2) gorilla
   (3) dolphin
   (4) sparrow
   (5) horse

2. Animals that show similarity in body structure may also have similarity in what else?

   (1) genetic codes
   (2) interests
   (3) life spans
   (4) behavior patterns
   (5) brain sizes

3. What is the best example of appendages that have similar bone structures but very different uses?

   (1) the leg of an elephant and the leg of a human
   (2) the wing of a falcon and the wing of a bat
   (3) the arm of a human and the arm of a monkey
   (4) the leg of a human and the leg of a dog
   (5) the forelimb of a bird and the arm of a human

Questions 4–6 refer to the following passage.

The publication of Charles Darwin's ideas on evolution and natural selection started a bitter controversy among biologists, religious leaders, and the general public. This controversy centered around Darwin's conclusions that both plant and animal species change over time and that new species may develop in the process. A particular point of contention was Darwin's suggestion that human beings, like other animals, evolve as a result of natural selection.

The process of human evolution remains today one of the most debated ideas in biology. Many scientists now believe that human beings did, in fact, evolve from a simpler life form, most likely an apelike primate that lived millions of years ago. According to this idea, the evolution of these prehuman primates resulted in the formation of several new species. One of these species is *Homo sapiens* (human beings). If this conclusion is correct, human beings are related to other modern primates much more closely than scientists before Darwin's time could ever have imagined.

4. Charles Darwin noticed certain similarities between the physical features of chimpanzees and those of orangutans. Based on his beliefs, which of the following conclusions could he most likely have drawn?

   (1) Chimpanzees are not biologically related to orangutans in any way.
   (2) Either the chimpanzee or the orangutan, but not both, evolved from an apelike primate that lived millions of years ago.
   (3) Chimpanzees evolved from orangutans that lived millions of years ago.
   (4) Chimpanzees and orangutans both evolved from the same apelike primate that lived millions of years ago.
   (5) Neither chimpanzees nor orangutans have evolved at all.

5. Which of the following discoveries would be the best evidence that humans and modern apes may have evolved from a common ancestor?

   (1) An ape can be taught to communicate in simple sign language with humans.
   (2) Apes can be raised from babies to adulthood by humans.
   (3) Ancient skulls have been discovered that show both humanlike and apelike features.
   (4) Apes can walk upright on their two back legs similar to how humans walk.
   (5) Apes in the wild form family groups similar to the family groups formed by humans.

6. Which activity would accelerate the evolution of humans toward a better adapted species?

   (1) educating as many people as possible
   (2) encouraging all children to participate in physical exercise
   (3) providing an economic system where each person can succeed up to the level of his or her ability
   (4) using genetic engineering to cure inherited diseases
   (5) supporting research efforts to better understand the history of life

Answers are on page 446.

The Human Brain

The human brain is often described as the most marvelous yet mysterious organ in the human body. You use your brain in everything that you do. Because of your brain, you have special qualities that make you unique among all other living organisms. Your brain shapes the personality that is the "you" whom other people know.

As you read this page, your brain receives electrical signals from your eyes. Somehow your brain changes these signals into the thoughts of your conscious mind. As familiar as these processes are, scientists are not sure what the conscious mind is or how it is related to the brain. This mystery, often called the *mind-brain problem*, will undoubtedly remain one of the most challenging and exciting areas of brain research well into the twenty-first century. In this section we'll mention a few of the most important discoveries about the mind and the brain.

Seen from above, the human brain looks much like a large gray walnut. Its typical weight in an adult is about three pounds. Although we usually think of the brain as a single unit, it is actually divided into two halves. Each half, called a **hemisphere**, is joined to the other half by bundles of nerve fibers. Biologists believe that these nerve fibers enable the two halves of the brain to communicate with each other.

TOP VIEW OF HUMAN BRAIN

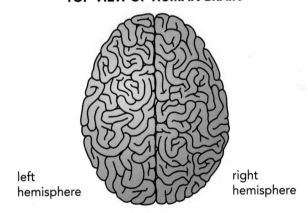

left
hemisphere

right
hemisphere

The two halves of the human brain are connected in the center by bundles of nerve fibers.

Brain tissue consists of nerve cells called **neurons.** Although the exact number of neurons is unknown, each human brain is believed to contain more than ten billion neurons! These neurons form a network of cells through which electrical and chemical messages pass. These messages occur 24 hours a day. Scientists believe that these messages are directly related to mental activities that take place both while we are awake and while we dream.

Because the brain has so many neurons, it has the capacity to store more information than all the libraries in the world. However, we don't use our brain power just to memorize information. We can use books and computers to do that. Instead, we use our brain power to carry out the more complex activities of intelligent humans. The brain thinks, feels, stores memories, and interprets. It also responds to sight, sound, touch, and other body sensations and controls body movement and body growth.

A neuron consists of a cell body, a nucleus, a long fiber called an **axon** through which a nerve impulse is sent, and a large number of branching fibers called **dendrites.** The ends of the axon of the neuron that is sending a "message" are in contact with the dendrites of many, many neurons that receive the message. The point of contact is called a **synapse.** No one knows how information is coded and sent from neuron to neuron, but scientists know that both chemical and electrical processes are involved.

TWO NEURONS IN SYNAPTIC CONTACT

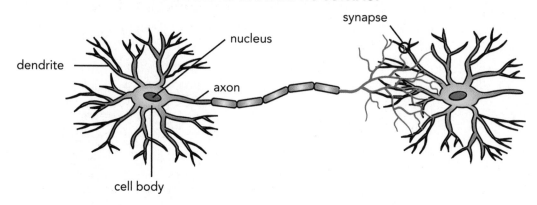

Localization of Brain Functions

Each of our body sensations and movements is controlled by one of the brain hemispheres. The left hemisphere controls the right side of the body. The right hemisphere controls the left side of the body. If one hemisphere is damaged, the opposite side of the body may be partly or completely paralyzed. This often occurs with accident and stroke victims.

Besides controlling sensations and movements, the brain provides us with intelligence and emotions. Intelligence is the ability to acquire and apply knowledge. Emotions are our inner feelings. Each hemisphere appears to play a special role in the many ways in which knowledge and feelings are acquired and remembered.

- The left hemisphere is primarily used for reasoning skills such as mathematics and science and for language skills.

- The right hemisphere is important for spatial-relations skills, imagination, and artistic skills such as painting and music.

The division of skills in the brain has led researchers to comment that the functions of the two halves of the brain are similar to the two ways in which we solve problems. The left half of the brain gives us logic. The right half of the brain gives us intuition.

FUNCTIONS OF THE LEFT AND RIGHT BRAIN HEMISPHERES

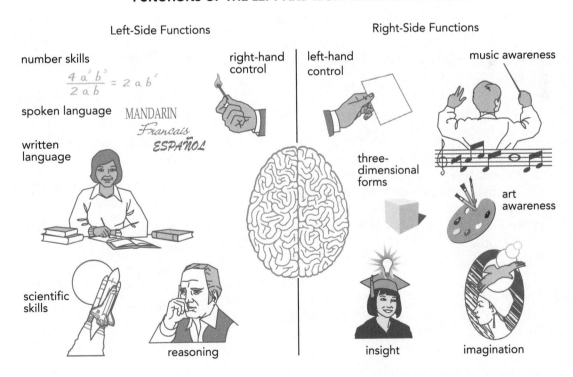

Left-Side Functions — Right-Side Functions

number skills

$$\frac{4a^2b^3}{2ab} = 2ab^2$$

spoken language — MANDARIN — Français — ESPAÑOL

written language

right-hand control

left-hand control

music awareness

three-dimensional forms

art awareness

scientific skills

reasoning

insight

imagination

Thinking About Science

Directions: Complete each sentence below by filling in the blank with the correct word(s).

1. The human brain is divided into _____ hemispheres.
    (number)

2. The _____ hemisphere of the brain controls the right side of the body, while the _____ hemisphere controls the left side of the body.

3. The cells that make up the human brain are called _____.

4. The two sides of the brain are connected by _____.

Answers are on page 446.

GED PRACTICE

Directions: Choose the <u>one best answer</u> to each question.

Questions 1–3 refer to the information on pages 225–227.

1. For what purpose do bundles of nerve fibers join the brain hemispheres?

    (1) to enable dreaming during sleep
    (2) to hold the two brain halves together
    (3) to enable the two brain halves to share information
    (4) to enable blood to flow from one side to the other
    (5) to separate the two brain halves

2. An elderly man has suffered a stroke that leaves the right side of his body paralyzed. What part of his body has most likely been affected by the stroke?

    (1) the left side of his heart
    (2) the right side of his heart
    (3) the right half of his brain
    (4) the left half of his brain
    (5) both halves of his brain

3. Carlos has incorrectly assumed that a larger brain size indicates greater intelligence. Which two facts show that Carlos is not correct?

    A. The brains of all human adults are about the same size.

    B. A teenager's brain is larger than a baby's brain.

    C. The brain of an elephant is larger than the brain of a human.

    D. The brain of a human is larger than the brain of a dog.

    (1) A and B
    (2) A and C
    (3) A and D
    (4) B and C
    (5) C and D

Answers are on page 446.

Taking Care of Your Body

A Long and Healthful Life

Have you ever wished for a magic pill that would let you live forever? If so, you are not alone. This natural wish has a long history. Spanish explorers of the sixteenth century even tried to find a fountain of youth in what is now the state of Florida. The water of this legendary fountain was believed to restore youth and good health to those who drank it.

Biologists today do not expect that anyone will find a fountain of youth. Growing older is a natural part of the life cycle. As humans grow older, organs such as the heart and lungs do not work as well as when they were younger. Sight and hearing become impaired. And, the human body becomes more likely to come down with serious illnesses from which it cannot recover.

Considered together, changes that bring about the decline of an organism are called **aging**. Because of aging, many biologists believe that there may be a maximum age limit to which even the healthiest organisms can live. For humans, this maximum age is about 110 years. Some biologists, though, say that a much longer life span, perhaps 150 years, may soon be possible as a result of advancement in health-related technology. However, it may be that body cells have an internal clock that determines the maximum life span of each species. No one knows for sure.

The most important thing you can learn from human biology is that you have a lot of control over how long and how well you live. Having a long and healthful life is not a matter of luck. You can plan for it. You have control of many physical and mental factors that have much to do with aging. Do you know that more than half of the deaths each year in the United States are caused by heart and blood vessel diseases? These diseases are almost unknown in many corners of the world. Why? The answer is related to lifestyle.

Medical research indicates that each of us can do many things to help prevent heart and blood vessel diseases and to reduce cancer.

Avoid Fatty Meat and Other Animal Products
Fatty animal meats, such as beef, pork, and chicken, and fatty products, such as eggs and cheese, add excess cholesterol and saturated fats to the diet. Both cholesterol and saturated fats are contributing factors in high blood pressure, heart disease, and obesity (excessive weight).

Reduce or Stop Smoking
Smoking causes lung cancer and emphysema and leads to heart and blood vessel diseases.

Reduce Alcohol Consumption
Excessive alcohol consumption impairs brain function, damages the liver, leads to digestive disorders, and can seriously harm the unborn fetus of a pregnant mother.

Reduce Sugar Consumption

Excessive sugar leads to an unhealthy change of events in the human body. Eat a large candy bar, and the insulin hormone is released in the blood. Insulin attempts to lower the body's sugar level, and within a couple of hours the body may additionally release anti-insulin antibodies. The presence of this surge of chemicals in the blood can leave a person feeling irritable and nervous. Also, excess sugar is stored in the body as unwanted fat.

Reduce Stress

Stress contributes to heart disorders such as high-blood pressure, heart disease, ulcers, cancer, and chronic pain problems.

Reduce Body Weight

Excessive body weight, which can lead to high-blood pressure and heart disease, is also a contributing factor in breast cancer and colon cancer.

Exercise Regularly

Regular exercise strengthens muscles and promotes good health in all body organs. Exercise also is valuable in weight control and stress reduction.

Keep Aware of Advances in Health Education

Keep aware of advances made in health education. For example, recent evidence suggests that eating a diet high in fiber may help to lower blood pressure, decrease the cholesterol level, and lower the risk of chronic disease. Good sources of fiber are fresh fruits and vegetables and foods made from whole grains. Information is often available free of charge from county health clinics or schools.

Thinking About Science

Directions: Circle *T* for each statement that is true and *F* for each statement that is false.

T   F   **1.** Many biologists believe that each species has a natural maximum life span.

T   F   **2.** There is much you can do to help prevent many diseases.

T   F   **3.** Mental attitude is not a factor that is related to good health.

T   F   **4.** Doctors believe that smoking increases a person's chances of getting both lung cancer and heart disease.

Answers are on page 446.

Directions: Choose the <u>one best answer</u> to each question.

Questions 1 and 2 refer to the information on pages 229 and 230.

1. What is the leading cause of death of people in the United States?

   (1) heart and blood vessel diseases
   (2) cancer
   (3) accidents
   (4) childhood diseases
   (5) alcoholism

2. People in the United States have a higher incidence of heart disease than people in many poorer countries. What factor is this problem most likely related to?

   (1) U.S. citizens pay more for medical insurance than people in poorer countries.
   (2) U.S. citizens get less exercise than do people in poorer countries.
   (3) U.S. citizens have a higher life expectancy than do citizens of poorer countries.
   (4) U.S. citizens do not handle stress as well as citizens of poorer countries do.
   (5) U.S. citizens eat more whole grains than do citizens of poorer countries.

Questions 3–5 refer to the following passage.

In 1900, U.S. citizens could expect to live an average of 47 years. By the end of the twentieth century, the average life expectancy in the United States had risen significantly—to more than 75 years. There are several reasons for this increase. First, fewer children are dying. Laws now prohibit child labor, which caused many deaths and injuries at the turn of the century. Better nutrition and new vaccinations against disease help ensure children's health. Second, adult Americans are healthier. Workplace safety laws and advances in medicine and technology have protected more and more adults. And finally, increased education at all levels has brought about a new public awareness of health and safety.

3. Which of the following is <u>not</u> one of the reasons given for the increase in average life expectancy in the United States during the twentieth century?

   (1) increased average income
   (2) better nutrition
   (3) improved working conditions
   (4) development of vaccines
   (5) increased education

4. Which of the following would be <u>least</u> important to a researcher studying ways to increase life expectancy in the United States?

   (1) the quantities and types of food eaten by people in the United States
   (2) the smoking and drinking habits of people in the United States
   (3) the leading causes of death of people in the United States
   (4) the amount of money the average American household spends on food each year
   (5) the percent of people receiving adequate medical care

5. By about how many years has the average life expectancy in the United States risen since 1900?

   (1) 5
   (2) 10
   (3) 30
   (4) 60
   (5) 90

Questions 6–8 refer to the following passage.

In order to observe the relationship between aging and the amount of food an organism consumes, a researcher did the following experiment. He placed four mice in each of two cages and fed each group of mice the same type of food. He kept the food trays in cage 1 full at all times. The mice in cage 1 could eat any time and any amount they wanted. He placed only small portions of food in cage 2. The food supply for the mice in cage 2 was purposely limited. The results of his experiment were as follows:

• The mice in cage 1 seemed to lack energy and were sick a lot. They all died before reaching the average life expectancy of a mouse.

• The mice in cage 2 were energetic and healthy. They all lived long beyond the average life expectancy of a mouse.

6. What is the most reasonable conclusion that you can draw from the results of this experiment?

   (1) The death of the mice in cage 1 was related to the type of food they ate.
   (2) The mice in cage 2 would probably have lived beyond their life expectancy even if their food supply wasn't limited.
   (3) Limited feeding slows the aging process in mice.
   (4) Overfeeding slows the aging process in mice.
   (5) Neither overfeeding nor limited feeding affects the aging process in mice.

7. Which of the following would be the <u>least</u> important item that the researcher would want to know before drawing a conclusion?

   (1) the causes of death of the mice in cage 1
   (2) the time of day that the mice in cage 2 were fed
   (3) the average daily amount of food consumed by each group of mice
   (4) the daily amount consumed by a normal mouse
   (5) the life expectancy of a mouse fed an average amount of food

8. Suppose these research results also apply to humans. Which statement <u>least</u> supports the opinion that overeating leads to poor health?

   (1) Overeating ensures that you have enough vitamins and minerals.
   (2) Overeating overloads your body's ability to deal with chemical pollutants found in food.
   (3) Overeating makes you uncomfortable and unable to get restful sleep.
   (4) Overeating requires a great amount of energy for digestion.
   (5) Overeating results in excess weight gain that is hard on the heart.

Answers are on page 446.

Nutrition

How does a piece of chocolate cake and a milk shake sound to you for lunch? If you're hungry, it may sound pretty good—unless, of course, you're on a diet. Then you may not want the weight gain this food will give you.

While a piece of cake and a milk shake provide lots of calories, they do not provide the nutrients, or food substances, that your body needs. **Calories** are a measure of food energy. We all need calories for daily activities and during sleep, but many people eat more calories than they need. These excess calories are stored as body fat. **Nutrients**, on the other hand, are food substances that the body can use for tissue growth and repair, as well as for energy. Without nutrients, the human body ceases to function properly, and sickness and death can result. A well-balanced diet is made up of foods that provide an adequate, but not excessive, number of calories while supplying all the nutrients needed for good health.

Nutrition is the study of the health value of food. Nutritionists have discovered that the most important nutrients found in food are carbohydrates, fats, protein, vitamins, and minerals. Many types of food are major sources of one type of nutrient but also contain smaller amounts of other nutrients.

- **Carbohydrates** are a main source of food energy. Bread, rice, potatoes, fruits, and grain cereals are healthful sources of carbohydrates. These sources also contain important vitamins, minerals, and protein. Less healthful sources include sugar and desserts such as cakes, cookies, doughnuts, and ice cream. Healthful sources are low in calories, while less healthful sources are high in calories and contribute to excess weight gain. Medical evidence now indicates that sugar and sugary products contribute to heart disease and diabetes as well as to tooth decay.

- **Fats** are another energy source. Some fats should be eaten only occasionally and in limited amounts. These fats are found in beef, pork, chicken, and many dairy products. As indicated on page 000, fats from meats and other animal products are known to contribute to heart and blood vessel diseases. For cooking, oil from vegetable sources should be used instead of oil made from animal fat.

  Recent research has shown that oil from salmon, though an animal source, does not seem to carry the risk for heart disease as other animal fats do. In fact, in small amounts, oil from salmon seems to have health benefits.

- **Protein** is vital to body growth and to the repair of body tissues. The most healthful sources of animal protein are lean beef, chicken, fish, and dairy products. Good sources of protein from vegetables include grain products, potatoes, and beans.

- **Vitamins** and **minerals** are chemicals that are used by the body in small amounts. Though they contain no calories, vitamins and minerals are important for proper body growth, for body activity, and for the prevention of certain diseases. The most common sources of vitamins and minerals are fruits and vegetables. Many people also supplement their diets with vitamins and minerals in the form of pills.

- Water, which makes up more than two-thirds of your body weight, is also an important part of your diet. Water is used in the digestion of food, in the production of blood, and in the elimination of body wastes. Water also helps regulate body temperature.

As a general rule, in a well-balanced diet 55 to 60 percent of the calories come from carbohydrates, no more than 30 percent come from fats, and 10 to 15 percent come from protein. The exact number of calories your body requires on a daily basis depends on your age, body size, and activity level. If you increase your activity level, you need more calories and nutrients. Information about diet and nutrition is available in bookstores, schools, and county health clinics.

Thinking About Science

Directions: Answer each question below.

1. Match each word on the left with the best descriptive phrase on the right. Write the letter of the phrase on the line before the correct number.

   _____ 1. calorie   (a) needed for cell growth and repair

   _____ 2. water   (b) a measure of food energy

   _____ 3. carbohydrate   (c) needed by the body in small amounts

   _____ 4. protein   (d) a main energy-providing nutrient

   _____ 5. vitamin   (e) helps regulate body temperature

2. Answer each question below.

   a. What two diseases can be caused by a diet high in sugar?

   _____ and _____

   b. In a well-balanced diet, what percent of calories should come from

   protein? _____ carbohydrates? _____

   fats? _____

   Answers are on page 446.

GED PRACTICE

Directions: Choose the <u>one best answer</u> to each question.

Questions 1–3 refer to the information on pages 233 and 234.

1. What does the human body do with the excess food calories present in such foods as chocolate cake and milk shakes?

    (1) It stores them as muscle tissue.
    (2) It stores them as nerve tissue.
    (3) It passes them through the digestive system.
    (4) It digests them only when the body needs them.
    (5) It stores them as fat tissue.

2. For which ailment is a doctor or nurse most likely to recommend that the patient drink lots of water?

    (1) chest cold
    (2) high fever
    (3) broken arm
    (4) toothache
    (5) plantar wart

3. Which of the following describes the relationship between food intake and exercise?

    (1) A person with an increased exercise program needs fewer nutrients.
    (2) A person with an increased exercise program must eat fewer calories to avoid gaining weight.
    (3) The amount of exercise a person gets has nothing to do with weight gain or weight loss.
    (4) A person with an increased exercise program can eat more calories without gaining weight.
    (5) A person who exercises little needs more nutrients than a person who exercises a lot.

Questions 4 and 5 refer to the following diagram.

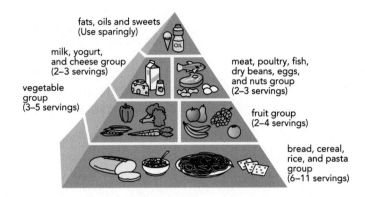

The U.S. Department of Agriculture and the Department of Health and Human Services developed the food pyramid shown above. The food pyramid divides foods into six groups, showing recommended servings of each.

4. According to the food pyramid, which food group should you get the most daily servings of?

    (1) fats, oil, and sweets
    (2) milk, yogurt, and cheese
    (3) vegetables
    (4) meat, poultry, fish, beans, eggs, and nuts
    (5) bread, cereal, rice, and pasta

5. Which food group is the major source of protein?

    (1) fats, oil, and sweets
    (2) milk, yogurt, and cheese
    (3) vegetables
    (4) meat, poultry, fish, beans, eggs, and nuts
    (5) bread, cereal, rice, and pasta

Answers are on page 446.

Systems of the Human Body

Skeletal System

Like the frame of a house, your **skeleton** gives form to your body. It also provides protection for internal organs. A typical human skeleton is made up of about 200 bones and numerous joints.

The shape of the skeleton allows for great freedom of movement while at the same time providing strength and protection. The skull surrounds and protects the brain, while the bones of the upper spine (backbone) support the skull and allow you to turn your head without turning your body. The ribs form an enclosed upper-body cavity that protects the most important internal organs. The numerous bones in the hands allow for many types of highly skilled thumb and finger movements, from tying shoes to assembling machines and playing musical instruments. The numerous bones of the feet help provide for balance and ease of movement while standing, walking, or running.

HUMAN SKELETON

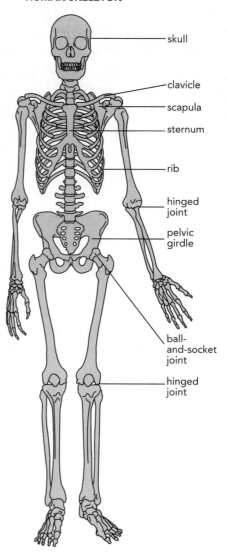

- skull
- clavicle
- scapula
- sternum
- rib
- hinged joint
- pelvic girdle
- ball-and-socket joint
- hinged joint

Joints

Joints are formed where two or more bones come together. Most bones are connected to each other by **ligaments**—tough strands of connective tissue. To prevent the bones from grinding against each other, the surfaces of contact are covered with cartilage, a tough but flexible tissue. Cartilage is also the tissue that makes up the tough part of both your nose and ears.

The human body has several types of joints.

- Ball-and-socket joints, found in the shoulders and hips, allow for movement in almost all directions.

- Hinge joints, found in elbows and knees, allow for movement in one direction.

- Gliding joints, found in wrists and ankles, allow limited movement in many directions.

- Pivot joints, found between vertebrae in the spine, mainly allow rotating movement from side to side.

- Fixed joints, found in the skull, hold the bones of the skull together and do not allow for any movement.

Muscular System

Movement in the human body is made possible by muscles. A **muscle** is tissue that can contract (shorten or pull together). Muscles are connected to bones by **tendons**—strong, fibrous connective tissue. Because a muscle can only contract, every joint is controlled by opposing muscles. This enables back-and-forth movement to occur. As shown below, you contract your biceps muscle to bend your arm. You contract your triceps muscle to straighten it.

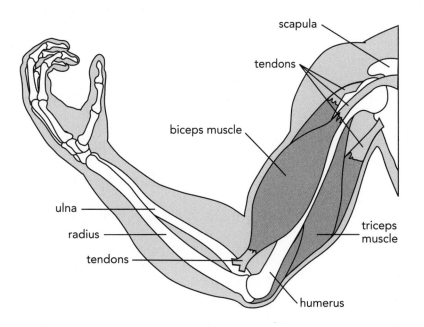

Muscles may be voluntary or involuntary.

- **Voluntary muscles** are those that you can consciously control. Skeletal muscles, used to control bone movement, are all voluntary muscles. To raise your hand, you consciously use skeletal muscles of the arm and shoulder.

- **Involuntary muscles** are those over which you normally have limited control. The smooth muscles of the lungs, intestines, and bladder are involuntary muscles. The cardiac muscles in the heart are involuntary muscles that cause heartbeat.

Both voluntary and involuntary muscles produce heat as they contract and relax. This is the reason you feel warm when you exercise and the reason people jump up and down to keep warm while waiting in line on a cold day.

Nervous System

To control the working of all its muscles and to sense stimuli, the human body contains a network of nerves that thread throughout the body. These nerves are like tiny wires that carry electrical signals called **nerve impulses**. Each nerve connects with the spinal cord, a large central nerve within the spine that serves as the communication link with the brain.

When you decide to move your arm, your brain sends a nerve impulse down the spinal cord and out to the correct nerve. The impulse reaches the muscles involved and causes them to contract and raise your arm.

If you cut your finger, a nerve impulse is sent from the point of the cut to the brain by way of the spinal cord. It is only when this impulse reaches the brain that you feel pain. Pain and all other sensations actually occur within your brain, although the stimulus that produces each sensation may occur anywhere on your body. As you can imagine, nerve impulses are very complex and race back and forth in a fraction of a second between your brain and points within your body.

Thinking About Science

Directions: Circle *T* if the statement is true and *F* if the statement is false.

T   F   **1.** A joint is a break in a bone.

T   F   **2.** Only involuntary muscles are controlled.

T   F   **3.** Voluntary muscles can be controlled.

T   F   **4.** Nerve impulses travel both to and from the brain.

Answers are on page 446.

Directions: Choose the <u>one best answer</u> to each question.

Questions 1–6 refer to the information on pages 236–238.

1. Which of the following is the best example of the use of voluntary muscles?

    (1) a heart beating
    (2) an eye twitching
    (3) a hand waving
    (4) an eyelid blinking
    (5) teeth chattering

2. Which of the following activities is the best example of a use of involuntary muscles?

    (1) jumping rope
    (2) driving a car
    (3) signing your name
    (4) lifting weights
    (5) sneezing

3. Which of the following phrases best sums up the function of the nervous system?

    (1) communication network
    (2) support structure
    (3) waste elimination
    (4) food processing
    (5) energy storing

4. Damage to the spinal cord can interfere with nerve impulses that flow to and from the brain. Suppose a person falls and seriously injures his lower back. Where might he experience temporary loss of feeling?

    (1) in the arms
    (2) on the right side of the body
    (3) on the left side of the body
    (4) in the legs
    (5) in the shoulders

5. A young girl quickly pulls her hand away from a hot burner on a stove. During this incident, four things quickly happen, although not necessarily in the following order:

    A. nerve impulse sent from brain to hand

    B. muscles contract to pull hand back

    C. nerve impulse sent from hand to brain

    D. heat felt

    What is the order in which these four things actually happen?

    (1) A, C, B, D
    (2) D, C, A, B
    (3) B, A, C, D
    (4) D, A, C, B
    (5) C, D, A, B

6. Which fact best supports the hypothesis that the purpose of shivering is to generate heat when the body is cold?

    (1) Shivering is an involuntary action.
    (2) Shivering occurs mainly in the upper part of the body.
    (3) Shivering is movement caused by muscles that rapidly contract and relax.
    (4) Shivering interferes with normal speech.
    (5) The amount that a person shivers may depend on how long it's been since he or she has last eaten.

    Answers are on page 447.

Digestive System

Among life's pleasures, eating rates pretty high for most people. However, when we talk about eating, we usually think only about tasting, chewing, and swallowing. That's the fun part, but it's only the first step of the process called **digestion**—the breaking down of food into nutrients that the body's cells can use. As shown below, the human digestive system consists of many more parts than just the mouth.

HUMAN DIGESTIVE SYSTEM

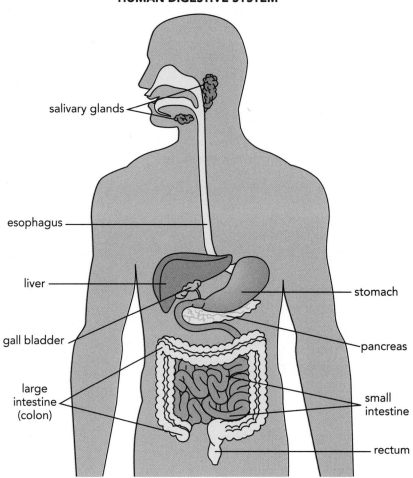

After food is chewed and swallowed, it passes down the esophagus and into the stomach, the body's main organ of digestion. In the stomach, the food is churned in digestive juices much like a washing machine churns clothes in soapy water. After being in the stomach for two to five hours, the partially digested food passes into the small intestine.

With the help of digestive juices from the liver and pancreas, the small intestine completes the digestion process. From here the digested nutrients and water pass through the walls of the small intestine and into the bloodstream, where they then travel to the body's cells. Waste products continue through the small intestine and move into the large intestine, where they are prepared for passage out of the body. At the end of the large intestine is the rectum, which stores the solid wastes until they are removed from the body through an opening called the anus.

Excretory System

Excretion is the process in which waste products are removed from the body. As we've seen, one form of waste products occurs during the digestive process and is eliminated from the body by the digestive system. In addition, human body cells produce waste as they process the nutrients they receive from the digestive system.

As blood passes through the body, body cells release into the blood both carbon dioxide gas and liquid waste products. Blood passes through both the lungs and the kidneys. The lungs remove carbon dioxide gas from the blood, and we exhale this waste gas to the atmosphere. The kidneys act as a blood filter and separate the waste product from the water, glucose, and minerals that the body needs. The waste product, called urine, passes through a tube called the urethra and is stored in the bladder. When the bladder is full, it contracts and pushes urine out of the body. In most instances, the emptying of the bladder is under the control of voluntary muscles.

In addition to producing digestive juices, the liver also filters harmful substances out of the blood. Before nutrient-rich blood moves throughout the body, the liver removes excess sugar from the blood. If this excess sugar is not needed, it is changed to glycogen, a carbohydrate, and stored.

HUMAN EXCRETORY SYSTEM

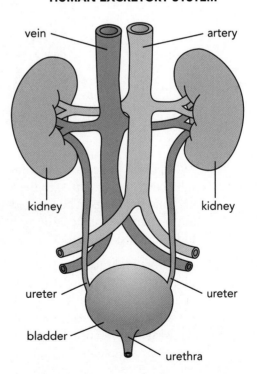

Respiratory System

Closely related to the body's need for food is its need for oxygen. Oxygen is only one of many gases found in air, but it is the gas that cells use for **respiration**—the process in which food sugar is broken down and energy and carbon dioxide gas are released. The energy powers all of the cells' activities, while the carbon dioxide gas is a waste product.

HUMAN RESPIRATORY SYSTEM

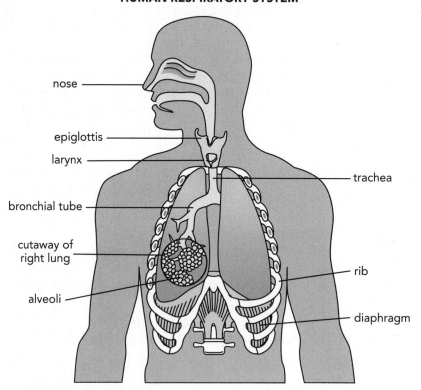

In order to get oxygen into our blood, we breathe air. As shown above, inhaled air passes through the nose and mouth, down the trachea (windpipe), and into the lungs. The epiglottis, a muscle that works like a trapdoor, allows air to enter the trachea during breathing. But, the epiglottis closes the opening to the trachea when food or liquids are swallowed.

Bronchial tubes branch off the trachea and carry the air into each of the two lungs. In the lungs the bronchial tubes branch into even smaller tubes that end in millions of little air sacs, called alveoli. It is in the alveoli that blood vessels absorb the oxygen from the air. At the same time, the blood releases the waste carbon dioxide gas it has brought from the body cells.

Circulatory System

Blood transports nutrients, water, and oxygen to all cells in the body and carries wastes to the organs that remove wastes. Blood is the fluid that flows through the circulatory system of the human body.

HUMAN CIRCULATORY SYSTEM
(major arteries and veins)

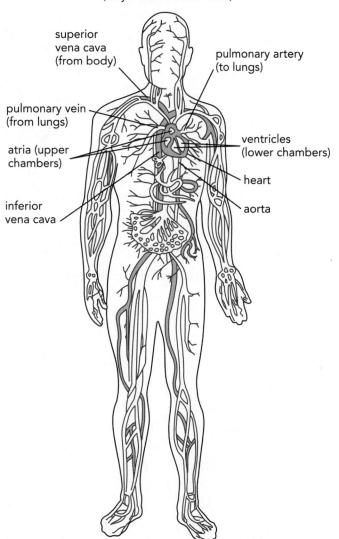

superior
vena cava
(from body)

pulmonary artery
(to lungs)

pulmonary vein
(from lungs)

ventricles
(lower chambers)

atria (upper
chambers)

heart

aorta

inferior
vena cava

The center of the circulatory system is the heart, the blood's pump. The heart is a fist-sized muscle that is divided into two atria, or upper chambers, and two ventricles, or lower chambers. The right atrium pumps blood into the right ventricle, which pushes the blood through the pulmonary artery to the lungs. While in the lungs, the blood absorbs oxygen gas and releases waste carbon dioxide gas that it has taken from body cells. The oxygen-rich blood returns through the pulmonary vein to the heart and passes through the left atrium and the left ventricle, where it is pumped away from the heart and out through the aorta to the rest of the body.

When it reaches body cells, the oxygen-rich blood gives up its oxygen and nutrients and picks up carbon dioxide gas. The blood, now rich in carbon dioxide, leaves the cells and returns to the heart through veins leading to the right atrium. From there the carbon dioxide-rich blood begins the flow cycle once again.

THE HUMAN HEART

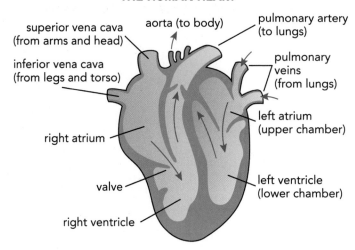

Reproductive System

The male reproductive system, shown below, has three main parts. The testes produce the male sex cells, called **sperm**. Millions of sperm are produced each day and are stored in the scrotum. During sexual activity, the sperm leaves the body through the penis.

MALE REPRODUCTIVE SYSTEM

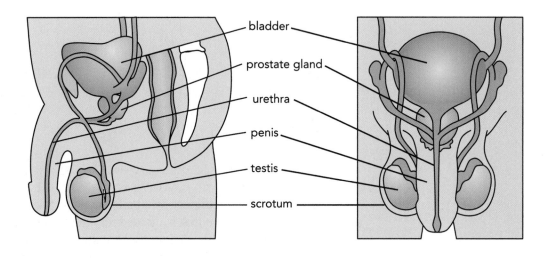

The female reproductive system is shown below. Female sex cells, called **eggs**, are produced in the ovaries. Usually one egg matures at a time. When the egg matures, it passes through the fallopian tube on its way to the uterus. If the egg gets fertilized by sperm, it attaches to the wall of the uterus. If the egg remains unfertilized, it passes out of the body through the vagina. The processes of both the female and male reproductive systems are controlled by special chemicals called **hormones**.

FEMALE REPRODUCTIVE SYSTEM

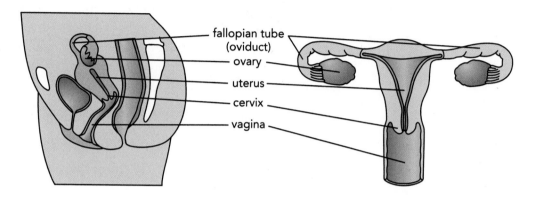

fallopian tube (oviduct)
ovary
uterus
cervix
vagina

The growth and release of a mature egg is called the **menstrual cycle.** The cycle starts when an egg begins to mature, and the lining of the uterus thickens. In about two weeks, the egg is ready to be released into the uterus. If the egg is not fertilized, the lining of the uterus breaks down and is shed through the vagina as menstrual blood. The cycle, which takes about 28 days, then begins again. If a mature egg and sperm unite, pregnancy results, and the menstrual cycle stops.

Endocrine System and Hormones

The endocrine system is a network of glands that produce hormones. **Hormones** are special chemicals produced within the body that regulate body functions. Glands that you may already be familiar with are sweat glands, which release water and salt from the body, and salivary glands, which release digestive juices into the mouth.

Endocrine glands release several types of hormones directly into the blood. Some of these hormones control body growth, energy use, and reproduction. Adrenaline is a hormone released into the body in times of danger. Adrenaline causes muscles to tense in anticipation and causes the heart rate to increase. Insulin is a hormone that controls the level of sugar in the blood. Testosterone and estrogen are hormones that control the sexual maturation and sexual activities of men and women.

Thinking About Science

Directions: Match each word on the left with the best definition on the
right. Write the letter of the definition on the line before the
correct number.

_____ **1.** kidneys

(a) organs in which blood takes oxygen
from the air

_____ **2.** lungs

(b) primary organ of digestion

_____ **3.** stomach

(c) organ from which digested food enters
bloodstream

_____ **4.** arteries and veins

(d) organ responsible for filtering waste
products

_____ **5.** small intestine

(e) tubes that carry blood

_____ **6.** ovary

(f) chemicals that control body processes

_____ **7.** hormones

(g) organ in which male sperm are stored

_____ **8.** uterus

(h) organ in which female egg is produced

_____ **9.** scrotum

(i) organ in which fertilized egg develops

Answers are on page 447.

Go to **www.GEDScience.com** for additional practice and instruction!

Directions: Choose the one best answer to each question.

Questions 1–6 refer to the information on pages 240–245.

1. What function is performed by the epiglottis?

   (1) It prevents food and liquids from entering the trachea.
   (2) It prevents food and liquids from entering the esophagus.
   (3) It prevents air from entering the trachea.
   (4) It prevents air from entering the esophagus.
   (5) It produces the sounds of speech.

2. Which of the following phrases best sums up the function of the circulatory system?

   (1) communication network
   (2) support structure
   (3) waste elimination
   (4) food processing
   (5) transport and delivery

3. What gas does blood release into the lungs during breathing?

   (1) oxygen
   (2) nitrogen
   (3) carbon monoxide
   (4) carbon dioxide
   (5) helium

4. According to the diagram on page 244, which of the following statements is correct?

   (1) Arteries carry blood both away from the heart and back to the heart.
   (2) Veins carry blood both away from the heart and back to the heart.
   (3) Ventricles carry blood both away from the heart and back to the heart.
   (4) Veins carry blood away from the heart; arteries carry blood back to the heart.
   (5) Arteries carry blood away from the heart; veins carry blood back to the heart.

5. What is the most likely reason that being overweight puts an extra burden on the heart?

   (1) A person who is overweight often feels self-conscious.
   (2) The heart of an overweight person must pump a greater amount of blood in order to nourish the extra fat cells.
   (3) An overweight person has an increased risk of developing diabetes.
   (4) The heart of an overweight person tends to be smaller than average.
   (5) An overweight person may not consume enough protein.

6. Which of the following comments about an artificial heart is most likely based on human values rather than on scientific evidence?

   (1) An artificial heart is a mechanical pump that takes the place of a seriously damaged human heart.
   (2) Implanted artificial hearts have shown a high failure rate because of unusual blood-clotting problems.
   (3) After its design is perfected, an artificial heart may give a patient a longer life expectancy than a transplanted human heart.
   (4) The decision to implant an artificial heart ought to be left solely up to the patient and his or her doctor, regardless of the risks involved.
   (5) Today's artificial heart may best be used as a temporary life-support measure that keeps a patient alive until a human heart can be obtained for transplant.

7. Which of the following is the first step in pregnancy?

   (1) movement of male sperm out of the scrotum
   (2) movement of female egg through the fallopian tube
   (3) fertilization of the female egg
   (4) shedding of the uterine lining
   (5) production of hormones that control male and female sexual activity

Answers are on page 447.

Reproduction and Human Genetics

Human reproduction starts with the union of a male sex cell (a sperm) and a female sex cell (an egg). The combined cell, called a fertilized egg cell, grows quickly into a ball of many cells that implants itself on the inner wall of the female uterus. Here it develops into a **fetus**, the developing stage of a baby, about two months after fertilization. For about nine months the fetus grows inside the uterus, receiving nourishment and oxygen from its mother.

Inherited Traits

Reproduction results in a new individual who has many of the features (traits) of each parent. These traits are passed from parents to child by **genes**, chemical messengers that make up the strands of chromosomes present in each body cell. Sperm and egg cells bring hereditary information from each parent and combine it to produce the unique mixture of traits acquired by the child.

In the nucleus of most human body cells is a set of 46 chromosomes. Most of these chromosomes are arranged in 22 pairs that contain about 100,000 genes. These genes determine all of an individual's traits. For example, genes determine whether a child has his or her mother's nose, the father's hands, or the grandfather's hairline.

The remaining pair of chromosomes is a special pair that determines the sex of the child. The mother always contributes an X chromosome, while the father can contribute either an X or a Y chromosome. If a fertilized egg contains two X chromosomes, it will develop into a female fetus. If it contains one X and one Y chromosome, it will develop into a male fetus.

The only human body cells that do not contain 46 chromosomes are the female egg cell and the male sperm cell. Each of these cells has only one set of 23 unpaired chromosomes. In a fertilized egg cell, the 23 unpaired chromosomes from the egg are joined by 23 from the sperm to give a total of 46 chromosomes. In this way, a fertilized egg receives exactly half of its genes from the male parent and half from the female parent.

Twins

In most cases, a single fertilized egg develops into a single fetus. Once in a while, though, a fertilized egg will separate into two cells that move away from each other. Each of these cells may develop into a fully formed fetus. The two children that are born are known as **identical twins**. Because they form from the same fertilized egg cell, identical twins are genetically identical. Each has exactly the same set of chromosomes and genes.

Fraternal twins develop when two egg cells are fertilized by two sperm cells during the same reproductive cycle. Although fraternal twins develop in the mother's uterus at the same time, they are no more alike than brothers and sisters who may be born years apart.

Prenatal Care

Protecting the health of a developing fetus is called prenatal care. To provide good prenatal care, a pregnant woman needs good nutrition, healthful exercise, and periodic medical checkups.

Substances in the mother's blood can affect the health of a developing fetus. Because of this, a pregnant woman should avoid smoking, drinking alcohol, or taking drugs. She should take only medicines prescribed by her doctor. She should also avoid all sources of chemical fumes such as garden sprays, oven cleansers, and other household chemicals. These fumes contain chemicals that can harm the fetus.

Genetic Disorders

A **genetic disorder** is a disease, disability, or difference caused by an abnormal gene. Many genetic disorders are inheritable traits that result in generation after generation of illnesses or disabilities. Many other genetic disorders, however, do not cause any problems that affect a child's health or abilities. Examples of more serious inheritable genetic disorders are sickle-cell anemia and hemophilia. An example of a less serious genetic trait is color blindness.

Many genetic disorders can be identified in adults. Anyone with a known genetic disorder can get genetic counseling before deciding to have children. Genetic counseling can provide parents with information about how the genetic disorder may affect the life of any child they may choose to have.

Genetic disorders can also be detected in a fetus during the early months of pregnancy. Doctors use a procedure called **amniocentesis** to examine fetal cells present in the amniotic fluid that surrounds the fetus. By studying these cells, doctors can identify certain types of genetic disorders that are present in the fetus.

Thinking About Science

Directions: Circle *T* for each true statement and *F* for each false statement.

T F **1.** Genetic counseling is an attempt to resolve marriage problems caused by differences in inherited traits.

T F **2.** Color blindness can be inherited.

T F **3.** Except for egg and sperm cells, all cells of a human body contain 23 pairs of chromosomes.

T F **4.** The health of a developing fetus depends in part on the care the mother-to-be gives to her own body.

Answers are on page 447.

Directions: Choose the <u>one best answer</u> to each question.

Questions 1–4 refer to the information on pages 248 and 249.

1. Which of the following is <u>not</u> true about identical twins?

   (1) Identical twins form from two fertilized eggs.
   (2) Identical twins have the exact same genetic makeup.
   (3) Identical twins form from a single fertilized egg.
   (4) Identical twins are more alike than are fraternal twins.
   (5) Identical twins are always the same sex.

2. How does the female egg cell differ from other cells in a woman's body?

   (1) The egg cell has twice as many chromosomes as all other cells.
   (2) The egg cell has 23 more chromosomes than all other cells.
   (3) The egg cell has no chromosomes.
   (4) The egg cell has 23 fewer chromosomes than all other cells.
   (5) The egg cell has chromosomes but does not have genes.

3. Which of the following activities should a mother-to-be avoid during the months of pregnancy?

   (1) going to music concerts
   (2) taking daily walks
   (3) cooking meals at home
   (4) taking naps
   (5) painting the house

4. Suppose a woman is a social drinker. If she discovers she is pregnant, what should she do to protect the health of the fetus?

   (1) reduce drinking alcoholic drinks for at least four more months
   (2) drink alcohol only with meals
   (3) decrease her use of alcohol over the remainder of the pregnancy
   (4) stop drinking alcohol until after the birth of the child
   (5) continue social drinking as usual

Questions 5–7 refer to the following passage.

Sickle-cell anemia is an inheritable blood disease that affects about 72,000 Americans each year. There is no known cure for this disease. Symptoms include enlargement of the abdomen and heart, swelling of the feet and hands, aching joints, and pain caused by clogged blood vessels. Many children die of sickle-cell anemia before they reach their teenage years.

Sickle-cell anemia affects red blood cells. A healthy red blood cell has a doughnut shape, but the red blood cell of a person who has sickle-cell anemia is shaped like a sickle; it is elongated and narrow. Sickle cells tend to clump together and clog blood vessels. This results in a lack of oxygen reaching body tissues and causes the symptoms mentioned.

Sickle-cell anemia is caused by a single gene that affects the shape and function of red blood cells. However, because this gene is recessive, only those who have inherited two sickle-cell genes display symptoms of the disease. Carriers of a single sickle-cell gene are said to have the sickle-cell trait but do not suffer symptoms of the disease. Because it is a genetic disease, sickle-cell anemia is not contagious.

Sickle-cell anemia is particularly common in people of Mediterranean or western African ancestry. An estimated 8 to 12 percent of all African Americans carry the sick-cell gene.

A blood test can determine if an individual carries the sickle-cell gene. If both potential parents are carriers, they may want to seek genetic counseling. Genetic counselors will explain how sickle-cell anemia can affect children they may have.

5. What is affected in a person who has sickle-cell anemia?

   (1) white blood cells
   (2) blood vessels
   (3) red blood cells
   (4) arterial walls
   (5) oxygen molecules

6. Which of the following phrases does not correctly describe sickle-cell anemia?

   (1) a blood disease
   (2) an inheritable disease
   (3) a contagious disease
   (4) a genetic disorder
   (5) symptoms include clogging of blood vessels

7. Which statement about sickle-cell anemia is true?

   (1) The symptoms of sickle-cell anemia occur just before blood clots.
   (2) The symptoms of sickle-cell anemia occur only in women.
   (3) The symptoms of sickle-cell anemia occur only in men.
   (4) A person will have the symptoms if he or she has a single sickle-cell gene.
   (5) A person can carry a single sickle-cell gene and not suffer any of the symptoms.

Answers are on page 447.

Human Biology Review

Directions: Choose the <u>one best answer</u> to each question.

Questions 1–3 are based on the following illustration and passage.

DEVELOPING FETUS

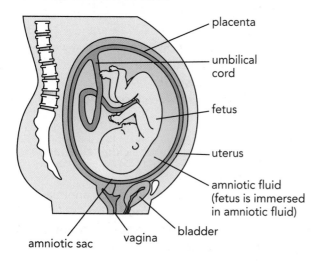

A human fetus develops within the mother's uterus. During development and prior to birth, the fetus is protected by an amniotic sac—a bag in the uterus that is filled with fluid. The amniotic sac keeps the fetus at a steady temperature, protects the fetus against injury, and provides the fetal skin with moisturizing fluids.

Prior to birth, the fetus neither eats through its mouth nor breathes through its lungs. Instead, it receives nourishment and oxygen through the umbilical cord attached to its abdomen. The umbilical cord runs through the amniotic sac to the *placenta*—a special tissue that lines the inner wall of the uterus. Nourishment and oxygen from the mother's blood cross through the placenta into the blood vessels of the fetus. Fetal waste products cross through the placenta to the mother's blood for elimination. The mother and fetus do not directly share blood.

During childbirth, the uterus undergoes a series of contractions that push the fetus out the vaginal canal. After the baby is out, the placenta is expelled. Birth is complete when the baby begins breathing on its own. The umbilical cord is cut, and the placenta is discarded. The scar left at the point of attachment of the umbilical cord to the child is called the navel but is most often referred to as the "belly button."

1. What is the name of the tissue through which fetal blood receives oxygen from the mother's blood?

   (1) navel
   (2) fetus
   (3) uterus
   (4) placenta
   (5) amniotic sac

2. During respiration, human body cells produce carbon dioxide gas as a waste product. This gas is carried to the lungs by blood and expelled during breathing. What most likely happens to the carbon dioxide gas produced by the body cells of a fetus?

   (1) It is expelled through the mother's lungs.
   (2) It remains in the fetus until birth.
   (3) It is absorbed by amniotic fluid.
   (4) It stays in the mother's blood.
   (5) It is reused by the fetus.

3. Drinking alcohol and smoking during pregnancy can harm a developing fetus. What is the most likely reason that this is true?

   (1) Mother and fetus share the same blood.
   (2) The mother's long-term health is at risk.
   (3) These products cost a lot of money.
   (4) Fetal tissue grows rapidly.
   (5) Substances in a mother's blood can enter the blood of the fetus.

Questions 4–8 refer to the following passage.

Cholesterol is a wax-like substance found in human blood. In small quantities, cholesterol is important to good health. The human body uses it to help produce hormones and bile acids that aid in digestion. However, in excess, cholesterol can interfere with proper blood flow and can lead to blood vessel disease and death.

Humans get excess cholesterol buildup in their blood in two ways: by eating an excess of foods that contain cholesterol and by eating an excess of foods that contain saturated fats. Foods that contain cholesterol are fatty animal meats such as beef, pork, and chicken. Foods that contain saturated fats are animal products and plant products high in oil content. Particularly high in saturated fats are coconut oil, palm oil, and chocolate. Cholesterol itself is not found in plant products.

To lower cholesterol level, doctors recommend a diet rich in fruits, vegetables, and grain products. In general, people should reduce the amount of meat and animal by-products such as eggs, cheese, and whole milk in their diets. Fish is a good substitute for red meat—beef, pork, and chicken. Reduced-fat or fat-free milk is a good substitute for whole milk.

Excess cholesterol plays a major role in causing *atherosclerosis*—a clogging of blood arteries. Excess cholesterol settles onto artery walls, leading to a buildup of arterial plaque (a substance made up of cholesterol, fat, protein, and cellular debris). As plaque builds up, blood flow through the arteries becomes restricted. Restricted arteries to the heart can result in a heart attack. Restricted arteries to the brain can lead to a stroke.

4. Which of the following statements is false?

   (1) Grains, fruits, and vegetables do not contain cholesterol.
   (2) Animal products are a main source of cholesterol in the American diet.
   (3) Cholesterol is made by the human body.
   (4) Coconut oil, palm oil, and chocolate contain cholesterol.
   (5) Low levels of cholesterol are important for human health.

5. What is atherosclerosis?

   (1) clogged blood arteries
   (2) an excessive cholesterol level
   (3) saturated fat in the blood
   (4) a heart attack
   (5) blood flow to the heart

6. What can be caused by excess cholesterol in a person's blood?

   (1) muscle spasms
   (2) excessive weight gain
   (3) excessive weight loss
   (4) arterial plaque buildup
   (5) heart enlargement

7. What fact best shows that a link exists between diet and atherosclerosis?

   (1) The first signs of atherosclerosis are seen in children as young as age three.
   (2) Men tend to develop atherosclerosis at a younger age than women.
   (3) People on low-fat diets have a lower than average incidence of atherosclerosis.
   (4) People on high-fat diets have a higher than average incidence of obesity.
   (5) Many vegetarians (nonmeat eaters) also develop atherosclerosis.

Answers are on page 447.

Life Science Writing Activities

The following topics will give you extra practice in thinking and writing about life science.

Directions: Choose one of the topics below and write a well-developed essay (approximately 250 words). You may wish to plan your essay before you write. Pay attention to your organization, development, and control of sentence structure, punctuation, grammar, word choice, and spelling. After you finish writing your essay, reread what you have written and make any changes that will improve your essay.

―――――――――― **TOPIC 1** ――――――――――

Many people carry cards in their wallets that state that in the event of their accidental death, they would be willing to donate organs to people in need of an organ transplant. Would you be willing to be an organ donor?

In your essay state whether you would be willing to be an organ donor. Give specific reasons to back up your opinion.

―――――――――― **TOPIC 2** ――――――――――

Botanists estimate that a considerable number of all species of organisms on Earth face extinction during the next 10 to 30 years. The endangered species include unique plants and animals that could possibly provide new forms of energy or even a cure for cancer. These species may die out because their habitat—the rain forests of Latin America, Africa, and Australia—is being destroyed. Is it important to protect these plants and animals, or would our money and time be better spent on other projects?

In your essay present your views on the protection of endangered species. Give specific reasons to explain your beliefs.

―――――――――― **TOPIC 3** ――――――――――

In order to test new products or develop cures for diseases, scientists often experiment on such animals as rats, monkeys, dogs, and cats. Do you believe that such experiments are fair and necessary?

In your essay state whether you think animal testing is a necessary practice. Give specific reasons to back up your opinion.

PART THREE

Readings in Physical Science

- Chemistry
- Physics

CHAPTER 9

Chemistry

Nature uses only the largest threads to weave her patterns, so each small piece of her fabric reveals the organization of the entire tapestry.

~ Richard Feynman

Have you ever wished that you could take a piece of iron—say, an old nail—and turn it into gold? The idea of turning iron into gold was more than just a fanciful wish to alchemists, the chemists of the Middle Ages (A.D. 500–1600). These early scientists searched for a way to change metal into gold and tried to create a medicine that would keep people from aging. Unfortunately for all of us, the alchemists did not achieve their goals. However, their experiments revealed a great deal about the substances with which they worked.

Modern chemistry has come a long way since the days of alchemy. Today's chemists seek to understand the structure, composition, and properties of all matter. **Matter** is anything that has weight and takes up space. Matter can be a solid such as gold, a liquid such as water, or a gas such as oxygen. All matter, from the smallest atom to the largest planet, is electrical, consisting of positive and negative charges.

By learning about the properties of matter, chemists have been able to improve traditional medical remedies. A well-known example is the development of aspirin. During the seventeenth and eighteenth centuries, Native Americans used the bark of willow trees as a treatment for fever. Later, chemists discovered that the salicylic acid in the bark was the chemical responsible for the pain-relieving effect. Chemists began to produce this acid in their laboratories. The drug proved to be helpful in easing pain, but it had unpleasant side effects, including stomach irritation. Chemists were able to reduce this irritation by adding another element to salicylic acid. The resulting drug, acetylsalicylic acid, is what we know today as aspirin.

In addition to improving traditional remedies, chemists are also developing new products at an ever-increasing rate. In fact, more than 90 percent of all the medicinal drugs now being used were not available in any form before World War II.

Chemists also have been able to create materials not found in nature. One example is plastic. Plastic has proven to be one of the most durable, inexpensive, and versatile materials known. Milk jugs, telephones, automobile parts, and clothes are just some of the products that can now be made of plastic. Yet, only a few decades ago, plastic was mainly a novelty material used to make children's toys.

Our study of chemistry in this chapter will involve four major topics:

- The structure of matter
- The chemistry of life
- The behavior of matter
- Chemical reactions

The Structure of Matter

The Atomic Theory of Matter

Long before scientists were able to prove it, ancient Greek philosophers had an idea of what an atom was. They believed that any substance could be divided only so far before the smallest possible piece of that substance was reached. Democritus (460–370 B.C.) called this smallest particle the **atom**, from the Greek word *atoma,* meaning "indivisible." He believed that atoms were indestructible and moved about in empty space. Democritus thought that atoms were made of the same matter but differed in shape, size, weight, and arrangement. Differences in substances were accounted for by the arrangements of atoms in space, not in differences among atoms.

Democritus is often thought of as the founder of the atomic theory of the universe. Our current understanding of atoms has many similarities with the ideas of Democritus. Today we know that all matter is formed from one or more of ninety-two naturally occurring chemical elements. Each **element**, such as gold, is a pure substance that is composed of identical atoms. Elements are the building blocks of matter. They combine to form all known substances in the same way that letters of the alphabet combine to form words.

Surprisingly, most of the natural elements are rare. In fact, only eleven elements make up more than 99 percent of all matter on Earth. You may already know some of the most common elements—the gases oxygen, hydrogen, and nitrogen, and the metals aluminum, iron, and nickel.

If a gold coin is divided into the smallest unit that still has the properties of gold, that unit is a single atom of gold. That atom, like the atoms of all other elements, is made up of three types of particles—protons, neutrons, and electrons. The protons and neutrons are located in a central **nucleus**, the core of the atom. The electrons are in orbits around the nucleus.

- **Protons** are particles that have a positive electric charge.

- **Neutrons** have no electric charge. They are electrically neutral.

- **Electrons** are particles that have a negative electric charge.

Electric force holds electrons in orbit around a nucleus. The negatively charged electrons are attracted to the positively charged protons. Unless disturbed by an outside force, each orbiting electron is in a stable orbit, determined by its own energy of motion and the energy associated with the electric force.

Nuclear particles (neutrons and protons) are held together in a nucleus by **nuclear force**. Nuclear force is much, much stronger than electric force. However, nuclear force acts only over very short nuclear distances. The weaker electric force acts over much longer atomic distances.

Protons and neutrons are almost exactly the same size. Each is more than 1,800 times as massive as an electron. Because of this size difference, almost all the **mass** (amount of matter) of an atom is concentrated in the nucleus.

In their natural state, all atoms are electrically neutral. This means that, in the natural state, atoms have the same number of electrons as protons. Although the exact orbital path of an electron is not known, it is often illustrated as shown in the diagram of a helium atom below.

THE HELIUM ATOM

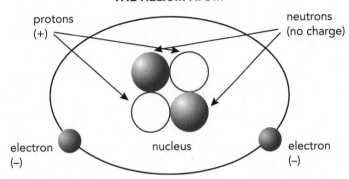

Electric force attracts electrons (-) to protons (+). Nuclear force holds nuclear particles (neutrons and protons) together.

 Thinking About Science

Directions: Answer each question below.

1. Complete each sentence by filling in the blank(s) with the correct word from the reading passage.

   a. Oxygen and iron are examples of _____.

   b. The three particles that are found in atoms are

      _____, _____ and

      _____.

   c. The _____ is the central core of an atom.

2. The statements below refer to the atomic theory of matter. Circle *T* for each statement that is true and *F* for each statement that is false.

   T F a. Almost the entire mass of an atom comes from its electrons and protons.

   T F b. Electrons, protons, and neutrons are found in an atom's nucleus.

   T F c. Electrons are the only negatively charged particles found in an atom.

Answers are on page 448.

Directions: Choose the <u>one best answer</u> to each question.

Questions 1 and 2 refer to Table I.

TABLE I

ELEMENTAL COMPOSITION OF THE HUMAN BODY

Element	Weight (nearest percent)
Oxygen	65
Carbon	18
Hydrogen	10
Nitrogen	3
Calcium	2
Phosphorus	1
Traces of others	1

1. Which two elements together make up about 5 percent of the human body?

   (1) hydrogen and phosphorus
   (2) calcium and phosphorus
   (3) carbon and hydrogen
   (4) nitrogen and calcium
   (5) oxygen and nitrogen

2. Water is made from combining hydrogen and oxygen atoms. About what percent of the human body can you conclude is made up of water?

   (1) 28%
   (2) 55%
   (3) 65%
   (4) 75%
   (5) 83%

Question 3 refers to Table II; question 4 refers to Tables I and II.

TABLE II

ELEMENTAL COMPOSITION OF EARTH'S CRUST, SEAWATER, AND ATMOSPHERE

Element	Weight (nearest percent)
Oxygen	49
Silicon	26
Aluminum	8
Iron	5
Calcium	3
Sodium	3
Potassium	2
Magnesium	2
Hydrogen	1
Traces of others	1

3. What is the third most abundant element by weight on Earth's surface?

   (1) sodium
   (2) aluminum
   (3) silicon
   (4) oxygen
   (5) hydrogen

4. Which conclusion below can be correctly drawn from the data shown in the two tables?

   (1) Although sodium is present on Earth, the human body contains no sodium at all.
   (2) The largest single source of oxygen on or near Earth is the atmosphere.
   (3) Iron is very important in a healthful diet.
   (4) Carbon is an element that is found in all forms of life that exist on Earth.
   (5) Although carbon is the second most abundant element in our bodies, the Earth's surface contains little carbon.

Answers are on page 448.

The Periodic Table

Do you ever wonder what makes one element different from another? Why, for example, is helium different from gold? Helium is a colorless, odorless gas used to fill balloons. Why is helium lighter than air and gold heavier than water? Gold is a shiny, yellow metal used in jewelry and in dentistry. Gold is also the basis of much of the world's money. Who hasn't seen a movie about the California gold rush of the mid-1800s? Can you imagine anyone getting excited about a "helium rush"?

Gold differs from helium because the atomic structure of gold differs from the atomic structure of helium. A gold atom has more electrons, protons, and neutrons than a helium atom has.

Every element has a unique atomic structure. No two elements have exactly the same combination of protons, neutrons, and electrons. Each element has its own atomic mass and atomic number.

- The **atomic mass** is the sum of the protons and neutrons in the nucleus. The atomic mass of aluminum is 27—aluminum has 13 protons and 14 neutrons.

- The **atomic number** is the number of protons in an atom. A neutral atom has an equal number of protons and electrons. The atomic number of aluminum is 13. A neutral aluminum atom has 13 protons in the nucleus and 13 orbiting electrons.

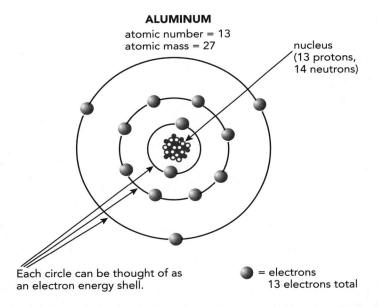

ALUMINUM
atomic number = 13
atomic mass = 27

nucleus
(13 protons,
14 neutrons)

Each circle can be thought of as an electron energy shell.

= electrons
13 electrons total

In each atom, electrons orbit in energy levels called **energy shells**. Each shell can hold only a certain number of electrons. Atoms with larger atomic numbers have electrons in several energy shells. In the diagram of the aluminum atom above, each circle represents a particular energy shell. The two electrons in the circle closest to the nucleus are in the lowest energy shell. The next higher energy shell contains eight electrons. The outer (highest) energy shell of aluminum contains only three electrons.

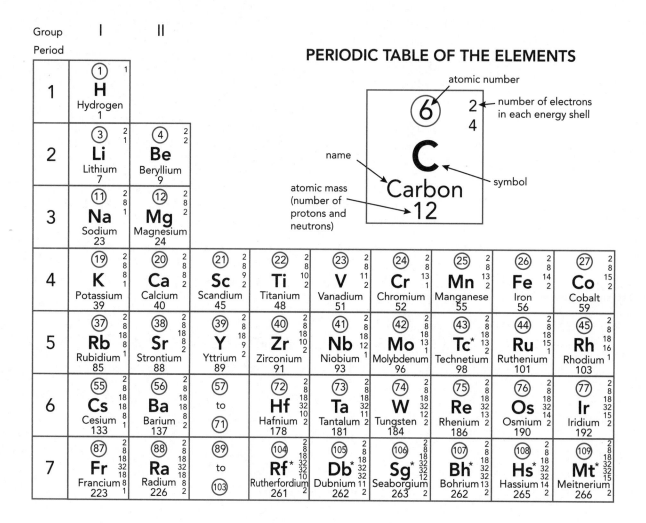

PERIODIC TABLE OF THE ELEMENTS

Group I II

Period

Rare Earth Elements

Periodic table (partial), showing groups III–VIII.

	III	IV	V	VI	VII	VIII
						(2) He — Helium — 2 — 4
	(5) B — Boron — 2,3 — 11	(6) C — Carbon — 2,4 — 12	(7) N — Nitrogen — 2,5 — 14	(8) O — Oxygen — 2,6 — 16	(9) F — Fluorine — 2,7 — 19	(10) Ne — Neon — 2,8 — 20
	(13) Al — Aluminum — 2,8,3 — 27	(14) Si — Silicon — 2,8,4 — 28	(15) P — Phosphorus — 2,8,5 — 31	(16) S — Sulfur — 2,8,6 — 32	(17) Cl — Chlorine — 2,8,7 — 35	(18) Ar — Argon — 2,8,8 — 40

(28) Ni — Nickel — 2,8,16,2 — 59	(29) Cu — Copper — 2,8,18,1 — 64	(30) Zn — Zinc — 2,8,18,2 — 65	(31) Ga — Gallium — 2,8,18,3 — 70	(32) Ge — Germanium — 2,8,18,4 — 73	(33) As — Arsenic — 2,8,18,5 — 75	(34) Se — Selenium — 2,8,18,6 — 79	(35) Br — Bromine — 2,8,18,7 — 80	(36) Kr — Krypton — 2,8,18,8 — 84
(46) Pd — Palladium — 2,8,18,18,0 — 106	(47) Ag — Silver — 2,8,18,18,1 — 108	(48) Cd — Cadmium — 2,8,18,18,2 — 112	(49) In — Indium — 2,8,18,18,3 — 115	(50) Sn — Tin — 2,8,18,18,4 — 119	(51) Sb — Antimony — 2,8,18,18,5 — 122	(52) Te — Tellurium — 2,8,18,18,6 — 128	(53) I — Iodine — 2,8,18,18,7 — 127	(54) Xe — Xenon — 2,8,18,18,8 — 131
(78) Pt — Platinum — 2,8,18,32,17,1 — 195	(79) Au — Gold — 2,8,18,32,18,1 — 197	(80) Hg — Mercury — 2,8,18,32,18,2 — 201	(81) Tl — Thallium — 2,8,18,32,18,3 — 204	(82) Pb — Lead — 2,8,18,32,18,4 — 207	(83) Bi — Bismuth — 2,8,18,32,18,5 — 209	(84) Po — Polonium — 2,8,18,32,18,6 — 209	(85) At — Astatine — 2,8,18,32,18,7 — 210	(86) Rn — Radon — 2,8,18,32,18,8 — 222
(110) Uun* — Ununnilium — 2,8,18,32,17,1 — 269	(111) Uuu* — Unununium — 2,8,18,32,18,1 — 272	(112) Uub* — Ununbium — 2,8,18,32,18,2 — 277						

* = Manmade

| (63) Eu — Europium — 2,8,18,25,8,2 — 152 | (64) Gd — Gadolinium — 2,8,18,25,9,2 — 157 | (65) Tb — Terbium — 2,8,18,27,8,2 — 159 | (66) Dy — Dysprosium — 2,8,18,28,8,2 — 163 | (67) Ho — Holmium — 2,8,18,29,8,2 — 165 | (68) Er — Erbium — 2,8,18,30,8,2 — 167 | (69) Tm — Thulium — 2,8,18,31,8,2 — 169 | (70) Yb — Ytterbium — 2,8,18,32,8,2 — 173 | (71) Lu — Lutetium — 2,8,18,32,9,2 — 175 |
| (95) Am* — Americium — 2,8,18,32,25,8,2 — 243 | (96) Cm* — Curium — 2,8,18,32,25,9,2 — 247 | (97) Bk* — Berkelium — 2,8,18,32,26,9,2 — 247 | (98) Cf* — Californium — 2,8,18,32,28,8,2 — 251 | (99) Es* — Einsteinium — 2,8,18,32,29,8,2 — 252 | (100) Fm* — Fermium — 2,8,18,32,30,8,2 — 257 | (101) Md* — Mendelevium — 2,8,18,32,31,8,2 — 258 | (102) No* — Nobelium — 2,8,18,32,32,8,2 — 259 | (103) Lr* — Lawrencium — 2,8,18,32,32,9,2 — 260 |

Reading the Periodic Table

The periodic table, shown on pages 262 and 263, identifies all the known elements. The elements are listed in order of atomic number (the number of protons in a neutral atom).

Differing shell structure is the basis of the rows and columns of the periodic table.

- Each row is read from left to right and is called a **period**. A period contains elements that have the same number of energy shells that are at least partially filled with electrons.

- Each column is read from top to bottom and is called a **group**. Each of the eight principal groups (indicated by Roman numerals at the top of the table) lists elements that have the same number of electrons in their outermost energy shell. Elements in the same group tend to have similar physical and chemical characteristics.

principal group
(same number of electrons in outermost shells)

period
(same number of electron shells)

Period		
2	③ 2,1 **Li** Lithium 7	④ 2,2 **Be** Beryllium 9
3	⑪ 2,8,1 **Na** Sodium 23	⑫ 2,8,2 **Mg** Magnesium 24
4	⑲ 2,8,8,1 **K** Potassium 39	⑳ 2,8,8,2 **Ca** Calcium 40	㉑ 2,8,9,2 **Sc** Scandium 45
5	㊲ 2,8,18,8,1 **Rb** Rubidium 85	㊳ 2,8,18,8,2 **Sr** Strontium 88	㊴ 2,8,18,9,2 **Y** Yttrium 89

Reading from left to right, elements are listed in order of atomic number. Each element in the table is shown with its name, symbol, atomic number, and atomic mass.

 **Thinking About Science**

Directions: Answer each question below.

1. Complete each sentence by filling in the blank(s) with the correct word(s) from the reading passage.

   a. The number of protons in an atom is known as that atom's

   _____ .

   b. Atomic mass is the sum of the number of an atom's

   _____ and _____ .

2. Sodium (atomic number 11) has an atomic mass of 23.

   a. How many protons does a sodium atom have in its nucleus?

   _____

   b. How many neutrons does a sodium atom have in its nucleus?

   _____

   c. How many electrons does a neutral sodium atom have?

   _____

   Answers are on page 448.

GED PRACTICE

Directions: Choose the <u>one best answer</u> to each question.

Questions 1 and 2 refer to the information on pages 261–264.

1. Calcium (Ca, atomic number 20) has two electrons in its outermost electron energy shell. Which element also has two electrons in its outermost shell? [Hint: Identify the elements in the same <u>group</u> as calcium.]

   (1) potassium (K)
   (2) carbon (C)
   (3) magnesium (Mg)
   (4) helium (He)
   (5) scandium (SC)

2. Which element has the same number of energy shells as oxygen (O, atomic number 8)? [Hint: Identify the elements in the same <u>period</u> as oxygen.]

   (1) sulfur (S)
   (2) lithium (Li)
   (3) phosphorus (P)
   (4) selenium (Se)
   (5) helium (He)

Questions 3 and 4 refer to the following passage and diagram.

An *isotope* of an element is a form of the element that has the same atomic number as other forms but differs by atomic mass. The periodic table lists the most common isotope of each element. Shown below are the three isotopes of hydrogen, the most common isotope being protium—commonly just called hydrogen.

ISOTOPES OF HYDROGEN

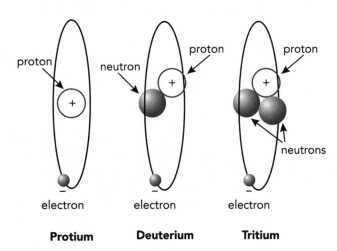

3. In what way do an element's isotopes differ from one another?

    (1) number of neutrons
    (2) number of protons
    (3) number of electrons
    (4) total positive charge
    (5) total negative charge

4. How does the mass of a tritium atom compare to the mass of a protium atom?

    (1) about one-third as much
    (2) about one-half as much
    (3) nearly equal
    (4) about two times as much
    (5) about three times as much

Questions 5 and 6 refer to the following passage.

One of the most amazing discoveries of the twentieth century was *antimatter*. Antimatter is composed of elementary particles that are a type of mirror image of particles normally found on Earth. *Antiparticles* have the same mass as regular particles but have opposite charges and other properties. The atomic antiparticles are the *positron* (antielectron), the *antineutron*, and the *antiproton*.

When a particle and an antiparticle collide, they destroy each other and produce a burst of gamma-ray energy (high-energy light waves). The meeting of groups of particles and antiparticles would result in all the particles disappearing in a flash of high-energy light.

Luckily, antiparticles do not exist on Earth, unless created during an experiment. When created, they exist for only a small fraction of a second before colliding with particles and disappearing. Most scientists believe that the universe contains mainly particles, and very few antiparticles. Why this is the case is a mystery that may be solved during the twenty-first century.

5. Which of the following is a property of an antiproton?

    (1) positive charge
    (2) negative charge
    (3) same mass as an electron
    (4) abundant on Earth
    (5) twice the mass of a proton

6. How is the collision of a particle and an antiparticle most likely detected in an experiment?

    (1) as a vibration
    (2) as a loud sound
    (3) as a group of electrons
    (4) as a burst of gamma rays
    (5) as newly formed particles

Answers are on page 448.

Elements in Combination

Look around you and notice the variety of things in your everyday life. You might see chairs, tables, curtains, windows, water, people, and much, much more. It's hard to believe that this incredible variety is made up almost entirely of combinations of eleven elements.

When two or more atoms combine, a **molecule** is formed.

- A molecule of water is made up of one atom of oxygen and two atoms of hydrogen.

- A molecule of salt is made up of one atom of sodium and one atom of chlorine.

When the atoms of two different elements combine, a completely new substance is formed. Each newly created substance, water or salt, is called a **compound**. A compound is made up of molecules that each contain the atoms of two or more elements.

Chemical Formulas

A **chemical formula** is a shorthand way of showing which elements are contained in a molecule. Symbols identify the elements, and small numbers (subscripts) tell the number of each type of atom.

- H_2O is the chemical formula for water. The subscript 2 indicates that there are two atoms of hydrogen (H) in one molecule of water. The symbol O, written without a subscript, indicates that one atom of oxygen (O) is in each molecule of water.

- C_3H_8 is the formula for propane gas. Each molecule of propane contains three atoms of carbon (C) and eight atoms of hydrogen (H).

A number written in front of a formula indicates that more than one molecule is represented.

- The formula $4H_2O$ represents four molecules of water. Notice that four molecules of water contain eight atoms of hydrogen ($4 \times 2 = 8$) and four atoms of oxygen ($4 \times 1 = 4$).

- The formula $6CaCO_3$ represents six molecules of $CaCO_3$, known as calcium carbonate. Each $CaCO_3$ molecule contains one atom of calcium (Ca), one atom of carbon (C), and three atoms of oxygen (O). The formula $6CaCO_3$ represents a total of six atoms of calcium, six atoms of carbon, and eighteen atoms of oxygen ($6 \times 3 = 18$).

Thinking About Science

Directions: Answer each question below.

1. In the formula Al_2O_3, how many atoms of aluminum are represented?

   _____

2. In the formula $5C_3H_8$, how many molecules of propane are represented? _____

3. In the formula $3H_2O$, how many atoms of hydrogen are represented?

   _____

Answers are on page 448.

GED PRACTICE

Directions: Choose the <u>one best answer</u> to each question.

Questions 1 and 2 refer to the information on page 267.

1. One molecule of the iron oxide commonly called *rust* contains two atoms of iron (Fe) and three atoms of oxygen (O). Which of the following is the correct formula for two molecules of rust?

   (1) $Fe_2O_3 2$
   (2) $2Fe_3O_2$
   (3) Fe_4O_6
   (4) $2Fe_2 2O_3$
   (5) $2Fe_2O_3$

2. How many total atoms are contained in six molecules of water ($6H_2O$)?

   (1) 10
   (2) 12
   (3) 16
   (4) 18
   (5) 20

3. Glucose is a sugar that is made by green plant cells. According to its chemical formula ($C_6H_{12}O_6$), which elements make up one molecule of glucose?

   (1) 6 atoms of hydrogen and 12 atoms of oxygen
   (2) 6 atoms of carbon, 12 atoms of hydrogen, and 6 atoms of oxygen
   (3) 6 atoms of carbon, 12 atoms of oxygen, and 6 atoms of hydrogen
   (4) 1 atom of carbon, 6 atoms of hydrogen, and 12 atoms of oxygen
   (5) 6 atoms of carbon, 12 atoms of helium, and 6 atoms of oxygen

Answers are on page 448.

Chemical Bonding

The combining of atoms occurs through a process called **chemical bonding**. Chemical bonding results from one of two processes:

- The transfer of one or more electrons from one atom to another

- The sharing of electrons by two or more atoms

Ionic Bonds

An **ionic bond** is formed when an electron in the outermost energy shell of one atom transfers to the outermost shell of a second atom to form a compound. Ordinary table salt, sodium chloride, is a compound formed by the ionic bonding of sodium atoms to chlorine atoms. As illustrated below, a sodium atom has one electron in its outer shell, while a chlorine atom has seven electrons in its outer shell. The smaller inner circle represents the nucleus of each atom. The outer circle represents the outer electron energy shell.

SODIUM AND CHLORINE ATOMS
(Only the electrons in the outermost energy shells are shown.)

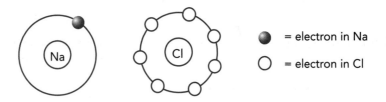

● = electron in Na

○ = electron in Cl

When the two atoms combine, the outer electron of the sodium atom transfers to the chlorine atom. After the transfer neither atom is electrically neutral any longer. Each is an **ion**, an atom that has either lost or gained an electron.

SODIUM CHLORIDE

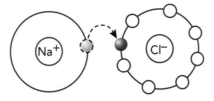

The Na electron has transferred over to the Cl atom.

Having lost an electron, the sodium atom now has a positive charge. The chlorine atom has gained an electron and now has a negative charge. The ionic bond, the electric force between ions, holds the positive sodium ion close to the negative chlorine ion.

Covalent Bonds

In a **covalent bond**, electrons are not transferred from one atom to another. Instead, electrons are shared by the bonded atoms of a molecule. Covalent bonds can occur between different types of atoms or between the same types of atoms. The most common form of oxygen, for example, is O_2, formed by the covalent bonding of two oxygen atoms.

A molecule of water is formed by the covalent bonding of two hydrogen atoms to one oxygen atom. An oxygen atom has six electrons in its outermost shell. A hydrogen atom has one. When a water molecule forms, each hydrogen atom shares its electron with the oxygen atom. At the same time, the oxygen atom shares one of its electrons with each hydrogen atom. Altogether, four electrons are shared in a water molecule, two in each covalent bond.

SEPARATED HYDROGEN AND OXYGEN ATOMS

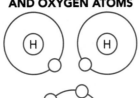
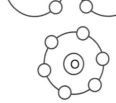

WATER MOLECULE

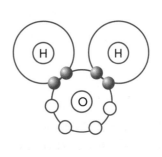

= electrons shared by hydrogen and oxygen atoms

Thinking About Science

Directions: Match each item on the left with the best description on the right. Write the letter of the phrase on the line before the correct number.

_____ **1.** chemical bonding

(a) an atom that has either a positive or negative charge

_____ **2.** water

(b) a compound formed by ionic bonding

_____ **3.** ion

(c) the chemical combining of two or more atoms

_____ **4.** sodium chloride

(d) a compound formed by covalent bonding

Answers are on page 448.

Directions: Choose the <u>one best answer</u> to each question.

Questions 1 and 2 refer to the following passage.

A special type of covalent bond, called a metallic bond, occurs in metals such as gold, silver, copper, and iron. In a metallic bond, the electrons in outer energy shells are loosely bound and are shared among all the atoms. These shared electrons are able to move easily through the whole solid. The atomic nuclei form a rigid lattice of positive charges through which the electrons move.

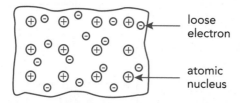

Silver

The "looseness" of shared electrons enables metals to easily conduct electricity and to be good conductors of heat energy.

1. How does a metallic bond differ from an ordinary covalent bond?

   (1) Metallic atoms do not have electrons.
   (2) Electrons in metals are not shared.
   (3) Electrons in metals are shared among many atoms.
   (4) Only one electron is shared for each atom in a metal.
   (5) Electrons in a metal are shared between two atoms only.

2. What makes one metal a better conductor of electricity than another?

   (1) ease in which electrons can move
   (2) spacing of atomic nuclei
   (3) weight of atomic nuclei
   (4) average distance between atomic nuclei
   (5) number of electrons in each atom

Questions 3–5 refer to the following passage.

Two different elements may combine in more than one way and form compounds with very different properties. For example, the elements carbon and oxygen can combine to form carbon monoxide or carbon dioxide.

Carbon monoxide (CO) is an odorless gas given off whenever fuel, such as gas, oil, wood, or kerosene, is burned. Breathing concentrated carbon monoxide can quickly lead to unconsciousness and death. Many people have died accidentally from carbon monoxide poisoning caused by faulty heating systems and by idling cars.

Carbon dioxide gas (CO_2), on the other hand, is very much a part of the life process. CO_2 is given off when people breathe. CO_2 is used by plants during photosynthesis.

3. Which of the following may result from breathing carbon monoxide?

   (1) blistered skin
   (2) unconsciousness
   (3) photosynthesis
   (4) bad breath
   (5) increased heart rate

4. What is the most important safety consideration in the design of an automobile repair shop?

   (1) a separate lunch room
   (2) a centrally located telephone
   (3) comfortable work benches
   (4) good ventilation
   (5) storage areas for repair manuals

5. Runners often complain of feeling lightheaded or dizzy while running near busy city streets. What gas may be present near busy streets that could explain this complaint?

   (1) carbon dioxide
   (2) oxygen
   (3) carbon monoxide
   (4) water vapor
   (5) very dry air

Answers are on page 448.

The Chemistry of Life

Properties of Carbon

On the morning of July 20, 1976, the *Viking I* lander slowly drifted, with parachutes open, down to the dusty, red surface of the plain of Chryse. *Viking I* began a search of Martian soil for signs of life. *Viking I* was soon aided by *Viking II*, which touched down on the Martian plain of Utopia on September 3. Disappointingly, neither craft found any evidence of organic molecules, the fingerprints of life, on the windy Martian surface. A visit by the more complex *Pathfinder* spacecraft on July 4, 1997, also failed in this quest. The disappointment continued with the loss of the *Surveyor 98* climate orbiter on September 23, 1999, and of its sister polar lander on December 3, 1999. Still, NASA's Mars Exploration Program has continued into the new millennium with several proposed voyages over the next decade. The hope of finding signs of life on Mars remains strong, but it may have to await the landing of astronauts during the decades ahead.

Organic, from the word *organism,* refers to compounds produced by living things. All organic compounds contain the element carbon. Organic molecules form easily in environments that are rich in carbon and water. Scientists know that water is present in the polar ice caps of Mars. They also know that the Martian atmosphere consists mostly of carbon dioxide gas. The presence of water and carbon dioxide on Mars gives rise to the possibility of organic molecules.

Carbon is now thought to be so important to the life process that chemists have named the study of carbon **organic chemistry**. Organic chemistry is often called the "chemistry of life." Several properties of carbon make it such an important element.

Carbon atoms can form covalent bonds with four other atoms at the same time. One or more of the other atoms can be another carbon atom. By linking with one another, carbon atoms can form closed rings, long chains, or branching networks. Each carbon atom in line can then combine with atoms of other elements. In this way, very large organic molecules can form. Below is an example of a carbon chain molecule and a carbon ring molecule.

ORGANIC MOLECULES

Butane

Benzene

carbon chain

carbon ring

Thinking About Science

Directions: Answer each question below.

1. a. What two substances present on Mars gave scientists hope that there might be life on Mars? _____ and

    _____

    b. What element do all organic compounds contain?

    _____

2. What is the proper name for that branch of chemistry that is often referred to as the "chemistry of life"? _____

Answers are on page 448.

GED PRACTICE

Directions: Choose the one best answer to each question.

Questions 1 and 2 refer to the following passage and diagrams.

Because of the ease with which carbon atoms can bond to one another, carbon molecules can take a variety of different shapes. Some carbon molecules, called isomers, have the same number of carbon atoms but different molecular structures—different arrangements of atoms. Isomers often differ in their physical, chemical, and biological properties.

An example of isomers is normal butane (written as *n*-butane) and isobutane.

1. Which of the following properties differs between an *n*-butane and an isobutane molecule?

    (1) number of carbon atoms
    (2) number of hydrogen atoms
    (3) total number of atoms
    (4) shape of molecule
    (5) weight of molecule

```
        H   H   H   H
        |   |   |   |
   H —  C — C — C — C — H
        |   |   |   |
        H   H   H   H
```
n–Butane

```
        H   H   H
        |   |   |
   H —  C — C — C — H
        |   |   |
        H   |   H
            |
       H —  C — H
            |
            H
```
Isobutane

2. In an isobutane molecule, how many carbon atoms does the middle atom in the longest carbon chain bond with?

    (1) 0
    (2) 1
    (3) 2
    (4) 3
    (5) 4

Answers are on page 448.

Hydrocarbons

Carbon atoms link so easily that there is almost no limit to the number of different molecules that may be possible. At present, more than 3 million carbon compounds are known. Most of these are **hydrocarbons**, compounds composed of only carbon and hydrogen.

The main hydrocarbons found in nature are coal, natural gas, and petroleum (oil). You may be familiar with natural gas fuels—methane (CH_4) and propane (C_3H_8). Distillation of petroleum creates fuels such as kerosene ($C_{12}H_{26}$) and gasoline, a mixture of hydrocarbons. From petroleum we also get hydrocarbon compounds that are used to make perfumes, pesticides, medicines, and many other consumer products.

Methane

Propane

Kerosene

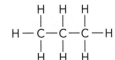
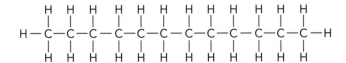

The word **polymer** refers to any long-chain hydrocarbon—a hydrocarbon containing a large number of carbon atoms. Most modern-day synthetic polymers have been made within the last sixty years. An example is polyethylene, a type of plastic. Polyethylene contains between 2,500 and 25,000 carbon atoms in each molecule. Polyethylene and other synthetic polymers are used to produce textiles, shoes, toys, plastics, construction materials, medical supplies, cooking utensils, recreational equipment, synthetic rubber, and synthetic leather.

Thinking About Science

Directions: Answer each question below.

1. Briefly define each of the following words.

   a. hydrocarbon: _____

   b. polymer: _____

2. Write a rule that tells how the number of hydrogen atoms is related to the number of carbon atoms in a polymer. _____

   _____

Answers are on page 448.

GED PRACTICE

Directions: Choose the <u>one best answer</u> to each question.

Questions 1 and 2 refer to the information on page 274.

1. Which one of the following is <u>not</u> a common property of the fuels methane, propane, and kerosene?

    (1) Each fuel contains only carbon and hydrogen atoms.
    (2) Each fuel has carbon atoms that link together with more than one hydrogen atom.
    (3) Each fuel is a polymer.
    (4) Each fuel has more hydrogen atoms than carbon atoms.
    (5) Each fuel is a hydrocarbon.

2. Propane and kerosene are examples of *alkane polymers*. Based on the diagram on page 274, how many hydrogen atoms would you expect to find in an alkane polymer with 20 carbon atoms?

    (1) 22
    (2) 24
    (3) 38
    (4) 40
    (5) 42

PERCENT BREAKDOWN OF PETROLEUM USE IN THE UNITED STATES

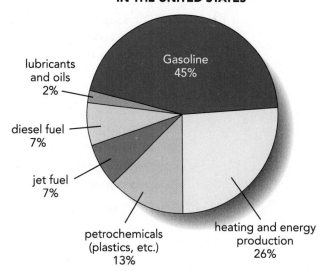

Questions 3 and 4 refer to the graph above.

3. What is the main petroleum product used in the United States?

    (1) petrochemicals
    (2) diesel fuel
    (3) heating and energy production
    (4) gasoline
    (5) jet fuel

4. What total percent of petroleum is used for the production of transportation fuels?

    (1) 7 percent
    (2) 14 percent
    (3) 59 percent
    (4) 72 percent
    (5) 98 percent

Answers are on page 449.

Go to **www.GEDScience.com** for additional practice and instruction!

Behavior of Matter

Phases of Matter

A chemical formula tells us a great deal about a substance, but not everything. For example, the formula H_2O stands for a water molecule. But what form of water—ice, liquid, or steam? If you say, "All three," you are right! The formula H_2O identifies a water molecule that may be in any of its three forms—solid water (ice), liquid water, or water vapor (steam).

The three forms of a substance—solid, liquid, and gas—are called the three **phases of matter**. Each phase of a substance is determined by the distance and angles between the molecules and atoms along with the energy that binds them together. To understand the properties of each phase, you need only think about everyday objects.

- **Solids:** Pick up a piece of wood or a metal spoon. Though these two objects don't look alike, they do share the two properties of all solids—definite size and definite shape. Place a spoon and a piece of wood in a dish, and neither will change in size or shape. This is because the molecular structure of a solid is nearly rigid.

- **Liquids:** Pour a glass of water into a dish. The water quickly takes the shape of the dish. Also, the volume of water in the dish is equal to the volume of water that was in the glass. Water has the property of every liquid—definite volume but not definite shape. A liquid takes the shape of the container that holds it. This is because the atoms and molecules in its structure move around each other without moving apart.

- **Gases:** Add air to a soft soccer ball. The ball does not change shape. The entering air takes the shape of the ball and crowds in as necessary. Air has the property of all gases: neither definite shape nor definite volume. A gas will spread out or contract as needed to fill any container that encloses it. This is because its molecular structure is relatively loose, allowing atoms to move apart independently of each other.

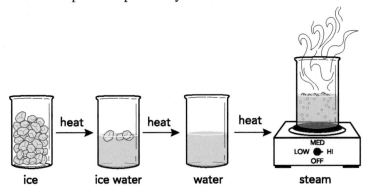

The three phases of water: ice, liquid, and steam.

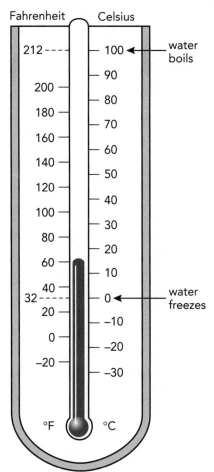

Fahrenheit — Celsius

212 — 100 ← water boils
200 — 90
180 — 80
160 — 70
140 — 60
120 — 50
100 — 40
80 — 30
60 — 20
40 — 10
32 — 0 ← water freezes
20 —
0 — −10
−20 — −20
— −30

°F   °C

Changing from One Phase to Another

All substances change from one phase to another when their temperature is raised or lowered to certain points. The temperature affects the rate at which a substance's molecules move—the greater the temperature, the greater the motion, and vice versa.

- **Melting:** If the temperature of ice (a solid) is raised to its melting-point temperature, the molecules begin to move around each other causing the ice to turn into liquid water. With enough heat, even solid iron can be liquefied.

- **Boiling:** In a similar way, a liquid can be changed to a gas. If the temperature of water is raised to its boiling point, the molecules move even faster and farther apart. The water becomes steam, or vapor—the gaseous phase of a substance that is normally a liquid.

- **Condensing:** A gas becomes liquid when its temperature is lowered to its condensation point. This causes the molecules to condense, or move closer together. Steam from a shower condenses and forms water droplets on cool mirrors and water pipes.

- **Freezing:** When the temperature of a liquid drops to its freezing point, the molecules move so close together that they can barely move. Liquid water placed in a freezer turns to solid ice.

Because the freezing and melting points of water appear so often in science, it is useful to remember these values for water at sea level:

- The freezing point of water (melting point of ice) is 32°F (Fahrenheit), which is 0°C (Celsius).

- The boiling point of water (condensation point of steam) is 212°F, which is 100°C.

Thinking About Science

Directions: Complete each sentence below by filling in the blank(s) with the correct word(s) from the reading selection.

1. The temperature at which a liquid turns into a gas is called the liquid's

   _____.

2. The temperature at which a liquid turns into a solid is called the

   liquid's _____.

3. The freezing point of water is _____ °F or _____ °C.

4. The boiling point of water is _____ °F or _____ °C.

Answers are on page 449.

Directions: Choose the <u>one best answer</u> to each question.

Questions 1–4 refer to the following passage and graph.

Antifreeze is added to a car's cooling system to protect the engine from the effects of very cold weather. Without antifreeze, a car's cooling system would contain only water. The water would freeze solid when the air temperature dropped below 32°F, the freezing point of water, if the car were not running. Frozen coolant can crack the block of an engine.

Mixing antifreeze with the radiator water lowers the freezing temperature of the coolant to below 32°F. With the proper amount of antifreeze, you can reduce the coolant freezing temperature to well below any temperature the outside air may reach.

FREEZING POINT TEMPERATURE OF COOLANT WITH ANTIFREEZE

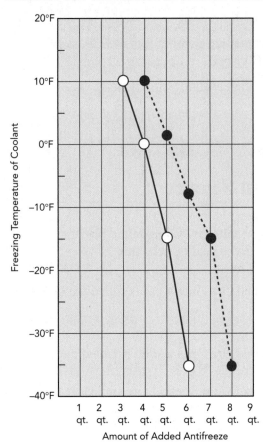

Amount of Added Antifreeze

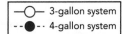
—○— 3-gallon system
--●-- 4-gallon system

1. For a car with a 3-gallon cooling system, about how many quarts of antifreeze are needed to protect the engine down to a temperature of −15°F?

   (1) three
   (2) four
   (3) five
   (4) six
   (5) seven

2. Assume you have a car with a 4-gallon cooling system that is now protected to about 0°F. How many more quarts of antifreeze should you buy to add enough to lower the protection temperature to −15°F?

   (1) one
   (2) two
   (3) three
   (4) four
   (5) five

3. For which range of temperature does the graph not provide information?

   (1) between 10°F and −35°F
   (2) below 10°F
   (3) above −35°F
   (4) above −10°F and below 10°F
   (5) above 10°F and below −35°F

4. What is a reasonable conclusion you can draw from the graph?

   (1) A large cooling system requires more antifreeze than a smaller system.
   (2) A large cooling system requires less antifreeze than a smaller system.
   (3) A large cooling system requires the same amount of antifreeze as a smaller system.
   (4) A large cooling system requires no antifreeze.
   (5) A small cooling system requires no antifreeze.

Answers are on page 449.

Physical and Chemical Changes

In nature, change continually takes place. Some changes are hardly noticeable, such as water evaporating from a lake. Some changes are welcome, such as a baby getting older. Some changes are not welcome, such as a car rusting. But change, welcome or not, is a daily part of our lives.

Changes are classified as physical or chemical:

- A **physical change** does not produce a new substance (example: melting ice cream).

- A **chemical change** produces a new substance (example: burning wood).

When ice cream melts, it changes from a solid to a liquid. The ice cream changes, but it is still ice cream. We know it by its color and taste, even though it may not be as cold as we'd like. Put back in the freezer, the ice cream returns to its more solid texture.

During a physical change, a substance may change shape, size, color, and state. The substance may look different, but it is the same substance. Melting, boiling, freezing, condensing, and cutting are all physical changes.

On the other hand, when wood burns, it is no longer wood. The wood has changed to ashes, carbon dioxide gas, and water. No simple act, such as placing the ashes in the freezer, can change the ashes back to wood.

During a chemical change, a substance breaks down or combines with other substances and becomes a new substance. This new substance has different qualities from those of the original substance. Other chemical changes are milk souring, iron rusting, and grapes fermenting.

Thinking About Science

Directions: Answer each question below.

1. Write a brief definition for each type of change:

   a. physical change: _____

   b. chemical change: _____

2. Write the type of change (physical or chemical) that is taking place in each action described below.

   _____ a. An iron nail, left in the rain, rusts.

   _____ b. A board is sawed into three smaller pieces.

   _____ c. Gasoline burns in a car's engine.

   _____ d. A glass vase shatters when it hits the floor.

Answers are on page 449.

Directions: Choose the <u>one best answer</u> to each question.

Questions 1–5 are based on the information on page 279.

1. Which of the following is a chemical property of a cube of sugar?

    (1) size
    (2) weight
    (3) color
    (4) feel when touched
    (5) smell when burned

2. Suppose that a quart of frozen ice cream is taken out of the freezer and left at room temperature for thirty minutes. Which of the following would be most important in determining whether all the ice cream melts?

    (1) the flavor of ice cream
    (2) the room temperature
    (3) the outdoor temperature
    (4) the size of the freezer
    (5) the shape of the ice cream container

3. When iron (Fe) combines with water and oxygen, it begins to rust. Which of the following actions will lead to this chemical change in a piece of iron?

    (1) placing it in a warm, dry place
    (2) heating it until it turns liquid
    (3) placing it in a cool, wet place
    (4) placing it in a cool, dry place
    (5) running electricity through it

4. Melting a cube of ice and sanding a rough board are both examples of physical changes. Thinking about these two examples, which of the following statements is (are) true?

    A. A physical change can always be reversed so that a substance is returned to its original form.

    B. A physical change cannot be reversed.

    C. Some physical changes can be reversed; some cannot.

    D. Both a change of phase and a change of shape are physical changes.

    (1) A only
    (2) B only
    (3) C only
    (4) A and D only
    (5) C and D only

5. Lighting a match and making toast are both examples of chemical changes. Referring to these examples, which of the following statements is (are) true?

    A. These chemical changes can be reversed—the match and toast can be returned to their original forms.

    B. These chemical changes cannot be reversed.

    C. These chemical changes change more than just the outward appearance of the match and the toast.

    D. These chemical changes are destructive, not purposeful.

    (1) A only
    (2) B only
    (3) B and C only
    (4) B and D only
    (5) C and D only

Answers are on page 449.

Solutions

If we had to choose a single word to describe the mixture of elements that appear on and within Earth, that word would be solution. Solutions are everywhere in nature.

- Air is a solution of gases.

- Ocean water is a solution of water, salt, and other minerals.

- Earth's interior is a molten sea of elements and compounds.

Think of what happens when you drop a cube of sugar into a glass of water. While you watch, the sugar disappears. But is it really gone? Taste the water, and you discover a sweet taste. The sugar is still there even if you do not see it.

When sugar disappears in water, we say the sugar has **dissolved**. As it dissolves, molecules of sugar become evenly distributed among molecules of water. Because of this, sugar water is equally sweet in every part of the mixture. A **solution**, such as sugar water, is a uniform mixing of substances.

Two components of a solution are the solvent and solute.

- The **solute** is the substance that is dissolved.

- The **solvent** is the substance that dissolves the solute.

In a sugar solution, sugar is the solute and water is the solvent. The water dissolves the sugar.

Although solutions are very common, not every mixture forms a solution. For example, when sand is mixed with water, it appears at first to go into solution. But if you wait a few minutes, the sand will settle to the bottom. Sand does not dissolve in water.

Thinking About Science

Directions: Match each word on the left with the best description on the right. Write the letter of the phrase on the line before the correct number.

_____ **1.** solution   (a) a solution of numerous gases

_____ **2.** solute   (b) a dissolving agent

_____ **3.** solvent   (c) a dissolved substance

_____ **4.** air   (d) a uniform mixture of substances

Answers are on page 449.

Directions: Choose the <u>one best answer</u> to each question.

Questions 1–5 refer to the following passage.

A solution is often thought of as a solid dissolved in a liquid or as a liquid dissolved in a liquid. Other solutions are also common.

Gases can be dissolved in gases. Air is a solution of gases dissolved in gases. Gases in air include nitrogen, oxygen, hydrogen, and helium.

Gases can be dissolved in liquids. In carbonated soft drinks, carbon dioxide gas is dissolved in water along with sugar and flavor additives.

Solids can be dissolved in solids. Metal alloys are made by dissolving one metal in another. To form an alloy, two or more metals are melted and then mixed as liquids. The solution of liquid metal is cooled and solidified. Brass is an alloy made by dissolving zinc in copper. Brass has qualities that are a mixture of the qualities of zinc and copper. Brass is stronger than copper but is less flexible.

1. Cola drinks are carbonated soft drinks. What type of solution are cola drinks?

   (1) liquid dissolved in liquid
   (2) solid dissolved in gas
   (3) gas dissolved in gas
   (4) gas dissolved in liquid
   (5) solid dissolved in solid

2. Water is added to latex house paint to thin the paint. What type of solution is this?

   (1) liquid dissolved in liquid
   (2) solid dissolved in liquid
   (3) gas dissolved in gas
   (4) gas dissolved in liquid
   (5) solid dissolved in solid

3. Powdered punch mix is added to water to make punch. How do you classify this punch solution?

   (1) liquid dissolved in liquid
   (2) solid dissolved in liquid
   (3) gas dissolved in gas
   (4) gas dissolved in liquid
   (5) solid dissolved in solid

4. An open bottle of carbonated cola sat in a refrigerator for two hours. A second open bottle of the cola sat on a countertop at room temperature for two hours. After this time, the warm cola tasted flat, whereas the cold cola did not. What is the best explanation of this discovery?

   (1) Lowering the temperature decreases the amount of carbon dioxide gas that a liquid can hold.
   (2) Raising the temperature decreases the amount of carbon dioxide gas that a liquid can hold.
   (3) Changing the temperature does not affect the amount of carbon dioxide gas a liquid can hold.
   (4) The warm cola was exposed to fresh air, but the cold cola was not.
   (5) Dissolved carbon dioxide gas escapes more quickly from a bottle of cola when it is shaken than when it is warmed.

5. A tablespoon of sugar is added to each of two glasses. One glass contains warm water, and the other contains cold water. The sugar dissolves more quickly in the warm water. Which phrase best describes how the rate of dissolving is affected by temperature?

   (1) increases with increasing temperature
   (2) decreases with increasing temperature
   (3) is not dependent on temperature
   (4) increases with stirring
   (5) decreases with stirring

Answers are on page 449.

Chemical Reactions

Chemical Equations

Chemists spend much of their time investigating chemical changes. In a chemical change, two or more substances combine to form one or more new substances. This process is called a **chemical reaction**.

To describe what happens in a chemical reaction, chemists use a shorthand method known as a **chemical equation**. The equation shows the formulas of the **reactants** (the substances combining) and the **products** (the new substances formed). An arrow shows the direction in which the reaction proceeds.

The equation for the formation of a water molecule is written as follows:

$$2H_2 + O_2 \longrightarrow 2H_2O$$

From left to right, the equation says that two molecules of hydrogen (H_2) combine with one molecule of oxygen (O_2) to form two molecules of water (H_2O). The formulas H_2 and O_2 indicate that both hydrogen and oxygen gas molecules are each made up of two atoms: H_2 means two atoms of hydrogen (H), and O_2 means two atoms of oxygen (O).

A chemical reaction also occurs when nitrogen (N) reacts with hydrogen (H) to form ammonia (NH_3). The chemical equation for the ammonia reaction is as follows:

$$N_2 + 3H_2 \longrightarrow 2NH_3$$

In words, one molecule of nitrogen (N_2) combines with three molecules of hydrogen (H_2) to produce two molecules of ammonia (NH_3).

The Law of Conservation of Matter

Chemists have observed that atoms neither appear nor disappear during a chemical reaction. If there are two atoms of nitrogen on the left side of a reaction equation, there must be two atoms of nitrogen on the right side. And, if there are six atoms of hydrogen on the left side, there must be six atoms of hydrogen on the right side. This fact is called the law of conservation of matter.

> **The Law of Conservation of Matter**
>
> Matter is neither created nor destroyed during a chemical reaction.

Chemical Reaction Rates

Chemical reactions will occur only if the following three conditions are met.

- Groups of reacting molecules must be close to one another.

- Reacting molecules must be able to collide with one another.

- There must be sufficient energy for reacting molecules to complete a reaction.

The speed at which a chemical reaction takes place is called the **reaction rate**. A greater reaction rate means that a reaction takes place in a shorter time. Some chemical reactions, such as a firecracker exploding, have a very high reaction rate and take place in a small fraction of a second. Other reactions, such as paint weathering, have a low reaction rate and may take several years.

Reaction rates depend on many variables, including both the molecular structure and the concentration of the reacting chemicals. Temperature also affects reaction rates. As a general rule, a higher temperature leads to a higher reaction rate. Heat increases the speed of molecular motion and helps bring reacting molecules into contact at a faster rate. Heat also adds energy to reacting molecules and makes them more likely to react.

- Cooking food is a familiar example of a chemical reaction that very much depends on temperature.

- The drying of oil paint is another example. Oil paint dries in a few hours on a hot, dry day. Chemicals in the paint freely mix with oxygen gas in the air, creating hardened paint. The same paint, though, dries very slowly on a cold, rainy day. Cold temperatures and the presence of moisture in the air slow these chemical reactions. Instead of drying in hours, oil paint may take several days to dry.

Stirring, as well as heating, increases reaction rates involving liquids.

- A clothes washer is a familiar example. Soap, dissolved in water, reacts with stains and dirt on clothing. The constant stirring and agitation of the solution increases both the rate and efficiency with which this reaction takes place.

- Mixing a two-part epoxy (glue) is another example. The more the two parts are mixed, the more quickly the epoxy hardens.

Reaction rates also increase in the presence of catalysts. A **catalyst** is a substance that provides a faster mechanism by which a reaction may take place. During the reaction, though, the catalyst is not changed. Hydrogen and oxygen gases are very explosive if mixed in the presence of a flame. However, at room temperature, this mixture by itself is stable. If you place powdered platinum with the gases, though, an explosion will take place. The platinum atoms become covered with oxygen atoms and weaken the oxygen bonding. The weakened oxygen atoms then more easily react with hydrogen atoms. An explosion occurs as oxygen and hydrogen atoms unite to form water. The powdered platinum is not changed during the reaction.

Some reactions take place only when a certain **activation energy** is reached.

- One example is a match. A match does not burst into flame until it is scratched by a hard surface. The scratching adds heat energy needed by the chemicals in the match before they will ignite.

- Another familiar example is the burning of paper. A piece of paper, when slowly heated, gets warmer and warmer until it reaches a temperature of about 450°F, at which point it bursts into flame.

 Thinking About Science

Directions: Answer each question below.

1. Complete each sentence by filling in the blanks with the correct word(s).

   a. A _____ is used to describe a chemical reaction.

   b. The _____ are substances that combine during a chemical reaction. The _____ are substances that are formed.

2. Respiration takes place in your body's cells to provide the energy necessary for your activities. During respiration, glucose reacts with oxygen obtained from your breathing. The products of the reaction are carbon dioxide gas, water, and energy. The chemical equation for respiration is written as follows:

$$C_6H_{12}O_6 + 6O_2 \rightarrow 6CO_2 + 6H_2O$$

   The following questions refer to the chemical equation for respiration.

   a. How many molecules of glucose are represented in the equation? _____

   b. How many molecules of carbon dioxide (CO_2) result when one molecule of glucose combines with six molecules of oxygen? _____

   c. How many atoms of hydrogen appear on each side of the equation? _____

Answers are on page 449.

Directions: Choose the <u>one best answer</u> to each question.

Questions 1 and 2 refer to the following passage.

Iron (Fe), one of the most abundant elements on Earth, is usually obtained for commercial purposes from the iron ore hematite (Fe_2O_3). To remove the iron, hematite is combined with carbon monoxide gas (CO). The chemical equation for this reaction is written as follows:

$$Fe_2O_3 + 3CO \longrightarrow 2Fe + 3CO_2$$

1. In the chemical equation for extracting iron (Fe) from hematite (Fe_2O_3), how many molecules of carbon dioxide gas (CO_2) are formed?

   (1) one
   (2) two
   (3) three
   (4) four
   (5) five

2. In the chemical equation for extracting iron (Fe) from hematite (Fe_2O_3), how many atoms of oxygen are represented on each side of the chemical equation?

   (1) two
   (2) three
   (3) four
   (4) five
   (5) six

Questions 3 and 4 refer to the following passage.

An *enzyme* is a specialized organic molecule that acts as a catalyst in a living organism. Enzymes regulate the speed of many chemical reactions involved in metabolism—the chemical reactions that take place within living cells. At present, there are more than 700 known enzymes.

In humans, enzymes play many roles. Some help regulate the digestion and use of sugar. Others release energy that causes the heart to beat and the lungs to expand and contract. Still others change food into substances the body uses for building tissue and replacing blood cells.

The fermentation of alcohol is the oldest known enzyme reaction. In 1897, Eduard Buchner, a German chemist, discovered that an enzyme created by yeast can cause fermentation—the chemical reaction in which sugar is used to make alcohol.

3. Which of the following is *not* a phrase that describes enzymes?

   (1) a type of catalyst
   (2) an organic molecule
   (3) found only in humans
   (4) have many functions
   (5) found in many living organisms

4. Which of the following can you infer to be true?

   (1) Enzymes are produced by the human body.
   (2) Enzymes are produced only by plants.
   (3) Enzymes are produced only by yeast.
   (4) Enzymes are present in all living organisms.
   (5) A human's main source of enzymes is from food.

Question 5 refers to the passage below.

Since the early 1980s, automobiles sold in the United States have come equipped with catalytic converters. The purpose of this device is to remove carbon monoxide and other harmful gases from the exhaust gases created by the car's engine.

A catalytic converter contains small beads that are coated with metals such as palladium and platinum. These metals act as catalysts and cause exhaust gases to undergo chemical reactions in which they are changed into carbon dioxide gas and water.

5. Which of the following acts as a catalyst in a catalytic converter?

   (1) carbon monoxide
   (2) exhaust gas
   (3) carbon dioxide
   (4) palladium
   (5) water

Answers are on page 449.

Chemistry Review

Directions: Choose the <u>one best answer</u> to each question.

Questions 1 and 2 refer to the following information.

The three phases of matter are solid, liquid, and gas. While kept at one atmosphere of air pressure, many common substances change from one phase to another when they are heated or cooled. Each change of phase usually takes place through one of the five processes described below.

freezing—the process of a liquid changing into a solid as its temperature is lowered

melting—the process of a solid changing into a liquid as its temperature is raised

evaporation—the process of a liquid slowly changing into a gas as a result of the slow escape of molecules from the liquid surface

boiling—the process of a liquid rapidly changing into a gas as its temperature is raised to the point at which vapor bubbles form in the liquid

condensation—the process of a gas changing into a liquid as its temperature is lowered

1. On a cool morning, water droplets of dew often cover the grass and flowers outside. Through what process does dew form?

    (1) freezing
    (2) melting
    (3) evaporation
    (4) boiling
    (5) condensation

2. Below −38°F, the element mercury is a solid. As its temperature is raised to −38°F, mercury turns into a liquid metal. What process does this exemplify?

    (1) freezing
    (2) melting
    (3) evaporation
    (4) boiling
    (5) condensation

Questions 3–5 refer to the following passage.

An *acid* is a substance that releases hydrogen when mixed with water. An acid is sour to the taste. *Organic acids* are not harmful and are found in foods. Citric acid is found in oranges, grapefruits, and lemons. *Inorganic acids* can be strong and dangerous. Hydrochloric acid, for example, is used as a metal cleaner and can burn exposed skin.

A *base* is a substance that combines with an acid and neutralizes its effect. Together, an acid and a base form a salt and water. Some weak bases, such as baking soda, are used as a mild stomach antacid. Stronger bases, such as ammonia and bleach, are used as household cleaners.

3. Suppose a small amount of baking soda is added to a glass of orange juice. How would the orange juice taste change?

    (1) more acidic
    (2) unchanged
    (3) sweeter
    (4) less acidic
    (5) colder

4. What is the most likely purpose of an antacid?

    (1) to neutralize excess stomach acid
    (2) to increase stomach acid
    (3) to prevent digestion of acidic food
    (4) to relieve a headache
    (5) to treat dehydration

5. The needles of evergreen trees are acidic, and lawn grass does not grow well in acidic soil. Gardeners often place lime on lawns near evergreen trees. What is the most likely chemical classification of lime?

    (1) inorganic acid
    (2) neutral, neither base nor acid
    (3) weak base
    (4) partly base and partly acid
    (5) organic acid

Questions 6–8 refer to the following passage.

Photosynthesis is a chemical reaction that naturally takes place in plant cells when they are exposed to sunlight. During photosynthesis, carbon dioxide gas reacts with water to produce glucose, oxygen gas, and water. The chemical equation for photosynthesis can be written as follows:

$$6CO_2 + 12H_2O \longrightarrow C_6H_{12}O_6 + 6O_2 + 6H_2O$$

This reaction is needed for a plant to live and grow. If photosynthesis does not occur, a plant will die.

6. In the equation for photosynthesis, how many molecules of water are produced in the formation of one molecule of glucose?

   (1) one
   (2) six
   (3) seven
   (4) twelve
   (5) eighteen

7. In the equation for photosynthesis, how many atoms of hydrogen (H) appear on each side of the equation?

   (1) two
   (2) six
   (3) twelve
   (4) twenty-four
   (5) forty-eight

8. From where do plants get the energy that is necessary for photosynthesis to occur?

   (1) glucose
   (2) water
   (3) chlorophyll
   (4) sunlight
   (5) oxygen

Questions 9 and 10 refer to the following passage.

In a chemical reaction atoms or molecules of one or more substances combine in new ways to form new substances. Because chemical bonds are broken and new bonds are made, energy may be both used and given up during these reactions. In *exothermic reactions*, more heat energy is produced than is used, and energy is released as the reaction takes place. For example, when wood burns, both heat and light energy are given off.

Endothermic reactions use more energy than they produce. Endothermic reactions require heat energy from an outside source in order to take place. The chemical change that takes place in bread while it bakes is endothermic.

9. What is true in an exothermic reaction?

   (1) Heat is required for the reaction to stop.
   (2) Heat is required for the reaction to proceed.
   (3) Heat is given off during the reaction.
   (4) Heat is a form of activation energy.
   (5) Heat is shared by the reacting substances.

10. The chemical equation for the fermentation of alcohol is as follows:

$$C_6H_{12}O_6 \longrightarrow 2C_2H_5OH + 2CO_2 + heat$$

Which phrase best describes this equation?

   (1) an endothermic reaction in which carbon dioxide gas (CO_2) is produced
   (2) an endothermic reaction in which carbon dioxide gas (CO_2) is used up
   (3) an exothermic reaction in which carbon dioxide gas (CO_2) is produced
   (4) an exothermic reaction in which carbon dioxide gas (CO_2) is used up
   (5) neither an exothermic nor an endothermic reaction

Answers are on page 450.

CHAPTER 10

Physics

In the world of human thought generally, and in physical science particularly, the most important and fruitful concepts are those to which it is impossible to attach a well-defined meaning.

~H. A. Kramers

Imagine that you wake up tomorrow and nothing works. There is no hot water, so you cannot shower. The stove will not get hot, so you cannot cook breakfast. The refrigerator is not running, and your television will not turn on! Sound like a world gone crazy? Maybe so—but that is what life would be like if the world ran out of energy.

Because the world's population is increasing and worldwide standards of living are rising, an ever-increasing number of people can afford energy-consuming products such as cars, stereos, and air conditioners. Since 1940 the total amount of energy used in the world has nearly doubled every 20 years. Many people are worried that we are headed for a serious energy shortage, a situation in which there will not be enough energy for everyone who needs it. A major challenge currently facing physicists is to develop new sources of safe energy.

The Science of Energy

When most people think about **energy**, they think about the gasoline that powers their cars and the electricity, oil, or natural gas that heats their homes. Besides these, though, there are many other important forms of energy. Sound and light are two examples. Energy carried by water and wind are two more.

Physicists study how energy is produced and how it can be used most efficiently. They try to learn as much as possible about each form of energy. The results of their research often lead to the development of new types of consumer products. For example, physicists have helped develop and improve entertainment products such as television sets, computers, video recorders, and cameras; appliances such as microwave ovens and electronic dishwashers; and medical equipment such as digital thermometers, CAT scanners (used to see inside the human body), and ultrasonic sound monitors (used to observe a growing fetus).

Processes that involve energy also play important roles in other areas of science. Because of this, several new fields have developed in recent years that link physics directly with these other sciences. For example, biophysicists apply the techniques and results of physics research to questions in life science. Astrophysicists study the birth and death of stars and planets. Physical chemists try to determine the atom-by-atom details of the structure of molecules. Environmental scientists use knowledge from both life science and physical science to answer questions concerning the health of our environment.

Physics, more than any other science, uses the language of mathematics to describe its theories and experiments. However, many of the concepts of physics can be understood without the aid of either algebra or geometry. These are the concepts that appear on the GED Science Test.

Thinking About Science

Directions: Match each word on the left with the best description on the right. Write the letter of the description on the line before the correct number.

_____ **1.** biophysics

_____ **2.** physical chemistry

_____ **3.** physics

_____ **4.** astrophysics

(a) the application of physics to problems in chemistry

(b) often called "the science of energy"

(c) the application of physics to research in astronomy

(d) the application of physics to research in biology

Answers are on page 450.

GED PRACTICE

Directions: Choose the <u>one best answer</u> to each question.

Questions 1–3 refer to the information on page 289.

1. Which of the following is a cause of the worldwide increase in energy use during the last century?

    (1) the possibility of serious energy shortage
    (2) the production of alternate energy sources
    (3) worldwide rising standards of living
    (4) the decreasing cost of energy production
    (5) the rise of the environmental movement

2. Which phrase best describes what physicists do?

    (1) rely on observation but not on mathematics
    (2) become involved in work that often has practical applications
    (3) support worldwide family planning efforts
    (4) avoid work in biology or chemistry
    (5) work mainly in universities

3. Which name is given to the application of the study of physics to organisms?

    (1) physical geology
    (2) physical chemistry
    (3) astrophysics
    (4) biochemistry
    (5) biophysics

Questions 4–6 refer to the circle graph below.

ENERGY PRODUCTION IN THE UNITED STATES (2000)

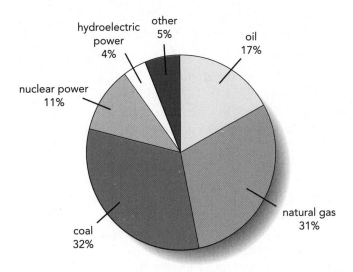

Questions 7 and 8 refer to the graph below.

ENERGY CONSUMPTION IN THE UNITED STATES (2000)

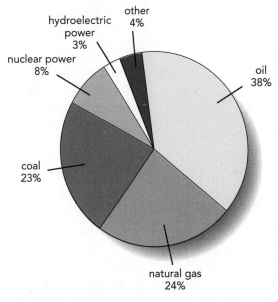

4. Which growing form of energy production is so limited at the present time that it is not included on the graph?

   (1) coal
   (2) nuclear power
   (3) solar
   (4) oil
   (5) natural gas

5. According to the graph, approximately what total percent of the energy produced in the United States comes from fossil fuels (coal, oil, and natural gas)?

   (1) 30 percent
   (2) 50 percent
   (3) 75 percent
   (4) 80 percent
   (5) 90 percent

6. Approximately how much more energy in the United States is produced from natural gas than from nuclear power?

   (1) about two times as much
   (2) about three times as much
   (3) about four times as much
   (4) about five times as much
   (5) about six times as much

7. Which of the following <u>most</u> likely accounts for the high rate of oil consumption in the United States?

   (1) use for home heating
   (2) use for making gasoline
   (3) use for making solar cells
   (4) use for making paint
   (5) use for making lubricants

8. Approximately what total percent of the energy consumed in the United States comes from fossil fuels (coal, oil, and natural gas)?

   (1) 30 percent
   (2) 50 percent
   (3) 65 percent
   (4) 85 percent
   (5) 95 percent

Answers are on page 450.

Laws of Motion

How would you answer the following two questions?

- How many angels does it take to keep the Moon moving around Earth?

- Why does an arrow, when shot into the sky, return to Earth?

If these questions seem a little odd to you, it's not surprising. These questions aren't often asked today! But such matters were taken very seriously in the time of Sir Isaac Newton (1642–1727), an English mathematician and physicist. Newton spent his life looking for an explanation of motion that didn't require the help of angels or natural resting places.

Newton's Laws of Motion

Newton began his study of motion by wondering what happens to an object, such as a ball, when a force acts upon it. A **force** is any push or pull that can affect an object either in motion or at rest. Newton made several discoveries that today are written as three laws of motion that still bear his name. Newton's laws of motion are now known to apply to all types of objects and all types of forces.

Newton's First Law: The Law of Inertia

Newton realized that unless some force stopped a rolling ball, the ball would roll forever. He also realized that without a force to start a ball rolling, the ball would stay at rest forever.

With these two ideas in mind, Newton wrote his first law:

The Law of Inertia

If no force is applied, an object at rest will remain at rest, and an object in motion will move in a straight line at a constant speed.

You've seen this principle in action if you've watched children slide along an icy sidewalk. Because there is only a very slight force to slow them down, they are able to slide a long distance.

This property of matter, a natural resistance to any change in its state of rest or motion, is called **inertia.** Every object, whether sitting or moving, has inertia.

Newton's Second Law: The Law of Acceleration

Newton's second law, most easily written in two parts, is based on two observations. First, Newton noticed that a ball can be thrown faster and farther simply by throwing it harder (applying more force).

> ### The Law of Acceleration, Part I
>
> An object's speed increases in proportion to the amount of force applied.

Second, Newton noticed that using as much force as you are able, you can throw a one-pound ball much faster and farther than you can throw a ten-pound ball. From this second observation, Newton concluded:

> ### The Law of Acceleration, Part II
>
> For the same amount of applied force, a lighter object accelerates—changes its speed—at a greater rate than a heavier object.

Think of how much easier it is to throw a baseball across a yard than to throw a bowling ball the same distance.

Newton's Third Law: The Law of Interaction

Finally, Newton thought about what happens when an object exerts a force on a second object. Imagine what happens when a child kicks a door shut. The foot exerts a force on the door. At the same instant, the foot feels a reaction force from the door. Newton stated his third law as follows:

> ### The Law of Interaction
>
> For every action, there is an equal and opposite reaction.

When an object exerts a force on a second object, the second object exerts an equal force in the opposite direction on the first object.

A reaction force can also act on an object that is not moving. Think about a telephone sitting on a desk. Due to gravity, the phone exerts a force (its weight) on the desk. At the same time, the desk exerts an upward reaction force on the phone. The phone remains motionless because the reaction force pushing the phone up exactly balances the force of gravity pulling the phone down.

BALLOON ROCKET

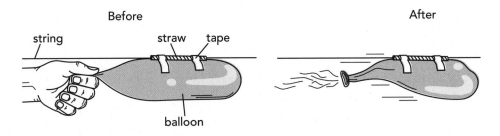

The balloon rocket demonstrates Newton's third law. The contracting balloon pushes gas out of the balloon, while the gas pushes against the balloon and causes it to move forward.

Thinking About Science

Directions: Answer each question below.

1. Briefly define each word.

a. force: _____

b. inertia: _____

2. Each of the four facts below demonstrates one of Newton's laws of motion.

On the line preceding each fact, write *1, 2,* or *3* to indicate which law is being demonstrated.

(1) The law of inertia: An object's motion will not change unless a force acts on the object.

(2) The law of acceleration: An object's speed increases when more force is applied.

(3) The law of interaction: For every action, there is an equal and opposite reaction.

_____ a. When a hammer hits a nail, the hammer bounces up off of the nail.

_____ b. Because the force of gravity is less on the Moon than on Earth, a rock dropped on the Moon falls more slowly than an equal-size rock dropped on Earth.

_____ c. A fast-moving barrel, rolling on a level floor, will roll until a force is applied to stop it.

_____ d. A track athlete can toss an eight-pound shot farther than she can toss a sixteen-pound shot.

Answers are on page 450.

GED PRACTICE

Directions: Choose the <u>one best answer</u> to each question.

Questions 1 and 2 refer to the information on pages 292 and 293.

1. Which fact is a good example of the law of inertia?

(1) A moving truck is difficult to stop.
(2) A telephone on a desk is acted upon by a reaction force.
(3) A basketball rebounds off of a floor.
(4) Light reflects off of a mirror.
(5) Air resistance slows a moving bicycle.

2. Which fact is a good example of the law of acceleration?

(1) A marble rolls more easily on a floor than on a carpet.
(2) A desk weighs more than a chair.
(3) A pebble is easier to throw than a boulder.
(4) Bumping a table can be painful.
(5) A car has moving parts.

Questions 3 and 4 refer to the information below.

Newton's second law can be written as a mathematical equation:

force = mass × acceleration

Force is any push or pull on an object.

Mass is the amount of matter that makes up the object.

Acceleration is the rate at which the object's speed is changing because of the force.

3. Tina and Lucy are each pushing a shopping cart. The weight of the food in Tina's cart is twice as much as the weight in Lucy's cart. For the acceleration of the carts to be the same, which of the following must be true?

   (1) Lucy must apply twice the force that Tina applies.
   (2) Tina must apply twice the force that Lucy applies.
   (3) Lucy must apply four times the force that Tina applies.
   (4) Tina must apply four times the force that Lucy applies.
   (5) The force Lucy applies must be exactly equal to the force that Tina applies.

4. What conclusion follows from Newton's second law?

   (1) An object moving at constant speed has no force acting on it.
   (2) An object that is not moving does not have any force acting on it.
   (3) If the speed of an object is changing, the object does not have any force acting on it.
   (4) If the speed of an object is changing, the object has one or more forces acting on it.
   (5) If the mass of an object is changing, the force on the object will also change.

Questions 5 and 6 refer to the illustration below.

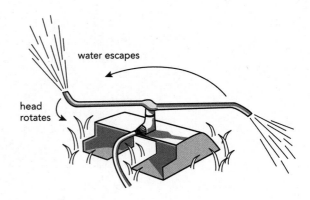

water escapes

head rotates

The head of the sprinkler rotates as reaction to the force of escaping water.

5. What exerts force on the sprinkler head, causing it to move?

   (1) the lawn
   (2) the garden hose
   (3) the escaping water
   (4) gravity
   (5) air pressure

6. What is demonstrated by the action of the sprinkler?

   (1) Newton's first law of motion, the law of inertia
   (2) Newton's second law of motion, the law of acceleration
   (3) Newton's third law of motion, the law of interaction
   (4) an exception to Newton's laws of motion
   (5) Newton's law of gravity

   Answers are on page 450.

Newton's Law of Universal Gravitation

Newton used his laws of motion to help discover the properties of gravity. Today, these properties are known as Newton's law of universal gravitation. This law is called universal because it applies to all objects in the universe.

The Law of Universal Gravitation, Part I

Gravitational force is an attractive force, a force that pulls two objects toward one another.

Gravity acts between pairs of objects in the universe. Gravitational force holds each of us on Earth's surface. It also holds the Moon in orbit around Earth and Earth in orbit around the Sun.

Gravity also acts between people. There is actually a gravitational force that pulls people toward each other. This force is so small, though, that you don't notice it.

The Law of Universal Gravitation, Part II

Gravitational force is greater for heavy objects (objects with more mass) than for light objects.

The only gravitational force that people are aware of is the force between themselves and Earth and between other objects and Earth. These forces are noticeable because Earth is so large (massive). Gravitational force between familiar objects, such as between you and this book, is much too weak to be noticeable or even measurable.

The Law of Universal Gravitation, Part III

The force of gravity decreases as the distance between objects increases.

Gravitational force drops to one-fourth its strength each time the distance between two objects doubles.

Thinking About Science

Directions: Each of the four facts below demonstrates one of Newton's laws of universal gravitation. On the line preceding each fact, write *1, 2,* or *3* to indicate which law is being demonstrated.

(1) Gravitational force is an attractive force, a force that pulls two objects toward one another.

(2) Gravitational force is greater for heavy objects (objects with more mass) than for light objects.

(3) The force of gravity decreases as the distance between objects increases.

_____ **1.** A balloon is more likely to break if a child sits on it than if a doll is placed on it.

_____ **2.** The gravitational force between the Sun and Venus is greater than the gravitational force between the Sun and Earth even though Earth and Venus are about the same size.

_____ **3.** The nine planets of the solar system orbit around the Sun.

_____ **4.** It is more difficult to lift a ten-year-old boy off the ground than it is to lift a 4-month-old baby.

Answers are on page 450.

Directions: Choose the <u>one best answer</u> to each question.

Questions 1 and 2 refer to the passage and graph below.

Weight is a measure of the force of gravity that holds a body on Earth. The graph below shows how the weight of a person would be different if Earth had a different radius (distance from center to surface) than it actually has. At the radius marked r_E on the graph, a given person weighs 200 pounds, his actual Earth weight. [r_E is the radius of Earth, about 4,000 miles.]

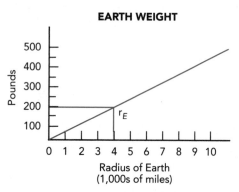

EARTH WEIGHT

1. The radius of the Moon is about 1,000 miles. If an astronaut weighs 200 pounds on Earth, what will be the astronaut's <u>approximate</u> weight while on the Moon? [Assume that Earth and the Moon are made of similar material.]

   (1) 25 pounds
   (2) 50 pounds
   (3) 100 pounds
   (4) 150 pounds
   (5) 200 pounds

2. Thinking about the graph, which of the following is a reasonable conclusion?

   (1) Most planets in our solar system are smaller than Earth.
   (2) Most planets in our solar system are larger than Earth.
   (3) Spacecraft would not be able to land safely on planets larger than Earth.
   (4) Humans may never be able to live on planets much smaller than Earth.
   (5) Humans may never be able to live on planets much larger than Earth.

Question 3 refers to the passage and line graph below.

The graph shows the rate at which the speed of an object increases as the object falls due to gravity. For example, an object, dropped from a tall building, reaches a speed of 96 feet per second after falling for three seconds.

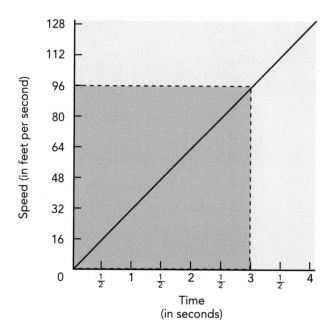

3. Under the action of gravity, how much does an object's speed increase each second it falls?

   (1) 10 feet per second
   (2) 16 feet per second
   (3) 32 feet per second
   (4) 64 feet per second
   (5) 100 feet per second

   Answers are on page 450.

Force, Work, and Machines

Force and Work

Scientists have a special definition of the concept **work**. Work is what happens when a force is applied to an object that moves in response to the force. Work is the product of the units of force times the units of distance.

work = force × distance

For work to occur, there must be force applied to an object and the object must move.

- If a woman pushes hard against a tree, no work is done unless the tree actually moves. She may put forth a tremendous effort without doing any work as defined by scientists.

- If a man lifts a weight off the ground he has done work. If a woman lifts twice as much weight the same distance, she has done twice as much work as the man.

Machines and Work

Machines are devices that are designed to make work easier. Simple machines do this in several ways:

- by changing the direction in which force is applied

- by changing the position where force is applied

- by changing a small force into a much larger force

The Lever

A **lever** is a simple machine that consists of a bar that moves freely around a pivot called a fulcrum. A lever makes work easier by multiplying the effort force, the force that is applied. When a person applies force to one end of a long lever, that force increases at the other end of the lever.

The crowbar pictured below is a lever that turns around a rock, the fulcrum. An effort force is applied to the top end of the crowbar. The load (stump) moves as the top end of the crowbar moves over a distance. The effort force felt by the stump is several times the effort force applied by the man.

LEVER

effort

load

fulcrum

The amount of work that goes into a simple machine equals the amount of work done by the machine. In other words,

force x distance = force x distance
      (work)   (work)

Wheel and Axle

A **wheel and axle** is a simple machine designed to make use of a principle similar to a lever. A wheel turns through a greater distance than does an axle. For the screwdriver shown below, this means that less force needs to be applied to the handle of the screwdriver to turn the axle and thus tighten the screw.

WHEEL AND AXLE

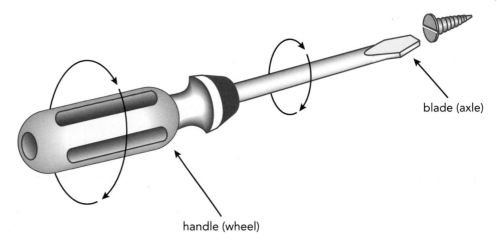

blade (axle)

handle (wheel)

Thinking About Science

Directions: Write a definition of each word below in the space provided.

1. work: _____

2. force: _____

3. machine: _____

4. fulcrum: _____

Answers are on page 451.

GED PRACTICE

Directions: Choose the <u>one best answer</u> to each question.

Questions 1 and 2 refer to the information on pages 299 and 300 and to the following reminder.

<u>Reminder:</u> The work done on one end of a lever (or wheel and axle) is equal to the work done by the other end.

force × distance = force × distance
  (effort end)   (load end)

1. Landon uses a crowbar to lift a stump. He applies 50 pounds of force to the handle of the crowbar. His end of the crowbar moves 20 inches. The stump moves 5 inches. What force was applied to the stump?

(1) 25 pounds
(2) 50 pounds
(3) 100 pounds
(4) 200 pounds
(5) 500 pounds

2. Carlita uses a pulley to lift a car engine. The engine weighs 300 pounds. She raises the engine 1 foot as she pulls the free end of the rope 5 feet. What force did Carlita apply to the free end of the rope?

(1) 30 pounds
(2) 60 pounds
(3) 150 pounds
(4) 300 pounds
(5) 1500 pounds

Answers are on page 451.

The Law of Conservation of Energy

When you turn on a lamp, electricity flows to the lightbulb. At the bulb, electrical energy is changed into light and heat, two other forms of energy. By studying how energy changes from one form to another, physicists discovered the basis for the law of conservation of energy.

The Law of Conservation of Energy

During interactions, energy may change from one form to another, but no energy is lost. The total amount of energy present remains constant.

Kinetic Energy and Potential Energy

There are two types of energy.

- **Kinetic energy** is energy of motion. A kicked soccer ball has kinetic energy.

- **Potential energy** is stored energy. A book sitting on the edge of a table has potential energy. If the book is pushed off of the table, its potential energy is changed to kinetic energy as the book falls to the floor. The energy changes form but is not lost.

Think about energy changes when a girl is swinging on a swingset.

- At the high point, she stops moving just before she reverses direction. At this point, all of her energy is potential energy (stored gravitational energy).

- At the low point, all of her energy is kinetic energy (energy of motion).

- At all points between the high and low points, her energy is partly potential and partly kinetic.

- As she swings from the high point to the low point, potential energy changes to kinetic energy. As she swings back up, kinetic energy changes to potential energy.

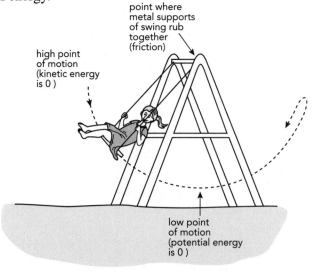

point where
metal supports
of swing rub
together
(friction)

high point
of motion
(kinetic energy
is 0)

low point
of motion
(potential energy
is 0)

The Force of Friction

Friction is a force that slows a moving object. Friction is one force that slows the swinging girl. Because there is friction, the swing slowly loses energy and comes to a stop unless it is pushed.

Friction changes the kinetic energy of the swing to heat energy. This is caused by electric forces between the atoms and molecules that make up the parts of the swing and the air.

- Heat energy is produced where the moving metal parts of the swing rub together.

- Heat energy is also produced in the air because of air friction—commonly called air resistance. You feel **air resistance** when you are traveling in a car and stick your hand out of the car window.

Friction always produces heat. The girl stops moving, but her kinetic energy is not lost. Her kinetic energy has been changed into heat—heat in the warm metal parts of the swing that have been rubbing together and heat in the air.

Types of Friction

Friction may be any of several types:

- *Sliding friction* occurs when a moving object rubs against a second object. The friction between the rubbing metal parts of the swing is an example.

- *Rolling friction* occurs when an object is placed on wheels and moved. When you pull a wagon, you feel the force of rolling friction.

- *Fluid friction* occurs when an object moves through a fluid, either a liquid or a gas. Swimming is an example of fluid friction in a liquid. Air resistance is an example of fluid friction in a gas.

- *Static friction* occurs when a force is applied to an object that does not move. If you push a book that is on a table, the friction you feel before the book starts to move is static friction. Once the book is moving, you feel sliding friction.

Friction can be a useful force or an annoying one. Friction between a pencil and paper makes writing possible, a useful activity. But, a similar type of friction causes holes to appear in your socks!

The force of sliding friction is much greater than the force of rolling friction.

Thinking About Science

Directions: Complete each sentence. Fill in each blank with the correct word(s) from the reading passage on pages 302 and 303.

1. According to the law of conservation of energy, the amount of energy in any given situation is _____.

2. Energy of motion is called _____, while stored energy is called_____.

3. _____ is a force that slows an object's motion.

Answers are on page 451.

GED PRACTICE

Directions: Choose the <u>one best answer</u> to each question.

Questions 1 and 2 refer to the following paragraph and illustration.

A pendulum consists of a suspended object that can swing freely back and forth. A wrecking ball swung by a crane is an example of a practical use of a pendulum. The wrecking ball illustrated below rises to its high point, A, before swinging back through its low point, C, and then over to the right side as indicated.

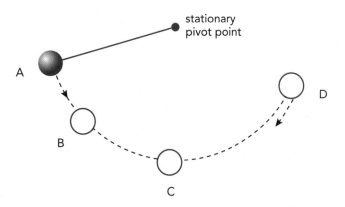

1. At which point is the energy of the wrecking ball partly kinetic and partly potential?

   (1) point A only
   (2) point B only
   (3) point C only
   (4) points A and B only
   (5) points B and C only

2. After striking a building, a wrecking ball hangs motionless, having lost the total kinetic and potential energy it had while swinging. Which conclusion below is best supported by the above observation and is consistent with the law of conservation of energy?

   (1) The energy will be recovered when the crane operator swings the ball back up.
   (2) The energy cannot be recovered.
   (3) Because it is attached to the crane, the ball never had its own energy.
   (4) The ball will continue moving on its own after a short time.
   (5) The energy has been changed into the energy used to break apart the building.

Answers are on page 451.

Forms of Energy

Heat: Energy of Molecular Motion

Ruben lives in a third-floor apartment in the city. In the summer, his apartment is very hot, even when the windows are open. In the winter the landlord keeps the heat turned down, and Ruben freezes!

Ruben's two predicaments are related to heat. **Heat** is the energy of moving atoms. When atoms move rapidly, an object is hot. When atoms move slowly, the object is cold. When Ruben is suffering in the heat, the atoms in the air of his apartment are moving very rapidly. When his teeth are chattering from the cold, the atoms in the air are moving much more slowly.

Temperature is a measure of heat energy. When an object absorbs heat, its temperature rises. When an object gives off heat, its temperature falls.

- When placed on a hot stove, water in a pan gains heat and boils.

- When put in a freezer, water loses heat and freezes.

What happens when two objects at different temperatures are brought together? Heat energy flows from the warmer object to the cooler object. This heat flow continues until both objects reach the same temperature. When you put ice cubes in a glass of tap water, the ice cubes warm and melt. At the same time, the water cools until both melted ice and water are the same temperature. Heat flows from the tap water to the ice cubes.

Expansion and Contraction

When an object is heated, it **expands**. As the object gets hotter, its atoms move more rapidly and farther apart. Have you noticed that doors sometimes stick in the summer? This is because the door expands more than the door frame. Most objects expand so little that you hardly notice. A pan heated on a stove expands only a small fraction of an inch.

When an object cools, it **contracts**. As the object cools, its atoms move more slowly and closer together. After taking a cake out of an oven, the cake must cool before you can remove it from the pan. As it cools, the cake contracts and loosens from the sides of the pan.

A gas expands more than a liquid, and a liquid expands more than a solid. When the outdoor temperature rises, the liquid inside a thermometer expands more than the glass—a solid—that contains it.

Thinking About Science

Directions: Each statement below refers to the effect of heat on matter. Circle *T* for each statement that is true and *F* for each statement that is false.

T F **1.** A penny, placed in the sunshine, expands as it becomes warmer.

T F **2.** A helium-filled weather balloon, released at ground level, expands when it reaches the cold upper atmosphere.

T F **3.** Air pressure in a car tire increases during a hot afternoon.

T F **4.** As the hot water in a bathtub cools, the water expands and may flow over the sides of a tub.

Answers are on page 451.

GED PRACTICE

Directions: Choose the <u>one best answer</u> to each question.

Questions 1 and 2 refer to the information on page 305.

1. When a piece of hot iron (temperature 380°F) is thrown into a barrel of cold water (temperature 50°F), which of the following will occur?

   (1) Heat will flow from the water to the iron until both are the same temperature.
   (2) Heat will flow from the iron to the water until both are the same temperature.
   (3) The water will be heated to 380°F.
   (4) The iron will be cooled to 50°F.
   (5) Nothing, because heat can't flow from iron to water.

2. When engineers design bridges they purposely place gaps between the points where large metal beams meet end to end. What is the most likely purpose of these gaps?

   (1) to allow for water drainage during rainstorms
   (2) to provide room for the beams to contract during times of cold weather
   (3) to prevent rust from forming at the point where the beams might rub together
   (4) to allow for errors in measurement during construction
   (5) to provide room for the beams to expand during times of hot weather

Questions 3–5 are based on the following reading selection and diagram.

Your body temperature is a measure of the heat produced within your body. Most of the time, your temperature remains about the same. However, during illness your temperature rises as your body fights infection.

A first sign of illness is an unusual increase in body temperature. This rise can be a symptom of a cold, the flu, or a much more serious illness such as meningitis, a disease that requires immediate medical attention. Also, extreme fever itself can be very harmful. A fever higher than 105.8°F (41°C) can cause permanent damage to a person's nervous system.

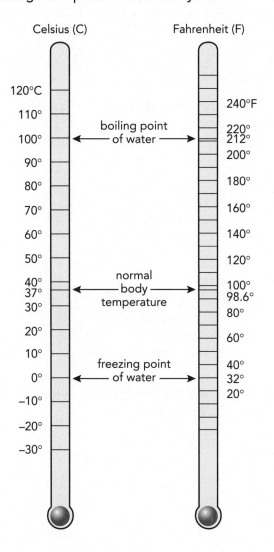

3. According to the diagram, what is the normal human body temperature?

   (1) 33°C or 91.4°F
   (2) 37°C or 98.6°F
   (3) 39°C or 102.2°F
   (4) 40°C or 104°F
   (5) 44°C or 111.2°F

4. Which temperature represents a slight fever?

   (1) 96°F
   (2) 37°C
   (3) 98.6°F
   (4) 38°C
   (5) 106°F

5. What is the best parental response to a child's waking in the middle of the night with a 105°F temperature?

   (1) Tell the child to go to sleep and see how the fever is in the morning.
   (2) Cool the child with a damp cloth, call the after-hours number at your doctor's office or hospital, report the child's symptoms, and get medical advice.
   (3) Wait for a few hours and see if the temperature goes down by itself.
   (4) Don't worry, because high temperatures in children are common.
   (5) Call a friend with children and ask for advice.

   Answers are on page 451.

Water and Sound Energy

During the afternoon of April 1, 1946, huge ocean waves pounded the shores of the Hawaiian Islands and left 173 people dead or missing, 163 people injured, and millions of dollars worth of property damage.

Where did the ocean along the normally peaceful Hawaiian shores get the energy to cause such extensive damage? Although difficult to believe, this tremendous energy came from an earthquake only five hours earlier in the Aleutian Trench. This trench is a gorge in Earth's crust that lies on the bottom of the Pacific Ocean off the shore of Alaska. The energy was carried to Hawaii by means of wave motion within the ocean water.

Two types of **waves** that carry energy by wave motion in material substances are water waves and sound waves.

Water Waves

If you look at waves on water, you can see many of the properties common to all waves. For example, Diagram A shows what happens when you drop a stone into a pond. The waves move directly away in a circular pattern from the place where the stone was dropped. Like all other types of waves, water waves travel in a straight line away from their source.

Diagram B is a cutaway drawing of the wave pattern. It illustrates the position of crests and troughs of the waves on the water's surface. The distance between two crests (or two troughs) is called the **wavelength**.

A

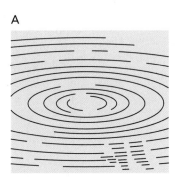

Circular water waves are produced by a stone dropped in a pond.

B

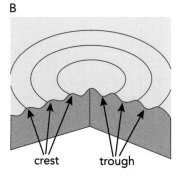

Cutaway shows portion of wave crests and troughs.

When a wave hits a smooth surface, it **reflects**, or bounces off the surface. In Diagram C, one series of waves spreads out away from the center. As the waves hit the barrier, they are reflected, causing the rainbow-shaped pattern.

As a wave crosses a boundary, it **refracts**, or bends, continuing its course but moving in a slightly different direction. In Diagram D, a straight water wave refracts as it crosses from an area of deep water to an area of shallow water. Water waves refract as they approach a beach.

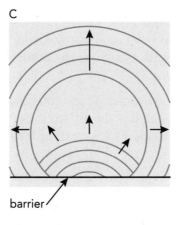

C

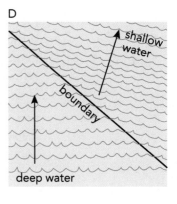

D

barrier

A circular water wave reflects as it strikes a solid barrier.

A straight water wave refracts as it moves across a boundary between deep and shallow water.

Finally, all waves **diffract**—they spread out into a region behind or around a barrier. You can see water waves diffracting in Diagram E below.

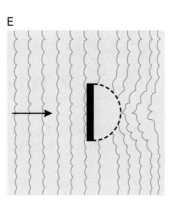

E

Waves diffract as they move around a barrier. A water wave diffracts, or spreads out, as it goes by an object.

Sound Waves

What does a cricket's shrill have in common with a rock concert? Your answer will depend upon your interest in rock music! One similarity between them is that both are forms of sound, a type of energy that travels to our ears as a wave.

Sound is produced by any vibrating object. For example, when a vibrating guitar string moves to the right, it compresses the air molecules to the immediate right. As the string moves to the left, the air molecules just to the right of the string become spaced farther apart. The result of the string's vibrating back and forth is a sound wave.

Like other waves, sound travels in a straight line and will reflect off a smooth surface. Reflection is most easily demonstrated by honking a car horn in a tunnel or by shouting in a canyon. The echoes that you hear are simply reflected sound waves.

Sound waves also diffract. When you stand in one room and speak with a person in another room, it is the diffraction of sound that allows you to hear the second person. Sound waves easily spread around corners and through doorways.

Listener   Speaker

Thinking About Science

Directions: Read each statement below. Circle *T* for each statement that is true and *F* for each statement that is false.

T F **1.** Sound waves carry energy, but water waves do not.

T F **2.** Water waves on the ocean move along the ocean's surface.

T F **3.** Sound waves move in a straight line away from the source.

Answers are on page 451.

Directions: Choose the <u>one best answer</u> to each question.

Questions 1–5 refer to the following passage and table.

The *frequency* of sound is the number of complete waves produced each second. Frequency determines pitch. A high-frequency sound like the high note on the piano is said to have a high pitch. A low-frequency sound like a bass drum has a low pitch. Each type of animal life on Earth has one frequency range in which it can hear and another frequency range in which it can speak or make sound. Several common frequency ranges are listed by cycles per second in the following table. A cycle is one complete vibration—one complete wavelength.

COMMON FREQUENCY RANGES

Animal	Hearing*	Making Sound or Speaking*
Human	20–20,000	85–1,100
Dog	15–50,000	450–1,080
Cat	60–65,000	760–1,520
Grasshopper	100–15,000	7,000–100,000
Dolphin	150–150,000	7,000–120,000
Robin	250–21,000	2,000–13,000
Bat	1,000–120,000	10,000–120,000

*in cycles per second (cps)

1. What is the frequency range in which dogs bark?

   (1) 85–1,100 cycles per second
   (2) 15–50,000 cycles per second
   (3) 450–1,080 cycles per second
   (4) 60–65,000 cycles per second
   (5) 250–21,000 cycles per second

2. Which animal has the greatest hearing range?

   (1) grasshopper
   (2) dog
   (3) cat
   (4) dolphin
   (5) bat

3. Of the animals listed in the table, which is the only animal that can hear sounds of a lower frequency than human beings can hear?

   (1) dolphin
   (2) dog
   (3) cat
   (4) bat
   (5) grasshopper

4. Of the animals listed in the table, which is the only animal that can "speak" at frequencies far greater than the highest frequencies it can hear?

   (1) dolphin
   (2) dog
   (3) cat
   (4) bat
   (5) grasshopper

5. Which of the following conclusions is best supported by the information given in the table?

   (1) In most cases, the smaller an animal is, the more sound frequencies it can hear.
   (2) Human beings can speak at higher frequencies than other animals can "speak."
   (3) The hearing range of most animals includes both lower and higher frequencies than their speaking range.
   (4) Human beings can hear at higher frequencies than other animals can.
   (5) Four-legged mammals such as dogs and cats can hear sounds of much higher frequencies than are heard by birds or sea animals.

Answers are on page 451.

Electromagnetic Energy

When you look into the sky on a clear, moonless night, stars appear as pinholes of light shining through a black canvas. Yet, seen through a telescope, starlight reveals distant galaxies—worlds that have existed billions of years longer than our own. Starlight, as well as all other forms of light, is a type of energy that travels as a wave through the vast distances of space. Today, scientists analyze this starlight with the hope of discovering how distant stars and planets formed. Information contained in this light may someday help explain the origin of Earth.

Electromagnetic Waves

Light is a special form of wave called an **electromagnetic wave**. Unlike water and sound waves, electromagnetic waves can travel through a **vacuum**—space that contains no matter. In fact, all the light we receive from the Sun, Moon, and stars travels to us through the vacuum of space. This light moves in a straight line on its long journey to us. Interestingly, it is only because sunlight moves in a straight line that we have clearly defined shadows on Earth.

Electromagnetic waves exist over a very wide range of wavelengths, called the **electromagnetic spectrum**. The range of wavelengths that humans can detect is usually called **light** or **visible light**. Visible light is a small part of the total electromagnetic spectrum. Wavelengths that we are unable to see include radio waves, microwaves, X rays, and gamma rays. Starlight consists of visible light and many of these other wavelengths. Scientists use specially designed detectors to study electromagnetic waves that are not visible to the human eye.

Light and Color

You may think of sunlight as white light, but sunlight is actually made up of a spectrum of colors. This spectrum is beautifully displayed as a rainbow arching across the sky after a light rain. The same bands of color can also be created by passing sunlight through a **prism**, a triangular piece of glass.

As you know, refraction occurs when a wave strikes a boundary and begins to move in a different direction. In a prism, the edge of the glass is a boundary. When the sunlight strikes it, the light bends, or refracts. The white light separates into its component colors because each color of light refracts by a different amount.

Each color of light can be thought of as a wave with a certain wavelength. As the prism diagram on page 313 shows, the amount of refraction depends on the wavelength of the color.

- Red light has the longest wavelength. Red light refracts the least.

- Violet light has the shortest wavelength. Violet light refracts the most.

Sunlight is made up of many colors. Why is it, then, when we look at most objects, we see only a single color? The answer is that objects reflect some wavelengths of light and absorb others. For example, a green leaf reflects wavelengths associated with green. This reflected light is what we see. The leaf absorbs all other wavelengths (colors).

A black surface absorbs almost all the light that strikes it. A mirror or white surface reflects almost all light. During reflection, light changes its direction of travel much as a tennis ball changes direction after striking a solid wall.

THE FORMATION OF A RAINBOW   **THE REFRACTION OF LIGHT BY A PRISM**

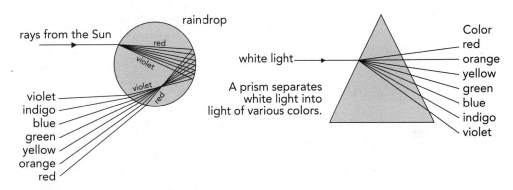

Thinking About Science

Directions: From the information given in the reading passage, determine if each of the following statements is true or false. Circle *T* if it is true or *F* if it is false.

T   F   **1.** An asphalt road appears almost black because it reflects all of the sunlight that strikes it.

T   F   **2.** A red car appears red because it absorbs all wavelengths of light except wavelengths associated with red light.

T   F   **3.** On a hot summer day, a green shirt will keep you cooler than a white shirt.

T   F   **4.** A mirror reflects almost all the light that strikes it.

Answers are on page 451.

Directions: Choose the <u>one best answer</u> to each question.

Questions 1–4 refer to the following passage and diagram.

The diagram below shows the electromagnetic spectrum. Shorter wavelengths (higher energy waves) are shown on the left; longer wavelengths (lower energy waves) are shown on the right.

ELECTROMAGNETIC SPECTRUM

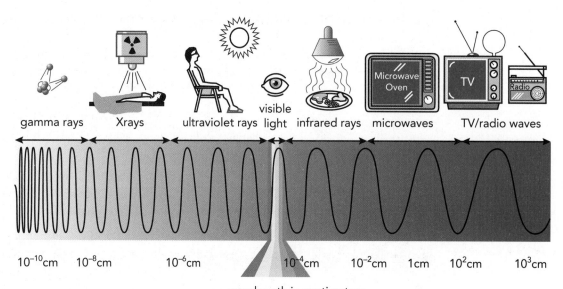

wavelength in centimeters

1. Which of the following statements is true?

   (1) Ultraviolet rays are higher energy than visible light.
   (2) Ultraviolet rays are lower energy than visible light.
   (3) Ultraviolet rays and visible light have the same energy.
   (4) Ultraviolet rays have the same energy as infrared rays.
   (5) Ultraviolet rays have lower energy than infrared rays.

2. Of the following, which has the longest wavelength?

   (1) microwaves
   (2) X rays
   (3) gamma rays
   (4) ultraviolet rays
   (5) radio waves

3. High-energy electromagnetic waves are harmful to humans. Which of the following should humans limit their exposure to?

   (1) microwaves and radio waves
   (2) visible light and television
   (3) X rays and ultraviolet rays
   (4) infrared rays and visible light
   (5) television and X rays

4. Which of the following is the <u>least</u> useful form of electromagnetic energy?

   (1) Radio waves are used to transmit radio signals.
   (2) Ultraviolet rays cause sunburn.
   (3) X rays are used to take pictures of bones inside the human body.
   (4) Visible light is used for seeing.
   (5) Microwaves are used for cooking food that has a high water content.

Answers are on page 451.

Electrical Energy

In 1877 the famous physicist Hermann von Helmholtz was taking members of the Imperial Court on a tour of his laboratory in Berlin. One of his guests looked at the electric wires and asked in amazement, "But, professor, how is it possible for electricity to flow through these thin little tubes?"

History doesn't tell us how Helmholtz answered this question. However, the atomic theory of matter today tells us that all matter is composed of atoms that have negatively charged electrons and positively charged protons. Electricity involves the motion of some of these electrons. Electricity is one of two types—static electricity or electric current.

Static Electricity: Electric Charges at Rest

Most objects in nature are electrically neutral, having the same number of electrons as protons. Here are two examples of what happens when the balance of positive and negative charges are upset:

- When you rub a comb through your dry hair, the comb picks up extra electrons. These electrons electrically stick to the comb and can then make your hair stand on end.

- When you walk across a woolen carpet, your body can pick up excess electrons from the wool. You can get quite a shock by touching a metal door handle, as electrons jump from your fingers to the metal.

Each scenario above is an example of **static electricity**—electricity in which electrons are transferred from one object to another. This transfer of electric charge takes place because the outermost electrons in many atoms are held loosely by the nuclei and can easily be removed.

Electric Current: Electric Charges in Motion

In static electricity you see the effects of transferred electric charges. Now, what is electric current?

Electric current is the flow of electrons in a material such as copper wire. In a way, you can think of this flow of electrons as being similar to the flow of water in a hose.

- A material in which electrons can be made to flow is called a **conductor**. Most good conductors are metals such as copper and silver.

- A material in which electrons cannot be made to flow is called a **nonconductor**, or an insulator. Glass is a nonconductor. The rubber material that covers electric wires is a nonconductor and is called **insulation.** Electric current cannot flow through insulation. Insulation protects you from electric shock when you touch wires carrying a current.

- A material in which only a small amount of electric current can be made to flow is called a **semiconductor**. A semiconductor, such as silicon, does not conduct current as easily as a conductor but will conduct current under certain conditions. Semiconductors have properties that make them very valuable in the electronics industry.

Direct Current

Electric current that moves in one direction only is called **direct current** (DC). You can create a direct current by attaching a battery to the ends of a copper wire. The battery produces an electric force that pushes electrons away from the negative terminal and toward the positive terminal. For a current to flow from terminal to terminal, there must be a complete circuit. A wire must connect the terminals so that electrons can move from one battery terminal to the other. A break anywhere in the circuit will stop the current's flow.

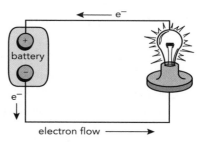

In a direct current circuit, electrons flow in a complete path from the negative terminal of the battery to the positive terminal.

Alternating Current

The most common household power source is the wall socket. A wall socket provides an **alternating current** (AC)—a current in which the electrons flow first in one direction and then in the opposite direction. The current in most homes is called 60-cycle AC—the current goes back and forth in a circuit 60 times in one second.

An electric circuit can be either a series circuit or a parallel circuit.

- In a **series circuit** there is only one path for electric current to take. A break anywhere in this circuit stops the electric current flow to every light or other device in the circuit. A string of holiday lights uses a series circuit. When one bulb in the string goes out, the entire strand of bulbs go out.

- In a **parallel circuit** there is more than one path for electric current to take. A break in one part of the circuit does not always stop the electric current from flowing through other lights or devices in the circuit. For example, a dining room chandelier may have several lightbulbs. When one bulb burns out, the others still remain lit.

SERIES CIRCUIT   **PARALLEL CIRCUIT**

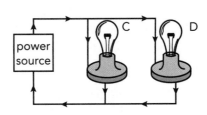

If bulb A burns out, bulb B goes out.   If bulb C burns out, bulb D stays lit.

The amount of current that flows from any power source depends on the voltage. Commonly used batteries you see around home are the $1\frac{1}{2}$-volt flashlight battery and the 9-volt smoke alarm battery. A wall socket, which produces a 120-volt signal, provides a much greater amount of current. This is why you can safely handle batteries but should not, under any circumstances, stick your finger in a wall socket!

Thinking About Science

Directions: Match each item on the left with the phrase that best describes it on the right. Write the letter of the phrase on the line before the correct number.

_____ **1.** alternating current

_____ **2.** voltage

_____ **3.** insulator

_____ **4.** electrons

_____ **5.** direct current

(a) flows in one direction only

(b) moving particles that make up an electric current

(c) a number that tells the strength of a battery

(d) flows first in one direction and then in the other direction

(e) a material in which electric current cannot flow

Answers are on page 451.

Directions: Choose the <u>one best answer</u> to each question.

Questions 1 and 2 refer to the information on pages 315–317.

1. Which statement best describes what happens in a series circuit of lights if one light goes out?

   (1) One other light goes out.
   (2) All of the other lights go out.
   (3) All of the other lights stay on.
   (4) Half of the other lights go out.
   (5) A circuit breaker trips.

2. One light in the dining room burns out. The rest of the lights in the room remain as bright as ever. What is the most reasonable conclusion you can draw from this fact?

   (1) The lights are in a parallel circuit.
   (2) The burned-out light caused a circuit breaker to trip to off.
   (3) The lights are in a series circuit.
   (4) Another light will burn out soon.
   (5) There is a power shortage at your house.

Questions 3 and 4 refer to the following diagram.

3. The following three statements refer to circuit A.

   A. Direct current is flowing in circuit A.

   B. Electrons are flowing from the positive terminal of the battery to the negative terminal.

   C. Disconnecting the wire at the positive terminal of the battery will turn off the light but not the bell.

   Which of the statements above is false?

   (1) A only
   (2) B only
   (3) C only
   (4) A and B only
   (5) B and C only

4. When a switch in any circuit is opened, the flow of current in that circuit stops. Referring to circuit B, choose which of the three switches (a, b, and c) you could open in order to turn off light 1 only.

   (1) a only
   (2) b only
   (3) c only
   (4) either a or c
   (5) either b or c

   Answers are on page 452.

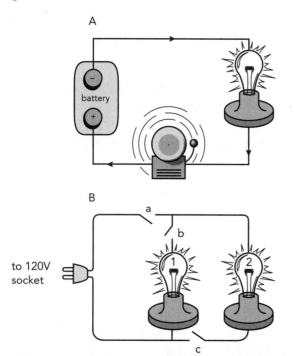

Superconductivity

Imagine trains that float on cushions of magnetic force and speed across the country at hundreds of miles per hour. Imagine computers only a fraction of the size they are now and powerful electric motors the size of your thumb. Will such devices be in our future? "Yes!" say many excited physicists today. In fact, scientists predict that these consumer products are just three of many that may result from one of the most exciting advances to take place in physics in decades: superconductivity.

Superconductivity is an amazing phenomenon that involves electric current—the flow of electrons through a conductor. In today's conductors of electricity, such as copper wire, electrons bump into atomic nuclei and into each other, thus experiencing resistance to flow. Electrical resistance causes heat and results in a loss of energy. About 20 percent of the electrical energy carried by high-voltage power lines is lost as heat.

In a **superconductor**, on the other hand, electrons do not lose energy in collisions. There is no electrical resistance. There are no collisions. No energy is lost when electrons flow, and no heat is created. Superconductors are perfect conductors of electricity.

No one knows exactly why superconductivity occurs. A popular hypothesis is that electrons in a superconductor move in pairs in a coordinated motion. Somehow this coordinated motion enables electrons to avoid collisions. Think of this motion as similar to the organized movement of two-lane traffic on a very busy street.

Although superconductivity was first discovered in the element mercury in 1911, no practical applications were developed in the years that immediately followed. The most important obstacle was that materials that became superconductors would do so only at extremely low temperatures. Mercury, for example, was found to become superconducting only when its temperature was lowered to −452°F! At any higher temperature, mercury is as resistant as a regular conductor. What's more, cooling mercury to −452°F requires immersing it in a bath of liquid helium, a very expensive and inefficient coolant.

Between 1911 and the present, other superconducting materials have been discovered. In the mid-1980s, physicists found that certain types of ceramics become superconductors and that they do so at liquid nitrogen temperature (−321°F). In the 1990s other superconductors were discovered that function at temperatures as high as −207°F. As new types of superconducting ceramics are developed, the hope is that room-temperature superconductors may someday be in common use.

Thinking About Science

Directions: Match each item on the left with the phrase that is the best description on the right. Write the letter of the phrase on the line before the correct number.

_____ 1. helium

(a) the absence of electrical resistance

_____ 2. mercury

(b) any material that transmits electricity

_____ 3. superconductivity

(c) a recently discovered superconductor

_____ 4. conductor

(d) the first known superconductor

_____ 5. ceramic

(e) a coolant when in liquid form

Answers are on page 452.

GED PRACTICE

Directions: Choose the <u>one best answer</u> to each question.

Questions 1 and 2 refer to the information on page 319.

1. Which theory below attempts to explain superconductivity?

   (1) The magnetic field surrounding a superconductor becomes strong as the electric current increases.
   (2) A superconductor's electrical resistance disappears when electric current flows.
   (3) A superconductor's electrons become very small and move rapidly through the conductor.
   (4) Electric current in a superconductor is not carried by electrons.
   (5) Electrons in a superconductor join in pairs and move through the material in a coordinated way.

2. The use of superconducting electric power lines could save utility companies billions of dollars each year. What assumption is made by scientists who claim that this will result in lower electricity costs to consumers?

   (1) After utility companies install superconducting power lines, consumers will use less electricity.
   (2) Consumers will get rebates for the installation of superconducting power.
   (3) Superconducting power lines will permit the construction of faster trains and result in lower train fares.
   (4) The money saved by utility companies in the transmission of electricity on superconducting lines will be passed along as savings to consumers.
   (5) After superconducting power lines are installed, many people who presently heat by gas or oil will switch to electricity.

Answers are on page 452.

Magnetism

Centuries ago, the Greeks discovered that small pieces of a certain iron ore could both attract and repel other pieces of the same ore. Today this ore is called magnetite, and pieces of magnetite are referred to as natural magnets. The phenomenon the Greeks observed is called **magnetism**.

HAVE YOU SEEN MAGNETS DO THESE THINGS?

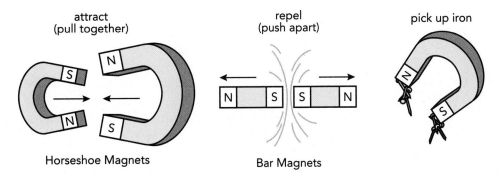

attract
(pull together)

repel
(push apart)

pick up iron

Horseshoe Magnets

Bar Magnets

Magnets have two poles, or regions, where the magnetic force is very strong. When magnets are brought close together, their poles act similar to electric charges.

- Opposite poles attract each other. The north pole of one magnet is strongly attracted to the south pole of a second magnet.

- Like poles repel each other. North poles repel each other; so do south poles.

Two common magnets that you may recognize are the horseshoe magnet and the bar magnet. A horseshoe magnet, as its name implies, looks like a horseshoe. The poles are the two ends of the magnet. A bar magnet is in the shape of a straight bar. One end is the north pole, and the other end is the south pole. Horseshoe and bar magnets differ only in shape. Like all other magnets, each of these magnets has one north pole and one south pole.

When you use magnets, you will discover two more of their properties.

- A magnet strongly attracts iron, which itself is not a magnet. Iron is attracted to both the north pole and the south pole of a magnet.

- Magnetic force, whether it attracts or repels, becomes weaker as the distance from the magnet increases.

Another type of magnet is called an electromagnet. An **electromagnet** is made by coiling a wire around a piece of iron and running an electric current through the wire. The magnetic field that results is very strong. You may have seen pictures of small electromagnets being used to lift cars in a junkyard.

Thinking About Science

Directions: The statements below refer to magnetism. Circle *T* for each statement that is true and *F* for each that is false.

T   F   **1.** The north pole of a magnet is always attracted to the south pole of another magnet.

T   F   **2.** A bar magnet differs from a horseshoe magnet in that a bar magnet will not attract iron.

T   F   **3.** Magnetite is a name given to a type of natural magnet.

T   F   **4.** The strength of a magnet increases as the distance from the magnet increases.

T   F   **5.** Horseshoe and bar magnets differ only in shape.

Answers are on page 452.

GED PRACTICE

Directions: Choose the <u>one best answer</u> to each question.

Questions 1 and 2 refer to the following passage.

When a wire carries an alternating electric current, both an alternating electric field and an alternating magnetic field are produced near the wire. These combined fields are called electromagnetic fields. In recent years, the presence of strong electromagnetic fields near electric power lines has become a topic of concern. Some scientists have suggested that long-term exposure to strong electromagnetic fields may be harmful. People living near high-voltage power lines have complained of excessive fatigue, unusual memory loss, headaches, and a feeling of discomfort. In response to these claims and out of concern for public health, scientists are investigating these health-and-safety issues. No one yet knows what dangers, if any, are posed by strong electromagnetic fields. Until answers become available, however, the smart response is to reasonably limit your exposure to them.

1. Which of the following does not have a surrounding electromagnetic field when it is turned on?

   (1) hair dryer
   (2) car radio
   (3) television set
   (4) gas barbecue
   (5) toaster

2. Suppose you are in the presence of a strong electromagnetic field near power lines. Which of the following is the *least* risk factor?

   (1) your distance from the power lines
   (2) the time of day
   (3) the time you spend in the field
   (4) the strength of the field
   (5) your personal sensitivity to the field

Question 3 refers to the illustration below.

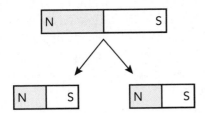

3. Suppose you cut a bar magnet in half. Which of the following statements are true?

   A. Two new magnets are formed.

   B. The magnetism of the bar is destroyed.

   C. The poles of the new magnets are in the same direction as the original poles.

   D. The poles of the new magnets are in the opposite direction of the original poles.

   (1) A and B
   (2) A and C
   (3) A and D
   (4) B and C
   (5) B and D

Question 4 refers to the illustration below.

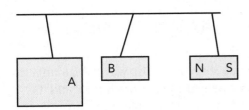

4. Which could be true for the three magnets?

   (1) Both A and B are south poles.
   (2) Both A and B are north poles.
   (3) A is a north pole; B is a south pole.
   (4) A is a south pole; B is a north pole.
   (5) Only the magnet to the right has poles.

Questions 5–7 refer to the following definitions.

nonmagnetic—not attracted to a magnet at all

naturally magnetic—occurs in nature as a natural magnet

ferromagnetic—strongly attracted by a magnet

paramagnetic—only slightly attracted by a magnet

diamagnetic—weakly repelled by a magnet

5. While playing with a magnet and a box of thumbtacks, Laurie noticed that the tacks strongly clung to both poles of the magnet. How are these thumbtacks best classified?

   (1) nonmagnetic
   (2) naturally magnetic
   (3) ferromagnetic
   (4) paramagnetic
   (5) diamagnetic

6. The ancient Chinese used lodestone, a type of magnetic ore found in mountains, to make compasses for use in navigation. How is lodestone best classified?

   (1) nonmagnetic
   (2) naturally magnetic
   (3) ferromagnetic
   (4) paramagnetic
   (5) diamagnetic

7. When alchemists were trying to find a way to create gold, they knew that gold is weakly repelled by a magnet. How is gold best classified?

   (1) nonmagnetic
   (2) naturally magnetic
   (3) ferromagnetic
   (4) paramagnetic
   (5) diamagnetic

Answers are on page 452 .

Nuclear Energy

Radioactivity

What do CAT scans and nuclear power plants have in common? You may already know the answer—they both make use of **radioactivity**, a property of some types of atoms. The nuclei of radioactive isotopes are unstable and break apart on their own. As an unstable nucleus breaks apart, it shoots out certain types of particles and rays. Nine naturally occurring elements are known to be radioactive.

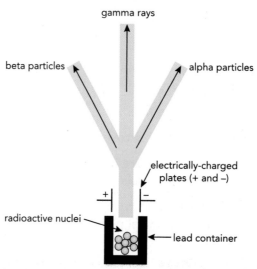

Alpha and beta particles and gamma rays are shot out as radioactive nuclei decay. Electrically charged plates can be used to separate the charged particles.

Three basic types of particles and rays are given off by a radioactive nucleus.

- An **alpha particle** is made up of two protons and two neutrons bound tightly together.

- A **beta particle** is an electron. It is identical to the electrons that orbit the nucleus of each atom.

- A **gamma ray** is a high-energy electromagnetic wave. A gamma ray differs from visible light in that its energy is much higher and its wavelength is much shorter.

A given amount of a radioactive substance will decay (change into other substances because its nuclei are splitting) over a period of time. The rate at which the substance decays is given as a number called a **half-life**. During one half-life, one-half of the radioactive nuclei present will decay by splitting into smaller nuclei. Each radioactive element has a different half-life.

- The half-life of uranium-238 is 45,510,000,000 years.

- The half-life of polonium is 138 days.

RADIOACTIVE DECAY OF URANIUM–238

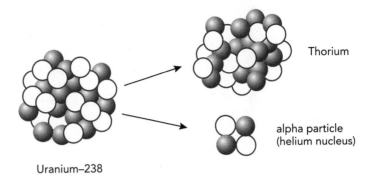

Thorium

alpha particle
(helium nucleus)

Uranium–238

Below is an illustration of a radioactive-decay curve for a fictitious element that has a half-life of one day. The element starts with 1,000 nuclei. Notice how many nuclei remain as each day (half-life) passes.

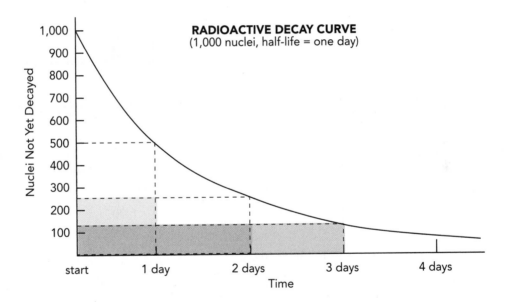

Notice that when one half-life (one day) has passed, only 500 nuclei have not yet decayed.

Thinking About Science

Directions: Answer each question below.

1. Name the three types of particles and rays given off by radioactive nuclei when they decay: _____, _____, and _____.

2. What is the name given to the length of time it takes half of a group of radioactive nuclei to decay? _____

3. What elements form when uranium-238 undergoes radioactive decay? _____

Answers are on page 452.

GED PRACTICE

Directions: Choose the <u>one best answer</u> to each question.

Questions 1 and 2 are based on the information on pages 324 and 325.

1. Which of the following statements is false?

   (1) Three types of particles and rays are given off by a radioactive nucleus.
   (2) Each radioactive element has a different half-life.
   (3) During radioactive decay, a nucleus breaks apart.
   (4) During one half-life, half of the radioactive nuclei will decay.
   (5) All elements are known to undergo radioactive decay.

2. According to the graph on page 325, how many nuclei remain after three half-lives have passed?

   (1) 1,000
   (2) 500
   (3) 250
   (4) 125
   (5) less than 100

Answers are on page 452.

Chain Reactions and Nuclear Power

The discovery of radioactivity in 1896 was the first step toward a complete understanding of atomic nuclei. Another discovery showed that many nuclei could be split into smaller nuclei if they were bombarded with particles such as protons or alpha particles.

The process of splitting a nucleus into two smaller nuclei is called nuclear fission. The **fission** of a nucleus causes the release of a large amount of nuclear energy. Scientists realized that a tremendous supply of energy could be released through the fission of very small amounts of elements such as uranium.

In 1942 Enrico Fermi, an Italian physicist working at the University of Chicago, produced the first controlled nuclear **chain reaction**. In a chain reaction nuclei are split apart in a controlled way, and as a result a great quantity of nuclear energy is produced. (An example of an uncontrolled nuclear reaction is the explosion of an atomic bomb.)

By the end of World War II, the first nuclear reactors were being built. A **nuclear reactor** is a device in which controlled chain reactions are carried out. Nuclear reactors are the heart of a nuclear power plant.

A nuclear power plant operates much the same way as a coal power plant. In each, heat energy is used to produce electrical energy. In the coal plant, heat is produced by the burning of coal in a boiler. In a nuclear plant, heat comes from the fission of nuclei in a nuclear reactor. In each plant, the heat created is used to boil water to produce steam. The steam turns a turbine that is connected to an electric generator. The generator produces electrical power, which then flows down electric power lines.

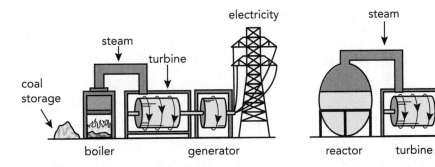

In both coal and nuclear power plants, water is heated to produce steam, which turns a turbine to create electricity.

Compared to other fuels, nuclear fuel produces an enormous amount of energy. A piece of U-235 (uranium 235, a rare form of uranium) the size of a grain of rice can produce energy equal to that contained in three tons of coal or fourteen barrels of oil! One pound of U-235 can produce energy equal to that produced by 3 million pounds of coal or 6,400 barrels of oil.

Nuclear Fusion

Someday it may be possible to obtain large amounts of power through a process called nuclear fusion. **Fusion** occurs when two nuclei are fused, or joined together to form one nucleus. Nuclear fusion is the process that provides the energy given off by stars, including the Sun. On the Sun, hydrogen atoms fuse, or combine, to form helium atoms, releasing tremendous energy in the process.

Unfortunately, fusion reactions can take place only in regions having an extremely high temperature—near 100 million degrees Celsius! Because it is so difficult to produce this high temperature, nuclear fusion is not yet a practical energy source. Whether it ever will be is still a debated question. However, hydrogen—the fuel needed for nuclear fusion reactions—is available in abundance on Earth. It can be taken directly from ocean water.

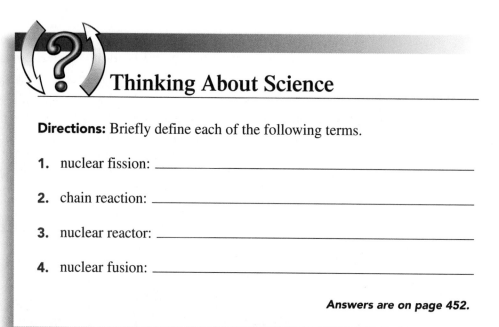

Thinking About Science

Directions: Briefly define each of the following terms.

1. nuclear fission: _____

2. chain reaction: _____

3. nuclear reactor: _____

4. nuclear fusion: _____

Answers are on page 452.

Go to **www.GEDScience.com** for additional practice and instruction!

Directions: Choose the <u>one best answer</u> to each question.

Questions 1–3 refer to the information on pages 327 and 328.

1. How is a nuclear power plant similar to a coal power plant?

   (1) Both use an electric generator to turn a steam-driven turbine.
   (2) Both produce nuclear waste.
   (3) Both use a steam-driven turbine to turn an electric generator.
   (4) Both burn coal as a source of heat energy.
   (5) Both use nuclear fission as a source of heat energy.

2. What is U-235?

   (1) a type of nuclear reaction
   (2) an electric generator in a nuclear power plant
   (3) a form of heat energy produced by nuclear fission
   (4) a type of fuel used in nuclear fusion
   (5) a type of fuel used in nuclear fission

3. All of the statements below were made by a scientist working at a nuclear power plant. Which statement is a prediction?

   (1) Nuclear fission produces radioactive by-products.
   (2) By the year 2050, nuclear power plants will be the world's primary method of producing electrical power.
   (3) Nuclear fusion power plants have not been developed because no one knows how to build one.
   (4) When U-235 fissions, tremendous energy is released.
   (5) Accidents such as the nuclear meltdown at Chernobyl remind us just how dangerous nuclear power plants can be.

Questions 4 is based on the following passage and illustration.

A nuclear chain reaction starts when a fast neutron strikes a U-235 nucleus. This nucleus splits into a cesium nucleus (Cs), a rubidium nucleus (Rb), and three fast neutrons. Each of these fast neutrons is then capable of striking and splitting another U-235 nucleus. As the reaction continues, the number of nuclei being split rapidly increases as does the energy produced.

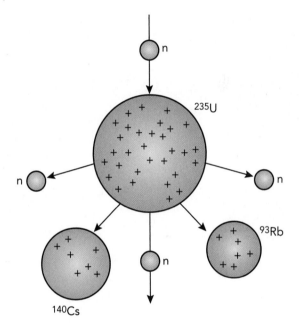

4. Control rods are used in a reactor to control the speed at which a nuclear chain reaction takes place. What is the most likely function of the control rods?

   (1) to absorb fast neutrons
   (2) to limit the amount of U-235 in the reactor
   (3) to measure the temperature of the reactor
   (4) to provide additional fast neutrons.
   (5) to collect Cs and Rb atoms

Answers are on page 452.

Our Energy Future

So far, we've discussed two forms of energy—fossil fuels (oil, coal, and gas) and nuclear energy. Each of these energy sources has disadvantages.

- Burning fossil fuels pollute the environment, and the supply of fossil fuels is limited.

- Nuclear energy produces hazardous radioactive waste. There is no known way to get rid of this waste. It can only be stored.

Scientists are doing research on alternative forms of energy, hoping that one of these, or a combination of them, may someday help fill our energy needs.

Water Energy

The most important form of water energy in the United States is **hydroelectric power**—the energy of flowing rivers. Flowing water can be used to turn turbines and produce electricity. At present, hydroelectric power provides about four percent of the energy used in the United States.

Ocean water also contains a great amount of energy, both as ocean waves and in the heat energy held in ocean water. But harnessing that energy has proved difficult. A machine large enough to capture a significant amount of energy from ocean waves would have to be more than a mile long. Many technical problems remain to be solved before the ocean can become a practical energy source.

Solar Energy

Solar energy is energy from sunlight. The great advantage of solar energy is that it is unlimited and does not pollute the environment. Homes and office buildings can be heated by solar energy.

- Passive solar heating can be achieved simply by capturing sunlight through the glass wall of a room. The sunlight heats the room.

- Active solar heating can be accomplished by using solar collectors. A solar collector (a device that is most often placed on a building's roof) uses sunlight to heat a fluid that slowly passes through the collector. The heated fluid is then pumped from the collector and is circulated through the pipes of a building's heating system.

A **solar cell** is a device that produces electricity when sunlight strikes it. Solar cells have a wide range of uses. At present, though, solar cell use is limited primarily to space satellites and to consumer items such as watches, electronic toys, portable radios, and calculators. Large solar cells are expensive and are not yet considered a reasonable large-scale power source. However, if technological advances lower the costs, you may one day see solar-powered automobiles, homes, and a wide range of consumer products.

Geothermal Energy

Geothermal energy is energy that comes from Earth's hot interior. You already know about two sources of geothermal energy that are not under our control—volcanoes and earthquakes. But some forms of geothermal energy can be controlled and used to advantage.

In certain places, scientists can drill wells into Earth's crust and tap into naturally occurring bodies of hot water or steam. This energy can be used to turn turbines that produce electricity. Iceland's electricity is produced in this way.

Although the amount of geothermal energy available in Earth's crust is unlimited and not polluting, technical difficulties prevent it from becoming a major energy source. Some of the hot springs are so far under Earth's crust that getting heat energy to the surface is very hard.

Wind Energy

Wind energy has been used for several centuries to power windmills in Europe. Now windmills are being set up around the world to provide small amounts of electricity to cities near strong wind areas. Although they prove useful, windmills will probably not supply a very large share of the energy needed by future generations.

Decisions About Energy Use

With all of these energy sources available, the United States itself will not run out of energy in the near future. We have enough fossil fuel alone to last for several centuries. But, as you've seen, having energy sources isn't the whole story. Today's most immediate concern is not whether energy sources are available. The concern is about the price we'll have to pay in order to use those sources.

The dangers of air pollution, the greenhouse effect, and nuclear waste will not go away by themselves. These dangerous by-products of energy production can only be kept to a safe level by laws that regulate energy industries.

The technological advances needed to develop safe, affordable energy sources cost a great deal of money, much of which will be paid by taxpayers. For these reasons, the safety of energy production in the United States and elsewhere in the world depends on what we citizens are willing to tolerate. In modern society, pollution control and technological advancement are political questions as well as scientific ones.

Thinking About Science

Directions: On each line below, write *controlled* or *uncontrolled* to indicate the use of energy being described.

_____ **1.** a raging house fire

_____ **2.** a race car moving at 200 miles per hour

_____ **3.** a glowing campfire

_____ **4.** an erupting volcano

_____ **5.** a ringing telephone

_____ **6.** an off-shore hurricane

Answers are on page 452.

GED PRACTICE

Directions: Choose the <u>one best answer</u> to each question.

Questions 1–3 refer to the information on pages 330 and 331.

1. What are the two main reasons that geothermal and solar energy are not being used more than they currently are?

   (1) excessive cost and pollution
   (2) scarcity and excessive cost
   (3) technical problems and pollution
   (4) technical problems and excessive cost
   (5) scarcity and technical problems

2. Magma is molten rock flowing in Earth's mantle. In which type of energy does magma play a role?

   (1) hydroelectric
   (2) nuclear
   (3) wind
   (4) solar
   (5) geothermal

3. Which factor is <u>least</u> likely to determine which type of energy the United States primarily uses in the twenty-first century?

   (1) profit made by power companies
   (2) unforeseen natural disasters
   (3) technological advances
   (4) the supply of remaining fossil fuels
   (5) competition from foreign countries

Answers are on page 452.

Physics Review

Directions: Choose the <u>one best answer</u> to each question.

Questions 1–3 refer to the information below.

Five forms of energy are listed below.

electrical—energy carried by a moving current of electrons

light—energy-carrying waves that can travel through a vacuum

sound—vibrations that travel through air or other substances and are detected by the ear

heat—energy of molecular motion

chemical—potential energy that can be released during a chemical reaction

1. What is the common name given to visible electromagnetic energy flowing from the Sun?

    (1) electrical
    (2) light
    (3) sound
    (4) heat
    (5) chemical

2. What type of energy does a superconductor carry without experiencing heat loss?

    (1) electrical
    (2) light
    (3) sound
    (4) heat
    (5) chemical

3. What type of energy does a car battery use to produce electrical energy?

    (1) electrical
    (2) light
    (3) sound
    (4) heat
    (5) chemical

Questions 4 and 5 refer to the diagram and passage below.

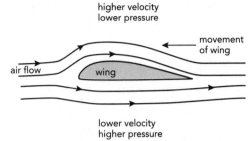

higher velocity
lower pressure

movement of wing

air flow

wing

lower velocity
higher pressure

An airplane is much heavier than air. So how is it able to fly? The answer is related to *Bernoulli's Principle*, which states that air pressure decreases as air velocity (the speed and direction of motion) increases.

The wings of airplanes are curved on top and flat on bottom. Air that flows over the curved top of the wing moves faster than air flowing along the bottom, because the air travels farther over the wing in the same amount of time as the air flowing under the wing. So, air pressure is lower on top of the wing and greater on the bottom. This pressure difference provides lift on the wing as the plane moves forward.

4. Which object below does <u>not</u> have a shape that makes use of Bernoulli's Principle?

    (1) a boomerang
    (2) an umbrella
    (3) a Frisbee
    (4) a sail on a sailboat
    (5) a seagull's wing

5. An airplane wing has flaps attached to the wing by hinges. Flaps are used during takeoff and landing. When the flaps are extended, the distance across the wing is increased. What is the most likely purpose of the flaps?

    (1) turn the plane
    (2) decrease lift
    (3) increase lift
    (4) reduce the plane's weight
    (5) increase the plane's weight

Questions 6 and 7 refer to the chart below.

As shown in the chart below, the loudness of sound is measured in units called decibels.

KIND OF SOUND	DECIBELS
softest sound we can hear	0 — hearing threshold
normal breathing	10 — barely audible (sound)
rustling leaves	20
soft whisper (15 ft.)	30
quiet office noise	50 — quiet noise
busy street traffic	70
average factory noise	80
heavy truck (45 ft.)	90 — constant exposure endangers hearing
subway train	100
loud thunder	110
rock concert with amplifiers	120 — pain threshold
jet taking off nearby	150

6. What is the approximate decibel level of normal conversation?

   (1) 3
   (2) 21
   (3) 31
   (4) 60
   (5) 102

7. Which of the following statements is false?

   (1) A whisper has a higher decibel level than a shout.
   (2) In a library the decibel level is lower than in a crowded lunchroom.
   (3) Decibel level decreases as you move away from the source of sound.
   (4) Decibel is a sound-loudness unit.
   (5) Hearing can be harmed by exposure to high decibel levels.

Questions 8 and 9 refer to the diagram below.

GAS KEPT AT CONSTANT VOLUME

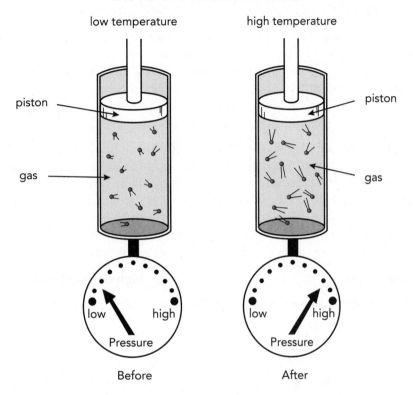

The volume of the gas is kept constant as the temperature of the gas is increased.

8. What is the main conclusion that can be drawn from the experiment shown in the diagram?

(1) Gas pressure increases as the gas volume increases.

(2) Gas pressure decreases as the gas volume decreases.

(3) Gas pressure increases as the gas temperature increases.

(4) Gas pressure decreases as the gas temperature increases.

(5) Gas pressure increases as both gas volume and temperature increase.

9. Which of the following is a result similar to the experimental finding?

(1) Air pressure in a car's tires increases with car speed.

(2) A hot-air balloon rises more quickly in cool air than warm air.

(3) A soccer ball feels softer as air leaks out.

(4) A window sticks on a hot day.

(5) Water expands as it freezes.

Answers are on page 453.

Physical Science Writing Activities

The following topics will give you extra practice in thinking and writing about physical science.

Directions: Choose one of the topics below and write a well-developed essay (approximately 250 words). You may wish to plan your essay before you write. Pay attention to your organization, development, and control of sentence structure, punctuation, grammar, word choice, and spelling. After you finish writing your essay, reread what you have written and make any changes that will improve your essay.

TOPIC 1

Applications of physics have produced the technology to create many machines and consumer products, such as computers. In some respects, computers have made our lives much easier, enabling us to do things we wouldn't even dream of trying if we didn't have a machine to organize the information for us. However, sometimes computers cause inconveniences. Have computers affected your life in a positive or negative way?

In your essay explain how computers have affected your life in a positive or negative way. Use specific examples to support your reasons.

TOPIC 2

In recent years, the United Nations has been working to eliminate the use of chemical weapons but has not banned the use of guns or tanks. Why do you think the UN is so concerned about chemical weapons? How different are they from guns and tanks?

In your essay state how chemical weapons are different from guns or tanks. Give specific examples to support your opinion.

TOPIC 3

In order to avoid an impending power crisis, the United States government is contemplating the increased use of nuclear power to provide additional sources of energy. While some people support the use of nuclear power, others are strongly opposed. Do you think the government should build more nuclear power plants to provide energy?

In your essay state whether you believe that the government should build more nuclear power plants. Give specific reasons to support your opinion.

PART FOUR

Readings in Earth and Space Science

- **Earth Science**
- **Space Science**

CHAPTER 11

Earth Science

Our loyalties are to the species and to the planet. We speak for Earth. Our obligation to survive is owed not just to ourselves but also to that Cosmos, ancient and vast, from which we spring.

~ Carl Sagan

Earth science is the study of Earth and the processes that affect it. Earth science involves the study of many topics concerning our planet:

- Origin and evolution

- Internal and external sources of energy

- Internal and surface structure

- Landmasses and bodies of water

- Atmosphere

- Forces acting upon and changing Earth

Fortunately for us, but unfortunately for space travelers, Earth is the most livable of all the known planets. In the study of earth science, separate branches of inquiry have developed. These four major branches are listed below.

Geology is the study of the composition and structure of Earth itself. Geologists seek to understand how land and water formations develop and change over time. Many geologists study natural events, such as volcanoes and earthquakes that threaten human safety.

Meteorology is the study of the atmosphere, the covering of air that surrounds Earth. Meteorologists use information about atmospheric conditions to help understand weather. Each day, using millions of temperature and air pressure readings from around the world, the United States' National Weather Service forecasts upcoming weather. Weather forecasts are especially useful as an early warning of approaching storms.

Oceanography is the study of Earth's oceans. Oceanographers study the movement of ocean water and the oceans' effects on weather. They also study the ocean floor, the mountains and valleys that lie below the ocean surface. As evidenced by offshore oil rigs, the ocean bottom is also a rich reserve of natural resources.

Paleontology is the study of prehistoric animal and plant life through the analysis of fossil remains. The work of paleontologists helps geologists understand the makeup of Earth's rock layers. Paleontologists also help make accurate geologic maps that are used in the search for underground water and for mineral and oil deposits.

In recent years new areas of study have arisen that overlap these four main branches.

Geochemistry is the study of the distribution of chemical elements in Earth's crust, mantle, and core. Geochemists often work for companies that are interested in the development of fuel resources, such as coal and oil, and valuable minerals, such as silver and gold.

Ecology is the study of organisms in relationship to their surroundings. Ecologists study the relationships of living communities to aspects of their nonliving environment, such as light, heat, solar radiation, moisture, and wind. Ecologists are involved in studies from life science, physical science, and earth science.

Environmental science is the study of how human beings interact with their environment, both living and nonliving. Many earth scientists who work in environmental science are concerned about the geological impact that human life is having on Earth and its ecosystems.

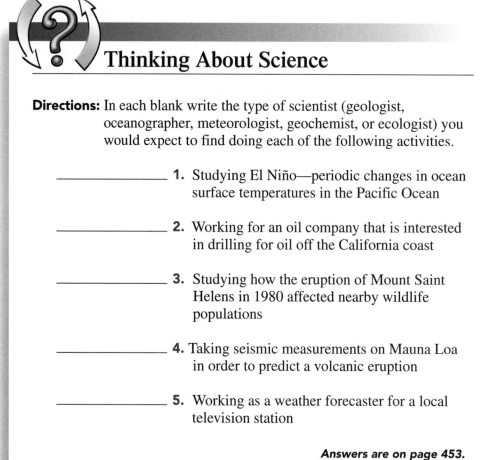

Thinking About Science

Directions: In each blank write the type of scientist (geologist, oceanographer, meteorologist, geochemist, or ecologist) you would expect to find doing each of the following activities.

_____ **1.** Studying El Niño—periodic changes in ocean surface temperatures in the Pacific Ocean

_____ **2.** Working for an oil company that is interested in drilling for oil off the California coast

_____ **3.** Studying how the eruption of Mount Saint Helens in 1980 affected nearby wildlife populations

_____ **4.** Taking seismic measurements on Mauna Loa in order to predict a volcanic eruption

_____ **5.** Working as a weather forecaster for a local television station

Answers are on page 453.

Directions: Choose the <u>one best answer</u> to each question.

Questions 1 and 2 refer to the information on pages 339 and 340.

1. A major oil company wants to explore for oil in an area that is close to a national park. Which of the following is most likely to be of concern to environmental scientists?

    (1) potential yearly profit
    (2) amount of oil available
    (3) impact on local wildlife
    (4) cost of the exploration
    (5) size of the oil company

2. Which of the following would be of most relevance to an environmental scientist working for the federal government?

    (1) cause of the extinction of dinosaurs
    (2) next week's weather forecast
    (3) yearly movement of an Alaskan glacier
    (4) life cycle of a star
    (5) underground storage of toxic waste

3. Which of the following discoveries would be of most relevance to a paleontologist?

    (1) fossils in Africa that are identical to fossils found in South America
    (2) the Earth's magnetic field periodically reverses in direction
    (3) the presence of rock fragments on Earth that came from an asteroid
    (4) the most recent ice age ended less than 20,000 years ago
    (5) there may be another planet in our solar system beyond the orbit of Pluto

Questions 4 and 5 are based on the following graph.

MAIN DISSOLVED SUBSTANCES IN SEA WATER
(by weight)

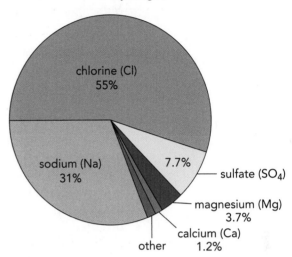

4. By weight, which dissolved substance is present in ocean water about one seventh as much as chlorine?

    (1) sodium
    (2) calcium
    (3) magnesium
    (4) sulfate
    (5) oxygen

5. What can you deduce is the main type of salt dissolved in seawater?

    (1) calcium chloride ($CaCl_2$)
    (2) Magnesium oxide (MgO)
    (3) sodium chloride (NaCl)
    (4) sulfuric acid (H_2SO_4)
    (5) potassium chloride (KCl)

Answers are on page 453.

The Early Earth

Earth has been around for a long time. In fact, scientists believe that Earth formed about 4.6 billion years ago! If this theory is correct, Earth is just one of the nine planets and their moons that were created by the gravitational collapse of a cloud of interstellar gas and dust, called the **solar nebula**. The Sun, comets, and asteroids most likely formed from this same nebula.

Of course no one saw the formation of Earth. But scientists have drawn conclusions from evidence and have proposed how the planet might have been developed.

The Solid Earth

Part of the nebula contracted and became dense enough to attract surrounding materials to it. These materials drew together in the center of the nebula, releasing kinetic energy as heat and making the center more dense. The gravity created by this dense center attracted materials still farther away. As the gravitational collapse of the nebula continued, thermonuclear reactions occurred in the center, and the Sun was formed. Meanwhile, gas and dust in the outer regions of the nebula settled in a disk shape around the Sun. The material in the disk cooled and condensed, clustering into clumps of rock that eventually became planets circling the Sun. At first, Earth, one of the newly formed planets, was relatively cool. Soon afterward, Earth heated up and became molten. The source of this heat was the continuing condensing of materials due to Earth's gravity and the heating effects of radioactivity.

At some point, the condensing stopped and the radioactivity lessened. The liquid Earth took shape and began to cool. As it cooled, a surface crust, a supporting mantle, and an interior core formed. Heavier elements such as iron tended to move into the core, while lighter elements such as aluminum tended to move to the crust. The formation of Earth to this point is believed to have taken place within the first few million years following the collapse of the solar nebula.

Scientists believe that Earth formed from a collapsing nebula.

The Atmosphere

Volcanic eruptions occurring as Earth's surface hardened brought carbon monoxide, carbon dioxide, water vapor, and methane out of the crust and mantle. Impacts from meteorites and comets added carbon, hydrogen, and oxygen. Varying amounts of these gases probably formed Earth's first atmosphere.

The emergence of life slowly changed Earth's first atmosphere to become more like the atmosphere we have today. Scientists believe that life most likely began in sheltered pools of water about 3.5 billion years ago. Simple life forms used energy from sunlight to carry out basic life functions and gave off oxygen gas as a by-product. By 2 billion years ago the oxygen level was $\frac{1}{100}$ the amount of oxygen in today's atmosphere.

The Oceans

Oceans probably began forming more than 4 billion years ago. By this time Earth had cooled enough for rain to stay on the surface, covering the crust. By 4 billion years ago a giant ocean covered Earth's surface. For the first several hundred million years after that, Earth did not yet have continents. The water that formed the oceans came from two main sources—water vapor from volcanic eruptions and ice from comets.

The Continents

As the crust developed, it went through cycles of melting and solidifying. During each cycle, heavier elements sank into the mantle and left lighter elements in the crust. At some point enough lighter rock reached the top to allow permanent areas of light rock to begin floating on the mantle. These areas gradually thickened and eventually rose above the ocean level. These early continents continually changed shape and position on the fluid mantle. By 1.5 billion years ago, the upper part of the mantle had cooled and solidified. As it cooled, it cracked and separated into separate regions that we now call **crustal plates**.

Thinking About Science

Directions: Complete each sentence below by filling in the blank(s) with the correct word(s) from the reading selection.

1. Scientists believe that Earth formed from the collapse of a

   _____.

2. The _____ is the central, spherical part of Earth.

3. Scientists believe that the age of Earth is about

   _____.

4. The buildup in oxygen in Earth's atmosphere was caused by

   _____.

Answers are on page 453.

GED PRACTICE

Directions: Choose the <u>one best answer</u> to each question.

Questions 1–3 refer to the passage on pages 342 and 343.

1. About how long after Earth formed did the oceans form?

   (1) 10 million years
   (2) 500 million years
   (3) 1.6 billion years
   (4) 3.2 billion years
   (5) 4.6 billion years

2. Where did early life forms most likely form on Earth?

   (1) in shallow pools of water
   (2) within volcanoes
   (3) in comet-impact craters
   (4) deep within oceans
   (5) in the atmosphere

Question 3 refers to the diagram below.

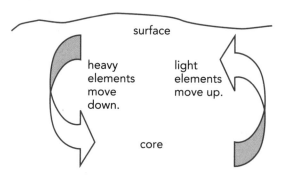

surface

heavy elements move down.

light elements move up.

core

3. Which of the following does the diagram help explain?

   (1) the temperature of Earth's core
   (2) the distribution of elements within Earth
   (3) the shape of Earth
   (4) the formation of continents
   (5) the formation of oceans

Answers are on page 453.

The Earth Today

Imagine for a moment that you're a sailor living in the fifteenth century. You're about to sail due west from the shore of Europe, out onto a vast unknown sea. Many of your friends say that the ocean leads to the edge of the flat Earth. Others tell of sailors who ventured out past the horizon and never returned. Still others warn of giant sea monsters swallowing up ships—like yours—that dare to sail too far from land.

Do these ideas sound funny? Sure they do today, but you probably wouldn't be laughing if you were about to set sail with Columbus in search of a new world. During those adventurous days, when very little was known about Earth, it was normal to have fears about the nature of our planet.

The Structure of Earth

Today we have a much better understanding of Earth.

- Earth's surface is about 71 percent water, divided into five large oceans.

- Earth's land portion, about 29 percent, is divided into seven continents and numerous islands. The oceans and land masses are the visible part of the **crust**, the outer skin of Earth. The crust varies in size, being about six miles thick under the oceans and as much as forty miles thick under high mountain ranges on the continents.

- The **mantle**, the supporting structure beneath the crust, is about 1,800 miles thick and is made up mainly of heavy rock.

- The **core** is divided into two parts: a solid inner core, made up of iron, and a liquid outer core that is composed mainly of melted iron. The inner core is shaped like a sphere. The radius (distance from the center to the edge) is about 800 miles. The outer core is about 1,400 miles thick.

THE STRUCTURE OF EARTH

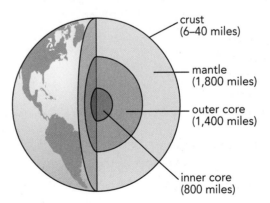

crust
(6–40 miles)

mantle
(1,800 miles)

outer core
(1,400 miles)

inner core
(800 miles)

Thinking About Science

Directions: Complete each sentence by filling in the blanks below with the correct word(s) from the reading selection.

1. The three main parts of the solid earth are the _____, _____, and _____.

2. About _____ percent of Earth's surface is covered by water.

3. There are _____ continents on Earth's surface.

4. Earth's inner core is mostly made of _____, and the outer core is mostly made of _____.

5. The approximate radius of Earth (inner core + outer core + mantle) is _____.

Answers are on page 453.

GED PRACTICE

Directions: Choose the <u>one best answer</u> to each question.

Questions 1–3 refer to the information on page 345.

1. What name is given to the part of Earth on which we live?

   (1) mantle
   (2) crust
   (3) outer core
   (4) inner core
   (5) tectonic

2. Which part of Earth contains most of the mass of Earth?

   (1) mantle
   (2) crust
   (3) outer core
   (4) inner core
   (5) atmosphere

3. Where on Earth's surface is the crust the thickest?

   (1) below icebergs
   (2) beneath plateaus
   (3) beneath the ocean
   (4) below valleys
   (5) below mountains

Answers are on page 453.

Energy in Today's Earth

Think about the energy that nature provides Earth. What do you think of first? Many people think about the Sun. They know that the Sun bathes Earth in sunlight and makes life possible. Not so well known is that Earth also has tremendous internal energy. Unfortunately, this energy is felt mainly in times of volcanic eruptions and earthquakes. Human life very much depends on both sources of Earth's energy.

Internal Energy

Earth's internal energy comes from two primary sources—the gravitational energy from Earth's formation, which led to a high temperature core, and radioactivity. As incredible as it may be, Earth's core reaches temperatures over 13,000°F. At this temperature, heavy metals and other elements slosh around like water. The extreme temperature at the core is most likely produced by the radioactive decay of uranium and other radioactive isotopes. The heat produced in the core radiates outward from the core and heats the mantle.

Convection currents of molten rock within the mantle carry much of the heat to Earth's surface. The energy contained in these convection currents causes the movement of plates on Earth's crust, volcanic eruptions, and earthquakes. Hot, molten rock flows as lava from volcanoes and also flows from fissures, or cracks, in Earth's crust in the mid-oceanic ridges along the bottom of the ocean.

External Energy

The Sun is the major source of Earth's external energy. Energy flows to Earth in the form of light waves. This electromagnetic energy is partially absorbed in the atmosphere and partially absorbed on Earth's surface. Part of the energy is radiated back out into space both as reflected light and as heat. Much of the energy stays within Earth's atmosphere. This atmospheric heat energy leads to temperature and pressure differences in the atmosphere and oceans that produce winds, ocean currents, and weather.

Geochemical Cycles

Earth consists of a relatively fixed number of atoms of each element, such as carbon. The amount of carbon on and in Earth today is approximately the same amount as when Earth formed. And carbon, like each other element, is found in several different chemical storehouses. Movement of carbon among these storehouses is driven by Earth's internal and external energy sources.

- Carbon occurs in the atmosphere as carbon dioxide gas.

- Carbon occurs in carbon-bearing rocks such as limestone.

- Carbon is found in water as dissolved carbon dioxide.

- Carbon is found in all organic molecules.

The movement of elements from one chemical storehouse to another is referred to as a **geochemical cycle**.

Thinking About Science

Directions: Answer each question below.

1. What is the main external energy source for Earth?

    _____

2. What is the main internal energy source for Earth?

    _____

3. How high does the temperature reach in Earth's core?

    _____

4. What is the source of energy in Earth's core?

    _____

5. Name four chemical storehouses of carbon on Earth.

    _____ , _____ ,

    _____ , _____

Answers are on page 453.

Go to **www.GEDScience.com** for additional practice and instruction!

Directions: Choose the <u>one best answer</u> to each question.

Questions 1 and 2 refer to the following diagram, which shows how four main types of rocks can be changed from one to another.

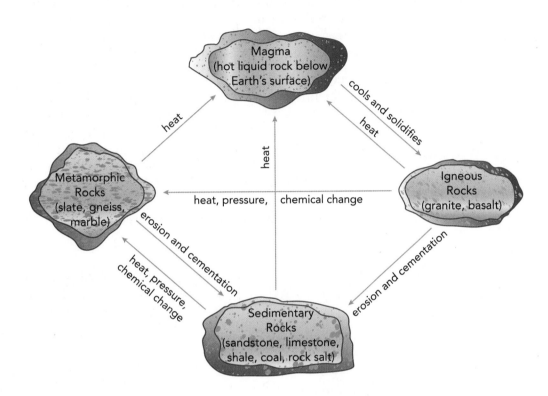

1. When granite is heated, it changes from which type of rock to which type of rock?

   (1) igneous rock to magma
   (2) metamorphic rock to igneous rock
   (3) igneous rock to sedimentary rock
   (4) sedimentary rock to magma
   (5) igneous rock to metamorphic rock

2. Which of the following are needed to change sedimentary rock into metamorphic rock?

   (1) cooling and chemical change
   (2) heat and erosion
   (3) heat and chemical change
   (4) erosion and chemical change
   (5) erosion and cementation

Answers are on page 454.

Plate Tectonics

Looking at a world map, you cannot help but notice that the east coasts of North and South America look like pieces of a jigsaw puzzle of which Greenland, Europe, and Africa are also a part. Suppose you could slide the Americas over, next to Europe and Africa—placing Greenland in the opening at the top. It appears that the coastlines would fit neatly next to one another. This fit has been noticed for many decades. However, it has only been in recent years that geologists have come to understand this remarkable pattern.

There is now evidence to suggest that the continents actually sat side by side about 200 million years ago. In fact, geologists have given the name **Pangaea** to this possible supercontinent. According to the most popular theory, called **plate tectonics**, Earth's crust is now made up of about twelve large plates and several small plates that slowly move around on the surface of the mantle. Although each crustal plate moves only about two inches a year, 200 million years is ample time for Pangaea to have separated into today's continents. The movement of the plates is most likely driven by convection currents in the mantle. These currents arise as heat flows from Earth's core.

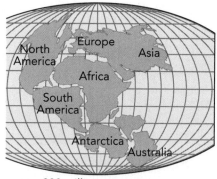

200 million years ago

present

The theory of plate tectonics does more than describe the movement of continents—often called **continental drift**. Plate tectonics also helps geologists understand earthquakes, volcanic eruptions, mountain building, and the formation of continents and oceans.

- Earthquakes and volcanic eruptions occur along the boundary lines where two plates collide. When slippage occurs between two plates, an enormous amount of energy is released. This energy release may result in earthquakes near the boundary between the plates. California experiences thousands of small quakes each year along the plate boundary known as the San Andreas fault.

- Volcanoes can be caused by the tremendous pressure that develops as one plate actually moves under a second plate. The molten rock that spews out of a volcano comes from the sea of molten rock in Earth's mantle just below the plates.

- Changes in mountains, continents, and the ocean floor occur when two plates collide. During such collisions, the crust is raised by faulting, folding, or arching up layers of rock. When plates move apart, some parts of the crust sink, creating valleys with rock towering above. Volcanic eruptions themselves also give rise to new mountains. The group of islands that now makes up Japan is an example of a string of volcanoes that formed near the boundary of two plates.

Thinking About Science

Directions: Circle *T* for each statement below that is true and *F* for each statement that is false.

T   F   **1.** 200 million years ago, Earth's continents formed one supercontinent.

T   F   **2.** Continental drift is caused by gravitational energy from Earth's core.

T   F   **3.** Earthquakes are caused by the pressure that develops as one plate moves under another plate.

T   F   **4.** Valleys are caused by the sinking of Earth's crust when plates move apart.

Answers are on page 454.

Directions: Choose the <u>one best answer</u> to each question.

Questions 1–4 are based on the information on pages 350 and 351.

1. Which of the following best summarizes the main idea of the theory of plate tectonics?

   (1) Earth's crust varies in thickness, being much thicker beneath mountain ranges than beneath bodies of water.
   (2) Earth's crust is made up of rigid plates that slowly move along Earth's surface.
   (3) Earth's continents are slowly being pushed apart by the movement of the oceans.
   (4) The coasts of several continents are similar in shape, giving Earth the appearance of a jigsaw puzzle.
   (5) Earth is round and not flat, as was once widely believed.

2. Which of the following is a hypothesis based on the Pangaea theory?

   (1) In the fifteenth century, no one knew for sure that Earth was round.
   (2) Seismic measurements (measurements of shock waves from earthquakes) suggest that Earth's crust is thicker beneath the continents than beneath the oceans.
   (3) About 71 percent of Earth's surface is covered by water and 29 percent by land.
   (4) Earth's continents look like a jigsaw puzzle because they were once part of a huge supercontinent that split apart.
   (5) Earth is the only planet in the solar system that looks blue when seen from space.

3. Which of the following is <u>not</u> evidence that Pangaea existed?

   (1) The discovery of fossils of the same extinct bird in both Europe and North America.
   (2) The discovery of rare plants living in both South America and Africa.
   (3) The discovery of ancient European pottery in diggings in Mexico.
   (4) The discovery that South America is still slowly moving away from Africa.
   (5) The discovery that the shape of the fault line that runs beneath the Atlantic Ocean is similar to the shape of the eastern coastlines of the Americas.

4. Which of the following would <u>not</u> be important to a geologist interested in predicting the possibility of a volcanic eruption from a peak in the Appalachian Mountains?

   (1) the history of volcanic activity in all parts of the eastern United States
   (2) the average amount of yearly rainfall in the Appalachian Mountains
   (3) the location of the nearest boundary between two crustal plates
   (4) the history of any earthquake activity in or near the Appalachian Mountains
   (5) the age and structure of the Appalachian Mountains

Answers are on page 454.

Earth's Atmosphere

Unless it is raining or the wind is blowing, we don't usually pay much attention to the **atmosphere,** the blanket of air that surrounds Earth. Yet without the atmosphere, Earth would be a desolate planet and would not be able to support human life.

The atmosphere plays three roles in making life possible. First, the atmosphere provides the three gases necessary for life—oxygen, nitrogen, and carbon dioxide. All animals, including human beings, breathe oxygen. Nitrogen and carbon dioxide are both needed for plant growth. Less important atmospheric gases include argon, neon, helium, and hydrogen.

Second, the atmosphere protects us from most of the Sun's high-energy **ultraviolet light,** which is harmful to life. Although ultraviolet rays are only a small part of the sunlight striking Earth, they are known to be very dangerous. Luckily, 99 percent of all ultraviolet rays are absorbed before they reach Earth's surface. They are absorbed by an atmospheric gas called **ozone,** a type of oxygen gas. The ozone layer surrounds Earth but is much thinner over the North Pole and South Pole than over other regions.

The 1 percent of ultraviolet light that passes through the atmosphere and reaches Earth's surface is known to cause sunburn and is now believed to cause skin cancer in many people. Because of this, doctors recommend that people limit the amount of time they spend in direct sunlight. They also recommend that people who like to sunbathe wear a suntan lotion that blocks ultraviolet rays.

Third, the atmosphere gives us weather—both clear blue skies and violent storms. The atmosphere acts as a huge energy machine, regulating the temperature at Earth's surface. The atmosphere controls both the amount of sunlight striking Earth and the amount of surface heat allowed to escape back into space.

- The atmosphere allows only 46 percent of sunlight striking it to pass through and reach Earth's surface.

- Carbon dioxide gas in the atmosphere controls the amount of heat on Earth's surface that is allowed to radiate back into space.

Through these two controlling devices, the atmosphere keeps Earth's surface temperature in a range that sustains life. The temperature at Earth's surface, together with Earth's rotation, gives us wind and water movements that are responsible for our daily weather.

LEVELS OF
EARTH'S
ATMOSPHERE

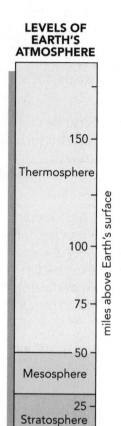

miles above Earth's surface

150 —

Thermosphere

100 —

75 —

50

Mesosphere

25 —

Stratosphere

Troposphere

When meteorologists talk about the atmosphere, they usually divide it into four, or sometimes five, layers:

- The **troposphere** is the layer closest to the ground. Most of the gas in the atmosphere is in this layer. In fact, more than half of all atmospheric gas is within an altitude, or height, of 3½ miles. It is in the troposphere that almost all weather occurs. Under normal conditions the temperature decreases about 10°F for each mile gained in altitude in the troposphere. The carbon dioxide gas in this layer regulates Earth's surface temperature.

- The second layer is called the **stratosphere.** The temperature is about the same throughout the stratosphere; it no longer decreases with increasing altitude. The stratosphere is especially important to us because it contains the ozone gas that protects us from harmful ultraviolet light.

- Outside the stratosphere is the **mesosphere,** a layer of atmosphere in which air temperature again drops with increasing altitude.

- The outermost layer of atmosphere is called the thermosphere, a region where the temperature rises with altitude. The **thermosphere,** together with the outer mesosphere, is often called the **ionosphere,** a region that reflects radio waves toward the ground. The ionosphere makes it possible for a radio station to broadcast over hundreds or even thousands of miles.

Thinking About Science

Directions: Write a brief answer to each of the following questions.

1. What is meant by the word *atmosphere?*

   _____

2. Why is ozone an important gas in the atmosphere?

   _____

3. Which atmospheric gas controls the amount of sunlight warmth that radiates back out into space?

   _____

4. What percentage of sunlight reaches the surface of Earth?

   _____

5. What form of sunlight is known to be harmful to human life?

   _____

Answers are on page 454.

GED PRACTICE

Directions: Choose the <u>one best answer</u> to each question.

Questions 1–4 are based on the following information about the layers of the atmosphere.

troposphere—the layer closest to Earth; weather conditions occur here; height: ground level to about 8 miles

stratosphere—the layer that contains ozone gas; height: about 8–30 miles

mesosphere—the region in which temperature decreases with increasing altitude; height: about 30–50 miles

ionosphere—the region in which radio waves are reflected; made up of the outermost area of the mesosphere and innermost area of the thermosphere

thermosphere—the outermost area of the of atmosphere; height: 50 miles and more

1. High-altitude clouds, called *cirrus clouds*, form at altitudes of between 5 and $7\frac{1}{2}$ miles. In which layer of the atmosphere must pilots be concerned about poor visibility caused by cirrus clouds?

   (1) troposphere
   (2) stratosphere
   (3) mesosphere
   (4) ionosphere
   (5) thermosphere

2. Which is the outside layer of the atmosphere that the space shuttle passes through as it leaves its orbit (from above the atmosphere) to return to Earth?

   (1) troposphere
   (2) stratosphere
   (3) mesosphere
   (4) ionosphere
   (5) thermosphere

3. Disturbances in the atmosphere often affect radio reception. In which layer of the atmosphere are disturbances most likely to affect the reception in Seattle, Washington, of stations broadcasting from Tokyo, Japan?

   (1) troposphere
   (2) stratosphere
   (3) mesosphere
   (4) ionosphere
   (5) thermosphere

4. In recent years synthetically produced chemicals called *fluorocarbons* have been banned from use as propellants in aerosol sprays such as spray paint. Scientists believe that these chemicals get into the atmosphere and wear away the layer of protective ozone gas. In which layer of atmosphere are the fluorocarbons believed to be causing the damage?

   (1) troposphere
   (2) stratosphere
   (3) mesosphere
   (4) ionosphere
   (5) thermosphere

Answers are on page 454.

Earth's Seasons

You may not realize it, but as you are reading this sentence you are racing through space at a speed of 66,000 miles per hour! As incredible as it may seem, this is the speed at which Earth travels in its **orbit** around the Sun. It takes about 365 days (one year) to make one complete trip (**revolution**). During this time, the only clue of Earth's orbital motion is the changing of the seasons.

As Earth moves (revolves) along its orbit, it also turns (rotates) on its **axis**—an imaginary line running through Earth's center from the North Pole to the South Pole. You can think of Earth as slowly spinning like a top around this axis. Earth makes one complete rotation during each twenty-four-hour period (one day). Because Earth turns from west to east, the Sun appears to rise over the eastern horizon each morning and set below the western horizon each evening. Earth's rotation causes day and night.

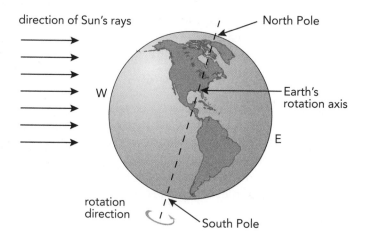

Earth rotates from west to east on its rotation axis. One complete turn takes 24 hours (one day).

As you can see from the illustration, Earth's axis is tilted, so some parts of Earth receive the Sun's rays more directly than do other parts. Direct sunlight produces more heat than indirect sunlight. Seasons are caused by this 23-degree tilt in Earth's axis.

- During summer the Northern Hemisphere is tilted toward the sun, receiving direct sunlight.

- During winter the Northern Hemisphere is tilted away from the sun, receiving indirect sunlight.

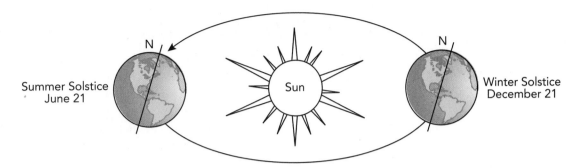

Summer Solstice
June 21

Sun

Winter Solstice
December 21

Seasons are caused by the tilt in Earth's axis. The first day of summer and winter for countries in the Northern Hemisphere is shown above.

The situation in the Southern Hemisphere is exactly the opposite.

- When the northern half of Earth receives direct light and more heat from the Sun, the southern half receives less.

- Summer occurs in the Northern Hemisphere while winter occurs in the Southern Hemisphere, and vice versa. While July is a warm month in the United States in the Northern Hemisphere, it is a cold month in Australia in the Southern Hemisphere.

Thinking About Science

Directions: Answer each question below.

1. Circle *T* for each statement below that is true and *F* for each statement that is false.

    T F a. The word *rotation* refers to the turning of Earth on its axis.

    T F b. The Northern Hemisphere and the Southern Hemisphere each receive the same amount of direct sunlight in January.

    T F c. The seasons occur because of Earth's rotation.

    T F d. The Sun appears to rise in the east and set in the west.

2. Complete each sentence by filling in the blank with the correct word(s) from the reading selection.

    a. Earth takes _____ to make one rotation.
       (time)

    b. Earth takes _____ to make one revolution.
       (time)

    c. Day and night are caused by Earth's _____.

    d. Seasons are caused by the _____ of Earth's axis.

Answers are on page 454.

Directions: Choose the one best answer to each question.

Questions 1 and 2 are based on the information on pages 356 and 357.

1. In which month are people most likely to be sunbathing in coastal cities in southern Brazil?

   (1) February
   (2) April
   (3) July
   (4) August
   (5) September

2. In which month are people most likely to be playing in the snow in Montreal, Canada?

   (1) May
   (2) July
   (3) September
   (4) January
   (5) April

Questions 3 and 4 refer to the following passage and diagram.

At any instant, people in different parts of the world see the Sun in a different position in the sky. For example, while people in San Francisco are watching the Sun come up, people in Moscow are watching the Sun go down.

To avoid confusion in telling time, scientists have divided Earth into twenty-four time zones. As you move from west to east, you add one hour to your clock for each new time zone that you enter. For example, when it is 2:00 P.M. in San Francisco, it is 5:00 P.M. in New York City. As shown on the time zone map below, you cross into three new time zones as you go from San Francisco to New York City.

THE WORLD TIME ZONES

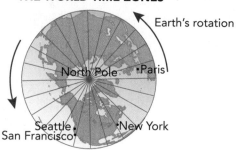

3. While vacationing in Paris, France, James calls his home in Seattle, Washington. He places the call at 6:00 A.M. on Saturday, July 9, Paris time. What time and day will it be in Seattle when the call is received?

   (1) 2:00 P.M. Friday, July 8
   (2) 10:00 P.M. Friday, July 8
   (3) 2:00 P.M. Saturday, July 9
   (4) 10:00 P.M. Saturday, July 9
   (5) 2:00 A.M. Sunday, July 10

4. If an airplane leaves San Francisco at 8:00 A.M. and flies nonstop to New York, what time will the airplane arrive in New York City (New York City time), assuming that the trip takes five hours of actual flying time?

   (1) 1:00 A.M.
   (2) 10:00 A.M.
   (3) 1:00 P.M.
   (4) 5:00 P.M.
   (5) 10:00 P.M.

Answers are on page 454.

Earth's Weather

The study of weather is the study of the changes that take place in Earth's atmosphere, the layer of gases that surrounds the planet. A local weather report usually includes the following four features:

- **Temperature** is a measure of the warmth of the air.

- **Humidity** is a measure of the water vapor in the air. Humidity readings are usually given as percentages. A humidity reading of 90 percent means that the air contains 90 percent of the water vapor it can possibly hold at that particular temperature.

- **Wind** refers to air movement. Both the speed and direction of the wind are usually cited. Wind direction refers to the direction from which the wind is blowing.

- **Air pressure (barometric pressure)** refers to the weight of the atmosphere. Air pressure depends on atmospheric temperature, humidity, and air movement. A high-pressure reading usually indicates clear, pleasant weather. A low-pressure reading indicates wet or stormy weather.

Although the exact causes of weather changes are not completely understood, meteorologists have discovered several characteristics of weather. For instance, they know that most changes in weather are caused by movements of large masses of air. **Air masses** are bodies of air with a certain temperature and with a certain moisture content.

Air masses that form over the polar regions tend to be very cold and dry. Air masses that form over tropical oceans tend to be warm and moist. An air mass takes on the characteristics of the region where it originated.

The movement of air masses is caused by temperature and pressure differences. Warm air masses tend to rise over cold ones, and air tends to flow from regions of high pressure to regions of low pressure. As an air mass moves, its direction of motion is also greatly affected by Earth's rotation.

Stormy or turbulent weather conditions form along a line called a **front**—the boundary line where a warm air mass collides with a cold air mass. Along a front, the moisture in the warm air condenses into water droplets when it cools. Clouds, rain, sleet, hail, or snow then occur along the front. The actual weather along a front depends on the air temperatures and moisture contents of the two colliding air masses. Because weather changes take place along a front, you often hear a weather forecaster say, "A front is moving in and bringing the weather with it!"

Thinking About Science

Directions: Match each item on the left with the best description on the right. Write the letter of the phrase on the line before the correct number.

_____ **1.** barometric pressure

_____ **2.** humidity

_____ **3.** temperature

_____ **4.** wind

(a) a measure of the water vapor content of the air

(b) air movement

(c) the weight of the atmosphere

(d) a measure of the warmth of the air

Answers are on page 454.

GED PRACTICE

Directions: Choose the <u>one best answer</u> to each question.

Questions 1 and 2 refer to the following passage and diagram.

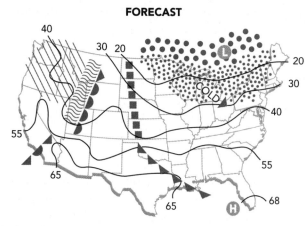

FORECAST

Symbols Used On the Map
Fronts:

rain — ▼▼ cold
snow — ◢◣ warm
showers — ▼◣ occluded
flurries — ■■■ stationary

Ⓛ low atmospheric pressure

Ⓗ high atmospheric pressure

isotherm: a line that connects points that have the same temperature

Probably the most common science diagram you'll ever see is a weather map. A weather map gives a brief summary of the weather conditions in a certain location.

Weather maps use symbols to stand for certain weather conditions. Most often, a brief definition of these symbols accompanies the map. Notice the example of a weather map. A key to the map symbols is shown at the right.

As seen on the map, the weather in the southern states was cool (55°F to 68°F) and dry, while the weather in the northern states was cold (20°F to 40°F) and wet. Rain is shown over the northwestern states, and snow is shown over the northern part of the central and eastern United States.

1. What do cities that lie on the same isotherm have in common?

   (1) weather
   (2) type of precipitation
   (3) temperature
   (4) humidity
   (5) wind speed

2. Which month is most likely represented by the weather map above?

   (1) April
   (2) June
   (3) August
   (4) October
   (5) December

Answers are on page 454.

The Changing Earth

Earth can be compared to a gigantic sculpture being shaped by the forces of nature. This comparison is especially meaningful to anyone who has seen the awe-inspiring canyons in the southwestern United States, the breathtaking waterfalls at Niagara Falls in New York, or the powerful photographs of the volcanic eruption at Mount Saint Helens in Washington in 1980.

At first glance, land on Earth's surface looks solid and unchanging. Although we don't usually notice it, changes take place on a daily basis. The Grand Canyon itself was once a highland plateau that was crossed by the Colorado River. Then, during millions of years—but one day at a time—the river, wind, and rain combined to carve and shape this mile-deep canyon.

Earth's surface is changed by processes that take place rapidly and violently as well as by those that take place slowly and gently. Rapid, violent changes are brought about by volcanic eruptions and earthquakes. Slow, gentle changes are brought about by weathering and erosion.

Weathering

Weathering is the breaking down of rock into smaller pieces by natural processes. Weathering helps produce **soil**, a mixture of tiny rock fragments and organic materials produced by living things. Most organic materials in soil are the decaying remains of plants and animals. Weathering may bring about both physical and chemical changes in rock.

Physical weathering, also called mechanical weathering, breaks rocks apart without changing the chemicals within the rocks. One type of physical weathering is caused by the action of freezing water. Water from rain, rivers, or streams flows over a rock and fills any small cracks in the rock's surface. In cold weather the water freezes and expands as it turns into ice. The force of the expansion widens the cracks and splits the rock.

Chemical weathering is the softening and crumbling of rock brought about by chemical changes. These chemical changes occur because rock is exposed to water and atmospheric gases. For example, when iron in a rock is exposed to water, the iron changes to rust. Rust is created from the chemical reaction of iron in the rock and oxygen gas in water.

Sometimes plants and animals contribute to both physical and chemical weathering. For example, roots growing in small cracks will increase in size and split rocks. Chemicals present in the roots bring about chemical changes that dissolve rock. Burrowing animals, such as gophers and worms, create tunnels that allow water and atmospheric gases to penetrate more easily into surface soil, exposing buried rocks to weathering.

Erosion

Erosion is the natural movement of rock fragments over the surface of Earth. The three main causes of erosion are gravity, wind, and water.

Gravity erosion is the falling of rock fragments due to gravity. If small rock pieces break off from solid rock high on a cliff, they fall until other rocks stop them. Hillsides covered with loose rocks are often the result of the gravity erosion of weathered rocks higher up.

Wind erosion is the movement of rocks by wind. Wind erosion acts mainly on small rock fragments such as loose soil and sand. Strong wind often carries fine, hard rock particles in a stream that acts like a sandblaster. Wind erosion can add to the effects of both weathering and gravity erosion.

Water erosion is the most powerful of all types of erosion. Rivers cause the breakup of rocks and move rock fragments along the direction of the river's flow. Arizona's beautiful Grand Canyon was created, in great part, by the water-erosion effects of the Colorado River.

The Grand Canyon was created by the combined forces of erosion and weathering.

Thinking About Science

Directions: Write the answer to each question below.

1. In what way do small ground animals play a part in the process of weathering?

   _____

   _____

2. After a new concrete slab is poured for a driveway, what will occur first, weathering or erosion? _____

Answers are on page 454.

GED PRACTICE

Directions: Choose the <u>one best answer</u> to each question.

Questions 1 and 2 refer to the following definitions.

physical weathering—weathering (the breaking up of rocks) that does not involve chemical change

chemical weathering—weathering involving chemical change

gravity erosion—rock movement is caused by gravity

wind erosion—rock movement caused by wind

water erosion—rock movement caused by water

1. When ocean waves move sand from the north end of a beach to the south end, what process is occurring most?

   (1) physical weathering
   (2) chemical weathering
   (3) wind erosion
   (4) water erosion
   (5) gravity erosion

2. Trapped carbon dioxide gas in a mineral reacts with water washing over the mineral and forms an acid that causes the mineral to crumble. Which process is occurring here?

   (1) physical weathering
   (2) chemical weathering
   (3) wind erosion
   (4) water erosion
   (5) gravity erosion

Question 3 refers to the following passage.

When a river goes round a bend, the river tends to erode the outside curve more than the inside curve. Because of this, a river that contains a slight bend can actually create a small lake that ends up cut off from the river. The small lake that is formed is called an oxbow lake because its U shape resembles the shape of an oxbow. In the illustration below, the four steps in the formation of an oxbow lake are not arranged in order.

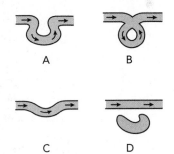

3. In what order should the drawings above be placed to show how an oxbow lake might develop from a slight bend in a river?

   (1) A, C, B, D
   (2) C, B, A, D
   (3) B, A, C, D
   (4) D, A, B, C
   (5) C, A, B, D

Answers are on page 455.

What Fossils Tell Us About the Changing Earth

There is no written record that tells about Earth's geological past. However, Earth itself has left a record in the form of **fossils**—trace remains of organisms of a past geological age. Along with giving clues about extinct forms of life, fossils enable scientists to better understand the aging process of Earth itself.

The Fossil Record

Fossils are most often found buried in rock, but they may also be found in caves, ancient tar beds, and the solid ice that covers Earth's polar regions. In each of these places, fossils are protected from the damaging effects of wind, water, and chemical interactions.

Usually, only the hard parts of a dead plant or animal are preserved. This is usually bones, shells, and woody tissues. Soft parts, such as flesh, either decay or are eaten by animals before they can be preserved. One exception is when an organism is subjected to extreme cold. Then the entire body may be preserved in ice. For example, the almost complete frozen bodies of extinct woolly mammoths have been found in Siberia.

Another type of fossil contains only the traces of an organism, not its remains. A familiar example is footprints left in mud that later hardened into solid rock. Paleontologists have found dinosaur footprints that are over 100 million years old.

Fossils help scientists understand the climate and land conditions of prehistoric times. As a general rule, organisms survive best in warm, humid climates and do less well in extreme hot or cold, dry climates. Fossils from ancient oceans provide clues to the water temperature and conditions in which these water organisms lived. In a similar way, fossils from ancient deserts provide clues to the land temperature and conditions in which these land organisms lived.

Because of ice ages and the movement of tectonic plates, each continent has experienced a variety of weather and surface conditions over time. This means that regions on each continent may at different times have been an ocean, a tropical forest, a desert, or a mountainous region. Fossils help scientists determine the changing characteristics of each geological region.

Fossils also provide evidence of continental drift. Fossils of the same extinct species have been found on separated continents. The presence of the same ancient organisms on widely separated land masses suggests that the continents were at one time linked together. On the other hand, fossils of more recently evolved species are found only on certain continents. This suggests that once the continents separated, they did not drift back together at a later time.

Thinking About Science

Directions: Circle *T* for each statement below that is true and *F* for each statement that is false.

T   F   **1.** Unless an organism is subjected to extreme cold, only its hard parts will remain as fossil evidence.

T   F   **2.** Fossils provide clues to Earth's climate in a previous geologic age.

T   F   **3.** Fossils of certain recently evolved species have been found on more than one continent.

Answers are on page 455.

GED PRACTICE

Directions: Choose the <u>one best answer</u> to each question.

Questions 1 and 2 refer to the following passage.

During its lifetime, every organism absorbs two types of carbon: stable carbon-12 and radioactive carbon-14. Carbon-12 is by far the most common type, but the isotope carbon-14 is present in measurable amounts.

By eating and breathing, an organism keeps its body level of each type of carbon at a constant level. From the time of death on, however, the level of carbon-14 in an organism's remains slowly decreases without being replaced. This fact enables a paleontologist to determine a fossil's age.

Carbon-14 undergoes radioactive decay with a half-life of 5,730 years. By measuring the level of carbon-14 in a fossil, a paleontologist can determine how many half-lifes have passed since the organism died. For example, if the carbon-14 level is one-fourth that seen in a living organism, then two half-lifes ($1/4 = 1/2 \times 1/2$) have passed since the organism died. Two half-lifes equal 11,460 years ($2 \times 5,730$).

1. What characteristic of carbon-14 allows its use as a dating tool?

   (1) atomic weight
   (2) presence in air and food
   (3) bonding properties with hydrogen
   (4) electrical properties
   (5) radioactive properties

2. Suppose a fossil contains one-sixteenth the amount of Carbon-14 that a living organism contains: $1/16 = 1/2 \times 1/2 \times 1/2 \times 1/2$. What is the approximate age of the fossil?

   (1) 11,500 years
   (2) 17,000 years
   (3) 23,000 years
   (4) 29,000 years
   (5) 34,500 years

Questions 3–6 refer to the following passage and diagram.

The side of a cliff may be made up of many individual layers of rock. Often, each layer is a different type of rock from the layers above and below it. The lower layers are the oldest ones, and the upper layers are newer. As you might guess, the very top layer is the most recent.

Rock layers are a clue to the past climate and land surface conditions of a region.

- *Limestone*, a rock made of the compressed remains of aquatic animals and plants, is almost always formed at the bottom of an ocean. A layer of limestone indicates that an ocean probably once covered the land.

- *Sandstone*, a rock made of fine sand grains cemented together, often indicates that the region was once a windswept desert.

- *Coal*, a rock made of the compressed remains of dense vegetation, indicates that the region was once a lush forest.

When several rock layers appear on top of one another, it is likely that the region has undergone many changes of climate and surface conditions.

CLIFF LAYERS

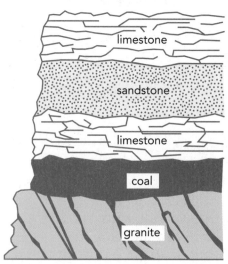

3. Which two layers of rock indicate that a lush tropical forest was covered by a rising ocean?

    (1) the granite layer and the coal layer
    (2) the sandstone layer and upper limestone layer
    (3) the coal layer and the lower limestone layer
    (4) the lower limestone layer and the sandstone layer
    (5) the granite layer and the upper limestone layer

4. Which fossil would most likely be found in the upper limestone layer?

    (1) a dinosaur footprint
    (2) a woolly mammoth
    (3) the leaf of an ancient redwood tree
    (4) a thorn from an extinct desert cactus
    (5) an impression of a small sea worm

5. Which of the following fossils would most likely be found in the sandstone layer?

    (1) an impression of a fin of an ancient fish
    (2) a bone fragment from the wing of an extinct species of penguin
    (3) a leg bone from an extinct species of camel
    (4) a jawbone from an extinct animal, similar to a gorilla
    (5) a wing print from an extinct insect that ate mainly vegetables and fruit

6. What is the best summary of information shown on the diagram?

    (1) This location was a desert that later was covered by a tropical forest.
    (2) This location has experienced many changes of climate and conditions.
    (3) This location has always been a hot, dry desert.
    (4) This location has mainly been an ocean.
    (5) This location has been under ice for most of its past.

Answers are on page 455.

Earth Science Review

Directions: Choose the <u>one best answer</u> to each question.

Question 1 refers to the following diagram and passage.

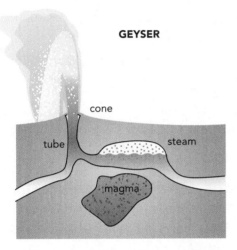

GEYSER

A geyser is an eruption of hot water up through Earth's surface. A geyser is produced by groundwater that has been heated by hot molten rock called magma. The heated groundwater sits in underground chambers and slowly builds up tremendous pressure until the water expands explosively and is jetted through a tube-like opening to the surface. Around the geyser's vent, or surface opening, a cone slowly builds from minerals dissolved in the hot geyser water.

After an eruption, groundwater again collects in the underground chambers. The time period between eruptions is determined by the supply of groundwater, the speed at which the water heats, and the size and shape of the geyser's tube-like opening and chambers. These factors do not change much underground, and a geyser's eruption cycle is usually predictable.

1. Which of the following is most likely to cause a decrease in the length of time between two eruptions of the same geyser?

   (1) a decrease in groundwater
   (2) an increase in groundwater
   (3) a decrease in pressure
   (4) a decrease in magma temperature
   (5) an increase in magma temperature

Question 2 refers to the following diagram and passage.

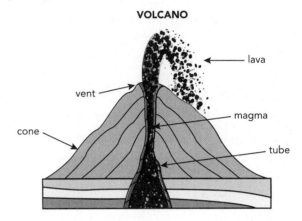

VOLCANO

A volcanic eruption is an explosion of magma through Earth's surface. The magma flows from the mantle deep inside Earth upward to the surface through a tubular crack in Earth's crust. The magma, together with hot gas and steam, is under high pressure and blows a vent in the surface. The magma breaks through the surface with enough force to blast a large part of a mountain out of its way. Magma that emerges from below the surface is called lava. An eruption forms a cinder cone, made of fragments of the ejected rocks and lava, around the vent.

Although predictions of volcanic eruptions aren't an exact science, scientists have discovered that many eruptions are preceded by small earthquakes, apparently caused by an increased movement of magma.

2. What do scientists think precedes a volcanic eruption?

   (1) a change in the weather pattern
   (2) weak earthquakes
   (3) decreased magma flow
   (4) increased tube size
   (5) decreased gas and steam buildup

Questions 3–6 refer to the following information.

EARTHQUAKE VIBRATION WAVES

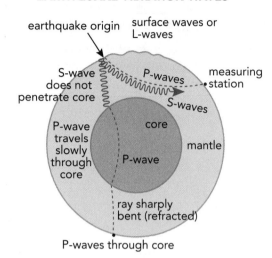

When an earthquake occurs, three types of vibration waves move out from the quake site:

Primary waves, or P-waves, result from the back-and-forth vibrations of rock. P-waves, traveling in all directions from the point of the quake, move through the mantle and core of Earth. P-waves move at a greater speed than do the other two types of waves.

Secondary waves, or S-waves, result from the shaking vibrations of rock that occur at right angles to the direction in which each S-wave travels. S-waves travel through Earth's mantle but not through its core.

Surface waves, or L-waves, result from the vibrations of rock on Earth's surface. L-waves are felt strongly near the quake site and travel over the surface in widening circles, like ripples made when a rock is thrown into a pond. Weaker L-waves form at distant points wherever P-waves or S-waves reach the surface. L-waves travel more slowly than either P-waves or S-waves.

3. According to the diagram, which statement is true?

(1) P-waves don't penetrate Earth's core.
(2) S-waves penetrate Earth's core.
(3) L-waves penetrate Earth's core.
(4) P-waves penetrate Earth's core.
(5) P-waves don't penetrate Earth's mantle.

RICHTER SCALE OF EARTHQUAKE MAGNITUDE

Magnitude	Earthquake Effects
0	Smallest measurable quake
2.5–3	Not felt, but measurable
4.5	Minor property damage
6.0	Considerable destruction in populated areas
7.0	Major damage to buildings, bridges, and other structures
7.9	1906 San Francisco quake
8.0 or more	Total destruction of nearby population centers

4. Which type of wave(s) will be first to reach a town located 500 miles from an earthquake?

(1) L-wave
(2) P-wave
(3) S-wave
(4) P-wave and S-wave at the same time
(5) L-wave and P-wave at the same time

5. An earthquake of Richter magnitude 8 occurs in Japan. What magnitude of P-wave will most likely be recorded by instruments but not felt by the general population later in Brazil?

(1) less than 0
(2) between 0 and 3
(3) between 4.5 and 6
(4) between 6 and 7
(5) between 7 and 8

6. A geologist wants to determine the location of a strong earthquake. Which of the following facts would be of least help to him?

(1) the time his instruments first started recording the arrival of the P-wave
(2) the speed at which a P-wave travels
(3) the time the earthquake occurred
(4) the magnitude of the P-wave that his instruments record
(5) the direction from which the P-wave is traveling

Answers are on page 455.

CHAPTER 12
Space Science

The Universe should be deemed an immense Being, always living, always moved, and always moving in an eternal activity inherent in itself, and which, subordinate to no foreign cause, is communicated to all its parts, connects them together, and makes the world of things a complete and perfect whole.

–Albert Pike

Look up at the clear night sky and what do you see? Nothing less than the universe! At least you see a small part of it, enough perhaps to evoke a sense of wonder. Through the centuries people have wondered at the majesty of the cosmos.

Today we know a little more about the universe than our ancestors did. This knowledge has come to us through scientific advancement. Here are three truly remarkable achievements in space science that occurred during the latter part of the twentieth century.

- In 1969 Neil Armstrong and Buzz Aldrin became the first human beings to walk on the Moon. As Armstrong stepped first onto the lunar surface, he made what has become perhaps the most memorable remark of the twentieth century: "That's one small step for man, one giant leap for mankind."

- In 1976 a spacecraft named *Viking* became the first space vehicle to land successfully on the surface of another planet. While on the surface of Mars, *Viking* sent back valuable data until it quit transmitting in 1982.

- In 1990 the Hubble Space Telescope (HST) was launched into orbit around Earth. The diameter of the primary mirror on the HST is about 8 feet. Located above the distortion effects of Earth's atmosphere, the HST is able to see more deeply and clearly into space than even the largest ground-based telescope.

Astronomy, one of the oldest sciences, is the traditional name given to the general study of all celestial bodies in the universe—the planets and their moons, stars, comets, meteoroids, asteroids, and interstellar clouds of material. Today, though, space science includes more than just astronomy. Space scientists come from all fields of science and mathematics.

Space scientists study the motion, the structure, and the life cycles of all celestial bodies. From this study, they hope to gain a better understanding of both the creation and the evolution of the universe, including Earth. With the further development of space vehicles, space stations, and Earth-orbiting telescopes, space science promises to play an important role in our lives.

The Universe As We See It

Thousands of years ago, ancient Greeks observed the night sky with religious wonder. Watching from night to night, they noticed lights in the sky that looked like stars but moved across the sky in strange paths. The Greeks believed that these celestial bodies traveled around Earth in complicated loops. They named these strange objects *planets*, a Greek word meaning "wanderers."

The belief that the wanderers circled Earth in loops persisted until 1543, when Nicolaus Copernicus (1473–1543) suggested a bold new idea. Copernicus, a Polish astronomer, proposed that Earth and all other planets traveled in **orbits** around the Sun. This is the theory that space scientists believe today. The acceptance of the idea that the Sun is at the center of the solar system came to be known as the **Copernican theory.** Together, the Sun and the planets are called the **solar system.**

The Solar System

OUR SOLAR SYSTEM

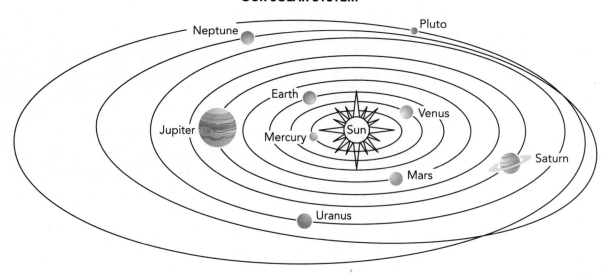

The solar system, as we know it today, consists of a central star we call the Sun, as well as nine major **planets** and their moons, the asteroids, and the comets that revolve around the Sun.

- The largest planets are Jupiter, Saturn, Uranus, and Neptune.

- Four smaller planets—Mercury, Venus, Earth, and Mars—are those closest to the Sun.

- Not much is known about Pluto, the smallest, outermost planet. Pluto's eccentric orbit sometimes crosses the orbit of Neptune.

Asteroids are very small planets that orbit the Sun. Most asteroids are found between the orbits of Mars and Jupiter. Asteroids vary in size; large asteroids may be 600 miles across while small ones can be the size of a grain of sand. When small asteroids enter Earth's atmosphere and appear as streaks of light in the night sky, they are called **meteors.** Fragments of meteors that are found on the surface of Earth are known as **meteorites.** The surface of the Moon shows thousands of impact craters formed by asteroids striking the Moon's surface during the early life of the solar system. Most impact craters on Earth have eroded away.

Comets are small objects that are made of dust and frozen gas. Most comets orbit the Sun in a predictable way. A comet can be seen from Earth only as it nears the Sun and part of its dust and frozen gas vaporizes to form a spectacular tail. The solid core of a comet may be small (three to nine miles in diameter), but the escaping gases can make a comet appear as large as the planet Jupiter. Many comets are periodically visible from Earth. One of the most famous is Halley's comet, which is visible about every 76 years. The first recorded sighting of Halley's comet may have occurred in 240 B.C., when Chinese astronomers reported seeing a "broom star."

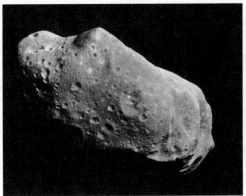

Asteroid 243 IDA, photographed by the Galileo spacecraft

Halley's Comet, last visible from Earth in 1986

Galaxies

The Copernican theory was an important step in our understanding of the universe. Although the size of the universe is unknown, evidence suggests that its age may be between 10 and 20 billion years old! What's more, scientists believe that the universe contains millions or even billions of widely separated **galaxies,** or large groups of stars. On average, each galaxy is believed to contain about 100 million stars.

Our own galaxy is called the Milky Way. The Milky Way contains the Sun and about 200 billion other stars. The distance across the Milky Way is estimated to be about 100,000 light-years. The distance between the Milky Way and the nearest similar galaxy is about 2 million light-years. (A **light-year** is the distance that light travels in one year, about 6 trillion miles. Light travels at the incredible speed of about 186,000 miles per second. Scientists believe that nothing can move more quickly than the speed of light.)

THE MILKY WAY GALAXY

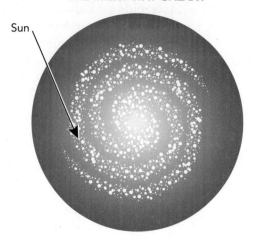

Sun

Earth is in the Milky Way galaxy.

Gravitational Force

The structure of the universe as a whole, including the Milky Way galaxy and our solar system, results mainly from the force of **gravity.**

- Gravity holds stars together in galaxies.
- Gravity holds each planet in its orbit around the Sun.
- Gravity holds the Moon and artificial satellites in orbit around Earth.
- Gravity holds objects, including ourselves, on the surface of Earth.

Thinking About Science

Directions: Complete each sentence by filling in the blanks below.

1. Earth is the_____ closest planet to the Sun.

2. The Copernican theory says that the _____ are in orbit around the _____.

3. One light-year is a distance of about _____ miles.

4. The Milky Way contains about _____ stars.

5. Most asteroids are in orbits between the planets _____ and_____.

Answers are on page 455.

Directions: Choose the <u>one best answer</u> to each question.

Questions 1–5 refer to the information on pages 369–372.

1. Which statement best expresses the idea proposed by Nicolaus Copernicus?

    (1) The Sun orbits Earth and all other planets.
    (2) The Sun is only one of billions of stars.
    (3) Earth is at the center of a system of orbiting planets.
    (4) The Sun is at the center of a system of orbiting planets.
    (5) The universe contains billions of galaxies.

2. Planets are seen as faint lights that move across the night sky. Yet, unlike stars, planets do not give off their own light. Knowing this, decide which of the following facts are needed in order to explain how we are able to see the other planets while standing on Earth.

    A. Planets close to the Sun have higher surface temperatures than planets farther away.

    B. Five planets are farther from the Sun than Earth while only three are closer.

    C. Planets reflect part of the sunlight that strikes them.

    (1) A only
    (2) B only
    (3) C only
    (4) A and C only
    (5) B and C only

3. Earth is about 93 million miles from the Sun. If light travels at 186,000 miles per second, about how long does it take light to travel from the Sun to Earth?

    (1) 8 minutes
    (2) 80 minutes
    (3) 8 hours
    (4) 8 seconds
    (5) 80 seconds

4. The ancient Greeks made the following observations:

    A. The Sun rises in the morning and sets at night.

    B. The Sun and the Moon look about the same size.

    C. The Moon changes shape during the month.

    D. Earth does not seem to move.

    Which of the above observations could the ancient Greeks use to support their belief that the Sun moved around Earth?

    (1) A and B only
    (2) A and C only
    (3) B and C only
    (4) B and D only
    (5) A and D only

5. One celestial object is often referred to by scientists as a "dirty snowball." Which object are they referring to?

    (1) planet
    (2) asteroid
    (3) star
    (4) meteorite
    (5) comet

Answers are on page 455.

Life and Death of Stars

Life of Stars

Stars are born, have a lifetime, and eventually die. Although the lifetime of a human being may be 100 years, the life of a star may be many billions of years. A star forms from a cloud of interstellar dust and gas, goes through a life cycle, and then dies, with much of the star's material returning to interstellar space. The exact life cycle of a star depends on the amount of material from which the star is made.

Energy of Stars

At the beginning of its life cycle, a star is a large, relatively cool contracting cloud of gas. The source of this gas is most likely the remains of other stars that have exploded. As the cloud is pulled together by gravity, the temperature of the cloud rises. The contraction and rising temperature continues up to a temperature of a few million degrees Fahrenheit. At this temperature, nuclear reactions begin taking place, and great amounts of additional heat are created.

At about the point at which a star begins acting as its own energy source, contraction stops. A star then goes through a series of steps as it consumes its own nuclear fuel. In the final step the star's only source of energy is its remaining hydrogen. When all of the hydrogen is consumed and converted to helium, the normal life of the star is over and it changes into another type of star.

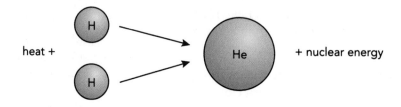

In a star, hydrogen is converted to helium, releasing nuclear energy.

Types of Stars

Depending on its original size, a star will likely become one of the following types:

- **Blue star**—a massive, hot star that uses up its hydrogen quickly, expands, and turns into a giant or supergiant.

- **Giant or supergiant star**—a star that is not as massive as a blue star, but has run out of hydrogen, resulting in the inner core shrinking and the outer core expanding. If the star glows a cool, red color, it is called a **red giant**. If the star is very large, it is called a **supergiant**.

- **White dwarf star**—a small, hot star that is the leftover core of a giant or supergiant. Our own Sun will eventually become a white dwarf.

- **Red dwarf star**—The smallest and coolest of stars, having the longest lifetime of all stars.

Death of Stars

When large stars get old, they often explode and turn into unusual but often beautiful structures.

- **Supernova**—a flash of light caused by the explosion of a massive blue star that has become too hot. Heavy elements are actually formed in supernova explosions.

- **Neutron star**—a very dense small star made up entirely of neutrons from the leftover materials near the center of a supernova. A teaspoon full of a neutron star would weigh a billion tons if brought back to Earth!

- **Pulsar**—a neutron star that spins. A pulsar sends out beams of pulsing radiation that can be detected by instruments on Earth.

- **Black hole**—the collapsed leftovers of a supernova. The gravity of a black hole is so strong that it may pull in material from nearby stars. Not even light can escape a black hole.

 Go to **www.GEDScience.com** for additional practice and instruction!

Thinking About Science

Directions: Complete each sentence below by filling in the blank with the correct word(s) from the reading selection.

1. A spinning neutron star is called a _____.

2. Our own Sun will eventually become a _____.

3. The flash of light that signals the death of a massive blue star is called a _____.

Answers are on page 455.

GED PRACTICE

Directions: Choose the <u>one best answer</u> to each question.

Questions 1–3 refer to the information on pages 374 and 375.

1. At about what point in a star's formation does contraction stop?

    (1) when a star dies
    (2) when nuclear reactions begin
    (3) when a star cools
    (4) when nuclear reactions stop
    (5) when all the hydrogen is consumed

2. Near the end of a star's life, what is its main source of energy?

    (1) gravitational energy
    (2) radioactive elements
    (3) light from nearby stars
    (4) hydrogen as a nuclear fuel
    (5) iron as a nuclear fuel

3. Which object listed below cannot be directly observed from Earth because light is not able to leave it?

    (1) blue star
    (2) red dwarf
    (3) supernova
    (4) pulsar
    (5) black hole

Answers are on page 455.

More About Galaxies

Origin of Galaxies

Where did all the nearly 50 billion galaxies and 100 million stars in each galaxy come from? No one knows. But the popular theory is that all objects in the universe, including galaxies and stars, probably formed from the same solar nebula.

As advances in telescopes have allowed scientists to look farther into space, they have made some interesting discoveries about galaxies:

- There are many types of galaxies, each with a different shape.

- Galaxies are not uniformly distributed in space. They tend to occur in groups.

- Groups of galaxies themselves form even larger groups called clusters.

- There are vast regions of space between galaxy clusters.

The universe has a pattern that is repeated in every direction. Huge galaxy clusters are separated by vast regions of space. Each cluster itself contains separated groups of galaxies. Why does the universe have this structure? Again, no one knows. The universe presents many mysteries that may be answered by future generations.

Types of Galaxies

Shown below are pictures of a **spiral galaxy** and an **elliptical galaxy**.

A spiral galaxy has a huge core of stars surrounded by spiral arms.

An elliptical galaxy looks like a sphere or an elongated sphere of stars.

Galaxies that differ from these two basic shapes are called **irregular galaxies.** An irregular galaxy is irregular in shape. It has no specific shape due to its random scattering of millions of stars.

Objects Within Galaxies

In addition to stars, a galaxy may contain other structures.

- **Gas cloud**—a vast cloud of gas and dust out of which a star may form. Spiral galaxies contain gas clouds, but it seems elliptical galaxies do not.

- **Globular cluster**—a group of older stars that looks like a ball of stars. Globular clusters are common in both spiral galaxies and elliptical galaxies.

- **Open cluster**—a small group of stars (a few thousand) that is located along the spiral disk of a spiral galaxy.

Thinking About Science

Directions: Complete each sentence below by filling in the blank(s) with the correct word(s) from the reading selection.

1. Scientists believe that the universe contains about

   _____ galaxies.

2. Groups of galaxies close to each other are called a

   _____.

3. A group of older stars in galaxies is called a

   _____.

Answers are on page 455.

GED PRACTICE

Directions: Choose the <u>one best answer</u> to each question.

Questions 1 and 2 refer to the information on page 377.

1. When a star explodes, its remains stay in the galaxy. What structure do these remains first form or become part of?

   (1) planets
   (2) new stars
   (3) gas cloud
   (4) globular cluster
   (5) open cluster

2. What do all galaxies most likely have in common?

   (1) same shape
   (2) same age
   (3) same contents
   (4) same number of stars
   (5) same distance from Earth

Answers are on page 456.

Origin and Evolution of the Solar System

Origin of the Solar System

What caused the formation of the Sun, the major planets, and the asteroids in our solar system about 4.6 billion years ago? The solar nebula theory is the most popular theory. According to that theory, the solar system began as a huge cloud of interstellar gas and dust, called the **solar nebula.** This cloud most likely formed from the remains of nearby exploding stars. As gravity pulled the gas and dust toward a central region, the cloud fragmented into separate smaller clouds that each condensed into a planet and its moons.

According to the solar nebula theory, the Sun formed at the central, most dense point of the cloud. The heaviest elements in the cloud moved toward this central region. As a result, planets that formed close to the Sun tend to be made up of the heaviest elements. Planets farthest from the Sun tend to be made up of the lighter elements. In fact, the largest planets, which are the planets farthest from the Sun, are primarily made up of the light gases hydrogen and helium.

The solar nebula theory suggests that planet formation is associated with star formation. And recent discoveries of planets around stars outside our solar system support this theory. The presence of moons around planets in our own solar system is also explained by this theory. Earth has a single moon, whereas the planets Jupiter and Saturn each have many. Analysis of moon rocks suggests that the Moon formed at about the same time as Earth formed.

Evolution of the Solar System

What will the solar system look like in the distant future? According to space scientists, the future of the solar system depends on the future of the Sun.

Scientists believe that the Sun has been in its present form for about 4.6 billion years, a little less than the age of the solar system itself. The primary energy-producing reaction within the Sun is the nuclear burning of hydrogen to produce helium. There appears to be enough hydrogen left in the Sun for this process to continue for another 4.6 billion years. According to this theory, the Sun is about halfway through its life cycle.

When the Sun runs out of hydrogen, this glorious star will start to expand. The inner planets, including Earth, will be engulfed as the Sun becomes a red giant star. The Sun will stay a red giant for about 500 million years and then shrink to a white dwarf star. As a white dwarf, the Sun will be about the size of present-day Earth and will remain a white dwarf as it cools for several billion additional years.

With the evolution of the Sun into a red giant and finally a white dwarf, life in the solar system as we now know it will no longer be possible.

Thinking About Science

Directions: Complete each sentence below by filling in the blank(s) with the correct word(s) from the reading selection.

1. Scientists believe that the Sun and Earth formed about

    _____ years ago.

2. What two gases are the main elements in the four largest planets in

    our solar system? _____ and

    _____ .

3. Scientists believe that the Sun will stay in its present form for about

    _____ years more.

Answers are on page 456.

GED PRACTICE

Directions: Choose the <u>one best answer</u> to each question.

Questions 1 and 2 refer to the information on page 379.

1. Which of the following do the four inner planets have in common with the four larger outer planets?

    (1) approximate age
    (2) size
    (3) distance from the Sun
    (4) elemental composition
    (5) orbital path

2. Which of the following supports the theory that planet formation is often associated with star formation?

    (1) the fact that the planets in our solar system orbit the Sun
    (2) the presence of the solar nebula
    (3) the age of the universe
    (4) the discovery of planets around stars other than our Sun
    (5) the discovery that galaxies are not uniformly distributed in the universe

Questions 3 and 4 refer to the following passage.

Solar wind is the name given to the stream of charged atomic particles (electrons, protons, and other light-element ions) that stream away from the Sun and into space. Solar wind is caused by the intense pressure of light radiating away from the Sun and the presence of electric and magnetic fields near the Sun's surface.

3. Which of the following is <u>not</u> a feature of the solar wind?

    (1) created on the Sun
    (2) flows away from the Sun
    (3) contains charged particles
    (4) is affected by magnetic fields
    (5) is created on Earth

4   Which of the following may be affected when solar wind strikes Earth?

    (1) long-term global climate
    (2) long-distance radio reception
    (3) height of ocean tides
    (4) time of sunrise and sunset
    (5) frequency of earthquakes

Answers are on page 456.

Origin and Evolution of the Universe

Origin of the Universe

How the universe began is still a mystery. One popular theory, called the **big bang theory**, sets the beginning of the universe with a tremendous explosion!

According to the big bang theory, the universe began 10 to 20 billion years ago as a very dense, hot, compact mass under extreme pressure. When the pressure became too intense, the big bang occurred and rapid expansion resulted. After a fraction of a second, the expansion slowed, with much of the available energy changing into fundamental particles—the particles that make up atoms of all matter in today's universe. In the early moments, as energy was converted to matter, the elements, stars, and galaxies formed, giving us pretty much the universe we see today. It's an incredible theory, but it's the best scientists have!

Evolution of the Universe

Today, scientists know that the universe is still expanding and cooling. Recent research suggests that it is expanding at an accelerated rate rather than the constant rate associated with the big bang theory. However, no one knows if this expansion will continue. There are currently three models of what may happen eventually. No one is sure which, if any, of these models is correct.

- **Open universe**—a universe that continues to slowly expand forever.

- **Flat universe**—a universe that at some future time reaches a size and then stays at that size.

- **Closed universe**—a universe that at some future time begins to contract and eventually collapses to its original state as a small, dense, hot mass.

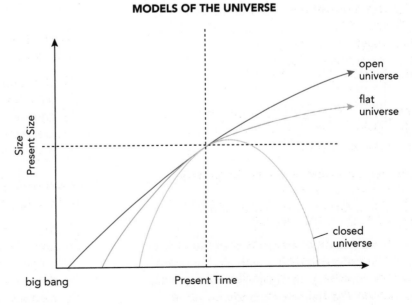

MODELS OF THE UNIVERSE

Thinking About Science

Directions: Complete each sentence by filling in the blank(s) with the correct word(s) from the reading selection.

1. According to the big bang theory, the universe began with an

   _____ .

2. According to the big bang theory, what was converted into the fundamental particles that make up the atoms in today's universe?

   _____ .

3. The three models of the eventual state of the universe are

   _____ , _____ ,

   and _____ .

Answers are on page 456.

GED PRACTICE

Directions: Choose the <u>one best answer</u> to each question.

Question 1 refers to the information on page 381.

1. Scientists jokingly use the phrase "the big crunch" to refer to one of the models of the universe. To what model are they most likely referring?

   (1) the big bang theory
   (2) the open universe theory
   (3) the flat universe theory
   (4) the closed universe theory
   (5) the accelerated universe theory

Questions 2–4 refer to the following passage.

The expansion of the universe is often compared to dots on a balloon:

Suppose you draw many dots on the surface of a balloon before you fill it with air. Then you fill the balloon with air and watch what happens to the dots as the balloon expands.

2. What happens to the dots on the balloon as you fill it with air?

   (1) They disappear.
   (2) They move closer together.
   (3) They move farther apart.
   (4) They form one large dot.
   (5) They remain at the same distance apart.

3. In this comparison what do the dots on the balloon represent?

   (1) elements
   (2) galaxies
   (3) energy
   (4) electrons
   (5) protons

4. In the balloon demonstration what does the balloon itself represent?

   (1) the universe
   (2) Earth
   (3) a star
   (4) the solar system
   (5) fundamental particles

Answers are on page 456.

Space Science Review

Directions: Choose the <u>one best answer</u> to each question.

Questions 1 and 2 refer to the following table.

COMPARING INTERPLANETARY DISTANCES

Planet	Distance from Sun in AU
Mercury	0.39
Venus	0.72
Earth	1.00
Mars	1.52
Jupiter	5.20
Saturn	9.54
Uranus	19.19
Neptune	30.06
Pluto	39.53

1. From the information in the table, what can you infer about the basis of the astronomical unit (AU)?

   (1) It represents the average distance from Earth to the Moon.
   (2) It represents the average distance from Earth to the Sun.
   (3) It represents the average distance of the planets from the Sun.
   (4) It represents the average diameter of the planets.
   (5) It represents the diameter of the Sun.

2. Earth is about 93 million miles from the Sun. About how far is Jupiter from the Sun?

   (1) 100 million miles
   (2) 200 million miles
   (3) 300 million miles
   (4) 500 million miles
   (5) 800 million miles

Questions 3 and 4 refer to the following table.

COMPARING THE FORCE OF GRAVITY

Planet	Percent of Earth's Gravity
Mercury	38%
Venus	91%
Mars	38%
Jupiter	236%
Saturn	92%
Uranus	89%
Neptune	112%
Pluto	7%

3. Suppose an astronaut weighs 150 pounds on Earth. What would the weight of this astronaut be on the surface of Mars?

   (1) 57 pounds
   (2) 76 pounds
   (3) 100 pounds
   (4) 112 pounds
   (5) 236 pounds

4. The diameter of Saturn is about ten times the diameter of Earth. With this being the case, what is the most likely reason that the force of gravity near the surface of Saturn is less than that of Earth?

   (1) Saturn is farther from the Sun.
   (2) Saturn has rings around it.
   (3) Saturn is mainly light gases.
   (4) Saturn has several moons.
   (5) Saturn has a very low surface temperature.

Questions 5 and 6 refer to the illustration below.

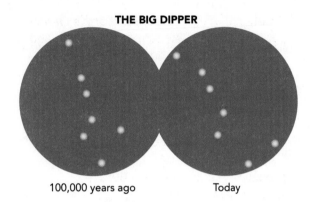

THE BIG DIPPER

100,000 years ago   Today

5. The group of stars known as the Big Dipper is shown above. What can you infer from this diagram?

   (1) The distance between the Sun and Earth changes over time.
   (2) Stars move relative to one another over time.
   (3) The universe is contracting.
   (4) This group of stars is not in the same galaxy as Earth.
   (5) Two different groups of stars are pictured.

6. What do you know is true about all of the stars in the Big Dipper?

   (1) They all are the same age.
   (2) They all are the same size.
   (3) They all are the same distance from Earth.
   (4) They all have the same surface temperature.
   (5) They all are visible from Earth.

Question 7 refers to the following passage.

   The star named *Polaris* is often referred to as the North Star because it is always located almost directly above Earth's North Pole. Polaris is in approximately the same position every hour of the day, every day of the year.

7. Suppose you look at Polaris on a clear night during a period of several hours. Which of the following would you observe?

   (1) Polaris slowly moves from west to east across the sky.
   (2) Polaris slowly moves from north to south across the sky.
   (3) The rest of the stars rotate around Polaris.
   (4) Polaris slowly moves toward the horizon directly below it.
   (5) No change occurs in the position of any of the stars, including Polaris.

8. At which location does Polaris appear closest to the horizon?

   (1) Anchorage, Alaska
   (2) Mexico City, Mexico
   (3) San Francisco, California
   (4) Sydney, Australia
   (5) Vancouver, Canada

9. At which location is Polaris not visible from Earth?

   (1) Europe
   (2) North America
   (3) the North Pole
   (4) the South Pole
   (5) the equator

Answers are on page 456.

Earth and Space Science Writing Activities

The following topics will give you extra practice in thinking and writing about Earth and space science.

Directions: Choose one of the topics below and write a well-developed essay (approximately 250 words). You may wish to plan your essay before you write. Pay attention to your organization, development, and control of sentence structure, punctuation, grammar, word choice, and spelling. After you finish writing your essay, reread what you have written and make any changes that will improve your essay.

----- TOPIC 1 -----

Earthquakes occur when the plates of Earth's crust shift and cause the ground to move. Opinions are mixed as to whether the public should be told about a predicted earthquake if scientists are not certain that the earthquake will occur. Some people say that earthquake warnings are necessary to prevent death and destruction. Others point to cases where people were needlessly evacuated from their homes on the basis of an erroneous prediction. Do you think the public should be told about a predicted earthquake?

In your essay explain whether it is wise to inform people about predicted earthquakes. Use specific examples to support your reasons.

----- TOPIC 2 -----

Think about the land features of the area where you live. If you live in a city, you might be able to see the effects of weathering and erosion on sidewalks, buildings, and small patches of grass or dirt. People who live in rural areas might see some of these effects on roads, hillsides, rivers, and fields. What do you think are the primary causes of erosion where you live?

In your essay describe one instance of weathering or erosion in your environment. State the probable causes of this erosion and the effects it may have on your environment in the future.

----- TOPIC 3 -----

In January of 1986, the space shuttle Challenger exploded after takeoff. All seven astronauts aboard the shuttle were killed. The Challenger accident caused many people to wonder if we should continue to send people into space. If you were in charge of the space program, would you support manned flights into space?

In your essay present your views about manned flights into space. Give specific reasons to support your opinion.

Science

This posttest will give you the opportunity to evaluate your readiness for the actual GED Science Test.

Directions: Choose the one best answer to each question. The questions are based on reading passages, charts, graphs, maps, and cartoons. Answer each question as carefully as possible. If a question seems to be too difficult, do not spend too much time on it. Work ahead and come back to it later when you can think it through carefully. You should take approximately 80 minutes to complete the test.

Posttest Answer Grid

1 ① ② ③ ④ ⑤	18 ① ② ③ ④ ⑤	35 ① ② ③ ④ ⑤
2 ① ② ③ ④ ⑤	19 ① ② ③ ④ ⑤	36 ① ② ③ ④ ⑤
3 ① ② ③ ④ ⑤	20 ① ② ③ ④ ⑤	37 ① ② ③ ④ ⑤
4 ① ② ③ ④ ⑤	21 ① ② ③ ④ ⑤	38 ① ② ③ ④ ⑤
5 ① ② ③ ④ ⑤	22 ① ② ③ ④ ⑤	39 ① ② ③ ④ ⑤
6 ① ② ③ ④ ⑤	23 ① ② ③ ④ ⑤	40 ① ② ③ ④ ⑤
7 ① ② ③ ④ ⑤	24 ① ② ③ ④ ⑤	41 ① ② ③ ④ ⑤
8 ① ② ③ ④ ⑤	25 ① ② ③ ④ ⑤	42 ① ② ③ ④ ⑤
9 ① ② ③ ④ ⑤	26 ① ② ③ ④ ⑤	43 ① ② ③ ④ ⑤
10 ① ② ③ ④ ⑤	27 ① ② ③ ④ ⑤	44 ① ② ③ ④ ⑤
11 ① ② ③ ④ ⑤	28 ① ② ③ ④ ⑤	45 ① ② ③ ④ ⑤
12 ① ② ③ ④ ⑤	29 ① ② ③ ④ ⑤	46 ① ② ③ ④ ⑤
13 ① ② ③ ④ ⑤	30 ① ② ③ ④ ⑤	47 ① ② ③ ④ ⑤
14 ① ② ③ ④ ⑤	31 ① ② ③ ④ ⑤	48 ① ② ③ ④ ⑤
15 ① ② ③ ④ ⑤	32 ① ② ③ ④ ⑤	49 ① ② ③ ④ ⑤
16 ① ② ③ ④ ⑤	33 ① ② ③ ④ ⑤	50 ① ② ③ ④ ⑤
17 ① ② ③ ④ ⑤	34 ① ② ③ ④ ⑤	

POSTTEST

Questions 1 and 2 refer to the following illustrations.

FRATERNAL TWINS

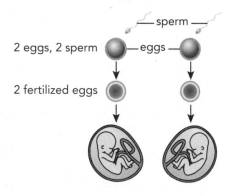

2 eggs, 2 sperm — eggs — sperm

2 fertilized eggs

Two genetically different individuals who develop within separate fetal sacs.

IDENTICAL TWINS

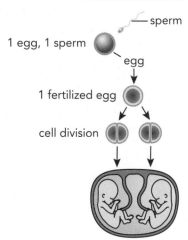

1 egg, 1 sperm — sperm

egg

1 fertilized egg

cell division

Cell division results in two genetically identical individuals who develop in the same fetal sac.

1. From which fact can you deduce that Gary's twin brother Frank is Gary's fraternal twin?

   (1) Both Frank and Gary are teachers.
   (2) Frank's ears have a different shape from Gary's ears.
   (3) Frank weighs about three pounds more than Gary.
   (4) Frank and Gary each have fraternal twin daughters.
   (5) Frank and Gary are about the same height.

2. Which of the following characteristics is <u>least</u> likely to be shared by identical twins?

   (1) height
   (2) shoe size
   (3) eye color
   (4) favorite color
   (5) gender (male or female)

3. In physics, work is defined as a process in which force is applied to an object with the result that the object moves. Which of the following activities would a physicist classify as work?

   (1) attempting to lift a rock that will not budge
   (2) mentally subtracting 194 from 331
   (3) swinging a bat and hitting a ball
   (4) watching the Super Bowl on television
   (5) trying unsuccessfully to open a jar of jam

POSTTEST

Questions 4 and 5 refer to the passage below.

Charles Darwin proposed the theory of natural selection in 1859. The theory holds that those species that are best adapted to the conditions of their environment will survive, and those that are not adapted will perish.

An example of this theory is illustrated by the peppered moth that was once common near Manchester, England. Before the Industrial Revolution, the light-colored form of this moth was common and the dark-colored form was rare. As Manchester's environment became increasingly polluted, however, the tree trunks on which the peppered moth lived became blackened by soot. The light-colored form of the moth stood out against the dark tree trunks and was eaten by birds. Ninety-nine percent of the light-colored moths disappeared.

In the absence of the light-colored moths, the rare dark moths became more common. In the 1950s, Manchester's industries were cleaned up, and the light-colored moth once more became the more common type.

4. Why did the number of light-colored moths decrease to such a low level?

   (1) They were eaten by birds.
   (2) The environment became polluted.
   (3) They were killed by an insecticide.
   (4) They had a low number of offspring.
   (5) They were white in color.

5. Which of the following can be inferred from the passage?

   (1) Air pollution is not harmful to all living organisms.
   (2) Moths can thrive in terrible conditions.
   (3) Darwin's theory works only under ideal circumstances.
   (4) To survive, all organisms must remain hidden in their environment.
   (5) Human activity can have a big impact on living organisms.

Question 6 refers to the following illustration.

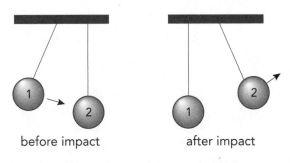

before impact   after impact

6. Kinetic energy is the energy that a moving body possesses. Potential energy is the energy that a body stores or has available for use. Which of the following statements explains the role that energy plays in the interaction shown above?

   (1) Kinetic energy is transferred from ball 1 to ball 2 at the time of impact.
   (2) Kinetic energy is transferred from ball 2 to ball 1 at the time of impact.
   (3) Potential energy is transferred from ball 1 to ball 2 at the time of impact.
   (4) Potential energy is transferred from ball 2 to ball 1 at the time of impact.
   (5) All kinetic energy is changed to potential energy at the time of impact.

POSTTEST

Questions 7 and 8 refer to the following passage.

When a squirrel hibernates, its bodily functions slow down. At the same time, the blood flow to the squirrel's brain almost ceases—a condition that leads immediately to a stroke in humans. Without a continual supply of blood, human brain cells break down and die. These cells are not replaced, and disability or death can result. The question is, why don't the brain cells of squirrels die during hibernation?

A clue may be found in the human brain, where a lack of blood causes brain cells to lose potassium and to gain calcium. Cells affected in this way die. By studying changes in potassium and calcium levels in a hibernating squirrel's brain, scientists hope to discover what protects the squirrel. The answer may someday enable doctors to help prevent strokes in some patients and to help stroke victims recover more fully.

7. According to the passage, which of the following can cause a stroke in a human?

   (1) a diet overly rich in calcium
   (2) an inability to hibernate
   (3) permanent disability or death
   (4) too little potassium in the blood
   (5) a restricted blood flow to the brain

8. Which is a hypothesis that is supported by information given in the passage?

   (1) Squirrels do not suffer strokes because they are able to replace dead brain cells.
   (2) A squirrel's brain cells break down during hibernation but the squirrel is not harmed.
   (3) The brain cells of a squirrel do not contain potassium and calcium.
   (4) A dead brain cell can be brought back to life by injecting it with potassium.
   (5) A squirrel's brain safely regulates its cells' potassium and calcium levels during hibernation.

Question 9 refers to the following diagram.

A PARTIAL SOLAR ECLIPSE
(seen from Earth)

Dashed line indicates the part of the Moon that cannot be seen from Earth.

9. Which of the following occur during a partial solar eclipse?

   A. The Sun is partially blocked from view.
   B. The Sun passes between the Moon and Earth.
   C. The Moon passes between Earth and the Sun.
   D. The amount of sunlight reaching Earth increases.

   (1) A and B only
   (2) A and C only
   (3) B and D only
   (4) C and D only
   (5) A, B, and D only

POSTTEST

Questions 10 and 11 refer to the following passage.

An *aurora* is a magnificent display of colored light that appears occasionally in the night sky. Auroras are seen most often in regions around the North and South Poles. Called northern or southern lights, auroras are caused by electrically charged particles from space colliding with air molecules in Earth's upper atmosphere.

The stream of fast moving, charged particles that cause an aurora comes from the Sun. Called a solar wind, this stream is created when hot gas storms occur on the Sun's surface. These storms, known as solar flares, emit highly energetic particles into space. As the resulting solar wind approaches Earth, its particles are guided toward the poles by Earth's magnetic field. A glowing curtain of colored light results.

10. According to the passage, what is an aurora?

   (1) a flow of electrically charged particles from the Sun

   (2) the guidance property of Earth's magnetic field

   (3) a luminous display in the sky seen at night

   (4) gas molecules in the upper atmosphere

   (5) a solar storm that emits electrically charged particles

11. What is the most reasonable conclusion you can draw about a year in which there was an above-average number of auroras?

   (1) The number of solar storms was above average.

   (2) The number of severe winter storms on Earth was above average.

   (3) The average distance between Earth and the Sun was less than normal.

   (4) An above-average number of people living in southern states reported seeing auroras.

   (5) More auroras occurred that year at the North Pole than at the South Pole.

Question 12 refers to the following illustration.

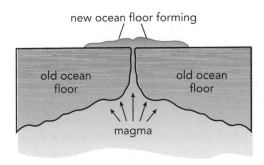

12. According to the illustration, what causes the formation of new ocean floor?

   (1) the change of old ocean floor into magma

   (2) erosion of underwater mountains due to the flow of magma

   (3) magma forcing its way down through a crack in the old ocean floor

   (4) magma forcing its way up through a crack in the old ocean floor

   (5) magma forming from minerals deposited in ocean water

13. *Adaptive radiation* refers to the pattern in which different species develop from a common ancestor.

Which of the following pairs is <u>not</u> an example of adaptive radiation?

   (1) a horse and a zebra

   (2) a deer and an elk

   (3) a shark and a salmon

   (4) a duck and a chicken

   (5) a giraffe and a frog

Questions 14–16 refer to the following passage.

Selective breeding is used to improve the traits of animals or plants. In selective breeding, only plants and animals with desirable traits are mated.

Hybridization is the selective breeding of two organisms that have distinct genetic differences even though they are members of the same species. The purpose of hybridization is to produce a new individual (a hybrid) that inherits desirable traits from each parent organism. However, hybrids may inherit undesirable traits as well.

An example of a hybrid animal is the mule, a cross between a female horse and a male donkey. The mule gets its size and strength from the horse. A mule's endurance and balance come from the donkey. Like many hybrids, though, the mule is sterile—unable to produce offspring.

Inbreeding, the opposite of hybridization, is the selective mating of plants or animals that have nearly identical genetic makeup. Inbreeding can produce generations of nearly identical offspring. In plants, inbreeding is done by self-pollination. Self-pollination ensures that only the one parent-plant's genes are passed on.

Inbreeding in animals is done by mating close relatives. The breeding of thoroughbred horses and purebred dogs are examples of inbreeding.

14. If a pet store advertises that a dog is a purebred cocker spaniel, which of the following can you assume to be true about the dog?

A. The dog will have traits that are very similar to the traits of other purebred cocker spaniels.

B. The dog will have only the favorable traits of its parents.

C. Both parents of the dog are purebred cocker spaniels.

D. Only one parent of the dog is a purebred cocker spaniel.

(1) A and B only
(2) A and C only
(3) A and D only
(4) B and C only
(5) B and D only

15. What is the sought-after feature of organisms produced by hybridization?

(1) inability to breed
(2) genetically identical features
(3) a unique combination of desirable traits
(4) no inheritable traits
(5) genetic similarity to one parent organism

16. Which of the following is <u>not</u> a hybrid?

(1) a pink rose, produced by crossing a red rose with a white rose
(2) a tangelo, produced by crossing a grapefruit with a tangerine
(3) a first-generation cockapoo, the result of breeding a purebred cocker spaniel with a purebred poodle
(4) a golden retriever, the result of breeding a purebred golden retriever with its cousin
(5) popcorn, usually created by crossing two kinds of corn

POSTTEST

Questions 17 and 18 refer to the following illustration and passage.

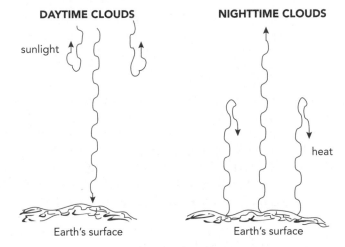

DAYTIME CLOUDS

sunlight

Earth's surface

NIGHTTIME CLOUDS

heat

Earth's surface

Earth's surface is heated by sunlight. During the day, clouds stop much of this light from reaching Earth's surface. Because of this, cloudy days are cooler than clear days. However, clouds in the night sky stop heat radiating off the warmed surface of Earth from escaping into space. Nighttime clouds form a protective blanket that keeps cloudy nights warmer than clear nights.

17. What property of clouds is the reason that they have a major effect on air temperature?

(1) Clouds reflect most heat-producing light rays.
(2) Clouds absorb most heat-producing light rays.
(3) Clouds transmit most heat-producing light rays.
(4) Clouds reflect most cold-producing light rays.
(5) Clouds absorb most cold-producing light rays.

18. During the winter, which of the following sky conditions produce the warmest nights?

(1) partially cloudy day and partially cloudy night
(2) cloud-covered day and cloud-covered night
(3) clear day and cloud-covered night
(4) cloud-covered day and clear night
(5) partially cloudy day and cloud-covered night

19. Which of the following is <u>not</u> the result of an interaction between electricity and magnetism?

(1) The needle of a compass deflects when the compass is near a lighted lamp.
(2) An electric current flows through a coiled wire while a magnet is moved near the coil.
(3) The needle of a compass points the wrong way when the compass is beneath electric power lines.
(4) A stereo speaker sounds fuzzy when a strong magnet is moved near it.
(5) A 12-volt battery causes twice as much current to flow through a lightbulb as does a 6-volt battery.

20. Glacial rock deposits found on the eastern coast of South America are almost identical to deposits found on the west coast of Africa.

Which of the following hypotheses is best supported by this discovery?

(1) South America and Africa were formed at about the same time.
(2) Glacial rock deposits were carried from Africa to South America by early explorers.
(3) Glacial rock deposits floated from Africa to South America.
(4) During the last Ice Age, glaciers formed near the poles and moved toward the equator.
(5) South America and Africa were once part of the same landmass.

Questions 21–23 refer to the following illustration and passage.

THREE PHASES OF WATER (H₂O)

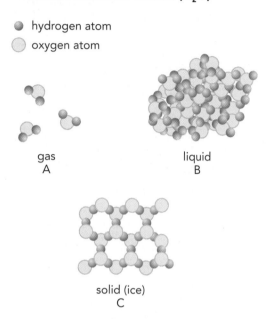

● hydrogen atom

○ oxygen atom

gas
A

liquid
B

solid (ice)
C

As a gas (water vapor), H₂O molecules are widely separated, being much farther apart on the average than H₂O molecules in water or ice. Unlike most other liquids, though, water expands when it freezes. As water forms ice, H₂O molecules form a lattice-like structure in which they are farther apart than H₂O molecules in water.

21. Suppose you compare equal volumes of water vapor, liquid water, and ice. From heaviest to lightest, how do the weights of these three phases of water compare?

(1) water heaviest, ice next, water vapor lightest
(2) ice heaviest, water next, water vapor lightest
(3) water vapor heaviest, ice next, water lightest
(4) water heaviest, water vapor next, ice lightest
(5) ice heaviest, water vapor next, water lightest

22. Which of the following is explained by the fact that H₂O molecules are farther apart in ice than in water?

(1) Heat energy is needed to melt ice.
(2) Ice sinks in water.
(3) Ice is hard enough to break a tooth if you chew it.
(4) Ice floats on water.
(5) Water transmits light better than ice.

23. To quickly cool a bottle of soda pop, Jenny placed it in the freezer at noon. She forgot about the glass bottle until 6:00 P.M. When she opened the freezer, she found the bottle in pieces. What is the best explanation of what happened?

(1) Lowering the temperature of glass below freezing causes glass to break.
(2) The soda pop expanded as it froze and broke the bottle.
(3) The water vapor in the freezer expanded as it froze and crushed the bottle.
(4) As the bottle froze, the glass expanded until it broke.
(5) The soda pop froze more quickly than the bottle.

POSTTEST

Questions 24 and 25 refer to the following passage.

AIDS (Acquired Immune Deficiency Syndrome) is a disease of the body's immune system—the system that enables the body to destroy germs that cause infections and illness.

The first symptoms of AIDS may be weight loss, swollen lymph nodes, body weakness, persistent cough, and chronic yeast infections of the mouth or genital areas. Other symptoms may include pneumonia or a type of cancer characterized by the presence of purplish spots. Eventually, an AIDS patient may develop life-threatening infections and cancers that usually don't affect people with normal immune systems.

AIDS is caused by a virus known as HIV, the Human Immunodeficiency Virus. Once infected with HIV, a person may feel fine and show no symptoms of AIDS for years. However, even though an "HIV-positive" person looks healthy, he or she is infectious and can transmit this virus to other people. The HIV virus spreads from the blood of an infected person to the blood of the uninfected. And, because blood cells are present in semen and other body fluids, the HIV virus can spread during sexual activity.

AIDS is most commonly spread in one of three ways:

• by having unsafe sex with an infected person

• by sharing a needle with an infected drug user

• from an infected mother to the fetus during pregnancy, or to the baby during delivery or breast-feeding

At present there are treatments for many of the symptoms of AIDS, but there is no cure for AIDS. You can, though, protect yourself from AIDS. You do this by making intelligent choices about sex partners and drugs. A high percentage of AIDS patients are people who have had unsafe sex with more than one partner and people who have shared needles during drug use.

24. Which of the following was <u>not</u> mentioned in the passage as a way AIDS can be spread from an infected person to an uninfected person?

(1) drug use
(2) sexual activity
(3) childbirth
(4) breastfeeding
(5) swimming

25. Against which type of diseases can a healthy immune system protect a person?

(1) sexually transmitted diseases
(2) all types of immune-system viruses
(3) some types of infectious diseases
(4) all types of infectious diseases
(5) some types of blood diseases

Questions 26 and 27 refer to the following drawing.

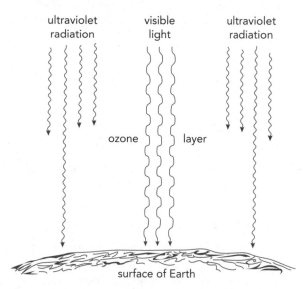

ultraviolet radiation   visible light   ultraviolet radiation

ozone))) layer

surface of Earth

26. Which of the following is the best summary of information provided in the drawing above?

(1) The ozone layer absorbs most ultraviolet radiation and visible light that strike it.
(2) The ozone layer absorbs most ultraviolet radiation that strikes it but allows visible light to pass through.
(3) The ozone layer protects Earth from all harmful effects of visible light.
(4) The ozone layer protects Earth from all harmful effects of ultraviolet radiation.
(5) Both ultraviolet radiation and visible light are present in sunlight.

27. What would most likely result if the ozone layer were partially destroyed by air pollutants?

(1) a decrease in the amount of visible light that reaches Earth's surface
(2) an increase in the amount of visible light that reaches Earth's surface
(3) a decrease in the amount of ultraviolet radiation that reaches Earth's surface
(4) an increase in the amount of ultraviolet radiation that reaches Earth's surface
(5) no change in the amount of ultraviolet radiation that reaches Earth's surface

28. *Electrolysis* is the use of an electric current to break down a substance into its component molecules. Electrolysis can be used to break down water (H_2O) into oxygen (O_2) and hydrogen (H_2).

Remembering that the number of atoms of each element must be the same on both sides of a reaction equation, decide which equation below correctly describes the electrolysis of water.

(1) $H_2O \rightarrow H_2 + O_2$
(2) $2H_2O \rightarrow 2H_2 + O_2$
(3) $3H_2O \rightarrow 3H_2 + 2O_2$
(4) $4H_2O \rightarrow 4H_2 + O_2$
(5) $5H_2O \rightarrow 4H_2 + 4O_2$

29. *Transpiration* is a process in which a plant loses water through tiny pores called stomata, located on the undersides of its leaves. Transpiration cools the plant and helps ensure a continual flow of mineral-rich water up the stem. Which of the following serves humans in a similar way?

(1) taste buds
(2) hair follicles
(3) sweat glands
(4) fingernails
(5) skin cells

POSTTEST

Question 30 is based on the following passage.

John Dalton (1766–1844), a British chemist, first developed the theory that matter is made up of atoms of differing weights. Dalton proposed that atoms combine in simple ratios by weight.

By studying gases, Dalton knew that an oxygen atom was sixteen times as heavy as a hydrogen atom. By breaking down water into oxygen and hydrogen gases and weighing the results, Dalton also knew that the resulting oxygen gas weighed eight times as much as the resulting hydrogen gas. From this information, Dalton correctly concluded that each water molecule is made up of two atoms of hydrogen and one atom of oxygen.

30. As a result of Dalton's work, what were scientists most likely able to begin doing for the first time?

    (1) determine the chemical makeup of simple substances
    (2) discover how water is able to put out fires
    (3) measure the pressure of gas as its temperature is raised
    (4) understand why oxygen is the gas used for respiration
    (5) understand the sunlight absorption properties of gases

Question 31 is based on the following diagram.

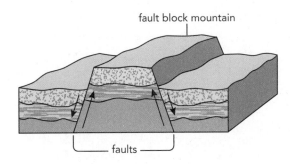

fault block mountain

faults

31. The Sierra Nevada in the western United States are fault-block mountains. Knowing this, what can you conclude about the fault lines that run beneath these mountains?

    (1) They are alternately spread apart and close together as they run deeper beneath Earth's surface.
    (2) They are close together as they run deeper beneath Earth's surface.
    (3) They stay the same distance apart as they run deeper beneath Earth's surface.
    (4) They spread apart as they run deeper beneath Earth's surface.
    (5) They cross each other beneath Earth's surface.

Questions 32 and 33 refer to the following graph and passage.

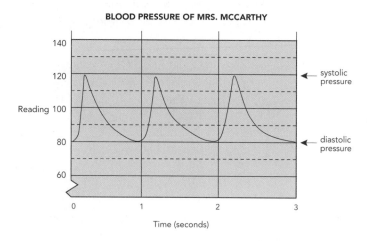

BLOOD PRESSURE OF MRS. MCCARTHY

The human heart is like a pump whose job is to force blood through arteries. One measure of how hard a heart is working is a blood pressure reading. A *blood pressure reading* such as 130/90 measures the pressure that blood exerts against the walls of a person's arteries during the heartbeat cycle.

The first number (130), the *systolic pressure*, is the point of highest blood pressure, measured as the heart beats. The second number (90), the *diastolic pressure*, is the point of lowest blood pressure, measured just before the heart beats. A rise in blood pressure can occur due to strenuous physical activity or to an illness or disease that causes the heart to work harder than normal.

The graph above records Ms. McCarthy's blood pressure for three complete heartbeat cycles.

32. What is Ms. McCarthy's blood pressure reading shown on the graph?

(1) 80/120
(2) 90/130
(3) 120/40
(4) 120/80
(5) 130/90

33. What was Ms. McCarthy's heartbeat rate (beats per minute) at the time this blood pressure reading was taken?

(1) forty-five beats per minute
(2) sixty beats per minute
(3) seventy-five beats per minute
(4) ninety beats per minute
(5) one hundred five beats per minute

---

34. Suppose the fossils of several types of extinct fish are found in the cliffs of an inland mountain. Which of the following are the two most reasonable hypotheses that might explain this discovery?

A. Prehistoric humans ate the fish and later moved to these cliffs, where they died.

B. The fish was a type of flying fish that flew to this mountain and died.

C. Birds carried the remains of the fish to these cliffs.

D. These cliffs were once under water.

(1) A and C
(2) A and D
(3) B and C
(4) B and D
(5) C and D

POSTTEST

Question 35 is based on the following passage.

Galileo (1564–1642) did much to increase human understanding of gravity and its effect on moving objects. Galileo discovered that objects falling toward Earth all fall at the same rate, regardless of their size or weight, as long as gravity is the only force acting on them.

Galileo incorrectly concluded, however, that planets, in their motion around the Sun, move in exact circles with no force acting on them—circles being the perfect shape according to religious beliefs of the time. He did not realize that the orbits of planets are actually ellipses (oval shapes) and that planetary orbits result from the force of gravity between the Sun and each planet.

35. Which of the following do scientists today know that sixteenth-century scientists such as Galileo did not know?

  (1) An ellipse is a more perfect shape than a circle.
  (2) The planets move around the Sun at the same rate.
  (3) Objects move in a curving path only when acted on by a force.
  (4) Falling objects on Earth tend to move straight toward the center of Earth.
  (5) The force of gravity is stronger between heavier objects than lighter ones.

36. A basketball is dropped from point A as shown in the drawing below. The ball hits the floor, rises to point C, and then drops again. The ball is momentarily motionless when its center is across from points A, B, and C.

At what point are kinetic (motion) energy and gravitational potential (stored) energy equal for the basketball?

  (1) point A
  (2) point B
  (3) point C
  (4) halfway between point A and point B
  (5) halfway between point A and point C

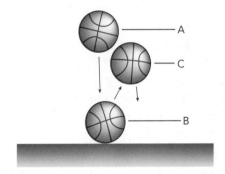

Question 37 is based on the following illustration.

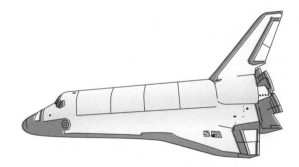

37. What is one of the destinations of the object pictured above?

  (1) New York City
  (2) bottom of the ocean
  (3) international space station
  (4) the Sun
  (5) inside a volcano

POSTTEST

Question 38 is based on the following passage.

Galen (129–c.199) is one of the most famous medical doctors in history. Galen's conclusions on how the human body worked were accepted as correct for 1,400 years, until the work of William Harvey during the Renaissance.

Galen made several important discoveries:

• Arteries carry blood, not air as had been believed up until that time.

• The brain controls the voice.

• Different muscles are controlled at different levels along the spinal cord.

Galen got one function completely wrong! Although he studied the heart, he believed that the liver was the central organ of the vascular (blood carrying) system. He also concluded that blood moves from the liver to the outer skin where it forms flesh. Galen did not realize that blood continually circulates through the body.

38. Which of the following would Galen likely believe could be a cause of skin burns being very slow to heal?

(1) liver disease
(2) heart disease
(3) spinal cord injury
(4) muscle disease
(5) bone disease

39. A heat pump is a process or a machine that transfers heat by mechanical means from a first object, which becomes cooled, to a second object, which becomes heated. Which of the following operates on the principle of a heat pump?

(1) a fan
(2) a refrigerator
(3) a stove
(4) a fireplace
(5) an automobile engine

Question 40 is based on the illustration below.

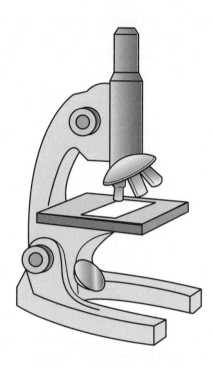

40. For what use is the device pictured above designed?

(1) weighing objects of very light weight
(2) splitting sunlight into a rainbow of colors
(3) testing the chemical makeup of a liquid
(4) measuring the distance between Earth and other planets
(5) seeing objects not visible to the naked eye

41. During photosynthesis, plants produce simple sugar in the chemical reaction represented below.

$$6CO_2 + 6H_2O \longrightarrow C_6H_{12}O_6 + 6O_2$$

What two compounds do plants use to produce sugar?

(1) water and carbon dioxide
(2) carbon dioxide and oxygen
(3) carbon dioxide and hydrogen
(4) water and oxygen
(5) carbon dioxide and sugar

POSTTEST

Question 42 is based on the following passage.

James Hutton (1726–1797) first proposed the theory of *uniformitarianism*. According to this theory, the natural processes that change Earth operate slowly over a long period of time. Hutton claimed that processes such as wind and water erosion have operated in a uniform way since the beginning of Earth's formation.

Hutton rejected the theory of *catastrophism*, which claimed that only major catastrophes such as severe earthquakes and volcanoes changed Earth's features. According to the theory of catastrophism, Earth is only a few thousand years old.

Uniformitarianism laid the groundwork for the modern study of Earth as a dynamic and continually evolving planet.

42. On what types of observations did Hutton base the theory of uniformitarianism?

   (1) Catastrophes such as volcanoes do not change Earth's features very much.
   (2) Small, everyday forces can act over time to change Earth's features.
   (3) Wind and water erosion change Earth's features in a very short period of time.
   (4) The features of many other planets are also changed by everyday forces.
   (5) Earth's surface is unchanging as far as it is possible to determine.

43. Humus is a dark-colored material that is made of the decaying remains of dead plants and animals. Which of the following is the only choice that would <u>not</u> be a good use of humus?

   (1) planting mixture
   (2) garden fertilizer
   (3) topsoil for a yard
   (4) walking path
   (5) food supply for home-grown worms

44. Which of the following would be <u>least</u> relevant in determining whether a newly discovered source of energy might have great practical value?

   (1) the amount of the energy-containing material that is available for use
   (2) whether the new source is a form of geothermal, chemical, nuclear, or solar energy
   (3) the cost of producing electricity or other types of power from the new source of energy
   (4) whether there are technical problems that must be solved before the energy can be used
   (5) whether use of the new source produces dangerous waste

45. Suppose a scientist wants to determine which personality traits are inherited and which are formed by a person's upbringing. Which of the following pairs could provide the best information for this study?

   (1) two adopted children who were raised separately in two families that live in the same city
   (2) an older sister and a younger brother who were raised in the same family
   (3) identical twins who were separated at birth and raised in different families
   (4) two unrelated children of the same age who were raised in different cultures
   (5) two unrelated adults who were raised in different cultures

POSTTEST

Questions 46 and 47 refer to the following circle graphs.

DAILY CALORIE CONSUMPTION

Current American Diet

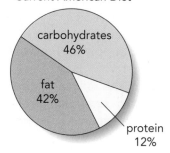

carbohydrates
46%

fat
42%

protein
12%

Recommended American Diet

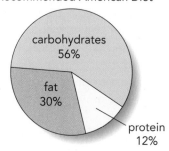

carbohydrates
56%

fat
30%

protein
12%

46. Which suggestion is the best summary of the recommended dietary changes shown on the graphs above?

(1) Eat less carbohydrates and more fat.
(2) Eat less protein and more carbohydrates.
(3) Eat less fat and more protein.
(4) Eat less fat and more carbohydrates.
(5) Eat less carbohydrates and more protein.

47. What assumption is most likely made by a person who decides to change his or her diet as recommended by the graphs above?

(1) These dietary changes are recommended only for overweight people.
(2) These dietary changes are recommended only for underweight people.
(3) The graphs result from a scientific study that relates eating habits to health.
(4) Food costs will not increase if these dietary changes are made.
(5) The dietary changes will result in the eating of fewer calories at each meal.

---

48. Which two of the following measurements would enable a scientist to compute the speed at which light travels through space?

A. measuring the distance between Earth and the Moon

B. measuring the time between sunrise and sunset

C. measuring the time it takes the Moon to revolve around Earth

D. measuring the time it takes for light to travel from Earth to the Moon and back

(1) A and C
(2) A and D
(3) B and C
(4) B and D
(5) C and D

POSTTEST

Questions 49 and 50 refer to the following passage.

Geologists believe that Earth's surface is made of many slowly moving rigid plates. Devastating earthquakes often occur along the boundary line where two plates meet. An example is the earthquake activity along the San Andreas fault, in California. Along this fault, or collision boundary, the slowly moving Pacific plate pushes against the continental plate and causes a buildup of pressure. Occasionally a sudden slippage occurs, and a tremendous amount of earthshaking energy is released. Such an earthquake destroyed the city of San Francisco in 1906.

The San Andreas fault can be drawn on a map as a line that runs throughout the length of California. This fault passes near San Francisco in the north and Los Angeles in the south, two major population regions on the West Coast. Slippage anywhere along the San Andreas fault can result in major earthquakes in nearby areas and smaller earthquakes throughout the entire state of California.

No one can predict for sure just where or when the next major earthquake will strike. Every point along the fault must be considered at equal risk. For this reason, many buildings in cities near the fault zone are specially designed to be earthquake-proof.

49. Which of the following is <u>not</u> a conclusion that can be drawn from the passage?

(1) In California some buildings are constructed with earthquake danger in mind.

(2) The San Francisco earthquake of 1906 resulted from slippage along the San Andreas fault.

(3) People living along the San Andreas fault are more likely to be injured in an earthquake than people living in other parts of California.

(4) Major earthquake danger is less in San Francisco than in Los Angeles because San Francisco has already had a major quake in this century.

(5) Because the islands of Japan also lie along a fault, Japan also faces the danger of earthquakes.

50. A geologist is trying to predict when an earthquake might occur in or near Redding, California. Which of the following would <u>not</u> be important to know?

(1) the pattern of yearly weather conditions in and around the city of Redding

(2) the history of earthquakes in and around the city of Redding

(3) the distance Redding lies from the San Andreas fault

(4) the types of land formations around Redding

(5) the history of earthquake activity in other areas of California that are geologically similar to the Redding area

Answers are on page 404.

Answer Key

1. (2) Ear shape is inherited. A difference in ear shape indicates a difference in genetic makeup. This fact tells you that Frank and Gary are fraternal, not identical, twins.

2. (4) Of the choices listed, only favorite color is something that identical twins have some control over. Height, shoe size, eye color, and gender are determined by genetics.

3. (3) Swinging a bat is work. A force is exerted and an object moves in response. None of the other choices involve actually moving an object.

4. (1) The light-colored moths disappeared because they were eaten by birds. The pollution is related to why they were eaten by birds but is not the reason the light moths decreased in number.

5. (5) Choice (5) is consistent with information given in the passage. None of the other choices can be inferred from the passage.

6. (1) Prior to impact, ball 1 has all kinetic energy and ball 2 is motionless. Immediately after impact, ball 2 has all kinetic energy, and ball 1 is motionless. Kinetic energy is transferred from ball 1 to ball 2 at the moment of impact. Each ball has potential energy when it is positioned away from the point of impact.

7. (5) According to the final paragraph in the passage, it is the lack of blood to the brain that causes brain cells to lose potassium and to gain calcium. So, choice (5) is correct. Choice (4) mentions the level of potassium in the blood, not in the brain cells.

8. (5) Only choice (5) is consistent with information given in the passage.

9. (2) Choices B and D are not correct. The Sun never passes between Earth and the Moon. And, during a solar eclipse, part of the sunlight is blocked from reaching Earth, thus decreasing Earth's sunlight, not increasing it.

10. (3) An aurora is a luminous display. The question does not ask what causes an aurora, only what it is.

11. (1) Because auroras are related to solar winds, it is reasonable to conclude that an increase in the number of solar storms would lead to an increase in auroras.

12. (4) Choice (4) says in words what the drawing shows: magma moving upward through a crack in the old ocean floor.

13. (5) Each of the choices, except choice (5) is a pair of animals that are closely related, even though they may not be the same species. Closely related animals are examples of adaptive radiation.

14. (2) A purebred results from inbreeding, the mating of nearly genetically identical animals. Thus, statements A and C must be true; B and D are incorrect.

15. (3) The passage states that hybrids are produced to create individuals with the desirable traits of each parent. None of the other answer choices is a correct restatement of information given in the passage.

16. (4) Each of the other choices is a result of breeding two organisms that are genetically very different. Choice (4) is an example of inbreeding, not hybridization.

17. (1) As the drawing indicates, clouds reflect much of the heat-producing light rays that strike them.

18. (3) A clear day allows the land surface to warm, while a cloudy night helps keep the warm land from radiating heat back into space.

19. (5) Choice (5) mentions a relationship between voltage and electric current; magnetism is not directly related to this particular result. Each other choice describes an interaction between magnetism and electric current.

20. (5) Choices (1) and (4) do not explain the similarity between the separate continents. Choices (2) and (3) are not reasonable. Only choice (5) is a reasonable hypothesis that explains the similarity of two separate landmasses.

21. (1) Water is heaviest because it is most dense. Water molecules are packed more closely together than either ice or water-vapor molecules are. Water vapor is the lightest phase of water.

22. (4) Ice floats because a given volume of ice weighs less than the same volume of water. Ice is not as dense as water.

23. (2) This has happened to just about everyone. Most drinks are mainly water, and water expands as it freezes, easily breaking a glass container that holds it.

24. (5) There is no evidence that the HIV virus can be transmitted from person to person while swimming.

25. (3) A healthy immune system does protect against some, but not all, infectious diseases. An example of a common infectious disease that the immune system does not prevent is the common cold.

26. (2) The drawing indicates that most of the ultraviolet radiation does not pass through the ozone layer, but visible light does. Choice (2) says in words what the drawing shows.

27. (4) Choice (4) is a logical conclusion. A thinner ozone layer would allow more ultraviolet radiation to pass through. There is evidence that this is happening today. Worldwide concern is now being expressed about protecting the ozone layer.

28. (2) Choice (2), the correct reaction equation, shows 4 atoms of hydrogen and 2 atoms of oxygen on each side of the arrow.

29. (3) Sweat glands produce droplets of water on human skin, allowing cooling as the water (sweat) evaporates.

30. (1) Dalton's work enabled chemists to determine the ratio of elements (the number of atoms of one element compared to the number of atoms of other elements) in simple substances.

31. (4) As the drawing shows, fault lines along the edges of a fault-block mountain spread apart as they run deeper beneath Earth's surface.

32. (4) As shown on the graph, the first number (systolic pressure) is 120, while the second number (diastolic pressure) is 80.

33. (2) Because three complete beats occur in three seconds, you can conclude that Ms. McCarthy's heart rate is one beat per second, or sixty beats per minute (60 seconds = 1 minute).

34. (5) Choices C and D are possible. Neither choice A nor B seems likely. Any edible parts of a fish would be digested and lose their identities. Fish being able to fly to mountain cliffs seems unlikely.

35. (3) Had Galileo known this fact, he would have realized that planets move in curving paths precisely because of the force of gravity.

36. (4) At points A, B, and C, the ball is motionless and has no kinetic energy. Only when the ball is halfway between point A and point B is half of its energy kinetic and half potential.

37. (3) The space shuttle is used to carry astronauts and supplies into orbit around Earth, where the international space station is located.

38. (1) Galen believed that the liver controlled the movement of blood to the skin, and that new skin came from blood.

39. (2) A refrigerator is a heat pump, transferring heat from food (which is then cooled) to the air (which becomes warmed) outside the refrigerator. Of the other choices, only a fan is used for cooling, but it does not work by directly transferring heat.

40. (5) A microscope is used to see objects not clearly visible to the unaided human eye.

41. (1) Sugar is produced by combining carbon dioxide (CO_2) and water (H_2O).

42. (2) Hutton realized that wind and water erosion, though operating slowly, could change land features substantially over a long period of time.

43. (4) Humus, being moist and slippery, would not be a good material for a walking path.

44. (2) The form of the energy source is not as important as the other considerations listed in choices (1), (3), (4), and (5).

45. (3) Identical twins can provide the best possible direct information about inherited traits and indirect information about learned traits.

46. (4) Choice (4) says in words what the graph recommends.

47. (3) The person assumes, though the graphs do not specify, that these graphs are based on scientific studies of healthful diets.

48. (2) The speed of light can be determined by dividing the distance between Earth and the Moon by the time it takes light to travel this distance. The speed of light is 186,000 miles per second, and it takes light about 1.3 seconds to travel from the Moon to Earth.

49. (4) According to the passage, it is impossible to predict exactly where the next major quake will strike. San Francisco and Los Angeles are at equal risk.

50. (1) Weather conditions are not relevant in determining earthquake danger. Land formations, occurrence of previous quakes, and the distance from major fault lines all provide information relevant to the chance of other quakes occurring.

Evaluation Chart

On the following chart, circle the number of any item you answered incorrectly. Pay particular attention to areas where you missed half or more of the questions. For those questions that you missed, review the skill pages indicated.

Subject Area / Theme	Life Science (45%) (pages 157–254)	Physical Science (35%) (pages 255–336)	Earth and Space Science (20%) (pages 337–385)
Fundamental Understandings	13 questions 1, 2, 4, 5, 7, 14, 15, 16, 32, 33, 43, 46, 47	9 questions 6, 10, 11, 19, 21, 22, 28, 36, 41	6 questions 12, 17, 18, 20, 31, 34
Unifying Concepts and Processes (pages 27–48)	2 questions 13, 29	1 question 3	0 questions
Science as Inquiry (pages 49–94)	2 questions 8, 45	1 question 48	1 question 9
Science and Technology (pages 95–114)	1 question 40	1 question 39	1 question 37
Science in Personal and Social Perspectives (pages 115–138)	4 questions 24, 25, 26, 27	2 questions 23, 44	2 questions 49, 50
History and Nature of Science (pages 139–155)	1 question 38	2 questions 30, 35	1 question 42

This practice test will give you a second opportunity to evaluate your readiness for the GED Science Test.

Directions: Choose the one best answer to each question. The questions are based on reading passages, charts, graphs, maps, and cartoons. Answer each question as carefully as possible. If a question seems to be too difficult, do not spend too much time on it. Work ahead and come back to it later when you can think it through carefully. You should take approximately 80 minutes to complete the test.

Practice Test Answer Grid

1 ① ② ③ ④ ⑤	18 ① ② ③ ④ ⑤	35 ① ② ③ ④ ⑤
2 ① ② ③ ④ ⑤	19 ① ② ③ ④ ⑤	36 ① ② ③ ④ ⑤
3 ① ② ③ ④ ⑤	20 ① ② ③ ④ ⑤	37 ① ② ③ ④ ⑤
4 ① ② ③ ④ ⑤	21 ① ② ③ ④ ⑤	38 ① ② ③ ④ ⑤
5 ① ② ③ ④ ⑤	22 ① ② ③ ④ ⑤	39 ① ② ③ ④ ⑤
6 ① ② ③ ④ ⑤	23 ① ② ③ ④ ⑤	40 ① ② ③ ④ ⑤
7 ① ② ③ ④ ⑤	24 ① ② ③ ④ ⑤	41 ① ② ③ ④ ⑤
8 ① ② ③ ④ ⑤	25 ① ② ③ ④ ⑤	42 ① ② ③ ④ ⑤
9 ① ② ③ ④ ⑤	26 ① ② ③ ④ ⑤	43 ① ② ③ ④ ⑤
10 ① ② ③ ④ ⑤	27 ① ② ③ ④ ⑤	44 ① ② ③ ④ ⑤
11 ① ② ③ ④ ⑤	28 ① ② ③ ④ ⑤	45 ① ② ③ ④ ⑤
12 ① ② ③ ④ ⑤	29 ① ② ③ ④ ⑤	46 ① ② ③ ④ ⑤
13 ① ② ③ ④ ⑤	30 ① ② ③ ④ ⑤	47 ① ② ③ ④ ⑤
14 ① ② ③ ④ ⑤	31 ① ② ③ ④ ⑤	48 ① ② ③ ④ ⑤
15 ① ② ③ ④ ⑤	32 ① ② ③ ④ ⑤	49 ① ② ③ ④ ⑤
16 ① ② ③ ④ ⑤	33 ① ② ③ ④ ⑤	50 ① ② ③ ④ ⑤
17 ① ② ③ ④ ⑤	34 ① ② ③ ④ ⑤	

PRACTICE TEST

Questions 1 and 2 refer to the illustration below.

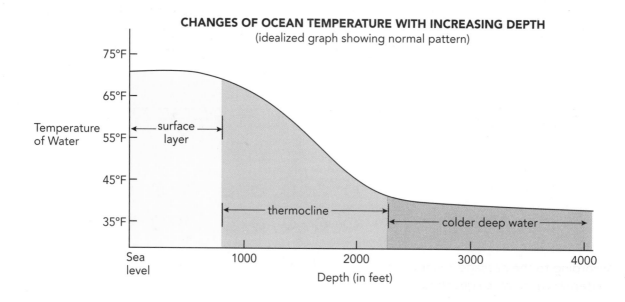

CHANGES OF OCEAN TEMPERATURE WITH INCREASING DEPTH
(idealized graph showing normal pattern)

1. Which phrase is the best definition of a thermocline?

   (1) temperature distribution in the ocean
   (2) layer of warm water close to the surface
   (3) layer of cold water beneath the warm surface
   (4) transition region between the warm surface and the much colder deep water
   (5) region of nearly constant temperature just beneath the warm surface

2. Which of the following would be the <u>most</u> likely to upset the ocean's normal temperature distribution?

   (1) an earthquake near the ocean shore
   (2) an erupting volcano on the ocean bottom
   (3) a violent rainstorm on the ocean surface
   (4) a hot sunny day when there is no wind
   (5) a hurricane passing over the ocean surface

3. Any object that moves through air feels the effect of air resistance, a force that pushes against the object and slows it down. Which of the following objects is the only one listed that is <u>not</u> specifically designed to take advantage of air resistance?

   (1) a parachute
   (2) a kite
   (3) an electric fan
   (4) a golf club
   (5) a Frisbee

PRACTICE TEST

Questions 4 and 5 refer to the passage below.

Did you ever wonder why the sky appears so blue on a clear day? What happens to the other colors of the rainbow that are also present in sunlight? The answer has to do with the scattering of sunlight by the atmosphere.

When you look at the daytime sky, you see only the light that travels to your eyes from the direction of your gaze. This light is blue, because more blue light than any other color of light is scattered by atoms of nitrogen and oxygen, the main gases found in Earth's atmosphere. Other colors of light are less apt to be scattered, and they continue their straight-line movement through the atmosphere and away from your eyes.

4. According to the passage, what does scattering cause blue light to do?

   (1) change color
   (2) return to space instead of striking Earth
   (3) change direction of movement
   (4) lose energy
   (5) become invisible

5. What information would scientists first need to know before they could determine the color of the daytime Martian sky as it is seen from the surface of Mars?

   (1) the types of gases that make up the Martian atmosphere
   (2) the amount of sunlight that strikes the Martian atmosphere
   (3) the color of the Martian surface
   (4) the average temperature on the Martian surface
   (5) the types of rocks and soil that make up the Martian surface

Question 6 refers to the drawings below.

The picture below shows the *lytic cycle*, the attack by a virus on a living cell.

THE LYTIC CYCLE

Step 1. A virus attacks a host cell and injects the virus's genes into the cell.

Step 2. The virus's genes turn the host cell into a virus factory.

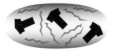

Step 3. The new viruses leave the host cell. The new viruses look for new host cells.

6. Which of the following facts <u>cannot</u> be inferred from the drawings?

   (1) A virus can use a host cell to produce many more viruses.
   (2) A host cell is often destroyed by the action of a virus.
   (3) A virus does not reproduce in the ways a cell reproduces.
   (4) A virus contains genetic material.
   (5) A virus can stay inactive for years.

Questions 7 and 8 refer to the following illustration.

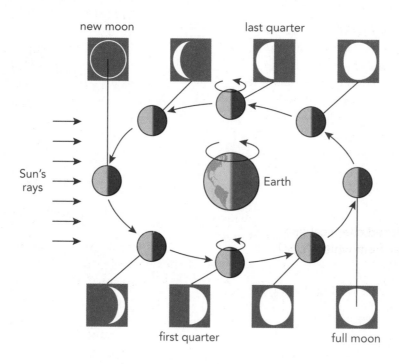

7. When a full moon occurs, which of the following is true?

(1) The Moon is between the Sun and Earth.
(2) The Moon is not visible from Earth.
(3) The Sun is between Earth and the Moon.
(4) The Moon and Earth are the same distance from the Sun.
(5) Earth is between the Sun and the Moon.

8. What can you conclude by observing the different shapes in which the Moon appears to us on Earth?

(1) Moonlight is light produced by the Moon.
(2) Moonlight is light from Earth that reflects off the Moon's surface.
(3) Moonlight is sunlight that reflects off the Moon's surface.
(4) The direction of the Moon's rotation (spinning motion) is opposite to that of the Earth.
(5) During a full moon, the entire surface of Earth is lit by sunlight.

PRACTICE TEST

Questions 9 and 10 refer to the following passage.

Potential energy is stored energy—energy available to be used. There are four common forms of potential energy: gravitational, chemical, nuclear, and elastic.

When a rock is positioned on top of a mountain, the rock has gravitational potential energy. If the rock is knocked loose, it rolls down the mountain due to the pull of the force of gravity. As the rock rolls and gains speed, its gravitational potential energy is changed to kinetic energy—energy of motion.

Chemical potential energy is stored chemical energy such as that found in a flashlight battery. When a flashlight is turned on, the battery's stored energy is changed into light energy. Another example of stored chemical energy is glucose, the food sugar from which your body cells get their energy. During exercise, your muscles change the chemical potential energy stored in this sugar into body heat and into the kinetic energy of body movement. A third example is the energy stored in coal. Coal's chemical potential energy is changed to heat when it is burned.

The energy stored in the nucleus of atoms is called nuclear potential energy. At a nuclear power plant, this energy is released and changed to heat. The heat is used to boil water and create the high-pressure steam needed to turn the electricity-producing turbines.

Elastic potential energy is energy that is stored in a stretched or compressed object such as a spring. A spring in a windup watch is an example. As the spring slowly unwinds, its elastic potential energy is changed to the kinetic energy of the watch's moving parts.

9. Which of the following is the best restatement of information given in the passage?

(1) Potential energy and kinetic energy are both forms of stored energy.
(2) Potential energy and kinetic energy are both forms of energy of motion.
(3) Potential energy is energy of motion, while kinetic energy is stored energy.
(4) Potential energy is stored energy, while kinetic energy is energy of motion.
(5) Potential energy always changes into kinetic energy.

10. Of the following, which is the only object that is <u>not</u> designed to make practical use of stored chemical energy?

(1) a bathtub drain
(2) a fireplace
(3) a flashlight
(4) a gas furnace
(5) an automobile engine

Question 11 refers to the passage and graphs below.

The bar graphs below show the relative amounts of pigment color in deciduous (leaf-dropping) trees during summer and fall seasons.

PIGMENT COLOR IN DECIDUOUS TREES

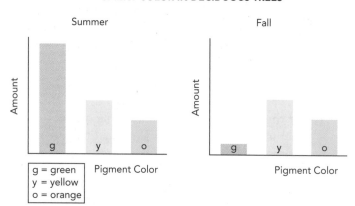

g = green
y = yellow
o = orange

11. For what reason do the leaves of deciduous trees appear orange and yellow each fall season?

(1) Green pigment changes color, to orange and yellow.
(2) Green pigment disappears, leaving orange and yellow.
(3) New leaves are starting to grow.
(4) Orange and yellow pigments increase in the fall.
(5) The leaves are dying and are about to drop to the ground.

12. Ancient alchemists used a process called calcination to convert limestone ($CaCO_3$) into lime (CaO). The same process, which is simply the controlled heating of limestone, is still used today in the cement industry. By comparing the chemical formulas of limestone and lime, determine the gas that is given off during calcination.

(1) O_2
(2) CO
(3) CO_2
(4) C_2O
(5) C_2

13. A new roller coaster in an amusement park travels in a loop as shown in the illustration below.

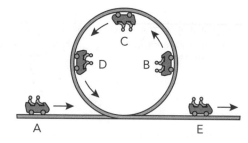

In which of the five indicated positions is the potential energy (stored energy) of the passenger car the greatest?

(1) A
(2) B
(3) C
(4) D
(5) E

14. Large plants have a vascular system, a system of tubes through which plants transport water, minerals, and food to all parts of the plant: from the roots, through the stems, and throughout the leaves. Which of the following human systems is functionally most like a plant's vascular system?

(1) respiratory system
(2) reproductive system
(3) digestive system
(4) circulatory system
(5) nervous system

PRACTICE TEST

Question 15 refers to the following graphs.

Each graph below shows the air temperature taken at various heights in a room.

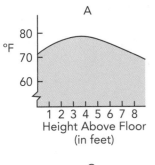

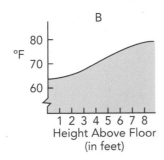

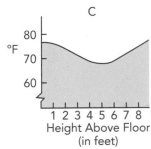

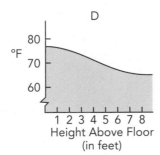

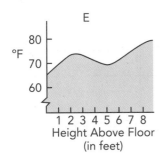

15. Remembering that warm air tends to rise above cold air, which graph most likely represents the temperature readings taken in a room in which the doors and windows are closed?

(1) A
(2) B
(3) C
(4) D
(5) E

Question 16 is based on the passage below.

Before the 1900s, Western thinkers, unlike Greek thinkers before them, came to believe that Earth had a beginning. They believed that Earth has an age that can be measured.

One way to measure Earth's age was proposed by James Ussher—an Anglican archbishop of the 1600s. Ussher counted generations in the Christian Bible. He concluded that Earth was created in 4004 B.C., making Earth about 6,000 years old.

Another method was tried in the 1700s by Georges Leclerc, a French scientist. By measuring the cooling rate of an ironball, Leclerc calculated that Earth must be about 75,000 years old.

Modern dating methods of the twentieth century, based on radioactivity, show that the true age of Earth is several billion years.

16. What do early theories about the age of Earth tell us about the use of evidence in a search for scientific facts?

(1) Religious teaching is always the best scientific evidence to use.
(2) Scientists tend to rely on any evidence, no matter how questionable.
(3) Evidence seldom leads scientists to scientific facts.
(4) Scientists often reject the best sources of available evidence.
(5) Scientists try to rely on the best evidence they have at the time.

PRACTICE TEST

Questions 17–19 refer to the diagram and chart below.

WATER POLLUTION AND YOUR HEALTH

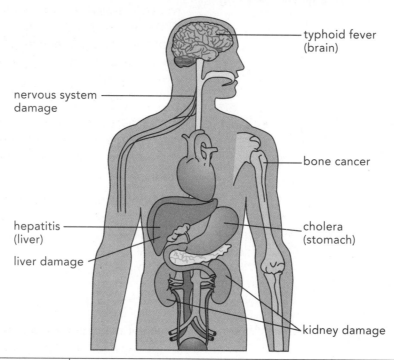

Bacteria (from human waste)	Chemicals (from factories and agriculture)	Radioactive Compounds (found in some soils and wastes created by humans)
• typhoid fever • cholera • hepatitis	• nervous system damage • liver damage • kidney damage	• bone cancer • other cancers

17. What water pollutants are most likely to affect people in underdeveloped countries?

(1) car exhaust
(2) acid rain
(3) radioactive compounds
(4) chemicals
(5) bacteria

18. What water pollutants are most likely to lead to kidney damage?

(1) chemicals
(2) tobacco products
(3) bacteria
(4) human waste
(5) radioactive waste

19. What is the best summary of the information provided by the diagram and chart?

(1) Water pollutants are generally less harmful than air pollutants.
(2) Boiling drinking water can clear the water of all pollutants.
(3) Water pollutants can affect most major systems of the body.
(4) Radioactive compounds are found in most countries of the world.
(5) Factories produce more chemical waste than do agricultural products.

PRACTICE TEST

Questions 20 and 21 refer to the following illustration and passage.

Glaciers

Earth passes through periods called *ice ages*, when much of its surface is covered with *glaciers*—huge sheets of ice. During an ice age the temperature on Earth drops about 42.8°F (6°C) lower than the temperature today. Land formations are changed, and species of animals and plants die out.

20. Which of the following is a hypothesis that attempts to explain why an ice age begins?

(1) The next ice age may begin within the next million years.
(2) Variations in the energy output from the Sun may lower Earth's temperature.
(3) An ice age may have been responsible for the extinction of dinosaurs.
(4) An ice age is a time during which much of Earth's surface is covered with ice.
(5) During the last ice age, the average temperature of Earth was about 42.8°F (6°C) lower than it is today.

21. The total amount of water (both liquid water and ice) on Earth has changed very little since Earth formed. Which of the following conclusions can be drawn from this fact?

(1) During an ice age, ocean levels are lower.
(2) During an ice age, ocean levels are higher.
(3) During an ice age, there is mainly snow and very little rain.
(4) During an ice age, there is mainly rain and very little snow.
(5) During an ice age, the oceans freeze.

Question 22 is based on the following passage.

Accurate timepieces were first invented in the seventeenth century. Before this, the motion of the Sun across the sky was used as a basis for measuring time. At any locality, noon occurs when the Sun is at the highest point in the sky. The time between noon on one day and the next was by custom divided into 24 hours.

With the invention of accurate timepieces, time could be kept mechanically and measuring the position of the Sun in the sky became unnecessary.

22. Before the seventeenth century, what limits were there on the accurate measurement of time?

A. Time could not be measured when clouds hid the Sun.

B. Time could not be measured at the equator.

C. Time could not be measured before sunrise or after sunset.

(1) A only
(2) B only
(3) C only
(4) A and B
(5) A and C

23. While on the surface of the Moon, astronauts noticed that they could jump much higher than back home on Earth. What can you conclude from this discovery?

(1) The Moon is at a very great distance from Earth.
(2) Earth's gravity is not felt very strongly on the Moon.
(3) The gravitational force of Earth is less than the gravitational force of the Moon.
(4) The gravitational force of Earth is greater than the gravitational force of the Moon.
(5) The Moon has no atmosphere.

Questions 24–26 refer to the following passage.

An ecosystem is a community of plants, animals, and nonliving things. Ecosystems may be found in forests, grasslands, deserts, mountains, and bodies of water. Each type of ecosystem depends on three cycles that make community life possible.

In the *carbon dioxide–oxygen cycle*, plants take carbon dioxide gas from the atmosphere and use it for photosynthesis, the production of food sugar. As plants use carbon dioxide gas, they give off oxygen gas. Animals, on the other hand, breathe in oxygen and give off carbon dioxide as a waste product. The cycle is completed when plants and animals die and carbon dioxide gas forms from their decomposing bodies.

In the *water cycle*, both plants and animals take in water for life activities. To complete the cycle, plant leaves give off water vapor in a process called transpiration. While transpiring, a plant uses evaporating water to help eliminate waste products formed from plant activity. Animals give water back to the atmosphere when they exhale and when they perspire (sweat).

In the *nitrogen cycle*, plants get the nitrogen that they need for plant tissue growth from nitrates (nitrogen compounds) in the soil. Nitrates are produced in the soil by a two-step process. First, nitrogen-fixing bacteria break down the proteins of decaying plant and animal remains and produce ammonia. Then, nitrifying bacteria change this ammonia to nitrates. The nitrates are used to produce healthy plants that then become food for animals. With the death and decomposition of plants and animals, the nitrogen cycle is completed.

24. Which animal is well known for being adapted to an ecosystem in which the water cycle may be very unpredictable?

    (1) penguin
    (2) swordfish
    (3) frog
    (4) camel
    (5) duck

25. According to the passage, what process produces carbon dioxide gas and returns it to the atmosphere?

    (1) the breathing of animals
    (2) photosynthesis in plants
    (3) the perspiring of animals
    (4) transpiration in plants
    (5) the evaporation of water

26. In soil that is overwatered and does not drain well, a second type of bacteria, called denitrifying bacteria, thrives. This bacteria breaks down ammonia before it is converted to nitrates. What can you conclude may be a result of overwatering a house plant?

    (1) a decreased rate of plant growth
    (2) the death of denitrifying bacteria
    (3) the birth of many small insects
    (4) plant roots not getting carbon dioxide
    (5) an increased rate of plant growth

PRACTICE TEST

Questions 27 and 28 refer to the passage and diagrams below.

A lever is a simple tool that is used to help a person do some types of work. As shown in the diagrams below, a lever is a rigid bar that is free to rotate about a fixed point called the fulcrum. The fulcrum is the only part of the lever that doesn't move. The object to be moved is called the load. The position on the lever where the person applies force (pushes or lifts) is called the effort.

Depending on the relative positions of the fulcrum, load, and effort, each lever is placed in one of three classes. The first two classes of levers are shown below.

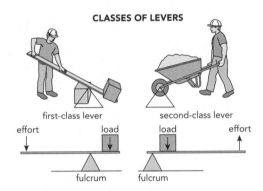

27. A bottle opener is a familiar lever used to pry the cap off a bottle. Referring to the definitions in the passage and to the diagrams, how is the bottle opener pictured below classified?

   (1) first-class lever, with fulcrum at point A
   (2) second-class lever, with fulcrum at point A
   (3) second-class lever, with fulcrum at point C
   (4) first-class lever, with fulcrum at point B
   (5) second-class lever, with fulcrum at point B

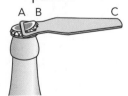

28. A double lever is a tool made by combining two levers of the same class. For example, the pair of pliers shown below is a double lever. Notice that in a double lever, the object on which work is performed is considered the load. In the pliers, for example, the gripped nut is the load in the nutcracker.

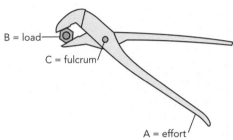

The nutcracker below is also a double lever. Which of the following correctly identifies the effort, fulcrum, and load?

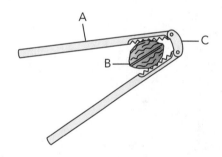

   (1) A = effort, B = fulcrum, C = load
   (2) A = fulcrum, B = effort, C = load
   (3) A = load, B = fulcrum, C = effort
   (4) A = fulcrum, B = load, C = effort
   (5) A = effort, B = load, C = fulcrum

Question 29 refers to the graph below.

The graph below shows the cycles of the female hormone *estrogen* and the male hormone *testosterone* in humans.

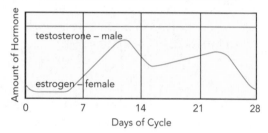

FEMALE AND MALE HORMONAL CYCLES

29. Which of the following statements is the best summary of information presented by the graph?

(1) Both estrogen and testosterone levels vary considerably over a 28-day cycle.
(2) Estrogen levels vary over a 28-day cycle while testosterone does not.
(3) Testosterone varies over a 28-day cycle while estrogen does not.
(4) Neither estrogen nor testosterone vary over a 28-day cycle.
(5) Estrogen and testosterone levels both increase over a 28-day cycle.

30. What is the most likely reason that humans and chimpanzees have many similar body features?

(1) All primates, including humans and chimpanzees, have similar needs.
(2) Humans have not evolved from their original form.
(3) Chimpanzees evolved from humans.
(4) Neither humans nor chimpanzees evolved from their original forms.
(5) Humans and chimpanzees evolved from a common ancestor.

Question 31 refers to the passage and graph below.

The line graph shows how the amount of *antibodies* (pathogen-fighting cells) in a person's blood varies between the first exposure to a pathogen and a later, second exposure.

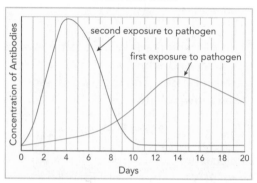

IMMUNE RESPONSE

31. What can you conclude to be true about the human immune system—the system that produces antibodies?

(1) The immune system may not destroy all of a pathogen during the first infection.
(2) The immune system reacts differently to different pathogens.
(3) The immune system remembers an invading pathogen.
(4) The immune system itself can come under attack.
(5) Second exposures to a pathogen are always more dangerous than first exposures.

PRACTICE TEST

Question 32 is based on the following illustration.

32. For what purpose is the pulley being used?

    (1) to change the direction of force applied
    (2) to increase the force applied
    (3) to decrease the force applied
    (4) to decrease the weight of the engine
    (5) to increase the weight of the engine

Question 33 is based on the following photograph.

33. What does the photograph above show is possible?

    (1) sending unmanned spacecraft to Mars
    (2) measuring the distance between Earth and the Moon
    (3) making a pressurized space suit
    (4) working underwater for long periods of time
    (5) sending humans to other heavenly bodies

Question 34 is based on the following passage.

    August Weismann (1834–1914), a German biologist, first proposed the germ-plasm theory of heredity. According to this theory, the only way a parent can pass on characteristics to its offspring is by the transfer of germ cells (eggs and sperm) prior to birth. He called the transferred material germ-plasm. Germ-plasm was thought to be a type of hereditary substance.

    Weismann was the first scientist to reject the accepted belief that parent organisms can pass on many acquired characteristics to their offspring. An acquired characteristic is one that a parent acquires during its own lifetime by its own effort, such as skill at the piano.

34. Which of the following is a characteristic that Weismann would claim cannot be inherited?

    (1) favorite food
    (2) overall body shape
    (3) natural hair color
    (4) shape of ears
    (5) finger length

PRACTICE TEST

Questions 35–38 refer to the following chart and passage.

OBSERVATIONS AT THE END OF EACH WEEK

	First Week	*Second Week*	*Third Week*
Open Toast	No mold is observed.	Several spots of mold are observed.	Mold covers most of the toast.
Enclosed Toast	No mold is observed.	No mold is observed.	Two spots of mold are observed on the toast.

Bread mold is the common fungus that is often seen growing on bread and other foods made from wheat. To study the factors that influence the growth of this tiny plant, Kristen, a nutritionist, performed an experiment.

In her experiment, Kristen wanted to find out if bread-mold spores (seeds) are airborne (present in and carried by air). To investigate this question, Kristen toasted a piece of bread until it was crisp. Then, she quickly placed it in a jar. She immediately sealed the jar with a tightly fitting lid. She then placed another piece of crisply toasted bread in a second jar. She did not place a lid on this second jar. She placed the two jars side by side on a table and observed them for three weeks. The results of her experiment are recorded in the chart.

35. In her experiment, why did Kristen toast the bread?

   (1) Toasting attracts bread-mold spores.
   (2) Toasting keeps bread from spoiling.
   (3) Toasting provides nutrients for bread-mold spores.
   (4) Toasting destroys bread-mold spores that may already be on the bread.
   (5) Toasting gives the bread a pleasant smell.

36. Which of the following is the best summary of the information presented in the chart?

   (1) Bread mold forms on bread whether or not the bread is toasted.
   (2) Bread mold forms on toast only when the toast is enclosed.
   (3) The rate of bread-mold growth on toast depends on exposure to fresh air, moisture, and temperature.
   (4) The rate of bread-mold growth on toast depends on the length of time the toast is exposed to fresh air.
   (5) Bread mold forms on toast less quickly than it forms on bread that is not toasted.

37. Which of the following is a hypothesis that is <u>not</u> supported by evidence presented in the chart?

   (1) Even a temporary exposure to air can result in bread becoming contaminated with airborne bread-mold spores.
   (2) Bread-mold spores grow better on bread that is not toasted because heat destroys certain nutrients.
   (3) More bread-mold spores grow on open toast than on enclosed toast because open toast has more exposure to bread-mold spores in the air.
   (4) Bread-mold spores can be made inactive and possibly destroyed by the high temperatures resulting from toasting.
   (5) By increasing the number of bread-mold spores on a piece of toast, you increase the amount of mold that actually grows.

PRACTICE TEST

38. Assuming that bread-mold spores are present in air, which of the following experiments would provide the best evidence concerning the effect of moisture on bread-mold growth?

    (1) Place two pieces of fresh bread in a single dry jar and leave the jar open for two hours. Then seal the jar.
    (2) Place one piece of fresh bread in each of two dry jars. Seal one jar and leave the second jar open.
    (3) Place one piece of fresh bread in each of two dry jars. Add ten drops of water to each jar, and seal both jars.
    (4) Place one piece of fresh bread in a dry jar, and a second piece in a jar to which ten drops of water have been added. Seal both jars.
    (5) Place one piece of fresh bread in each of two dry jars. Add ten drops of water to each jar and leave each jar open.

Question 39 is based on the illustrations below.

Light is given off *(emission)* and captured *(absorption)* by an atom in packets of energy called *photons* (⌇⌇→).

PHOTON EMISSION   PHOTON ABSORPTION

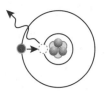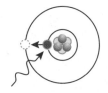

● electron
⚬ position to which electron moves

39. According to the illustrations, what process is involved in the atomic emission of a photon?

    (1) an electron moving from a higher energy level to a lower energy level
    (2) an electron moving from a lower energy level to a higher energy level
    (3) a photon moving from a higher energy level to a lower energy level
    (4) a photon moving from a lower energy level to a higher energy level
    (5) an electron changing into a photon

40. Hardening of the arteries (arteriosclerosis) is most prevalent among elderly patients. Arteries become less flexible and less able to carry blood, causing the heart to work harder during each beat. Which of the following most likely happens to a person's blood pressure when hardening of the arteries occurs?

    (1) Blood pressure increases.
    (2) Blood pressure decreases.
    (3) Blood pressure remains the same.
    (4) Blood pressure increases at first and then decreases weeks later.
    (5) Blood pressure decreases at first and then increases weeks later.

PRACTICE TEST

Questions 41 and 42 refer to the passage and graphs below.

In the only study of its kind on the causes and effects of lead pollution in the United States, the Environmental Protection Agency compiled the data shown in the graphs.

GRAPH A: LEAD USED IN GASOLINE

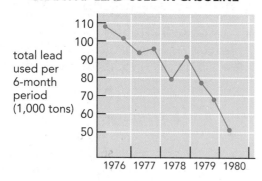

GRAPH B: AVERAGE BLOOD LEAD LEVEL IN AMERICAN ADULTS

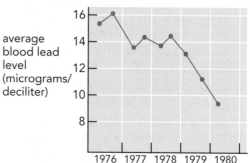

41. Which of the following is a conclusion that is supported directly by information in either of the graphs above?

   (1) Lead is a dangerous pollutant present in exhaust gases of cars that burn leaded (regular) gasoline.

   (2) By 1980, Americans were using less than half the yearly amount of gasoline that they had used in 1976.

   (3) Government regulations were responsible for the decrease in the amount of lead used in gasoline after 1976.

   (4) By 1980 the amount of lead pollution in the environment had been reduced to less than half of its 1976 value.

   (5) By 1980 the amount of lead used in gasoline had decreased to less than half its 1976 value.

42. Which of the following facts is needed in order to establish a cause-and-effect relationship between the two graphs?

   A. Americans bought more unleaded gasoline in 1976 than in 1980.

   B. When leaded gasoline burns, particles of lead enter the atmosphere.

   C. Lead can enter the human bloodstream when a person breathes in air.

   (1) A only
   (2) B only
   (3) A and C only
   (4) B and C only
   (5) A, B, and C

PRACTICE TEST

Questions 43–45 refer to the following passage.

One of the most controversial medical advances of the late-twentieth century is the method of pregnancy known as surrogate motherhood. A surrogate mother is a woman who, on behalf of a couple (or a single person), carries a fetus throughout pregnancy and birth. Then, immediately after delivery, the surrogate gives the child to the waiting couple.

A woman may become a surrogate mother by one of two methods. In the first method, she is artificially inseminated. A doctor uses a tube to place the man's sperm (sex cells) inside her uterus. She becomes pregnant when one of her own eggs becomes fertilized. In this type of pregnancy, the surrogate is actually the biological mother of the fetus she is carrying.

In the second method, a doctor implants a fertilized egg inside the surrogate mother's uterus. In this case the surrogate is not the biological mother of the fetus. The couple for whom she is carrying the fetus are the biological parents. The surrogate's only role is to provide the uterus in which the fetus grows until childbirth. For both methods, the surrogate is known as the birth mother because she actually carries and gives birth to the baby.

Most often, a surrogate mother is sought by a couple who are unable to have a child of their own. They choose this method of pregnancy because they desire that at least one or both of them be the biological parent, even though a second woman carries the fetus. A surrogate mother may be hired, or she may be a friend or relative who volunteers her services.

Surrogate motherhood is controversial because it raises issues concerning both law and human values. There are legal concerns about the rights of the couple, the rights of the surrogate mother, and the rights of the fetus. These rights are hard to determine, especially in a situation in which either the couple or the surrogate wants to change any part of the agreement concerning the child.

43. Which of the following is <u>not</u> a restatement of information presented in the passage?

(1) A surrogate mother may be paid.
(2) A surrogate mother is unable to have children of her own.
(3) A surrogate mother may be the biological mother of the fetus she carries.
(4) A surrogate mother may be made pregnant by artificial insemination.
(5) A surrogate mother may or may not be the biological mother of the fetus she carries.

44. When a couple hires a woman to be a surrogate mother, risks are taken by everyone. Choose the situation below that poses the <u>least</u> risk to the surrogate mother.

(1) The surrogate mother gives birth to a child with a birth defect, and the couple who hired her bring a lawsuit against her.
(2) The couple change their minds after the pregnancy is under way and decide that they don't want a baby.
(3) The couple refuse to pay the surrogate mother.
(4) The surrogate mother becomes emotionally attached to the baby and does not want to give up the baby.
(5) The child, born from a surrogate mother, may someday have difficulty adjusting to the facts surrounding his or her birth.

45. Which of the following is most likely the belief of a couple who chooses to seek a surrogate-mother arrangement?

(1) Surrogate motherhood is against the laws of nature.
(2) Surrogate motherhood is very risky.
(3) Surrogate motherhood is a reasonable option for people who cannot have children.
(4) Surrogate motherhood is unfair to the child.
(5) Surrogate motherhood is not fair to either mother.

PRACTICE TEST

Question 46 is based on the illustration below.

Question 47 is based on the drawing below.

CHANGING VIEW OF AN ATOM

Ancient Greeks
(2,400 years ago)

solid sphere

Rutherford Model
(early 20th century)

planetary system

Schrodinger Model
(present-day model)

mathematical description telling
most-probable location of atomic particles

ACTION OF CONVEX LENS

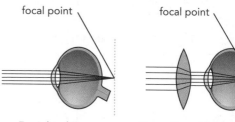

focal point   focal point

Farsighted Eye   Correction with Convex Lens

46. Which phrase best describes how the model of the atom has changed from the time of the ancient Greeks to the present?

(1) from a solid sphere to a planetary-type system

(2) from a strange mathematical model to a solid sphere

(3) from a strange mathematical model to a planetary-type system

(4) from a solid sphere to a strange mathematical model

(5) from a planetary-type system to a solid sphere

47. What function is performed by a convex eyeglass lens?

(1) protecting the eyes from rocks

(2) changing eye color

(3) changing eye shape

(4) moving the focal point of light entering the eyes

(5) changing the amount of light entering the eyes

PRACTICE TEST

Question 48 refers to the graph below.

The following bar graph shows the average length of time that food remains in each portion of your digestive system.

LENGTH OF TIME IN DIGESTIVE ORGANS

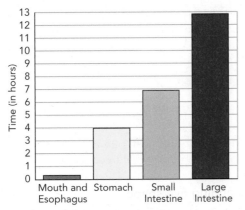

Organs of the Digestive Tract

48. On average, how much longer does food stay in the large intestine than in the stomach?

(1) 4 hours
(2) 5 hours
(3) 7 hours
(4) 9 hours
(5) 13 hours

Questions 49 and 50 refer to the passage below.

Many U.S. scientists hope that during the next few decades the United States will place a permanent colony on the Moon. As a first step to possibly colonizing Mars and other planets, the Moon colony would initially consist only of professional astronauts. These astronauts would spend several months at a time on the lunar surface. Later, as the colony grew, other citizens could visit and perhaps choose to reside permanently on the Moon.

Reasons given in support of a Moon colony include:

A. Gravitational effects are less on the Moon than on Earth.
B. Building a colony on the Moon is a way to unite U.S. citizens in a common goal: the colonization of other planets.
C. The Moon has no atmosphere.
D. The medical research that would be done as part of the Moon-colonization effort would greatly benefit all people.
E. The Moon is rich in minerals that could be used for building the Moon colony.

49. Which statements in support of a Moon colony are related to social benefits for people on Earth?

(1) A and B
(2) A and D
(3) B and D
(4) B and E
(5) D and E

50. Which statements are related to conditions on the Moon that may be advantageous for certain types of scientific experiments?

(1) A and B
(2) A and C
(3) B and D
(4) A, C, and E
(5) B, D, and E

Answers are on page 428.

1. (4) As shown on the graph, the surface layer is about 70°F, and the deep water is about 40°F. The thermocline is the transitional region between the surface layer and the deep water.

2. (2) An undersea volcano would be most disruptive because it would cause deep ocean water to boil, thus creating a region of hot water in what is normally a cold region of ocean. The other answer choices would do little to upset the normal pattern of ocean temperatures.

3. (4) A golf club is designed to efficiently transmit energy from the club head to the ball. Each other object listed is designed to take advantage of air resistance.

4. (3) The fact that the sky is blue in every direction you look indicates that scattering changes the direction of movement of blue light everywhere in the visible atmosphere.

5. (1) By knowing the types of gases in the Martian atmosphere, scientists could predict what colors of sunlight would be most readily scattered. The predominantly scattered colors of light would give Mars the color of its sky as seen from the Martian surface.

6. (5) The drawings do not give any information concerning the length of time a virus can stay inactive.

7. (5) A full moon is indicated by a box at the lower right-hand side of the diagram. As you can see from looking at the Moon in its orbit, a full moon occurs only when Earth is between the Sun and the Moon.

8. (3) Half of the Moon's surface is lit by sunlight at any given point in its orbit. However, we see only part of this lit surface. As you see on the diagram, most of the time part of the side of the Moon that faces us is sunlit and part of it is dark. The moonlight that we see is reflected sunlight.

9. (4) The passage refers to each form of stored energy as potential energy and to kinetic energy as energy of motion.

10. (1) A bathtub drain is designed to allow water to flow down through it, a use of stored gravitational energy. A fireplace uses chemical energy stored in wood; a flashlight makes use of stored chemical energy in the battery; a gas furnace uses chemical energy stored in the gas; an engine uses chemical energy stored in gasoline.

11. (2) Each fall, the leaves in deciduous trees lose chlorophyll, the green color in leaves. With the loss of green pigment, the orange and yellow colors of a leaf become predominant.

12. (3) CaO differs from $CaCO_3$ by one carbon atom (C) and two oxygen atoms (O): CO_2.

13. (3) The stored energy is the greatest when the passenger car is at its greatest height.

14. (4) In the human body, the circulatory system carries oxygen and nourishment to all of the body's cells.

15. (2) You would expect a room in which the air is not moving to have a temperature distribution as shown in graph B. The lower temperature air is near the floor, while the higher temperature air is near the ceiling, with a smooth transition region in between.

16. (5) As more evidence becomes available in the future, many theories that are accepted today may in fact be shown to be incomplete or perhaps incorrect.

17. (5) Underdeveloped countries are most likely to have poor sanitation practices, which means that human waste is likely a problem. These countries are least likely to suffer from chemical and radioactive wastes, which plague highly developed countries.

18. (1) This information is contained in the middle column of the chart.

PRACTICE TEST

19. (3) As indicated by the diagram and chart, water pollutants can affect almost all major systems of the human body.

20. (2) Only choice (2) is a hypothesis that explains the conditions that might have caused an ice age. The other choices are predictions or facts that do not explain why ice ages occur.

21. (1) The ocean is the main reservoir of water on Earth, and during an ice age ocean levels decrease as glaciers form. Water that falls as rain becomes part of glaciers instead of returning to the ocean as it does in today's climate.

22. (5) Statements A and C identify times when the Sun is not visible and thus accurate time could not be kept.

23. (4) Earth's gravity holds objects to the Earth and the Moon's gravity holds objects to the Moon. The fact that astronauts weigh less on the Moon than on Earth is due to the fact that the Moon's gravity is less than Earth's.

24. (4) A camel can go for a long period of time without drinking water. A camel does this by storing water within its own body, an adaptation that enables the camel to survive in the uncertain conditions of a desert.

25. (1) Animals give off carbon dioxide as a waste product of respiration (breathing).

26. (1) When ammonia is broken down before it is converted into nitrates, the nitrogen cycle is interrupted. A decrease in nitrates results in a decreased rate of plant growth.

27. (2) The fulcrum is at point A, the point that does not move. Point B is the load because the edge of the cap is lifted. Point C, the handle, is the effort—the point where force is applied. The relative positions of these three points make this a second-class lever.

28. (5) The effort is the place where force is applied at (A). As with the pliers, the gripped object at (B) is the load. The fixed point at (C) is the fulcrum.

29. (2) Unlike testosterone, estrogen levels vary over a considerable range during an average 28-day cycle.

30. (5) Though a controversial idea to many people, this is the most likely scientific explanation of the observed similarities between humans and chimpanzees.

31. (3) As shown by the graph, the human immune system reacts much more quickly and strongly to a second exposure. The immune system has a type of exposure "memory."

32. (1) As shown in the drawing, the purpose of this pulley is to allow the man to pull down while lifting the engine up.

33. (5) This is a famous picture of Neil Armstrong as he became the first human being to step onto the surface of the Moon.

34. (1) Favorite food is most likely an acquired taste and is not a hereditary trait.

35. (4) To see if bread-mold spores come from air, Kristen first had to eliminate any spores that might be present on the bread. She toasted the bread to kill or deactivate any spores that might be present.

36. (4) Only choice (4) is a summary of information obtained from the chart. Choice (2) is false. The other choices may also be true, but the chart itself does not provide any supporting evidence.

37. (2) Only choice (2) is a hypothesis for which no supporting evidence is available on the chart. The chart says nothing about untoasted bread.

38. (4) Only choice (4) gives evidence in which moisture is the only variable that differs when comparing one bread sample with the other.

39. (1)   Light is absorbed when an electron moves from a lower energy level to a higher one. Light is given off when an electron moves from a higher energy level to a lower energy level. A packet of light energy is called a photon.

40. (1)   Anything that causes the heart to work harder as it pumps blood will cause blood pressure to increase. Hardening of the arteries is a common cause of elevated blood pressure in older patients.

41. (5)   Graph A shows this decline. Answer choices (1), (3), and (4) are true, but no information about exhaust gases, government regulations, or forms of lead pollution (other than lead used in gasoline) is given in either graph. Answer (2) is not true and cannot be inferred as true from either graph.

42. (4)   Both statements B and C are needed to establish a cause-and-effect relationship between the two graphs. The graphs show a decline in the average amount of lead in Americans' blood during the same time that the use of lead in gasoline declined. Knowing B, you can reasonably conclude that less lead in gas results in less lead in the atmosphere. Knowing C, you can reasonably conclude that less lead in the atmosphere results in less lead in human blood.

43. (2)   Choice (2) is not always true, because a surrogate mother may have children of her own. When a woman is artificially inseminated, the fetus may grow from one of her own eggs. The other choices are true and are restatements of information in the passage.

44. (5)   Only choice (5) is not a direct risk to the surrogate. This is a potential problem that the parents who raise the child may someday face.

45. (3)   People who seek a surrogate-mother arrangement are likely to believe that they are making a reasonable choice.

46. (4)   The original concept of an atom as being a solid sphere of matter has been replaced by the modern mathematical view of an atom with electrons found in cloud-like orbits.

47. (4)   Eyeglasses change the focal length of the eye, resulting in corrected vision.

48. (4)   13 hours − 4 hours = 9 hours

49. (3)   Statements A, C, and E are statements of scientific fact not related to social benefits.

50. (2)   Statements A and C describe conditions on the Moon that may be advantageous for some types of scientific experiments. Statement E is true but is not directly related to experimentation.

Evaluation Chart

On the following chart, circle the number of any item you answered incorrectly. Pay particular attention to areas where you missed half or more of the questions. For those questions that you missed, review the skill pages indicated.

Subject Area / Theme	Life Science (45%) (pages 157–254)	Physical Science (35%) (pages 255–336)	Earth and Space Science (20%) (pages 337–385)
Fundamental Understandings	12 questions 6, 11, 19, 24, 25, 29 30, 35, 36, 37, 43, 48	9 questions 4, 9, 10, 12, 13, 23, 28, 32, 39	6 questions 1, 2, 7, 15, 20, 21
Unifying Concepts and Processes (pages 27–48)	3 questions 14, 26, 38	1 question 27	0 questions
Science as Inquiry (pages 49–94)	2 questions 31, 40	1 question 5	1 question 8
Science and Technology (pages 95–114)	1 question 47	1 question 3	1 question 33
Science in Personal and Social Perspectives (pages 115–138)	4 questions 17, 18, 44, 45	2 questions 41, 42	2 questions 49, 50
History and Nature of Science (pages 139–155)	1 question 34	2 questions 22, 46	1 question 16

Answer Key

Chapter 1

Thinking About Science, page 29

Sample answers:

1. Frogs are often seen near rivers and ponds and are plentiful after rain falls.
2. If meat is left to rot in open air, maggots will soon appear on it.

GED Practice, page 29

1. (4) The sea (ocean) looks almost flat when seen from the shore. This led many early thinkers to conclude that Earth was either flat or shaped like a disk.
2. (3) Thales had no way to determine the distance from Earth to the Moon.

Thinking About Science, page 33

Sample answers:

1. A system is an organized group of related objects or components that scientists choose to study in order to gain a better understanding of the world as a whole.
2. By order, scientists mean predictable properties and behavior.
3. Three parts of the digestive system are the mouth, stomach, and the small intestine.
4. If you dropped several ice cubes into a heated pan on a hot burner, the ice would quickly melt. The water that would form would begin to boil and would quickly evaporate (disappear) from the pan.

GED Practice, page 33

1. (4) Systems may be living or nonliving.
2. (3) Babies cry from the moment of birth. Crying is the one listed activity for which no learning is required.

Thinking About Science, page 35

1. H
2. F
3. O
4. F
5. H

GED Practice, page 36

1. (3) This is the one fact that might be related to the bees' behavior.
2. (2) The color of the shirt is important only if bees have color vision.
3. (5) This is Jerry's possible explanation of the bee's behavior.
4. (1) The sound wave with the shortest wavelength has the highest frequency.

Thinking About Science, page 39

Sample answers:

1. a. Change: the position of the balloon in the sky.
   b. Remain constant: the amount of gas within the balloon.
2. a. Change: the amount of water in the glass.
   b. Remain constant: the shape of the glass.
3. a. millimeters, centimeters, meters, kilometers
   b. tablespoons, fluid ounces, quarts, gallons

GED Practice, page 40

1. (5) The phases of the Moon occur on a monthly (cyclical) basis.
2. (3) The fact about the shirt is based on light absorbing properties of color, not on the principle of expansion/contraction.
3. (4) Pierced ears are the result of a personal decision.
4. (2) Leg strength can be purposely increased by exercise.

Thinking About Science, page 42

Sample answers:

1. The statement "the universe evolves" means that the universe changes through time.
2. earthquakes, volcanoes, and wind erosion

3. According to the condition of entropy, the cards will be randomly distributed. For example, it will be very unlikely to find four queens in a row.

GED Practice, page 43

1. (2) The purpose of sweating is to keep the human body at a constant temperature.
2. (5) Any movement of the body helps to generate heat. Sitting does not.
3. (4) This order shows the sugar cube slowly dissolving in water.

Thinking About Science, page 46

Sample answers:
1. the tail of a cow: to swat flies
2. the trunk of an elephant: to drink water
3. the tail of a fish: to aid in swimming

GED Practice, page 46

1. (3) Molars are used for chewing.
2. (1) Incisors are used for biting.

Concepts and Processes in Science Review, page 47

1. (5) Vestigial organs have no known use in today's organisms.
2. (1) This hypothesis would explain why vestigial organs exist—because they once served a purpose.
3. (4) Light may be reflected, absorbed, or transmitted depending on the material it strikes.
4. (1) Material that is transparent transmits most of the light that strikes it.
5. (2) The materials are classified according to the amount of light they transmit.
6. (4) The ducks are responding to the presence of crackers in the pond.
7. (3) By definition, a stimulus always occurs before a response.
8. (4) Beaks used to capture fish and to sieve food particles from water are designed for getting food from rivers, lakes, and oceans.
9. (5) Birds who sieve food particles from water are least dependent on keen eyesight.

Chapter 2

Thinking About Science, page 51

Sample answers:
1. Beaches form when waves move more rock fragments toward the shore than away from it.
2. During the process of absorption, food molecules leave the bloodstream and enter cells.

GED Practice, page 52

1. (4) All the supporting sentences in the paragraph relate to the idea of using chimpanzees in medical research.
2. (2) Paper makes up the largest portion of the graph (46%).
3. (3) Sixty-four percent is found by adding the percents for paper, metal, and glass— recyclable products of interest to the author.
4. (1) The author is expressing concern about the increasing levels of CO_2 in the atmosphere.
5. (2) The writer wants the reader to know that any message from space would have been sent very long ago.

Thinking About Science, page 54

Sample answers:
1. Light reflecting from the Moon's surface allows the Moon to be visible from Earth.
2. Miguel experienced a shock when he touched an exposed wire.
3. A scab formed on Carlina's finger after she cut it.

GED Practice, page 55

1. (3) DDT is a pesticide—a type of insect poison.
2. (4) The second paragraph states that DDT is banned in the United States.
3. (3) The final paragraph explains how rain washes pesticides into groundwater and streams.
4. (4) Precipitation is rain, hail, snow, etc.
5. (5) The label *evaporation* refers to all forms of moisture that return to the atmosphere (shown by arrows pointing upward).
6. (3) This answer summarizes all aspects of the diagram.

Thinking About Science, page 57

Sample answer:
1. The writer has a positive attitude toward robots.

GED Practice, page 58

1. (2) The writer believes that humans have a lot to do with extinction.
2. (5) The writer sounds very concerned about endangered species and most likely belongs to an environmental protection group.
3. (1) The point on the line above 20 minutes corresponds to a temperature about midway between 40°F and 60°F. The best answer is 52°F.
4. (4) At about the 45-minute point, the temperature levels off at 32°F.
5. (3) At 50 minutes, the water is partially, but not completely, frozen.

Thinking About Science, page 59

1. Light energy from the flashlight is changed into electrical energy in the calculator.
2. Chemical energy from the match is changed to light energy when the match is lit. This light energy is transferred to the candle.

GED Practice, page 60

1. (2) Iron at 212°F is the warmest and most dense substance given as an answer choice.
2. (3) Since sound travels faster through higher densities, lead must be denser than aluminum.
3. (5) Sound will not travel through empty space no matter where it is found.
4. (2) The angle of reflection is equal to the angle of incidence.
5. (3) Of the choices listed, only radios are not directly related to the property of light being discussed.
6. (4) A roughly textured ceiling reflects light in all directions, regardless of how light strikes it. The principle of reflection is only true for *smooth* reflective surfaces.

Thinking About Science, page 61

1. The relationship of bass to minnows and small crustaceans is a predator-prey relationship.
2. The relationship of the lice to the bird is a parasitic relationship.

GED Practice, page 62

1. (5) The relationship is commensal because the beetles nutritionally benefit but do not harm the ants.
2. (3) The relationship is parasitic because the fungus harms the chestnut tree as it takes nutrients from it.
3. (2) The relationship is saprophytic because the bacteria take nutrients from the remains of dead organisms.
4. (1) The relationship is predator-prey because the lioness kills and eats another organism.
5. (4) The relationship is mutualistic because both fungus and algae benefit from living together as a lichen.

Thinking About Science, page 63

Sample answers:
1. Ducks and geese flock to a warmer climate before winter begins in order to find a food source.
2. Wind might be a cause of erosion of the Rocky Mountains.

GED Practice, page 64

1. (4) This is the only answer choice that seems to be a reduced effort to help understand and fight air pollution.
2. (3) A car battery produces electricity as a result of chemical reactions taking place within it.
3. (2) Dressing warmly may help you feel better and help you get well more quickly but does little to stop the spread of a cold virus.
4. (5) This information would not help a doctor to treat the person.
5. (2) Sunlight reflects off a smooth water surface, such as might be found on an empty wading pool.
6. (4) Furniture polish is applied as a thin film on furniture surfaces, which creates a shiny appearance.
7. (3) Most ceilings are finished in rough, white plaster. The purpose of this finish is to reflect light equally in all directions.

Comprehending and Applying Science Review, page 65

1. (2) The passage mainly discusses why objects feel cool to the touch.
2. (4) Metal is a good conductor of heat and will feel warm to the touch if its temperature is above 98.6°F.
3. (2) Both biotic and abiotic factors affect an organism's chances for survival.
4. (4) Pesticides are nonliving chemicals.
5. (1) A zoo environment is closely monitored and controlled by humans.
6. (3) In both illustrations, there are breezes when cool moves toward warm air. If the air were the same temperature over land and ocean, no breeze would flow.
7. (5) If air over the land became colder than air over the ocean, the breeze would reverse its direction.
8. (2) Of the animals shown, the wolf and the dog are most closely related to one another and most likely evolved from a common ancestor.
9. (4) A buffalo is more closely related to a cow than to any other pictured animal.

Chapter 3

Thinking About Science, page 68

1. O
2. F
3. H
4. F
5. O
6. H
7. O
8. F
9. H
10. O
11. H
12. F
13. O
14. O

GED Practice, page 69

1. (3) This answer is a fact that is stated in the first paragraph.
2. (5) This answer is a valid hypothesis based on the information in the passage.
3. (2) This answer is a personal belief that is not supported by facts.
4. (2) Of the diseases listed, cancer is second only to heart disease as the leading cause of death for people age 65 and older.
5. (1) This answer is an opinion that cannot be proved.
6. (4) This answer expresses a reasonable explanation of an observed fact.

Thinking About Science, page 71

Sample answers:

1. The writer is assuming that life exists on other planets.
2. The astronaut is making the assumption that unmanned space probes cannot gather sufficient information about distant planets.
3. Rhoda is making the assumption that cold water will turn to ice more quickly than room temperature water.

GED Practice, page 72

1. (3) To support nuclear power, a person would have to believe that a way of safely storing radioactive waste is possible.
2. (1) This assumption is correct because many of the problems involved in storing radioactive waste, such as leaking storage drums, have become known only in recent years.
3. (5) Statements B and C are likely assumptions of people who are seeking to shut down nuclear power plants because of perceived dangers.

Thinking About Science, page 74

1. c
2. e
3. b
4. a
5. d

GED Practice, page 75

1. (5) This answer is the only direct effect of the ice age.
2. (2) The sudden occurrence of an ice age signaled the end of the Mesozoic era.
3. (3) An ice age began because the sunlight reaching Earth decreased, most likely from a large amount of dirt in the atmosphere.
4. (2) Dinosaurs most likely died because of the death of tropical forests, their food supply.
5. (3) Energy from the sun warms a fluid that is circulating in the heating system.
6. (2) The pump is the only part of the system that controls fluid circulation.
7. (1) The heat exchanger warms the air that passes next to it.
8. (3) The solar panel is not heated by sunlight at night. So, you can infer that the heat storage device is used as a source of stored heat at night.

Thinking About Science, page 78

1. moderate breeze
2. gale
3. strong gale

GED Practice, page 79

1. (5) Based on the experiment, this answer is the most reasonable conclusion.
2. (5) The main idea of the illustration is to point out the differences in how worker bees and drones are produced.
3. (4) Because they mate with each other, both the queen and the drone are exceptions to this rule.
4. (4) The small arrow on the graph indicates that the exercise ended after three minutes.
5. (3) The greatest distance between the two lines occurs just before the end of the exercise.
6. (5) By the three-minute point, student A's heart rate has leveled out at 170 beats per minute. You can infer that this rate would continue during two more minutes of exercise.
7. (1) An hour after quitting the exercise, student A's heart rate would most likely return to near its normal resting rate of 70 beats per minute.

8. (4) If two students exercise at different rates, differences in heart rates are to be expected. In this case you would be unable to compare physical condition, which is not as dependent upon students being the same sex, height, or age or exercising at the same time of day.

Thinking About Science, page 82

1. Checks should be placed next to *b* and *e*.
2. Checks should be placed next to *b*, *d*, and *e*.

GED Practice, page 83

1. (3) This is the only answer choice that mentions a legal definition of being too drunk to drive.
2. (4) Any car could have a burned-out headlight, regardless of whether the driver had been drinking.
3. (2) You determine that light, the faster of the two, will reach you more quickly.

Thinking About Science, page 84

Answer: Choice (3) would best determine whether owls and hawks would be in competition for the same sources of food if they lived in the same part of the forest.

GED Practice, page 85

1. (2) This is the only answer choice that gives a link between a high-fat diet and a known health risk.
2. (5) The teeter-totter will balance when stopped only if the weight of each child is the same. To determine if this is the case, you need to know the weight of each child.
3. (4) Gasoline will float on water only if the two liquids are not miscible and if water has a greater density than gasoline.
4. (5) For alcohol to float on oil, alcohol and oil cannot be miscible, and the density of alcohol must be less than that of oil.

Thinking About Science, page 86

Sample answers:
1. Betty's religious beliefs are in conflict with her personal desires.
2. Jay's personal values are in conflict with his job requirements.

GED Practice, page 87

1. (4) The artist is portraying the uncertainties that are associated with genetic engineering.
2. (2) The artist is illustrating an example of dangerous consequences that can result from genetic engineering if precautions are not taken.

Thinking About Science, page 90

1. Lauren grew both a control group of plants as well as an experimental group of plants so she would have something to compare the experimental group to that grew at the same time in similar conditions.
2. A single plant would not give Lauren as much confidence in the data as several plants. If the single plant had a defect of some sort, Lauren would have nothing in the same container to compare with that single plant.

GED Practice, page 91

1. (3) In each experiment, the pair of objects fell at the same rate.
2. (4) A strong wind might affect the rate at which a light object, such as a paper clip, falls.
3. (4) Although the leaf is about the same weight as the paper clip, its surface area is much greater.
4. (2) Of the choices given, an envelope and a small plastic spoon are the closest in weight with very different surface areas.
5. (4) The surface of the Moon is an ideal place for this experiment. In fact, astronauts actually performed this experiment on the Moon and concluded that, in the absence of air resistance, all objects fall at the same rate.

Analyzing and Evaluating Science Review, page 93

1. (2) There is no way to interview birds to find out how they experience taste.
2. (4) The robber fly's appearance helps it to approach its food source—the bumblebee.
3. (5) This choice describes the use of both a control group and an experimental group with identical conditions.
4. (1) The most relevant evidence would come from studies of people who live in crowded conditions, such as a city.

5. (3) A movie theater showing a popular movie is most likely to contain a crowd of people who might panic in the event of a fire.
6. (2) The diameter of Venus is very similar to the diameter of Earth.
7. (3) Earth has the largest diameter of the five smallest planets in the solar system.
8. (5) These are also two of the lightest elements that exist.
9. (1) The planets that rotate most slowly have the longest days, measured in Earth hours.

Chapter 4

Thinking About Science, page 96

Sample answers:

1. The goal of science is to understand the natural world.
2. The goal of technology is to improve human life.

GED Practice, page 96

1. (3) Patents do not keep inventions a secret. They just keep them from free public use.
2. (5) This choice will not improve the quality of life; it will advance our knowledge of the natural world.

Thinking About Science, page 99

Sample answers:

1. A technological milestone is an invention that changes human life from that time onward.
2. Answers will vary (Examples: a car, a plane, a semi-truck, a motorcycle)

GED Practice, page 99

1. (4) Electronic word processors are the most commonly used application in modern-day computers.
2. (2) Word processing entails creating, editing, storing, and printing documents with the use of a computer.
3. (1) *E-mail* is the common name for *electronic mail*, a type of messaging system that is delivered over the Internet.
4. (2) As mentioned in the passage, the intake valve allows gasoline and air to enter the cylinder.

5. (5) The expanding gas in the cylinder is what creates the mechanical energy that powers the car.

6. (3) Gas burns (chemical energy) and the car moves (mechanical energy).

Thinking About Science, page 103

Sample answers:

1. Technology often provides scientists with tools to use in more advanced scientific research.

2. Percival Lowell believed there was life on Mars because he observed canals on the surface of the planet.

3. Advancements in technology have allowed scientists to disprove Percival Lowell's theory.

GED Practice, page 104

1. (2) Modern computers are much, much faster than their predecessors, but you can't tell this by looking at them.

2. (4) Microchips are a modern electronic invention that is at the heart of the computer.

Thinking About Science, page 107

Answers will vary based on personal values.

GED Practice, page 108

1. (4) Some people have referred to surrogate parenting as "renting a uterus," a derogatory phrase. Selling this service is a very controversial practice.

2. (4) In general, tests should be done on a fetus only to determine important information. The less important the information, the more controversial it is likely to be.

3. (4) Of the choices listed, only gender was the same at the moment of birth.

4. (1) Dolly has genes only from the sheep from which the original cell was cloned.

5. (3) Obviously, Tamara has no reason to feel happy about this event, because important information has been withheld from her.

6. (5) It is most likely that the manufacturer is the only organization to have access to this information.

Thinking About Science, page 111

Answers will vary based on personal philosophy and beliefs.

GED Practice, page 112

1. (2) The potential danger at a nuclear power plant is the unwanted release of radioactive gas and material.

2. (4) Many radioactive substances remain lethal for a long period of time, and their effects on an environment may not be seen for many years.

3. (3) This must be considered the most important lesson if we want to protect our environment.

4. (3) A catalytic converter helps make exhaust gas less toxic.

5. (1) Exhaust gases are released in the atmosphere.

Science and Technology Review, page 113

1. (4) Of the jobs listed, a pilot is the least likely to be thought of as an information-age job.

2. (1) The main purpose of a microwave is to cook food.

3. (3) This would be the hypothetical result if the asteroid theory for the disappearance of the dinosaurs is true.

4. (5) As technology improves, the danger that Earth faces from asteroids will hopefully decrease.

5. (2) A chemical energy light source (fire) and an electrical energy light source (lighthouse beam) both give off light and heat.

6. (4) Modern lights use electric power.

7. (3) Regardless of commercial claims, electric lightbulbs do not last very long.

8. (5) The simple life of prehistoric people has been a weekend attraction for many of us.

Chapter 5

Thinking About Science, page 118

1. A pathogen is a harmful bacterium, virus, or fungus that invades the body.

2. Answers will vary. (Examples: AIDS, influenza, the common cold)

3. Answers will vary. (Examples: Diabetes, hemophilia, sickle-cell anemia)

4. Antibiotics are helpful in curing infectious diseases caused by bacteria.

GED Practice, page 119

1. (3) As long as Carlita washes her hands before touching her nose or mouth, she will not be infected by the virus.
2. (4) Adaptive immunity starts before a fever develops. Also, not all invading pathogens cause a fever.
3. (4) While heredity may play a role, a healthy lifestyle will greatly reduce a person's risk of cancer.

Thinking About Science, page 123

1. b
2. d
3. e
4. a
5. c

GED Practice, page 123

1. (1) The Endangered Species Act was designed merely to protect species that are found in the United States. There are organizations that work to protect endangered species worldwide.

Thinking About Science, page 127

Sample answers:
1. The world population has increased dramatically over the last century.
2. World population increased after 1950 because of better medical care, better nutrition, the decreased spread of diseases, and safer conditions in the workplace.

GED Practice, page 128

1. (4) As shown by the first data bars on the graph, the birth rate for the world is more than twice the death rate.
2. (2) The birth and death rates in Asia are most nearly equal to the proportion of those same rates for the world as a whole.
3. (5) In Latin America, the birth rate is almost five times the death rate, the greatest ratio of any of the regions shown.
4. (4) In Europe, the birth rate is only slightly higher than the death rate, indicating a very low growth rate.

Thinking About Science, page 132

Sample answers:
1. air pollution, water pollution, soil pollution
2. A landfill is used to bury human-produced trash.
3. strength, versatility, durability
4. seabirds, sea lions, turtles

GED Practice, page 133

1. (3) Method A leads to ocean pollution, and method C leads to air pollution.
2. (4) Resistance to weathering and decay make plastic difficult to dispose of, and this is the reason for environmental concern.
3. (1) Many people are wary of the effects that pesticides may have on the food they eat.
4. (2) The definition is stated in the first sentence of the passage.
5. (4) An organic compound contains carbon.
6. (5) Bioremediation has been used to help clean up oil spills.

Thinking About Science, page 135

1. The glass-sided, glass-roofed buildings often found in plant nurseries are called *greenhouses*.
2. Carbon dioxide causes Earth's atmosphere to increase in temperature as levels of carbon dioxide increase.

GED Practice, page 136

1. (2) Like a nursery greenhouse, a car lets sunlight in but does not allow trapped heat to escape.
2. (5) The other choices are results of the greenhouse effect. This answer choice is the only cause listed.
3. (3) The protection of polar bears is not directly related to the greenhouse effect.
4. (1) Because all hydrocarbon fuels contribute to the greenhouse effect, it would be beneficial for us to reduce our use of them.

Science in Personal and Social Perspectives Review, page 137

1. (2) Though not specifically mentioned, premature aging does follow from the other effects of famine.
2. (1) Overpopulation is a social disaster that can be controlled by humans. The other choices are natural disasters that cannot be controlled.

3. (1) Each of the other choices is mentioned in the passage.
4. (2) This fact becomes a greater problem as humans move into areas once inhabited only by forest dwellers.
5. (4) The chemicals produced by rosy periwinkle are used to fight certain types of cancer.
6. (3) The plant is in danger of extinction because its habitat is being destroyed.
7. (1) Cancer patients will not be able to obtain the chemicals produced by the plant.
8. (3) Every community has a landfill.
9. (1) 70% of 100 pounds equals 70 pounds.

Chapter 6

Thinking About Science, page 142

1. Answers will vary.
2. Answers will vary.

GED Practice, page 143

1. (4) It is not in the spirit of good science to be secretive.
2. (3) This type of research has led to negative relationships between nations.
3. (5) Once their research has been made public, scientists have no control over society's response.
4. (5) Smoking, whether firsthand or secondhand, is unhealthful for everyone.
5. (1) This claim is contradicted by massive amounts of medical evidence.

Thinking About Science, page 147

1. Aristotelian
2. modern
3. primitive
4. Renaissance
5. Aristotelian

GED Practice, page 148

1. (5) This is the only one of the choices that early scientists would have had the ability to observe.
2. (4) Religious objection to this idea remained until only a few hundred years ago. The feeling was that placing the Sun at the center diminished the importance of humans in God's universe.
3. (5) Thales introduced the concept of observation to explain ideas instead of using myths to explain ideas.
4. (1) The color of water was most likely the least important of its properties to Thales.
5. (4) This fact would give much support to his theory.

Thinking About Science, page 151

1. The evolution of Earth refers to the changing of Earth's features over time through natural processes.
2. The evolution of species refers to the changing of species through variations that get inherited by offspring.
3. The atomic theory of matter refers to the idea that all substances are made up of atoms.
4. The molecular basis of heredity refers to the idea that coded instructions are contained in the DNA of each cell in every organism and are passed from parents to offspring.

GED Practice, page 152

1. (4) Lamarck theory would suggest that with a lack of ground-level vegetation, giraffes are forced to reach up for leaves and other food sources.
2. (3) According to modern genetic theory, dyed hair color would not be able to be passed from a mother to her child.

History and Nature of Science Review, page 153

1. (5) Scientists who believed in the catastrophe theory thought that a species, once created, did not change.
2. (2) With no new catastrophe to change them, each of Noah's species would be alive and unchanged.
3. (3) This would help us to prove the common link between humans and apes.

4. (1) The dating techniques that were used to prove that Piltdown man was fake were not invented until 1953—41 years after Piltdown man was discovered.

5. (1) In a nuclear power plant, matter is converted to pure energy. In a fossil-fuel plant, matter is chemically changed (burned) to produce energy.

6. (4) The mass of the Sun is slowly decreasing as matter is converted to energy. Much of this energy leaves the Sun as light.

7. (2) Eventually the food supply may not be able to accommodate the human population.

8. (3) There will not be enough food to feed the growing population.

9. (1) Scientists of that time believed that Earth was the center of the universe.

10. (3) Scientists now know that the Sun is the center of our solar system. Earth orbits the Sun, and the Moon orbits Earth.

Chapter 7

Thinking About Science, page 160

1. d
2. c
3. a
4. e
5. b

GED Practice, page 160

1. (3) The first two paragraphs point out a variety of life forms living their lives.

2. (1) While it is true that frogs eat insects, it is only an opinion that frogs are more important to humans than are worms.

3. (5) The meat in the control jar must be kept away from flies for the experiment to give conclusive results.

4. (4) Flies were only able to lay eggs on the jar that wasn't covered.

5. (2) Redi needed to start the experiment with meat that did not already contain fly eggs.

Thinking About Science, page 163

1. growth
2. decline
3. beginning
4. death
5. maturity

GED Practice, page 163

1. (2) Animals that are slow to respond to danger are not likely to live long.

2. (4) This choice deals with survival, the most important motive for an animal's response, a motive not available to nonliving objects.

Thinking About Science, page 166

1. c
2. e
3. d
4. a
5. b

GED Practice, page 166

1. (5) A cell wall is only found in plants.

2. (3) Mushrooms have no use for chloroplasts, because they do not produce their own food.

3. (1) The nucleus contains all genetic information within a cell.

4. (2) The crunchy texture of carrots, celery, and other vegetables is due to the presence of a cell wall.

5. (4) A virus does contain genetic material, but it is much less complete than that contained in a living cell.

6. (2) A virus is not capable of reproducing on its own. It must use a cell to create more viruses.

7. (3) Unfortunately, antibiotics do not destroy viruses. That is why there is no shot to take for the common cold.

Thinking About Science, page 170

1. e; c; a; d; f; b
2. F; T; F; T

GED Practice, page 170

1. (1) A vacuole stores liquid in a plant cell.
2. (5) Animal cells do not produce sugar, an energy substance produced during photosynthesis in a plant cell.
3. (4) Every living organism starts life as a single cell.
4. (5) Only the structure of the cells themselves tell the function of a tissue. Certain organs have tissues that perform the same functions.

Thinking About Science, page 173

1. heredity
2. genes or DNA; nucleus
3. genes
4. two
5. chromosomes

GED Practice, page 173

1. (4) This statement provides a summary of the information on pages 171 and 172. The other statements list supporting details.
2. (2) Genes will be least similar in animals whose features are least similar.
3. (4) All plants with at least one *T* gene are tall. Therefore, the *T* gene is dominant.
4. (4) Taking the four possible combinations of the two gene sets gives you the following combinations: *TT, Tt, Tt,* and *tt.*

Thinking About Science, page 177

1. A unicellular organism is an organism that consists of a single cell.
2. A prokaryote is a unicellular organism that does not contain a nucleus.
3. A eukaryote is a unicellular organism that does contain a nucleus.
4. Binary fission is a method of reproduction in which a unicellular organism divides into two new organisms.
5. A moneran is one of the simplest living things.
6. A protist is a single-celled organism that can display the traits of fungi, plants, or animals.

GED Practice, page 177

1. (4) Bacteria cause strep throat and tuberculosis; amoebas cause amebiasis and dysentery.
2. (3) Unicellular organisms cannot be seen by the unaided eye.
3. (2) Milk, juice, and some alcoholic beverages are usually pasteurized.
4. (4) Boiling water for 10 minutes can kill harmful amoebas or bacteria that live in freshwater lakes or streams.
5. (1) Pasteur was able to prove that anthrax was caused by bacteria.
6. (5) The development of modern vaccines have helped to almost eliminate dreaded bacterial diseases, such as polio.

Thinking About Science, page 181

1. F
2. F
3. T
4. F
5. T

GED Practice, page 181

1. (3) Spores help plants spread out to new locations.
2. (3) This answer choice lists the correct reproductive steps in the correct order.

Thinking About Science, page 185

1. a. Roots anchor a plant and absorb water and minerals.
   b. Stems hold up the leaves and carry water and nutrients.
   c. Leaves are the sites where photosynthesis is carried out.
   d. Flowers are where reproduction occurs.
2. a. The stamen is the male reproductive structure.
   b. The stigma is the sticky top part of a pistil where pollen is deposited.
   c. The style is the tube that connects the stigma to the ovary.
   d. Pollen is a grain that contains the male sex cell.
3. Answers will vary (Examples: bees, hummingbirds)
4. T; F; F; F

GED Practice, page 186

1. (2) The Venus flytrap responds to touch.
2. (5) Morning glories open their petals on a 24-hour cycle.
3. (3) The tulip bulb was growing toward the direction of gravity even though it had been planted upside down.
4. (1) Chemical changes in the stem of a plant make phototropism possible.
5. (4) The stem of the corn plant grew away from the direction of gravity, as if knowing that sunlight was in the opposite direction.

Thinking About Science, page 191

1. c
2. e
3. b
4. a
5. d

GED Practice, page 191

1. (2) Lacking a backbone is the definition of *invertebrate*.
2. (4) The resting stage only takes place in complete metamorphosis.

Thinking About Science, page 195

1. a. A vertebrate is an animal with a backbone.
   b. Cold-blooded means unable to control body temperature.
   c. Gills are special organs that take oxygen out of water.
   d. Cartilaginous means made out of cartilage instead of bone.
2. c; e; d; a; b

GED Practice, page 195

1. (2) Fish, reptiles, and amphibians are all cold-blooded.
2. (1) An amniotic egg gives many kinds of protection to the embryo but none to the parent.
3. (3) As different as insects and amphibians are, it is remarkable that both go through such a similar process.
4. (3) Without lungs, life on land would not be possible.

Thinking About Science, page 199

1. birds; mammals
2. scales
3. sight, hearing, smell, touch, and taste
4. monotremes, marsupials, and placentals

GED Practice, page 199

1. (3) Penguins are warm-blooded, so their body temperature does not change in a cold climate.
2. (1) Birds, though, do not leave their eggs as do many reptiles.
3. (4) This organ helps mammals to breathe.
4. (2) This feature allows mammals to have three-dimensional vision.

Thinking About Science, page 203

1. b
2. e
3. c
4. a
5. d

GED Practice, page 204

1. (3) A turtle withdraws into its shell in times of danger.
2. (2) Sight has little value to an animal living in dark underground tunnels.
3. (4) Sharks are especially sensitive to the smell of blood, indicating an injured animal that may be easy prey.
4. (4) Although choice (5) is true, choice (4) better summarizes the passage.
5. (5) It was only by observing animals in their natural habitats that knowledge about toolmaking was obtained.
6. (3) The mouse is running for its life!
7. (2) This is a complex activity that the penguin just knows how to do, without being taught.
8. (4) Scruffy is accustomed to getting a reward for this type of behavior.

Thinking About Science, page 207

1. c
2. e
3. b
4. a
5. d

GED Practice, page 208

1. (4) More organisms must be born than the number of dying organisms in order to do more than merely replace the dying organisms.
2. (5) This factor would not directly affect fish.
3. (1) If the food source for frogs decreases, then both frogs and snakes (which eat frogs) will suffer.

Thinking About Science, page 211

1. c
2. e
3. d
4. a
5. b

GED Practice, page 212

1. (2) Many people believe that modern society, by taking care of its least able, is changing the relevance of Darwin's theory to modern life.
2. (1) Beak shape is directly related to a bird's eating activities and habits.
3. (4) Becoming a more efficient fish eater would be a very useful trait in these conditions.
4. (5) This proves that modern day organisms are descendants of extinct organisms.

Thinking About Science, page 215

1. Scientists believe that life first began on Earth about 3.5 billion years ago.
2. The fossils of blue-green algae were the first to be discovered.
3. The disappearance of dinosaurs from Earth led to the rise of mammals as Earth's dominant life form.

GED Practice, page 216

1. (4) Each of the other choices can be determined by dating a fossil or by analyzing its size and shape.
2. (1) Any member of the cat family or bear family is likely to be related to the saber-toothed tiger.
3. (3) Minerals may contain the detailed cell structure of an organism.
4. (5) The number of rings indicates the tree's age when it died.

Plant and Animal Science Review, page 217

1. (2) Besides being present as a gas itself, hydrogen is a component of each of the other three gases.
2. (3) The first step in Oparin's theory involves the breakdown of methane and other gases in the atmosphere.
3. (4) Nothing in the passage indicates that Oparin had either plant or animal cells in mind—only living cells in general.
4. (1) Oparin's theory hypothesizes how life may have started from *nonliving* substances.
5. (2) The head of a seahorse looks similar to the head of a horse.
6. (3) This is an interesting adaptation that is very similar to that of kangaroos.
7. (5) The streamlined body shape and pointed snout is the same design that is used for modern airplanes and submarines.
8. (3) Beetles make up the largest percentage of the graph.
9. (4) Mammals, which have the least number of species, have animals with the highest level of intelligence.
10. (1) The second paragraph indicates ways in which social insects work together.
11. (4) Part of the worker bee's job is to care for and protect the queen. It is the worker bees that attack when the hive is disturbed.
12. (3) Giving up one's life as part of a natural process, such as mating, is not characteristic of human social groups.

Chapter 8

Thinking About Science, page 223

Sample answers:

1. a. Human beings have similarities in body structures to other animals.
   b. Human beings have similarities in genetic codes to other animals.
2. a. body structure; function
   b. *Homo sapiens*

GED Practice, page 223

1. (2) Primates can walk erect on two legs and have eyes that face forward. Gorillas have each of these characteristics and are the most like humans.
2. (1) Genetic codes are the sets of instructions that determine body structure, among other things.
3. (5) A bird's forelimb is used for flying, while the forelimb of a human is used for hand and arm activity that does not involve flying.
4. (4) Because Darwin believed that all organisms evolve, it is most reasonable that he would conclude this hypothesis.
5. (3) This evidence would suggest a relationship between early humans and early apes.
6. (4) Human evolution occurs as changes take place in the human genetic code. Positive changes in this code may be brought about someday by genetic engineering, possibly the curing of what are now genetic diseases.

Thinking About Science, page 228

1. two
2. left; right
3. neurons
4. bundles of nerve fibers

GED Practice, page 228

1. (3) These nerve fibers allow the two halves of the brain to communicate with each other.
2. (4) The left half of the brain controls the right half of the body.
3. (2) Some people are extremely intelligent, yet their brains are not larger than average. Also, a human is generally considered to be more intelligent than an elephant.

Thinking About Science, page 230

1. T
2. T
3. F
4. T

GED Practice, page 231

1. (1) About half the deaths in the United States each year are caused by heart and blood disease.
2. (2) This is true as a general rule.
3. (1) Increased average income is not mentioned in the passage, nor is it necessarily related to life expectancy.
4. (4) Money spent on food is not important to know.
5. (3) 75 − 47 = 28, or about 30
6. (3) This conclusion is most reasonable when you consider that only the underfed mice lived beyond average life expectancy.
7. (2) The researcher is interested in the quantity of food eaten, not the time of feeding.
8. (1) This choice may be a positive benefit of overeating.

Thinking About Science, page 234

1. b; e; d; a; c
2. a. heart disease and diabetes
   b. 10 to 15 percent; 55 to 60 percent; 30 percent

GED Practice, page 235

1. (5) Excess calories from any source are stored as body fat.
2. (2) During a high fever, a patient sweats off a lot of water. Drinking water replaces the lost fluid and helps to lower body temperature.
3. (4) Exercise uses up energy (food calories). Thus, the more a person exercises, the more calories are burned up and not stored as fat.
4. (5) This group is the largest group on the food pyramid.
5. (4) All of these foods are high in protein.

Thinking About Science, page 238

1. F
2. F
3. T
4. T

GED Practice, page 239

1. (3) This is an intentional movement.
2. (5) Sneezing usually occurs without conscious control.
3. (1) The nervous system is the body's communication system, carrying electrical messages through nerves.
4. (4) An injury to the spinal cord in the lower back may affect all nerve impulses that try to move lower than that point, namely to and from the legs.
5. (5) First the nerve impulse goes from the hand to the brain, where it is interpreted as pain. Then, the brain sends a signal to the hand, after which the hand moves in response.
6. (3) When muscles contract and relax, they give off heat.

Thinking About Science, page 246

1. d
2. a
3. b
4. e
5. c
6. h
7. f
8. i
9. g

GED Practice, page 247

1. (1) According to the passage, the epiglottis performs this protective function.
2. (5) The circulatory system transports nutrients and oxygen to the body cells and waste carbon dioxide to the lungs.
3. (4) In the lungs, oxygen is absorbed by the blood and carbon dioxide is released as a waste product.
4. (5) Arteries transport blood to the lungs and other organs of the body; veins transport blood back to the heart from the lungs and other parts of the body.
5. (2) The heart has to work harder to pump this extra blood.
6. (4) This is the only statement that is an opinion for which evidence is of little help.
7. (3) This is the beginning of pregnancy.

Thinking About Science, page 249

1. F
2. T
3. T
4. T

GED Practice, page 250

1. (1) Identical twins form from a single fertilized egg.
2. (4) The female egg has 23 unpaired chromosomes, compared with 46 for all other cells in the body.
3. (5) Avoiding all inhalable chemicals, including drying paint, is important to a healthy pregnancy.
4. (4) A pregnant woman should stop all social drinking.
5. (3) Sickle-cell anemia causes red blood cells to become elongated and narrow.
6. (3) Sickle-cell anemia can be inherited, but it is not contagious.
7. (5) According to the passage, this is the only statement that is true.

Human Biology Review, page 252

1. (4) Both oxygen and nourishment are passed to fetal blood through the cells of the placenta.
2. (1) Fetal waste products (carbon dioxide being one) enter the mother's blood for later elimination.
3. (5) These substances can harm a fetus directly from the mother's blood.
4. (4) The foods mentioned in this choice do not contain cholesterol, but they do contain high levels of saturated fat, which the body may convert to cholesterol.
5. (1) This is defined in the final paragraph of the passage.
6. (4) This is a common result of high cholesterol.
7. (3) This shows a direct link between diet and atherosclerosis.

Chapter 9

Thinking About Science, page 259

1. a. elements
   b. electrons, protons, and neutrons
   c. nucleus
2. F; F; T

GED Practice, page 260

1. (4) nitrogen (3%) + calcium (2%) = 5%
2. (4) oxygen (65%) + hydrogen (10%) = 75%
3. (2) Aluminum at 8% by weight is the third most abundant element.
4. (5) In Table II, carbon is not listed separately. Carbon is part of the 1% listed as "traces of others."

Thinking About Science, page 265

1. a. atomic number
   b. protons and neutrons
2. a. 11
   b. 12 (23 - 11)
   c. 11

GED Practice, page 265

1. (3) Magnesium (Mg) is in the same column as Ca in the periodic table. Both are in the second column.
2. (2) Lithium (Li), is in the same row as oxygen. Both are in the second row.
3. (1) Isotopes differ by the number of neutrons. The number of protons and electrons is the same for all isotopes.
4. (5) Most of the mass of each isotope is found in the nucleus. Because neutrons and protons have about the same mass, a tritium atom is about 3 times as massive as a protium atom.
5. (2) An antiproton has the opposite charge of a positive proton.
6. (4) Antiprotons and protons come together and then disappear in a burst of light energy called gamma rays.

Thinking About Science, page 268

1. 2
2. 5
3. 6 (3×2)

GED Practice, page 268

1. (5) The 2 in front of the formula indicates that there are two molecules.
2. (4) There are six molecules in which each molecule contains three atoms.
3. (2) Remember: C stands for carbon, H for hydrogen, and O for oxygen.

Thinking About Science, page 270

1. c
2. d
3. a
4. b

GED Practice, page 271

1. (3) This sharing of electrons makes the flow of electricity possible.
2. (1) A good conductor is a material in which electrons can easily flow.
3. (2) This effect is mentioned in the second paragraph.
4. (4) Good ventilation is the first concern whenever car exhausts are involved.
5. (3) Most likely this is the result of nearby car exhausts.

Thinking About Science, page 273

1. a. carbon dioxide and water
   b. carbon
2. organic chemistry

GED Practice, page 273

1. (4) Isomers differ only in molecular shape.
2. (4) The carbon atom bonds with three other carbon atoms.

Thinking About Science, page 274

1. a. A hydrocarbon is a molecule containing only hydrogen and carbon atoms.
   b. A polymer is a hydrocarbon molecule containing a large number of carbon atoms.
2. To find the number of hydrogen atoms, multiply the number of carbon atoms by 2 and then add 2 to the product.

GED Practice, page 275

1. (3) Methane is not a polymer because it contains only one carbon atom.
2. (5) Each carbon atom bonds with two hydrogen atoms. Each carbon atom on the end of the chain bonds with one additional hydrogen atom—(20 + 20 + 2).
3. (4) This is because of the great number of cars in American society.
4. (3) 45% + 7% + 7% (gasoline + jet fuel + diesel fuel)

Thinking About Science, page 277

1. boiling point
2. freezing point
3. 32°F; 0°C
4. 212°F; 100°C

GED Practice, page 278

1. (3) Find the point on the three-gallon system line that is directly to the right of −15°F on the vertical axis. This point lies directly above five quarts on the horizontal axis.
2. (2) Protection to 0°F takes about 5 quarts, while protection to −20°F takes about 7 quarts. The answer is found by subtraction: 7 qt −5 qt = 2 qt.
3. (5) No information is given for these temperature ranges.
4. (1) The graphed data shows that a larger system requires more antifreeze for every level of protection.

Thinking About Science, page 279

1. a. A physical change is a change that does not produce a new substance.
   b. A chemical change is a change that does produce a new substance.
2. a. chemical
   b. physical
   c. chemical
   d. physical

GED Practice, page 280

1. (5) Burning sugar is a chemical change.
2. (2) Room temperature determines how long it takes the ice cream to melt. The warmer the room, the faster the ice cream will melt.
3. (3) Left in a cool wet place, iron will rust, a chemical change. None of the other actions will cause a chemical change in iron.
4. (5) Statement C is correct because melting can be reversed by freezing. Sanding, however, cannot be reversed. Statement D is true because melting is a change of phase, while sanding is a change in shape.
5. (3) Statement A is not true because a lighted match cannot be restored to its original form. Statements B and C are true. Statement D is not true because neither of the changes are destructive; each serves a useful purpose.

Thinking About Science, page 281
1. d
2. c
3. b
4. a

GED Practice, page 282

1. (4) Cola drinks are a solution of carbon dioxide dissolved in flavored sugar-water.
2. (1) This solution is liquid water dissolved in liquid paint.
3. (2) The punch solution is solid punch mix dissolved in water.
4. (2) Warming a carbonated drink (or shaking it) results in reducing the amount of gas the drink can hold.
5. (1) Warming creates molecule motion, which increases the rate at which one substance can dissolve in another.

Thinking About Science, page 285

1. a. chemical equation
   b. reactants; products
2. a. one
   b. six
   c. twelve

GED Practice, page 286

1. (3) The is shown by the large 3 on the right side of the reaction equation.
2. (5) On the left side: 3 + 3 = 6; On the right side: 3 × 2 = 6
3. (3) Enzymes are found in all living organisms.

4. (1) This can be inferred because human life would not be possible, even at birth, if enzymes were not produced in the body.

5. (4) This information is given in the final paragraph.

Chemistry Review, page 287

1. (5) Dew is formed from water vapor in the air condensing on cool leaves.

2. (2) For a substance to melt, it must be warmed to the point where its atoms have enough energy to break the bonds that hold them tightly together.

3. (4) The baking soda would lower the acid level of the orange juice without altering its taste much.

4. (1) The stomach naturally contains acid to help break down food. In an acidic stomach, this acid level is too high and feels uncomfortable.

5. (3) Lime is placed on grass to help neutralize the acidity of the soil.

6. (2) Six molecules of water are produced, as shown by the large 6 on the right-hand side of the reaction equation.

7. (4) Left side: $12 \times 2 = 24$; Right side: $12 + 12 = 24$

8. (4) Sunlight energy is required for photosynthesis.

9. (3) This is discussed in the first paragraph.

10. (3) As shown on the right side of the reaction equation, both heat is given off and carbon dioxide gas (CO_2) is produced.

Chapter 10

Thinking About Science, page 290

1. d
2. a
3. b
4. c

GED Practice, page 290

1. (3) As the standard of living rises, more and more products are being developed that use energy.

2. (2) Many concepts in physics are used in everyday life.

3. (5) This illustrates a combination of the word *biology* (the study of life) and *physics*.

4. (3) Solar power will become more abundant as we deplete our other energy sources.

5. (4) $32\% + 17\% + 30\% = 79\%$

6. (2) 30% compared to 11%

7. (2) The United States has more automobiles per person than any other country in the world.

8. (4) $23\% + 38\% + 24\% = 85\%$

Thinking About Science, page 294

1. a. A force is a push or pull that causes an object to change its state of motion.
   b. Inertia is a natural resistance to any change in motion.

2. a. 3
   b. 2
   c. 1
   d. 2

GED Practice, page 294

1. (1) Inertia is related to mass, the amount of matter in an object. A truck has a large mass (is very heavy!).

2. (3) This is an example of the second part of Newton's Second Law.

3. (2) For the acceleration to be the same, twice the force must be used to push twice the mass.

4. (4) An object's speed changes only when one or more forces are acting on the object.

5. (3) The water pushes on the sprinkler head as it sprays out.

6. (3) This is an example of action/reaction.

Thinking About Science, page 297

1. 2
2. 3
3. 1
4. 2

GED Practice, page 298

1. (2) as shown on the graph

2. (5) If you tried to walk on a planet that was similar to Earth but had 10 times the diameter of Earth, your weight would be 10 times what it is now. Do you think you could survive on that planet?

3. (3) The acceleration of gravity near Earth's surface changes a falling object's speed by 32 feet per second each second the object falls.

Thinking About Science, page 301

1. Work occurs when a force is applied to an object that moves in response to the force.
2. A force is a push or pull that causes an object to change its motion.
3. A machine is a device that is designed to make work easier.
4. The fulcrum is the point around which a lever turns.

GED Practice, page 301

1. (4) $50 \times 20 = 5 \times \underline{200}$ (Each product equals 1,000.)
2. (2) $300 \times 1 = 5 \times \underline{60}$ (Each product equals 300.)

Thinking About Science, page 304

1. constant
2. kinetic energy; potential energy
3. friction

GED Practice, page 304

1. (2) At the top of its swing at points A and D, the wrecking ball energy is all potential. At point C, the energy is all kinetic.
2. (5) The ball's energy is not lost during impact. This energy is transferred to the building, breaking the building apart and creating both sound and heat.

Thinking About Science, page 306

1. T
2. F
3. T
4. F

GED Practice, page 306

1. (2) Heat always flows from a hotter object to a colder one.
2. (5) These gaps are called *expansion joints*.
3. (2) This is shown on the thermometer.
4. (4) Choice (5) is a dangerously high fever.
5. (2) A fever of 105°F is very high and should be dealt with immediately.

Thinking About Science, page 310

1. F
2. T
3. T

GED Practice, page 311

1. (3) A dog barks in a frequency range of 450–1080 cycles per second.
2. (4) The greatest hearing range is that of a dolphin, from 150 to 150,000 cycles per second.
3. (2) A dog can hear frequencies as low as 15 cycles per second, compared to 20 for humans.
4. (5) Grasshoppers "speak" at frequencies as high as 100,000 cycles per second and hear only as high as 15,000. No other animal listed has this unusual ability.
5. (3) Most animals hear at both higher and lower frequencies than those at which they "speak."

Thinking About Science, page 313

1. F
2. T
3. F
4. T

GED Practice, page 314

1. (1) Ultraviolet (UV) rays have a shorter wavelength, higher frequency, and higher energy content than visible light.
2. (5) Radio waves are very low energy and that is why they are not dangerous even though space around us is full of them.
3. (3) The most common source of x-rays is the dental office and doctor's office. Ultraviolet rays are part of sunlight.
4. (2) Ultraviolet rays are more harmful than useful!

Thinking About Science, page 317

1. d
2. c
3. e
4. b
5. a

GED Practice, page 318

1. (2) If a light goes out in a series circuit, it causes a break in the whole circuit.
2. (1) Houses are wired in parallel circuits so that a single light failure does not result in all the lights going off.
3. (5) Electrons flow from the negative terminal to the positive terminal in this series circuit.
4. (2) Opening switch b will not cause a break in the circuit that powers light 2.

Thinking About Science, page 320

1. e
2. d
3. a
4. b
5. c

GED Practice, page 320

1. (5) This is known as the BCS theory of superconductivity.
2. (4) Unfortunately, money saved by companies using new technology is not always passed along to consumers.

Thinking About Science, page 322

1. T
2. F
3. T
4. F
5. T

GED Practice, page 322

1. (4) A magnetic field surrounds any wires or other conductors that carry an electric current. A gas barbecue does not operate on electricity.
2. (2) The time of day is not related to the possible danger of strong electric and magnetic fields.
3. (2) The drawing shows that statements A and C are true.
4. (3) The right side of the middle magnet must be N because it is pushing away from an N end. That means that B is a south pole (S). Then, A must be a north pole (N) because it is attracted to B, a south pole.
5. (3) All iron is ferromagnetic

6. (2) Lodestone was the first naturally magnetic material ever discovered.
7. (5) Gold is an unusual metal in having this property.

Thinking About Science, page 326

1. alpha particles, beta particles, and gamma rays
2. half life
3. thorium and alpha particle

GED Practice, page 326

1. (5) Only nine elements are known to be radioactive.
2. (4) This is $\frac{1}{8}$ of 1000 ($\frac{1}{2} \times \frac{1}{2} \times \frac{1}{2}$).

Thinking About Science, page 328

1. Nuclear fission is the process of splitting a nucleus into two smaller nuclei.
2. A chain reaction is the splitting of nuclei in a controlled way.
3. A nuclear reactor is a device in which controlled chain reactions are carried out.
4. Nuclear fusion is the joining of two nuclei together.

GED Practice, page 329

1. (3) This is a fact you will want to remember.
2. (5) This nuclear fuel produces much more energy than any other type of fuel.
3. (2) Of the choices given, only (2) is a prediction, a statement about what may happen in the future.
4. (1) Fewer fast neutrons mean fewer nuclei get stuck, which yields a slower reaction.

Thinking About Science, page 332

1. uncontrolled
2. controlled
3. controlled
4. uncontrolled
5. controlled
6. uncontrolled

GED Practice, page 332

1. (4) These are nonpolluting sources of energy that would be in much wider use if it were not for the cost.
2. (5) Molten rock is the source of heat used in geothermal energy.

3. (2) Natural disasters will probably have little to do with what energy sources are used throughout the 21st century.

Physics Review, page 333

1. (2) Visible light is a very small part of the entire electromagnetic spectrum that we know about.
2. (1) A superconductor carries an electric current without the normal heat-creating resistance that is a property of regular conductors.
3. (5) Chemical changes in a battery are changed into electrical energy available at the battery terminals.
4. (2) Of the objects listed, only an umbrella is not designed to move through the air.
5. (3) Flaps are used to increase lift during the time an airplane is traveling at slower than normal flying speeds.
6. (4) This level is slightly above quiet noise.
7. (1) The louder the sound, the higher the decibel level.
8. (3) The volume of the gas is shown to remain constant as temperature is increased. As the temperature of the gas is increased, its pressure increases.
9. (1) As a car speeds up, the tires feel more friction from the road. The added friction causes tire temperature to increase. The increase in temperature causes tire air pressure to increase.

Chapter 11

Thinking About Science, page 340

1. oceanographer or meteorologist
2. geologist or geochemist
3. ecologist
4. geologist
5. meteorologist

GED Practice, page 341

1. (3) Environmental scientists are mainly concerned about the impact human activity has on wildlife, and land and water resources.
2. (5) Storage of toxic waste is a problem in which government regulations must play an

important role if the environment is to be protected.
3. (1) Fossils would be most relevant to a paleontologist's study of Earth's history.
4. (4) There is just over seven times as much chlorine (55%) in ocean water as there is sulfate (7.7%).
5. (3) Sodium chloride is made up of sodium and chlorine, which are the new main substances dissolved in seawater.

Thinking About Science, page 344

1. solar nebula or cloud of interstellar gas
2. core
3. 4.6 billion years
4. the emergence of life

GED Practice, page 344

1. (2) Earth formed about 4.6 billion years ago, the oceans a little over 4 billion years ago.
2. (1) Most scientists agree that life most likely formed in water.
3. (2) Heavier elements tend to be found in and around the core, with the lighter elements being found near Earth's surface.

Thinking About Science, page 346

1. crust, mantle, and core
2. 71%
3. seven
4. solid iron, liquid iron
5. a little more than 4000 miles

GED Practice, page 346

1. (2) The ocean floor and the visible continents are the surface layer of the crust.
2. (1) The mantle, the supporting structure below the crust, is made of heavy rock.
3. (5) Mountains tend to form where parts of the crust have come together and bulged upward and downward, creating a thickened crust.

Thinking About Science, page 348

1. the Sun
2. heat produced in the core
3. over 13,000°F
4. radioactive elements

5. atmospheric carbon dioxide gas, limestone, carbon dioxide gas dissolved in water, and organic molecules

GED Practice, page 349

1. (1) Magma forms when igneous rocks are heated.
2. (3) Heat and a chemical change are necessary to change sedimentary rock into metamorphic rock.

Thinking About Science, page 351

1. T
2. F
3. F
4. T

GED Practice, page 352

1. (2) This movement is a result of Earth's liquid interior.
2. (4) This thought has occurred to many people who are familiar with the shape of the continents.
3. (3) Ancient European pottery would be, at most, several thousand years old, far too recent to have any relevance to questions concerning Pangaea.
4. (2) Of the choices given, only (2) involves something (rain) that is not related to volcanic activity.

Thinking About Science, page 354

1. The atmosphere is the blanket of air that surrounds Earth.
2. Ozone absorbs much of the dangerous ultraviolet light from the sun that strikes Earth's atmosphere.
3. carbon dioxide (often called the *greenhouse gas*)
4. about 46%
5. ultraviolet light

GED Practice, page 355

1. (1) The troposphere extends to an altitude of about eight miles and contains the cirrus clouds.
2. (5) The shuttle passes through the top layer of atmosphere, called the thermosphere.

3. (4) The ionosphere is the layer that affects long-distance radio reception.
4. (2) The damage is caused in the stratosphere, the layer, contains ozone.

Thinking About Science, page 357

1. a. T
   b. F
   c. F
   d. T
2. a. 24 hours
   b. about 365 days
   c. rotation
   d. tilt

GED Practice, page 358

1. (1) February weather in Brazil is similar to August weather in the United States.
2. (4) Canada and the United States are both in the northern hemisphere and have winter during the same months.
3. (2) Paris is eight time zones earlier than Seattle. Eight hours before 6:00 A.M. Saturday is 10:00 P.M. Friday.
4. (4) The flight takes five hours, and an extra four hours are "lost" because of time zone changes. Thus, the flight reaches New York City at 5:00 P.M. (8:00 A.M. + 9 hours).

Thinking About Science, page 360

1. c
2. a
3. d
4. b

GED Practice, page 360

1. (3) The word *isotherm* means *line of constant temperature*.
2. (5) The map shows winter conditions in the United States. December is the most likely month.

Thinking About Science, page 363

1. Small ground animals play a part in the process of weathering by digging in the soil, exposing underlying soil to air and moisture.
2. weathering

GED Practice, page 363

1. (4) Ocean waves create water erosion.
2. (2) An acid is a type of chemical.
3. (5) Arranged in order, the steps show how a river with a slight bend caused the bend to increase and then get cut off to form an oxbow lake.

Thinking About Science, page 365

1. T
2. T
3. F

GED Practice, page 365

1. (5) By calculating the amount of half-lifes in carbon-14, a scientist can trace the approximate age of a fossil.
2. (3) Since four half-lifes have passed, the amount of years in one half-life are multiplied by four: 5,730 x 4 = 22,920 or approximately 23,000.
3. (3) Coal is formed from the remains of a tropical forest, and limestone from the remains of ocean life.
4. (5) Of the choices given, only the sea worm is a form of ocean life, the types of fossils found in limestone.
5. (3) Of the choices given, the extinct camel is the one most likely found in a desert.
6. (2) The variety of types of layers indicates that choice (2) is the best answer.

Earth Science Review, page 367

1. (5) If the magma temperature increases, the geyser water will reach boiling temperature more quickly. The time between eruptions will then decrease.
2. (2) This is stated in the second paragraph.
3. (4) Only choice (4) is supported by the drawing. Each of the other choices is not a true statement.
4. (2) P-waves travel more rapidly than either L-waves or S-waves. Also, P-waves travel in all directions from the point of the quake.
5. (2) Only between a Richter magnitude of 0 and 3 is a quake measurable but too weak to be felt.
6. (4) The magnitude of the P-wave could help determine the strength of the quake but not its location.

Chapter 12

Thinking About Science, page 372

1. third
2. the planets; the sun
3. 6 trillion (6,000,000,000,000)
4. 200 billion
5. Mars and Jupiter

GED Practice, page 373

1. (4) This was a very controversial theory at the time it was proposed.
2. (3) Neither statement A nor B has anything to do with light coming to Earth from distant planets.
3. (1) This is a good math problem for you to solve: time = distance ÷ velocity (speed). (Remember: 8 minutes = 480 seconds.)
4. (5) Neither statement B nor C would have anything to do with the apparent motion of the sun.
5. (5) This is because a comet is made of dust and gas and looks like a dirty snowball with a long tail as it moves across the sky.

Thinking About Science, page 376

1. pulsar
2. white dwarf
3. supernova

GED Practice, page 376

1. (2) This is the point where a star begins creating its own energy.
2. (4) Near the end of its life cycle, a star gets almost all of its energy from nuclear fusion, the combining of hydrogen atoms to form helium.
3. (5) This may be the strangest object in the universe.

Thinking About Science, page 378

1. 50 billion
2. cluster
3. globular cluster

GED Practice, page 378

1. (3) Later, the gas cloud may condense to become a new star or planet.
2. (2) Most of the galaxies and stars that make them up were formed at about the same time, 10 to 20 billion years ago.

Thinking About Science, page 380

1. 4.6 billion
2. hydrogen and helium
3. 4.6 billion

GED Practice, page 380

1. (1) Scientists believe that all the planets in our solar system came into being at about the same time.
2. (4) This fact indicates that planets may be a common feature of stars, not a rare exception as was once commonly believed.
3. (5) The solar wind is created on the sun and strikes Earth.
4. (2) Because the solar wind contains charged particles, it can disturb long-distance radio reception. A similar effect occurs when a car radio passes near electric power lines.

Thinking About Science, page 382

1. explosion
2. energy
3. open universe, flat universe, and closed universe

GED Practice, page 382

1. (4) The "Big Crunch" would occur if all the galaxies in the universe came back together to a single point! Not many scientists believe that this will ever happen.
2. (3) They will mover farther away until the balloon bursts!
3. (2) This is an easy model to visualize and helps you understand the idea of an expanding universe.
4. (1) Like the balloon, the universe is rapidly expanding.

Space Science Review, page 383

1. (2) One AU is a distance of about 93,000,000 miles.
2. (4) 93,000,000 × 5.20 is approximately 484 million. 500 million miles is the best answer.
3. (1) 38% of 150 pounds is 57 pounds.
4. (3) The force of gravity depends both upon the size of a planet and the amount of matter the planet is made of. A planet made of light gases will likely have a force of gravity less than that of Earth, even if the planet has a larger diameter.
5. (2) Stars move through space, and move relative to one another because each moves at a different speed and in a different direction.
6. (5) Choice (5) is the only statement you know for sure is true.
7. (3) Being directly over the rotation axis, Polaris appears stationary in the sky as the other stars *appear* to rotate around it.
8. (2) Polaris appears closest to the horizon in the listed city that is closest to Earth's equator: Mexico City, Mexico.
9. (4) Standing on the South Pole, Polaris is directly below you! You would need to be able to see through Earth to see it.

Science Almanac

United States Customary Units of Measure

LENGTH
1 foot (ft) = 12 inches (in)
1 yard (yd) = 3 feet (ft)
1 mile (mi) = 1,760 yards (yds)

CAPACITY
1 pint (pt) = 16 fl. ounces (fl. oz)
1 quart (qt) = 2 pints (pt)
1 gallon (gal) = 4 quarts (qt)

WEIGHT
1 ounce (oz) = 16 drams
1 pound (lb) = 16 ounces (oz)
1 ton = 2,000 pounds (lbs)

Metric Units of Measure

LENGTH
1 centimeter = 10 millimeters
1 meter = 100 centimeters
1 kilometer = 1,000 meters

CAPACITY
1 milliliter = 1,000 microliters
1 liter = 1,000 milliliters
1 kiloliter = 1,000 liters

MASS
1 milligram = 1,000 micrograms
1 gram = 1,000 milligrams
1 kilogram = 1,000 grams

Scientific Units of Measure

UNIT	ABBREVIATION	MEASURES
ampere	amp	electric current
astronomical unit	AU	astronomical distance
calorie	cal	energy
hertz	Hz	frequency
joule	J	energy
kelvin	K	heat
ohm	Ω	electrical resistance
volt	V	electromotive force
watt	W	power

Classification of Organisms

HIERARCHY
Kingdom
Phylum
Class
Order
Family
Genus
Species

HUMAN CLASSIFICATION
Animalia
Chordata
Mammalia
Primates
Hominidae
Homo
Homo sapiens

OTHER EXAMPLES
Plantae, Fungi, Protista, Monera
Arthropoda, Mollusca, Platyhelminthes
Arachnida, Bivalvia, Cestoda
Scorpiones, Veneroida, Cyclophyllidea
Buthidae, Tricadnidae, Taeniidae
Centruroides, Tridacna, Taeniarhynchus
Centruroides vittatus, Tridacna gigas
(Striped Scorpion)   (Giant Clam)

Periodic Table of the Elements

See pages 262 and 263.

Planets in the Solar System

	DIAMETER *(in miles)*	DISTANCE FROM SUN *(in AU)*	LENGTH OF ORBITAL REVOLUTION *(in Earth days)*
Mercury	3,050	0.39	87.97
Venus	7,560	0.72	224.70
Earth	7,973	1.00	365.26
Mars	4,273	1.52	686.98
Jupiter	89,500	5.20	11.86
Saturn	75,000	9.54	29.46
Uranus	32,375	19.19	84.0
Neptune	30,937	30.06	164.8
Pluto	1,875	39.53	247.7

Interesting and Useful Web Sites

PLANT AND ANIMAL SCIENCE

The Cell
http://library.thinkquest.org/3564/
This site includes lessons, quizzes, and photographs related to basic cell biology.

Classification of Living Things
http://anthro.palomar.edu/animal/default.htm
This site provides an introduction to basic biological taxonomy with an emphasis on the evolution of humans.

Endangered Species Program, U.S. Fish & Wildlife Service
http://endangered.fws.gov
This site provides information on threatened and endangered species in the United States, including methods of preservation and protection.

HUMAN BIOLOGY

Evolution of Modern Humans
http://anthro.palomar.edu/homo2/default.htm
This site provides information on the biological and cultural evolution of modern humans.

Human Genome Project Information
http://www.ornl.gov/TechResources/Human_Genome/home.html
This site provides information about the Human Genome Project, including current research and ethical, legal, and social issues.

Nutrition.gov
http://www.nutrition.gov/
This site provides a wealth of information on food consumption, food safety, fitness, health, and disease.

CHEMISTRY

Chemical Elements.com
http://www.chemicalelements.com/
This site contains an online, interactive periodic table of the elements.

Chemtutor
http://www.chemtutor.com/
This site contains tutorials for basic concepts in chemistry.

Quia—Chemisty Activities
http://www.quia.com/dir/chem/
This site contains games and quizzes related to chemistry topics.

PHYSICS

Great Experiments–Physics
http://www.howstuffworks.com/exp-db11.htm
This site contains links to a variety of experiments that illustrate key concepts in physics.

Physics Central
http://www.physicscentral.com
This site, sponsored by the American Physical Society, provides information on physics as it relates to everyday life, including a column titled "How Things Work."

Exhibit Collection—Amusement Park Physics
http://www.learner.org/exhibits/parkphysics/
This site explores the physics involved in amusement park rides, such as roller coasters, carousels, and bumper cars.

EARTH SCIENCE

Discovery Channel's Planet Earth Guide
http://dsc.discovery.com/guides/planetearth/planetearth.html
This site provides information and interactive features that deal with all areas of Earth science.

The National Weather Service Homepage
http://www.nws.noaa.gov/
This site contains updated weather forecasts for the U.S. and various international locations, along with coverage of storm development.

National Museum of Natural History—Dinosaur Exhibits
http://www.nmnh.si.edu/paleo/dino/index.html
This site guides visitors through a virtual tour of several dinosaur exhibits. Photos of full and partial dinosaur skeletons, information on field work, and a list of dinosaur misconceptions are available.

SPACE SCIENCE

Astronomy Picture of the Day
http://antwrp.gsfc.nasa.gov/apod/astropix.html
Each day this site features a different image or photograph of some aspect of the universe, along with an explanation written by a professional astronomer.

Mars Exploration Homepage
http://mars.jpl.nasa.gov/index.html
This site presents detailed information on the Mars Exploration Program, along with a photo gallery, a history of previous missions, and updated information on current and future expeditions.

Space Telescope Science Institute/Hubble Space Telescope Public Information
http://oposite.stsci.edu/pubinfo/
This site contains a history of the Hubble Space Telescope and a gallery of photographic images of the universe.

Glossary

A

activation energy   the energy needed to enable a chemical reaction to take place

aging   the changes that bring about the decline of an organism

air mass   a body of air with a certain temperature and with a certain moisture content

air pressure   the weight of the atmosphere

air resistance   friction caused by air

alpha particle   a radioactive particle made up of two protons and two neutrons bound tightly together

alternating current   a current in which the electrons flow first in one direction and then in the opposite direction

amino acids   the building blocks of proteins

amniocentesis   a procedure that is used to examine fetal cells to identify certain types of genetic disorders present in a fetus

amniotic egg   a covering that protects and nourishes a developing embryo

asexual reproduction   a method of reproduction in which an organism is produced from a single cell

assumption   a belief that something is true without checking its validity

asteroid   any of the very small celestial bodies that orbit the Sun, mainly between Mars and Jupiter

astronomy   the study of all celestial bodies in the universe

atmosphere   the blanket of air that surrounds Earth

atom   the smallest particle of an element that can exist alone

atomic mass   the sum of the protons and neutrons in the nucleus of an atom

atomic number   the number of protons in an atom

ATP   a compound in which energy is stored for later use in a cell

axis   the imaginary line running through Earth's center from the North Pole to the South Pole on which the planet rotates

axon   a long fiber in a nerve cell through which a nerve impulse is sent

B

backbone   a segmented column of bones

barometric pressure   see **air pressure**

behavior   an organism's actions or reactions to its environment

beta particle   an electron emitted from the nucleus of a radioactive atom

big bang theory   the idea that the universe began with an explosion of a dense, hot, compact mass under extreme pressure

binary fission   a method of reproduction in which a cell simply divides into two new cells

biodegradable   organic materials that naturally decompose

biodiversity   a healthy variety of plant and animal species coexisting in an environment and making the environment more stable

biogenesis   the principle that living things only come from other living things

biological clock   an internal control of natural behavioral cycles

biological process   a fundamental property that is common to all living organisms

biology   the study of all living things

black hole   the collapsed leftovers of a supernova

blue star   a massive, hot star that uses up its hydrogen quickly, expands, and turns into a giant or supergiant

boiling the process by which a liquid changes to a gas

botany the study of plants

bud the part of a plant where new growth takes place

C

calorie a measure of food energy

camouflage a coloring pattern that enables an animal to blend into its surroundings and not be seen by predators

carbohydrate the main source of food energy

cartilage a tough, flexible material that covers bones and joints

catalyst a substance that provides a faster mechanism by which a reaction may take place

cause an action or condition that has a result associated with it

cell the basic unit of life

cell membrane the soft, flexible covering that holds a cell together and separates it from other cells

cell specialization the process in which the cells of an organism develop in different shapes, structures, and functions

cell wall a tough, flexible covering that surrounds the cell membrane of a plant cell

chain reaction a reaction in which nuclei are split apart in a controlled way, resulting in a great quantity of nuclear energy

chemical bonding the process through which atoms are combined

chemical change a change that produces a new substance

chemical equation a shorthand way of describing what happens in a chemical reaction

chemical formula a shorthand way of showing which elements are contained in a molecule

chemical reaction the process in which two or more substances combine to form one or more new substances

chemical weathering the softening and crumbling of rock brought about by chemical changes

chlorophyll the green substance in a plant cell that is used to capture light energy

chloroplast an organelle in a plant cell that contains chlorophyll

chromatin genetic material in the nucleus of a cell

chromosome a group of genes that carries genetic information for various traits

circadian clock a biological clock that controls daily activity

cloning the process of creating a genetically identical replica of an organism

closed universe the theory that the universe at some future time will begin to contract and eventually collapse into its original state as a solar nebula

cold-blooded a classification of an organism that cannot control its own internal body temperature

comet a small object made of dust and frozen gas that orbits in a predictable path around the Sun

complete metamorphosis a type of metamorphosis that takes place in four stages

composting the use of natural biological processes to aid in the decomposition of organic materials

compound a group of molecules that each contain the atoms of two or more elements

condensing the process by which a gas becomes a liquid

conductor a material in which electrons can be made to flow

conservation the controlled use and preservation of natural resources

constancy the tendency for things to remain unchanged

contaminants substances that harm the environment

continental drift the movement of continents

contraction a decrease in size of a substance due to its atoms moving closer together, often caused by a decrease in temperature

convection currents currents of molten rock within the mantle that carry much of the heat to Earth's surface

Copernican theory the idea that the Sun is at the center of the solar system

core the center of Earth

covalent bond a bond in which electrons are shared by the bonded atoms of a molecule

crust the outermost layer of Earth

crustal plates the exterior layer of Earth's crust (surface); also called tectonic plates

cytoplasm a jellylike fluid of water, salt, minerals, and many types of organic molecules that are essential to all life processes

D

dendrite a branching fiber on a nerve cell that receives messages from another nerve cell

diffraction the process in which a waves spread out into a region behind or around a barrier

digestion the breaking down of food into nutrients that the body's cells can use

direct current electric current that moves in one direction only

dissolve to become part of a solution

DNA a large, complex molecule formed by chains of chemical compounds

dominant gene one gene in a gene pair that determines the effect of the gene pair

drawing conclusions expressing unstated ideas that are logically connected to given information

E

ecology the study of the relationship of organisms to their environment

ecosystem a community of populations of organisms and the habitats and natural resources that affect the community

effect a result of an action or condition

egg the female sex cell

electric current the flow of electrons in a material

electric force the force that holds electrons in orbit around the nucleus of an atom

electromagnet a strong magnet that is made by coiling a wire around a piece of iron and running an electric current through the wire

electromagnetic spectrum the wide range of wavelengths over which electromagnetic waves exist

electromagnetic wave a wave that can travel through a vacuum

electron a particle with a negative electric charge that orbits the nucleus of an atom

element a pure substance composed of identical atoms

elliptical galaxy a galaxy that looks like a sphere or an elongated sphere of stars

embryo an organism in its early stage of development

endoplasmic reticulum a cell organelle that produces lipids, breaks down chemicals, and transports proteins for delivery to all parts of a cell

energy the capacity for doing work

energy shells the energy levels at which electrons orbit the nucleus of an atom

entropy the tendency of a system to become randomly disorganized

environment all the living and nonliving things that affect an organism's life in some way

environmental science   the study of how human beings interact with their environment

enzyme   a specialized protein that breaks down organic molecules

epidemic   the rapid spread of an infectious disease through an entire population

equilibrium   a condition in which change takes place in equal and opposite ways

erosion   the natural movement of rock fragments over the surface of Earth

eukaryote   an organism composed of one or more cells containing a nucleus and organelles

evidence   observations and data from experiments that support or oppose a stated point of view

evolution   a series of changes that occur over time

excretion   the process in which waste products are removed from the body

expansion   an increase in size of a substance due to its atoms moving farther apart, often caused by an increase in temperature

experiment   a procedure that is designed to test a hypothesis

explanation   the addition of newly acquired evidence to facts that are already known

extinction   the dying off of an entire plant or animal species

F

famine   widespread starvation

fat   an energy source derived primarily from animal products

fetus   the developing stage of a baby

fission   the splitting of the nucleus of an atom

flat universe   the theory that the universe will at some future time reach a size and stay at that size

flower   the part of a plant in which reproduction occurs

food chain   the interdependence of organisms for food

food web   a group of food chains that are linked together

force   any push or pull that can affect an object either in motion or at rest

fossil   a trace remain of an organism of a past geological age

fossil fuels   fuels, such as petroleum, coal, and natural gas, that are used to produce energy for industrialized societies

fraternal twins   two children who develop from two eggs fertilized by two sperm during the same reproductive cycle

freezing   the process by which a liquid turns into a solid

friction   a force that slows a moving object

front   the boundary line where a warm air mass collides with a cold air mass

fusion   the combining of two atomic nuclei to form one nucleus

G

galaxy   a large group of stars

gamma ray   a high-energy electromagnetic wave

gas   the phase of matter in which the molecular structure of a substance is relatively loose, allowing atoms to move apart independently of each other

gas cloud   a vast cloud of gas and dust out of which a star may form

gene   a strand of DNA that carries the information for a specific trait

genetic disorder   a disease, disability, or difference caused by an abnormal gene

genetics   the study of how characteristics are passed from one organism to another

geochemical cycle   the movement of elements from one chemical storehouse to another

geochemistry   the study of the distribution of chemical elements in Earth's crust

geology   the study of the composition and structure of Earth

geothermal energy   energy that comes from Earth's hot interior

giant   a star that is not as massive as a blue star, but has run out of hydrogen, resulting in the inner core shrinking and the outer core expanding

gills   special organs that take oxygen out of water

global warming   the overheating of Earth's surface

globular cluster   a group of older stars that looks like a ball of stars

glucose   a simple sugar that is used to produce energy in plants

Golgi complex   a cell organelle that receives proteins from the endoplasmic reticulum and modifies them for different functions

gravity   a force of attraction between two objects that is due to their mass

greenhouse effect   the natural heating of a planet by the process of atmospheric gases trapping heat energy

group   a column of the Periodic Table that lists elements that have the same number of electrons in their outermost energy shell

H

habitat   a home for a community of organisms

half-life   the rate at which a substance undergoes radioactive decay

heat   the energy of moving atoms

hemisphere   the left or right half of the human brain

hormone   a chemical produced within the body that regulates body function

humidity   the measure of the water vapor in the air

hydrocarbon   a compound composed of only carbon and hydrogen

hydroelectric power   electrical energy formed by the conversion of the energy of flowing water

hypothesis   a reasonable explanation of evidence or a prediction based on evidence

I

identical twins   two children who form from the same fertilized egg cell

immune system   molecules, cells, and organs that work together to defend the body against pathogens

implication   a point of view that another person presents to you

imply   to suggest

incineration   the burning of solid wastes

incomplete metamorphosis   a type of metamorphosis that takes place in three stages

inertia   the natural resistance of matter to change its state of rest or motion

infer   to guess at what is not stated directly

inference   a point of view that a person arrives at because of what he or she reads, hears, or sees.

insulation   material that protects against electric shock

invertebrate   an animal without a backbone or skull

involuntary muscle   a muscle over which a person has limited control

ion   an atom that has either lost or gained an electron

ionic bond   a bond that is formed when an electron in the outermost energy shell of one atom transfers to the outermost shell of a second atom

ionosphere   the region of Earth's atmosphere that reflects radio waves toward the ground

irregular galaxy   a galaxy that differs from the two basic shapes of galaxies

irrelevant information   information that includes any facts that do not directly affect a person's decision

J

joint   the spot where two or more bones come together

K

kinetic energy   the energy of motion

kingdom   the most general classification of an organism

L

landfill   a place where solid wastes are buried

larva   a wormlike creature that begins the process of complete metamorphosis

law of chance   a description of the probability of something happening

law of nature   a property of nature that does not change

leaves   the site of food production in a plant

lever   a simple machine in which a small force times a large distance at one end becomes a large force times a small distance at the other end

life cycle   the stages of life that all living things go through: beginning, growth, maturity, decline, and death

life science   see **biology**

ligament   a tough strand of connective tissue

light   the range of electromagnetic wavelengths that humans can visibly detect

light-year   the distance that light travels in one year: about 6 trillion miles

lipid   an energy-storing fat

liquid   a phase of matter in which a substance takes the shape of its container and has a definite volume

lysosome   a special organelle in an animal cell that gets rid of waste materials, protects the cell from foreign invaders, and destroys worn-out or damaged organelles.

M

machine   a device that is designed to make work easier

magnetism   a trait in which an object attracts and repels another object

mantle   the layer of Earth between the crust and the core

mass   the amount of matter an object or particle contains

matter   anything that has weight and takes up space

melting   the process by which a solid turns into a liquid

menstrual cycle   the growth and release of a mature egg

mesosphere   the layer of Earth's atmosphere in which air temperature drops with increasing altitude

metamorphosis   the process in which insects and amphibians go through stages of life

meteor   a bright streak of light in the night sky caused by a meteoroid burning up as it enters Earth's atmosphere

meteorite   a fragment of a meteor that is found on the surface of Earth

meteorology   the study of the atmosphere

migrate   to move from one place to another

milestone   a turning point or point at which everything changes

mineral   see **vitamin**

mitochondria a bean-shaped organelle that breaks down the chemical bonds of food molecules

mitosis the process of cell division

model an idea, drawing, or object that stands for a real thing

molecule a combination of two or more atoms

molting the process through which an organism sheds its exoskeleton

multicellular organism an organism that consists of more than one cell

muscle a contracting tissue that is responsible for bone movement

mutation a change in the genetic information within a cell

N

natural resources resources provided by nature that are available to support life

natural selection the idea that individuals with favorable traits are the most likely members of a species to survive, reproduce, and pass on those traits

nerve impulse electrical signals that travel to and from nerve cells throughout the body

neuron a nerve cell that makes up brain tissue

neutron a particle in the nucleus of an atom that has no electric charge

neutron star a very dense small star made up entirely of neutrons from the leftover materials near the center of a supernova

nonconductor a material in which electrons cannot be made to flow

nonrenewable resources resources that cannot be replaced or that take hundreds or thousands of years to replace

nonvascular plant a plant that has no specialized tissue to transport water and nutrients to parts of the plant

nuclear force the force that holds neutrons and protons together in the nucleus of an atom

nuclear reactor a device in which controlled chain reactions are carried out

nucleolus a body within the nucleus of a cell that is responsible for making protein

nucleus an organelle that controls the activities of a cell and stores heredity information; the core of an atom

nutrient a food substance that the body can use for tissue growth and repair, as well as for energy

nutrition the study of the health value of food

nymph a smaller version of an adult insect

O

oceanography the study of Earth's oceans

open cluster a small group of stars that is located along the spiral disk of a spiral galaxy

open universe the theory that the universe will continue to slowly expand forever

opinion a personal belief that is often based on a person's own value system

orbit the path in which a planet travels around the Sun

order the tendency of properties and behavior to be predictable

organ a group of different types of tissue that work together

organ system a group of organs that work together

organelle a specialized structure within the cytoplasm of a cell that performs a special life activity

organic a carbon-containing compound

organic chemistry the study of carbon

organism a living thing

ozone a type of oxygen gas that surrounds Earth and absorbs ultraviolet rays

P

paleontology   the study of prehistoric animal and plant life through the analysis of fossil remains

Pangaea   the massive supercontinent that split into the seven continents

parallel circuit   a circuit in which there is more than one path for electric current to take

pathogen   a harmful bacterium, virus, or fungus that invades the human body

period   a row of the Periodic Table that contains elements that have the same number of energy shells

phases of matter   the three forms of a substance: solid, liquid, and gas

photosynthesis   the process in which a plant changes sunlight, carbon dioxide gas, and water into glucose

physical change   a change that does not produce a new substance

physical weathering   a type of weathering that breaks rocks apart without changing the chemicals within the rocks

pistil   the female reproductive structure in a flowering plant

placenta   a special tissue through which a developing placental embryo receives nourishment from its mother

planet   a celestial body that revolves around the sun

plate tectonics   the theory of the movement of Earth's crustal plates

pollen   a grain that contains the male sex cell of a flowering plant

pollination   the process by which flowering plants reproduce

pollution   any form of contamination that affects the quality of life

population   all organisms of one type

potential energy   stored energy

polymer   a hydrocarbon that contains a large number of carbon atoms

predator   an animal that hunts other animals

prey   an animal that is hunted by another animal

prism   a triangular piece of glass that breaks light into a spectrum of colors

products   the substances formed during a chemical reaction

prokaryote   an organism whose cells do not contain a nucleus and other specialized cell structures

protein   a molecule that is necessary for cell growth and repair and sometimes energy

proton   a particle in the nucleus of an atom that has a positive electric charge

pulsar   a neutron star that spins, sending out beams of pulsing radiation

punctuated equilibrium   a form of rapid evolution in which species suddenly appear or disappear on Earth

pupa   a resting insect in the third stage of complete metamorphosis

R

radioactivity   a property of some types of atoms in which the nuclei are unstable and break apart, releasing particles and rays

reactants   the substances that combine in a chemical reaction

reaction rate   the speed at which a chemical reaction takes place

recessive gene   a gene that has no effect if a dominant gene is present

recycling   the breaking down of trash into its component substances and reusing them in new products

red dwarf star   the smallest and coolest of stars, having the longest lifetime of all stars

red giant   a giant star that glows a cool, red color

reflection the process in which a wave bounces off a smooth surface

refraction the process in which a wave crosses a boundary and begins to move in a slightly different direction

relevant information information that includes facts that directly affect a person's decision

renewable resources resources that can be used and then replaced over a relatively short period of time

reproduction the process by which an organism produces future generations of its own kind

resource recovery the process of burning trash to create electricity

respiration the process in which food sugar is broken down and energy and carbon dioxide gas are released

response the reaction of an organism to a stimulus

restate to use different words and phrases to express the same idea

revolution a planet's complete trip around the Sun

ribosome a cell organelle on which amino acids combine to make proteins

root the part of a plant that anchors it in the ground and absorbs water and minerals from the soil

root hairs the long extensions of a root that serve as the main point of entrance for water into the root

S

scientific fact a conclusion, based on evidence, that scientists agree on

scientific method a logical way to perform experiments and to draw conclusions that are supported by all available evidence

semiconductor a material in which only a small amount of electric current can be made to flow

series circuit a circuit in which there is only one path for electric current to take

sexual reproduction a method of reproduction in which two different sex cells meet and produce offspring

skeleton the frame of the human body

skull a bone that protects the brain and other organs in the head

social behavior the behavior of animals of the same species as they live together

soil a mixture of tiny rock fragments and organic materials produced by living things

solar cell a device that produces electricity when sunlight strikes it

solar energy energy from sunlight

solar nebula a cloud of interstellar gas and dust from which the solar system formed

solar system the system comprised of the Sun and the nine planets that revolve around it

solid the phase of matter in which the molecular structure of a substance is nearly rigid

solute the substance that is dissolved in a solution

solution a uniform mixture of substances

solvent the substance in a solution that dissolves the solute

species a group of organisms that have the same number of chromosomes and display similar traits

sperm the male sex cell

spiral galaxy a galaxy that has a huge core of stars surrounded by spiral arms

spore a tiny reproductive cell

static electricity electricity in which electrons are transferred from one object to another

stamen the male reproductive structure in a flowering plant

stem the part of a plant that holds the leaves up toward sunlight and transports water and minerals from the roots to the leaves

stigma   the sticky top part of the pistil in a flower

stimulus   something that causes a change in an organism's behavior

stomata   tiny openings in a leaf that allow gases to enter and exit the leaf

stratosphere   the second layer of Earth's atmosphere; contains ozone gas

style   a long tube through which pollen moves from the stigma to the ovary in a flowering plant

summarize   to briefly express a writer's key thought

superconductor   a conductor in which there is no electrical resistance

supergiant   a very large giant star

supernova   a flash of light caused by the explosion of a massive blue star that has become too hot

synapse   the point of contact between two nerve cells

system   an organized group of related objects or components that form a whole

T

technology   the use of knowledge, materials, and tools to solve human problems and to provide for human needs and wishes

temperature   the measure of heat energy; the measure of the warmth of the air in Earth's atmosphere

tendon   a strong, fibrous connective tissue that connects bones and muscles

thermosphere   the outermost layer of Earth's atmosphere in which the temperature rises with altitude

tissue   a collection of similar cells

troposphere   the layer of Earth's atmosphere that is closest to the ground

U

ultraviolet light   high-energy light from the Sun that is harmful to life

unicellular organism   an organism that consists of a single cell

uterus   a special organ in a female placental mammal in which an embryo develops

V

vacuole   a large compartment in a plant cell that stores water and other liquids

vacuum   a space that contains no matter

value   a principle or a quality that a person believes is important

vascular plant   a plant that has specialized tissue for transporting water and nutrients to parts of the plant

vertebrate   an animal with a backbone and a skull

vesicle   a membrane-covered compartment near the cell membrane that stores proteins and other organic substances

visible light   see **light**

vitamin   a chemical that is necessary for proper body growth, body activity, and the prevention of certain diseases

voluntary muscle   a muscle that a person can consciously control

W

warm-blooded   a classification of animals who can control their own internal body temperature

wave   a periodic disturbance that carries energy

wavelength   the distance between the highest or lowest points of two adjacent waves

weathering   the breaking down of rock into smaller pieces by natural processes

wheel and axle   a machine, consisting of a rope and axle, in which the force felt by the weight is much more than the force applied to the free end of the rope

white dwarf star   a small, hot star that is the leftover core of a giant or supergiant

wind   air movement

work   the process in which an object moves in response to an applied force

Z

zoology   the study of animals

Index